ADOBE®
Photoshop® CS/
ImageReady® CS
for the Web

Hands-On Training

lynda.com/books

Tanya Staples | with **Lynda Weinman**

Adobe Photoshop CS/ImageReady CS for the Web | H·O·T Hands-On Training

By Tanya Staples
developed with Lynda Weinman

lynda.com/books | Peachpit Press
800 East 96th Street • Indianapolis, IN • 46240
800.571.5840 • 317.428.3000 •
317.428.3280 (fax)
http://www.lynda.com/books
http://www.peachpit.com

lynda.com/books is published
in association with Peachpit Press,
a division of Pearson Education
Copyright ©2004 by lynda.com

ISBN: 0-321-22855-3

0 9 8 7 6 5 4 3 2

Printed and bound in the United States of America

H•O•T | Credits

Original Design: Ali Karp, Alink Newmedia (*alink@earthlink.net*)

lynda.com Director of Publications: Garo Green (*garo@lynda.com*)

Editor: Jennifer Eberhardt

Copy editor: Darren Meiss

Compositors: Rick Gordon, Deborah Roberti, and Gloria Schurick

Beta Testers: Robert Hoekman, Jr. and Crystal Waters

Cover Illustration: Bruce Heavin (*bruce@stink.com*)

Exercise Graphics: Domenique Sillett (*www.littleigloo.com*)

Indexer: Eric Schroeder

Proofreader: Beth Trudell

H•O•T | Colophon

The preliminary design for the H•O•T series was sketched on paper by Ali Karp | Alink Newmedia. The layout was heavily influenced by online communication—merging a traditional book format with a modern Web aesthetic.

The text in *Adobe Photoshop CS/ImageReady CS for the Web H•O•T* was set in Akzidenz Grotesk from Adobe and Triplex from Emigré. The cover illustration was painted in Adobe Photoshop and Adobe Illustrator.

This book was created using Adobe Photoshop CS, QuarkXPress 4, and Microsoft Office on Mac OS X 10.3. It was printed on 50 lb. Utopia at RR Donnelley, Crawfordsville, Indiana.

Photoshop CS/ImageReady CS | H•O•T _____ **Table of Contents**

Introduction_____ **xii**

1. Getting Started _____ **2**
Creating Web Graphics in Photoshop CS and ImageReady CS   3
When to Use Photoshop CS Versus When to Use ImageReady CS   7
What's New in Photoshop CS and ImageReady CS?   10

2. Interface _____ **18**
The Welcome Screen   19
Interface Overview   20
The Toolbox   22
Toolbox Fly-Out Menus   23
Jump To Buttons   24
Palettes   25
Exercise 1_Docking Palettes in Groups and Individually   26
Exercise 2_Docking Palettes Vertically   28
Exercise 3_Using the Options Bar   30
Exercise 4_Docking Palettes in the Palette Well   32
Exercise 5_Creating a Tool Preset   34
Resetting Tools   37
Exercise 6_Saving a Custom Workspace   38
Keyboard Shortcuts   40
Exercise 7_Customizing Keyboard Shortcuts in Photoshop CS   41
The File Browser   46
Exercise 8_Viewing and Organizing Images in the File Browser   47
Exercise 9_Assigning Keywords and Searching in the File Browser   57

3. Color _____ **64**
Color Profiles and the Web   65
sRGB for Windows   65
sRGB and Gamma for Macs   66
The Decline of Web-Safe Color   69

What Happens on an 8-bit System If You Don't Use Web-Safe Colors?   70

Exercise 1_Choosing Web-Safe Colors from the Color Picker   72

Exercise 2_Loading Color Swatches   77

Exercise 3_Creating Custom Swatches   81

Exercise 4_Recoloring Layered Images   89

Exercise 5_Using the Color Replacement Tool   95

Exercise 6_Copying Color as HTML   101

4.   Optimization _____ 104

What Affects Speed on the Web?   105

GIF, JPEG, or Macromedia Flash?   105

Transparency and Animation   106

Lossy or Lossless?   108

How Can You Make Small JPEGs?   108

How Can You Make Small GIFs?   109

What Is Bit Depth?   111

Photoshop CS JPEG and GIF Options   111

Macromedia Flash Export Options   117

Exercise 1_Saving for the Web Using JPEG   119

Exercise 2_Selective JPEG Optimization with Alpha Channels   124

Exercise 3_Saving for Web Using GIF   129

Exercise 4_Choosing the Right Color Reduction Palette   132

Exercise 5_Reducing Colors   136

Exercise 6_Locking Colors   138

Exercise 7_Changing the Dimensions of a Graphic   141

Exercise 8_Selective GIF Optimization with Alpha Channels   142

Exercise 9_Previewing Images in a Web Browser   146

ImageReady CS Palettes and Preference Settings   147

Exercise 10_Optimizing a JPEG in ImageReady CS   149

Exercise 11_Using a Matte Color on a JPEG in ImageReady CS   152

Exercise 12_Previewing and Writing HTML in ImageReady CS   154

Exercise 13_Exporting Images as Macromedia Flash   157

5.   **Layers** _____ **160**

What Are Layers?   161

Previewing and Writing HTML in ImageReady CS   154

Exercise 1_Using Layers   162

Exercise 2_Moving Layers   171

Exercise 3_Moving Linked Layers   174

Exercise 4_Aligning Linked Layers   176

What Are Layer Sets?   180

Exercise 5_Using Layer Sets   182

Exercise 6_Working with Multiple Layers in ImageReady CS   193

Comparing Linked Layers, Layer Sets and Multiple Layers   200

What Are Layer Comps?   202

Exercise 7_Using Layer Comps   203

Exercise 8_Exporting Layers as Files   210

What Are Fill Layers?   219

Exercise 9_Creating Solid Color Layers   220

Exercise 10_Creating Gradient Layers   223

Exercise 11_Creating Pattern Layers   228

What Are Adjustment Layers?   230

Exercise 12_Using Adjustment Layers   231

Exercise 13_Using Clipping Groups   236

6.   **Type** _____ **240**

Comparing Type in Photoshop CS and ImageReady CS   241

The Type Options Bar   243

Exercise 1_Using the Type Options Bar   244

The Character Palette   250

Exercise 2_Using the Character Palette   252

The Paragraph Palette   257

Exercise 3_Creating Paragraph Type   258

Exercise 4_Checking Spelling   263

Exercise 5_Finding and Replacing Type   265

Exercise 6_Creating Warped Type   266

Exercise 7_Creating Type on a Path   268

Exercise 8_Rasterizing Type   275

Exercise 9_Transforming Type   279

7. Shapes and Layer Styles _____ **282**

Comparing Bitmap Images and Vector Graphics   283

About Shape Tools   284

About Shapes   286

About Shape Layers   286

Exercise 1_Using Shape Tools and Shape Layers   288

About Layer Styles   296

Exercise 2_Creating Layer Styles   297

Exercise 3_Saving Custom Layer Styles   304

Exercise 4_Applying Custom Layer Styles from the Styles Palette   308

8. Background Images _____ **314**

What Is a Background Image?   315

About Background Image Sizes   317

Exercise 1_Defining, Previewing, and Resizing Background Images   319

Exercise 2_Saving Background Images   326

Exercise 3_Creating Symmetrical Background Images   332

Exercise 4_Creating Non-Symmetrical Background Images   338

Exercise 5_Creating Seamless Backgrounds from Photographs   346

Exercise 6_Creating Full-Screen Graphic Background Images   353

Exercise 7_Creating Full-Screen Photographic Background Images   357

Exercise 8_Using Directional Tiles to Create Background Images   363

9. Transparent GIFs _____ **366**

Understanding the Limitations of GIF Transparency   367

What Is Anti-Aliasing?   369

Recognizing Transparent Layers   370

Understanding GIFs, Masks, and Transparency   371

Understanding Offset Problems in Browsers   372

Exercise 1_Creating and Previewing GIF Transparency   373

Exercise 2_Fixing the Edges of Transparent GIFs   377

Exercise 3_Adding a Drop Shadow to Transparent GIFs   382

Exercise 4_Working with Transparent GIFs on Broad Backgrounds   385

Exercise 5_Diffusion Transparency Dither   389

Exercise 6_Saving Transparent Images in ImageReady CS   393

Exercise 7_Creating and Saving Transparent GIFs in Photoshop CS   396

Exercise 8_Creating Transparent GIFs from Non-Transparent Images   403

10.   **Slicing** _____ **408**

About Slices   409

About Slice Types   411

About Slice Lines, Slice Numbers, Slice Symbols, and Slice Colors   412

About the Web Content and Slice Palettes   413

Exercise 1_Creating User Slices   415

Exercise 2_Creating Layer-Based Slices   422

Exercise 3_Editing Slices   437

Exercise 4_Renaming Slices   442

Exercise 5_Optimizing Slices   446

Exercise 6_Saving Sliced Images   455

Exercise 7_Applying Alt Text and Status Bar Messages to Slices   458

Exercise 8_Assigning URLs to Slices   461

About Slice Sets   463

Exercise 9_Using Slice Sets   464

Exercise 10_Using Slices and Layer Comps   471

11.   **Rollovers** _____ **486**

About Rollovers   487

About Rollover States   488

About the Web Content Palette   489

Exercise 1_Creating Rollovers with Styles   490

Exercise 2_Creating Rollovers from Layer-Based Slices
and Creating Custom Rollover Styles   497

Exercise 3_Using Rollover Styles for Multiple Buttons   503

Exercise 4_Renaming and Saving Rollovers   507

Exercise 5_Creating Rollovers Using Layer Visibility   513

Exercise 6_Creating Rollovers from Layer Comps   518

Exercise 7_Creating Remote Rollovers   522

Exercise 8_Creating Remote Rollovers with Selected States   531

12. Image Maps _____ **542**

Server-Side and Client-Side Image Maps   543

What Does an Image Map Look Like?   544

Creating Image Maps in ImageReady CS   545

About the Web Content and Image Map Palettes   546

Exercise 1_Creating an Image Map with the Image Map Tools   548

Exercise 2_Creating an Image Map from Layers   560

Exercise 3_Creating Image Maps for Type   572

Exercise 4_Jumping to Photoshop CS with an Image Map   577

Exercise 5_Creating Image Map–Based Rollovers   580

13. Animated GIFs and Flash _____ **584**

The Animation Palette   585

Controlling the Timing of Animations   586

Animation Aesthetics   586

The Animated GIF Format   586

GIF Compression Challenges   587

The Macromedia Flash File Format   587

Animated GIFs Versus Macromedia Flash   588

Exercise 1_Creating Animations from Layer Visibility   590

Exercise 2_Setting the Looping and Speed   594

Exercise 3_Tweening with Opacity   598

Exercise 4_Selecting, Duplicating, and Reversing Frames   603

The Paste Frames Dialog Box   607

Exercise 5_Tweening a Tweened Sequence   608

Exercise 6_Tweening with Position   611

Exercise 7_Tweening with Layer Styles   615

Exercise 8_Creating an Animated Slideshow   618

Exercise 9_Optimizing and Saving Animated GIFs   621

Exercise 10_Creating Transparent Animated GIFs   623

Exercise 11_Creating Animated GIF Rollovers   627

Exercise 12_Exporting Animations as Macromedia Flash Files   631

Exercise 13_Exporting Frames as Files   635

Exercise 14_Designing Entire Web Interfaces   640

14. **Automation** _____**650**

What Is the Web Photo Gallery? 651

Exercise 1_Creating a Web Photo Gallery 653

Exercise 2_Customizing a Web Photo Gallery 657

What Do All the Web Photo Gallery Settings Do? 663

Exercise 3_Collaborating with a Web Photo Gallery 666

Exercise 4_Creating a PDF Presentation 669

What Are Actions? 675

Using Predefined Actions 675

Exercise 5_Creating Actions in ImageReady CS 676

Editing Actions 681

About Droplets 682

Exercise 6_Creating Droplets in ImageReady CS 683

Exercise 7_Creating Conditional Actions in ImageReady CS 688

15 **Data Sets** _____**692**

Buzzwords and Definitions 693

Exercise 1_Understanding Data Sets and Variables 695

Exercise 2_Creating Data Sets and Variables 698

Exercise 3_Creating Pixel Replacement Variables 702

Exercise 4_Importing Data Sets from Text Files 707

16   Integration with Other Programs _____ **710**

Exercise 1_Updating HTML in ImageReady CS   711

Exercise 2_Importing ImageReady CS Rollovers into GoLive CS   716

Exercise 3_Using Smart Objects in GoLive CS   723

Exercise 4_Using the Edit Original Feature in GoLive CS   729

Exercise 5_Working with ImageReady CS Data Sets in GoLive CS   733

Exercise 6_Importing ImageReady CS Rollovers
into Dreamweaver MX 2004   740

Exercise 7_Exporting Vector Images as Macromedia Flash Files   750

Exercise 8_Preserving the Appearance of ImageReady CS Files
with SWF Export   760

Exercise 9_Exporting Illustrator CS Files   765

Exercise 10_Exporting ImageReady CS Files to QuickTime   768

Exercise 11_Opening QuickTime Movies in ImageReady CS   771

Exercise 12_Converting PSD files to PDF   774

Appendix A Troubleshooting FAQ and Technical Support _____ **784**

Appendix B Online Resources _____ **790**

Index _____ **796**

Introduction

| A Note from Lynda | About the Author |
| Acknowledgments | How This Book Works |
| Making Exercise Files Editable on Windows Computers |
| Making File Extensions Visible on Windows Computers |
| System Requirements | What's on the CD-ROM? |

H·O·T

Photoshop CS/ImageReady CS for the Web

A Note from Lynda

In my opinion, most people buy computer books to learn, yet it is amazing how few of these books are actually written by teachers. Tanya Staples and I take pride in the fact that this book was written by experienced teachers, who are familiar with training students in this subject matter. In this book, you will find carefully developed lessons and exercises to help you learn Photoshop CS and ImageReady CS–two of the most well-respected graphics applications on the planet.

This book is targeted toward the beginning- to intermediate-level Web designers and Web developers who are looking for great tools to create graphics and Web content. The premise of the hands-on exercise approach is to get you up to speed quickly with Photoshop CS and ImageReady CS while actively working through the lessons in the book. It's one thing to read about a product and another experience entirely to try the product and get measurable results. Our motto is, "Read the book, follow the exercises, and you'll learn the product." I have received countless testimonials to this fact, and it is our goal to make sure it remains true for all of our hands-on training books.

Many exercise-based books take a paint-by-numbers approach to teaching. Although this approach works, it's often difficult to figure out how to apply those lessons to a real-world situation, or to understand why or when you would use the technique again. What sets this book apart is that the lessons contain lots of background information and insights into each given subject, which are designed to help you understand the process as well as the exercise.

At times, pictures are worth a lot more than words. When necessary, we have also included short QuickTime movies to show any processes that are difficult to explain with words. These files are located on the **H•O•T CD-ROM** inside a folder called **movies**. It's our style to approach teaching from many different angles, because we know some people are visual learners, others like to read, and still others like to get out there and try things. This book combines a lot of teaching approaches so you can learn Photoshop CS and ImageReady CS to create Web graphics as thoroughly as you want to.

This book didn't set out to cover every single aspect of Photoshop CS or ImageReady CS. The manual and many other reference books are great for that! What we saw missing from the bookshelves was a process-oriented tutorial that taught readers core principles, techniques, and tips in a hands-on training format. We've been making Web graphics since 1995, and it used to be a lot tougher than it is today. Photoshop CS and ImageReady CS are oriented toward making Web graphics faster to download and easier to create. In addition, ImageReady CS even writes JavaScript and HTML code, which is something traditional imaging programs have seldom broached.

I welcome your comments at **pscshot@lynda.com**. Please visit our Web site at **http://www.lynda.com**. The support URL for this book is **http://www.lynda.com/products/books/pscshot/**.

Tanya and I hope this book will raise your skills in Web design and digital imaging. If it does, we will have accomplished the job we set out to do!

–Lynda Weinman

NOTE | About lynda.com/books and lynda.com

lynda.com/books is dedicated to helping designers and developers understand design tools and principles. **lynda.com** offers hands-on workshops, training seminars, conferences, on-site training, training videos, training CDs, and "expert tips" for design and development. To learn more about our training programs, books, and products, visit our Web site at **http://www.lynda.com**.

About Tanya

Tanya Staples is a freelance author and educator teaching traditional and digital art. She has a bachelor's degree in fine art and art history and is currently completing a bachelor's degree in education. For the past five years, Tanya designed, taught, and wrote about graphics software, most recently as the Program Manager for the Corel Painter product line. When she's not in front of a computer or a classroom, you can find Tanya in the kitchen cooking up a storm for friends, or touring the back roads of Ontario on her motorcycle.

Snapshots

When Tanya isn't in front of a computer, you'll find her cruising the back roads of Ontario on her Suzuki Savage.

Tanya and Lynda take a break to smile for the camera.

Acknowledgments from Tanya

This book would not have been possible without the support of many dedicated, enthusiastic, and talented individuals.

My deepest thanks and appreciation to:

You, the reader. I hope you enjoy this book as much as I enjoyed creating it for you.

Lynda Weinman, my mentor and my friend, for giving me the opportunity to write this book; for allowing me to do what I love; and for your knowledge, support, and wisdom throughout this project. You have been a true inspiration to me, and your positive feedback has meant more than words can possibly say.

Garo Green, for keeping me organized and constantly making me laugh. Your energy is contagious, and it has been a blast working with you.

Domenique Sillett, for creating the fabulous imagery in this book. You are an amazing designer, and I have learned so much from working with you. See you at Anthropologie!

Auriga Bork, for your help recording the movies. Your bright smile and kind words always make the recording process so much fun!

The beta testers and **copyeditors** for your hard work, dedication, and attention to detail.

The folks at Adobe, for making more fantastic versions of Photoshop and ImageReady!

Patricia (my Savage Sister) and **Ifoma Smart**, **Alice** and **Rick Champagne**, **Heather Archibald** and **Mark Abdelnour**, and **Sean McLennan**, for always being there when I need you, for your constant encouragement and support, and for teaching me to just go out and giv'r.;-) You are the most amazing friends a girl could have.

Stephen Reese, for graciously giving so much of your time to peer-edit this book and for constantly challenging me to become a better writer. You have been an incredible resource, inspiration, and motivator throughout this project. The quality of this book would not be what it is without your dedication and friendship. You are a total rock star and I am so grateful to have you as my friend.

Matthew Hately, my husband, for your constant love and support, for putting up with the crazy hours I work, and for taking care of life maintenance when I just didn't have time! I could not have balanced going to school and writing this book without you.

And, to **Ewen MacMillan**, for reminding me what it really means to be strong. Your courage and determination is an inspiration.

How This Book Works

This book has several components, including step-by-step exercises, commentary, notes, tips, warnings, and movies. Step-by-step exercises are numbered, and file names and command keys are bolded so they pop out more easily. When you see italicized text, it signifies commentary.

- At the beginning of each exercise you'll see the notation **[IR]** if the exercise takes place in ImageReady CS, or **[PS]** if the exercise takes place in Photoshop CS.

- Whenever you're being instructed to go to a menu or to multiple menu items, it's stated like this: **File > Open**.

- Code is in a monospace font: **<HTML></HTML>**.

- URLs are in a bold font: **http://www.lynda.com**.

- Macintosh and Windows interface screen captures: The screen captures in the book were taken on a Macintosh, as I do most of my design work and writing on a Mac. I also own and use a Windows computer, and I noted important differences when they occurred.

Making Exercise Files Editable on Windows Computers

By default, when you copy files from a CD-ROM to a Windows 2000 computer, they are set to read-only (write protected). This will cause a problem with the exercise files because you will need to edit and save some of them. To remove the read-only property, follow the steps below:

Note: You do not need to follow these steps if you are using Windows XP Home Edition or Windows XP Professional Edition.

1. Open the exercises_files folder on the **H•O•T CD-ROM** and copy one of the subfolders (such as **chap_02**) to your **Desktop**.

2. Open the **chap_02** folder you copied to your **Desktop** and choose **Edit > Select All**.

3. Right-click one of the selected files and choose **Properties**.

4. In the **Properties** dialog box, click the **General** tab. Turn off the **Read-Only** option to disable the read-only properties for the selected files in the **chap_02** folder.

Making File Extensions Visible on Windows Computers

By default, you cannot see file extensions such as .gif, .jpg, or .psd on Windows computers. Fortunately, you can change this setting!

1. Double-click the **My Computer** icon on your **Desktop**. **Note:** If you (or someone else) have changed the name, it will not say **My Computer**.

2. Select **Tools > Folder Options**. This **Folder Options** dialog box opens automatically.

3. Click the **View** tab.

4. Turn off the **Hide extensions for known file types** option. This makes all file extensions visible.

Photoshop CS and ImageReady CS System Requirements

This book requires you use either a Macintosh (Power Macintosh running Mac OS 10.2.4 or later) or Windows 2000/XP. You will also need color monitor capable of 1024x768 resolution and a CD-ROM drive. I suggest you have at least 256 MB of RAM. Here are the minimum system requirements you need to run Photoshop CS and ImageReady CS.

Macintosh:

- PowerPC Processor (G3, G4, or G5)

- Mac OS X (10.2.4 or later)

- 192 MB RAM (256 MB recommended)

- 320 MB available hard disk space

- Color monitor with 16-bit color or higher

- 1024x768 or greater monitor resolution

- CD-ROM drive

Windows:

- Intel Pentium III or 4 processor

- Microsoft Windows 2000 with Service Pack 3 or Windows XP

- 192 MB RAM (256 MB recommended)

- 280 MB available hard disk space

- Color monitor with 16-bit color or higher

- 1024x768 or greater monitor resolution

- CD-ROM drive

What's on the CD-ROM?

Exercise Files and the H•O•T CD-ROM

The files required to complete the exercises are located inside a folder called **exercise_files** on the **H•O•T CD-ROM**. These files are divided into chapter folders, and you should copy each chapter folder to your **Desktop** before you begin the exercises for the chapter. Unfortunately, when files originate from a CD-ROM, under some Windows operating systems, it defaults to making them write-protected, meaning that you cannot alter them. You will need to alter them to follow the exercises, so please read the "Note to Windows Users" on page xvii for instructions on how to remove the read-only properties.

QuickTime Files on the H•O•T CD-ROM

There is a folder on the CD-ROM called **movies**, which contains several QuickTime tutorial movies for some of the exercises in this book. It's my hope that these movies will help you understand some of the more difficult exercises in this book by watching me perform them. If you like these movies, then you should definitely check out the *Photoshop CS and ImageReady CS for the Web* CD-ROM at **www.lynda.com**, which contains several hours worth of QuickTime movies about creating Web graphics in Photoshop CS and ImageReady CS.

Getting Demo Versions of Software

If you'd like to try the software programs used in this book, you can download demo versions as follows:

• Adobe Photoshop CS and Adobe ImageReady CS: **www.adobe.com**

• Adobe GoLive CS: **www.adobe.com**

• Adobe Illustrator CS: **www.adobe.com**

• Macromedia Flash MX 2004: **www.macromedia.com**

• Macromedia Dreamweaver MX 2004: **www.macromedia.com**

I.

Getting Started

| Creating Web Graphics in Photoshop CS and ImageReady CS |
| When to Use Photoshop CS Versus When to Use ImageReady CS |
| What's New in Photoshop CS and ImageReady CS? |

chap_01

Photoshop CS/ImageReady CS
H•O•T CD-ROM

This chapter offers an overview of the Web features in Photoshop CS and ImageReady CS. Here you'll find ideas for the kind of Web graphics you can create with these programs, advice on when to use each program, and an introduction to new Web features in Photoshop CS and ImageReady CS. The information in this chapter builds a foundation for what you'll learn in the hands-on exercises in the chapters that follow.

Creating Web Graphics in Photoshop CS and ImageReady CS

You can use Photoshop CS and ImageReady CS to create a variety of images for the Web. This section lists some examples of the kinds of Web graphics and content you can create. You'll get a chance to explore projects like the following in the chapters to come.

Photographs: Optimize photographs for the Web in Chapter 4, "*Optimization.*"

Logos and graphics: Create vector-based shapes in Chapter 7, "*Shapes and Layer Styles.*" Choose color and recolor images in Chapter 3, "*Color.*" Optimize logos and graphic art in Chapter 4, "*Optimization.*"

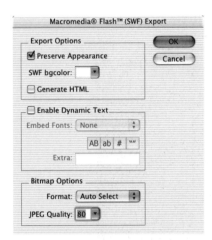

Macromedia Flash: Export static files as Macromedia Flash files in Chapter 4, "*Optimization*." Export animations as Macromedia Flash files in Chapter 13, "*Animated GIFs and Flash*."

Type: Create and edit vector-based type in Chapter 6, "*Type*." Type created in Photoshop CS or ImageReady CS is great for Web buttons or banners that require fancy fonts or special type effects.

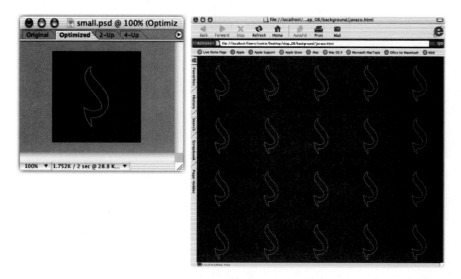

Background images: Create symmetrical and nonsymmetrical background images using the offset filter, define images as background images, and save the required HTML code to make background images work in a Web browser in Chapter 8, "*Background Images.*"

Slices: Slice images, edit slices, and save the required HTML code to make sliced images work in a Web browser in Chapter 10, "*Slicing.*"

Rollovers: Create simple Web buttons with rollovers, remote rollovers, and selected states, and save the required JavaScript and HTML code to make rollovers work in a Web browser in Chapter 11, "*Rollovers*."

Image maps: Create multiple hot spots in a single image and save the required HTML code to make image maps work in a Web browser in Chapter 12, "*Image Maps*."

Animations: Create animated Web buttons and graphics using the animation features in ImageReady CS. Save animations as animated GIFs and export animations as Macromedia Flash files in Chapter 13, *"Animated GIFs and Flash."*

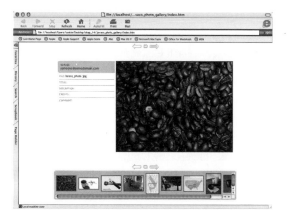

Web photo galleries: Create Web photo galleries to display images. Photoshop CS automatically creates all the elements for the Web site, and it optimizes the images, writes the HTML code, and designs the navigation buttons. Assemble Web photo galleries in Chapter 14, *"Automation."*

When to Use Photoshop CS Versus When to Use ImageReady CS

It's not always clear when you should use Photoshop CS and when you should use ImageReady CS to create Web graphics. Although Photoshop CS and ImageReady CS have many common features, there are many features exclusive to each program. Here are some recommendations:

• **Creating simple Web graphics:** Use either Photoshop CS or ImageReady CS to create simple Web graphics such as Web buttons and background images.

• **Performing complex image-editing tasks:** Use Photoshop CS to perform complex image-editing tasks such as retouching a photograph or making a collage. The reason is simple—Photoshop CS has more sophisticated image-editing tools than ImageReady CS.

- **Designing full Web page layouts:** Use Photoshop CS to create full Web page layouts. Photoshop CS has more advanced image-editing and creation tools. When you're finished designing the layout, you can always jump to ImageReady CS to create rollovers or animations and save the required JavaScript or HTML code required to make the Web page work.

- **Organizing images:** Use the File Browser in Photoshop CS when you want to organize, sort, or keyword images.

- **Optimizing images:** Use the program you have open at the time. The Save For Web window in Photoshop CS is similar to the Optimize palette in ImageReady CS; however, ImageReady CS gives you better access to the original image if you want to make changes during the optimization process.

- **Exporting images as Macromedia Flash files:** Use ImageReady CS if you want to export static images to the Macromedia Flash (SWF) format. The Macromedia Flash Export feature is only available in ImageReady CS.

- **Slicing images:** Use ImageReady CS when you're slicing an image. Although Photoshop CS gives you access to the slice tools, you don't have access to the Slice, Table, or Web Content palettes, which you'll need for performing complex slicing tasks and creating rollovers.

- **Creating rollovers:** Use ImageReady CS to create rollovers. ImageReady CS gives you access to the Web Content palette and all the controls you need to create rollovers. It also writes the required JavaScript and HTML code required to make the rollovers work in a Web browser. Although Photoshop CS does not have the features for creating rollovers, you can design the artwork in Photoshop CS and use ImageReady CS to create and save the rollovers.

- **Creating image maps:** Use ImageReady CS if you want to create image maps. ImageReady CS gives you access to image map creation tools and lets you save the required HTML code to make image maps work in a Web browser.

- **Creating animated GIFs and Macromedia Flash animations:** Use ImageReady CS if you want to create and save animations as animated GIF or Macromedia Flash (SWF) files. Although you can't build animations in Photoshop CS, you can create artwork in Photoshop CS, then build and save the animations in ImageReady CS.

- **Creating Web photo galleries:** Use Photoshop CS if you want to create a Web photo gallery from a series of images.

Don't worry if you're still unsure about which program to use when. You'll get hands-on experience completing all these tasks in the appropriate program as you work through the book. Plus, you can always glance back at the following handy reference chart.

When to Use Photoshop CS Versus When to Use ImageReady CS	
Task	Program
Creating simple Web graphics such as buttons or backgrounds	Photoshop CS or ImageReady CS
Performing complex image-editing tasks such as retouching and manipulating photographs or creating collages	Photoshop CS
Designing full Web page layouts	Photoshop CS
Organizing images	Photoshop CS
Optimizing images	Photoshop CS or ImageReady CS
Exporting images as Macromedia Flash files	ImageReady CS
Slicing simple images	Photoshop CS or ImageReady CS
Slicing complex images, editing slices, or using slices for rollovers	ImageReady CS
Creating rollovers	ImageReady CS
Creating image maps	ImageReady CS
Creating animated GIFs and Macromedia Flash animations	ImageReady CS
Creating Web photo galleries	Photoshop CS

What's New in Photoshop CS and ImageReady CS?

Photoshop CS and ImageReady CS have a number of new features to make it easier for you to design and output Web graphics. Here is a handy chart to help you identify some of the key new features in Photoshop CS and ImageReady CS you'll learn about in this book. For a complete list of new features, visit **http://www.adobe.com/photoshopcs.**

New Features in Photoshop CS and ImageReady CS	
Feature	**Description**
Welcome Screen	Photoshop CS and ImageReady CS each prompt you with a Welcome Screen when you first launch the program. The Welcome Screen provides quick access to information about new features, color management, tutorials, movies, and more. You'll see how the Welcome Screen works in Chapter 2, "*Interface*."
Customizable keyboard shortcuts	Photoshop CS lets you assign new keyboard shortcuts and redefine existing keyboard shortcuts for menu items, tools, and palette commands in an easy-to-use interface. You can save different sets of keyboard shortcuts for different workflows and print a list of keyboard shortcuts for future reference. You'll learn how to customize keyboard shortcuts in Chapter 2, "*Interface*."

continues on next page

New Features in Photoshop CS and ImageReady CS *continued*

Feature	Description
Enhanced File Browser	Photoshop CS provides an enhanced File Browser that lets you organize, sort, rename, rotate, preview, and flag images.

You can also apply keywords and metadata to images through the File Browser and search for images using the keywords and metadata. The File Browser offers a number of automation tasks for creating Web photo galleries, multipage PDFs, PDF presentations and contact sheets, and batch processing images. You'll learn how to use the File Browser in Chapter 2, "*Interface*."

| **Color Replacement tool** | Photoshop CS lets you change the color of an entire image or area of an image using the Color Replacement tool. The Color Replacement tool recolors images while keeping the original texture and shading of the original. You'll learn how to use the Color Replacement tool in Chapter 3, "*Color*." |

continues on next page

New Features in Photoshop CS and ImageReady CS *continued*	
Feature	**Description**
Export to Macromedia Flash	ImageReady CS lets you export layers, files, animations, and frames as Macromedia Flash (SWF) files. When you export files, ImageReady CS preserves vector objects and text as native SWF information. You'll learn how use the Macromedia Flash Export feature in Chapter 4, "*Optimization*," Chapter 5, "*Layers*," and Chapter 13, "*Animated GIFs and Flash*."
Web-focused Interface	ImageReady CS has a Web-focused interface that lets you select, manipulate, copy, and group objects quickly and easily. You can execute layer commands over multiple layers and apply font settings to multiple type objects at the same time. You'll learn how to work with multiple objects and layers in Chapter 5, "*Layers*."

continues on next page

New Features in Photoshop CS and ImageReady CS *continued*

Feature	Description
Nested layer sets	Photoshop CS and ImageReady CS let you group layers into nested layer sets up to five levels deep. Nesting layer sets is a great way to keep complex, layered images organized. You'll learn how to nest layer sets in Chapter 5, "*Layers*."
Layer Comps	Photoshop CS and ImageReady CS let you record any combination of layer visibility, position, and appearance using the new layer comps feature. Layer comps make it easy to create multiple layouts for a Web site in a single file and allow you to create alternate designs for client review and approval. You'll learn how to use layer comps in Chapter 5, "*Layers*."

continues on next page

New Features in Photoshop CS and ImageReady CS *continued*

Feature	Description
Export layers and frames as files	ImageReady CS lets you export layers and animation frames as files. You can export all layers in a file, top level layers and layer sets, or selected layers. You also export all layers using the same file format or specify a file format and individual optimization settings for each file. You can also export frames or selected frames in an animation as individual files. You can export layers and frames to a number of file formats, including Macromedia Flash (SWF) files. You'll learn how to export layers as files in Chapter 5, "*Layers*," and how to export animation frames as files in Chapter 13, "*Animated GIFs and Flash*."
Type on a path	Photoshop CS lets you create type on an open path or on a closed shape. You'll learn how to create type on a path in Chapter 6, "*Type*."

continues on next page

New Features in Photoshop CS and ImageReady CS *continued*	
Feature	**Description**
Web Content palette	ImageReady CS includes a new Web Content palette that makes it easy to create and edit slices, rollovers, and image maps. You'll learn how to use the Web Content palette in Chapter 10, "*Slicing*," Chapter 11, "*Rollovers*," and Chapter 12, "*Image Maps*."
Slice sets	ImageReady CS lets you create multiple slice sets in a single document. You can create multiple configurations of a Web site in the same file and use slice sets to slice each configuration. You'll learn how to use slice sets in Chapter 10, "*Slicing*."
Enhanced remote rollovers	ImageReady CS has a new workflow for creating remote rollovers. The new click-and-drag targeting method lets you create remote rollovers in a snap! You'll learn how to create remote rollovers in Chapter 11, "*Rollovers*."

continues on next page

New Features in Photoshop CS and ImageReady CS *continued*	
Feature	**Description**
Export multiple HTML files from selected states	ImageReady CS lets you export multiple HTML files for each selected state. You'll learn how in Chapter 11, "*Rollovers*."
Collaborative Web photo galleries	Photoshop CS lets you create Web photo galleries from images in the File Browser.

The new collaborative templates allow feedback from clients, colleagues, and friends with no extra HTML coding required! You'll learn how to create collaborative Web photo galleries in Chapter 14, "*Automation*."

PDF presentations and multipage PDFs	Photoshop CS lets you create PDF presentations and multipage PDFs. You'll learn how to do both in Chapter 14, "*Automation*."

continues on next page

New Features in Photoshop CS and ImageReady CS *continued*	
Feature	**Description**
Conditional actions	ImageReady CS lets you insert a conditional step into an action. When you play the action, ImageReady CS will scan for the characteristics you specified in the conditional action and perform a step only if the characteristics match the settings in the conditional action. You'll learn how to create conditional actions in Chapter 14, "*Automation*."
Import data sets from text files	ImageReady CS lets you import data sets from spreadsheets and databases as tab-delimited or comma-delimited text files. You'll learn how to do both in Chapter 15, "*Data Sets*."

Now that you've had a chance to see what Photoshop CS and ImageReady CS are all about, it's time to get started with the hands-on exercises. In the chapters that follow, you'll learn practical techniques for using Photoshop CS and ImageReady CS to design Web graphics and content. Enjoy! ;-)

2.

Interface

The Welcome Screen	Interface Overview
Using the Toolbox	Using Palettes	Using the Options Bar
Creating a Tool Preset	Resetting Tools
Saving a Custom Workspace	Keyboard Shortcuts
Using the File Browser

chap_02

Photoshop CS/ImageReady CS
H•O•T CD-ROM

Adobe has always been known for consistent, easy-to-use interfaces across products, platforms, and versions. Photoshop CS and ImageReady CS are no exception. This chapter takes you through the basic concepts of the Photoshop CS and ImageReady CS interface and teaches you how to customize your settings for Web graphics workflow.

This chapter begins with an overview of the main interface components: the new Welcome Screen, the Toolbox, the palettes, and the Options bar. You'll learn how to customize the interface to match your workflow by docking and undocking palettes, creating custom tool presets, saving custom workspaces, and creating custom keyboard shortcuts. You'll also learn how to use the File Browser, which was introduced in Photoshop 7, including some of the new features in Photoshop CS.

You might be anxious to start in on some of the step-by-step exercises contained in later chapters, but you should review this chapter first to understand the key elements that make up the Photoshop CS and ImageReady CS interfaces.

The Welcome Screen

When you open Photoshop CS or ImageReady CS for the first time, you will see the Welcome Screen. The Welcome Screen is a new feature in Photoshop CS and ImageReady CS and is designed to give you quick access to tutorials, tips and tricks, color management, and new feature information.

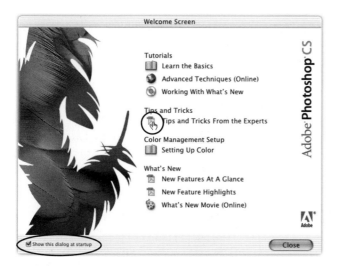

To view information from the Welcome Screen, click the icon beside the text and follow the instructions onscreen. **Note**: Some of the content is online and you will need to have an active Internet connection to view the information.

If you close the Welcome Screen, you can reopen it by choosing **Help > Welcome Screen**.

If you do not want the Welcome Screen to appear each time you launch Photoshop CS or ImageReady CS, turn off the **Show this dialog at startup** option located in the bottom-left corner of the Welcome Screen.

Interface Overview

Photoshop CS and ImageReady CS are separate applications that ship together. Fortunately, from an interface standpoint, you're in for an easy learning curve because Photoshop CS and ImageReady CS share similar toolboxes, palettes, and menu items, which are are organized in the same logical way.

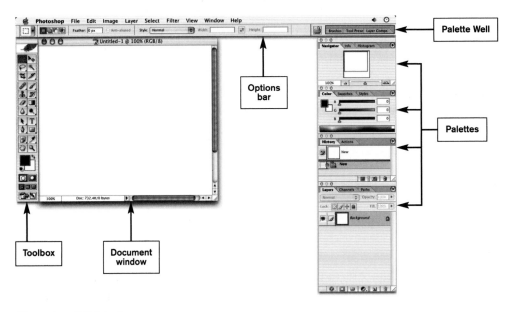

Photoshop CS interface

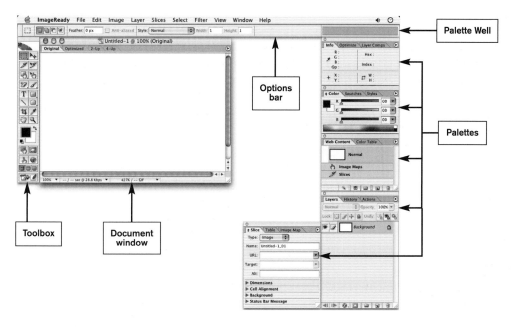

ImageReady CS interface

When you first open Photoshop CS or ImageReady CS, the Toolbox, Options bar, and key palettes are turned on by default. Even though different palettes are turned on in Photoshop CS and ImageReady CS, it's obvious from first glance these two programs have very similar interfaces. If you know Photoshop CS already, you'll have a huge advantage when learning ImageReady CS.

Tip: Pressing the **Tab** key in either application toggles the palettes on and off.

The Toolbox

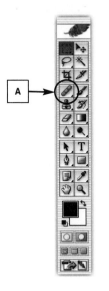

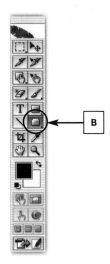

Photoshop CS Toolbox　　　　*ImageReady CS Toolbox*

The Toolboxes in Photoshop CS and ImageReady CS are vertical and are docked to the top-left corner of the screen by default. In both programs, the Toolbox can be undocked and moved to any location onscreen. Many of the tools have an associated keyboard shortcut, which is listed in parentheses in the tooltip. You can access the tooltips by hovering your mouse over a tool, without clicking.

The Toolbox in Photoshop CS is almost identical to the Toolbox in Photoshop 7. The key difference between Photoshop 7 and Photoshop CS is the addition of the Color Replacement tool, which is located beneath the Healing Brush tool (labeled A in the previous illustration). The Color Replacement tool samples the color of the original image and replaces it with the foreground color while maintaining the texture and shading of the original color. You'll learn how to use the Color Replacement tool in Chapter 3, "*Color.*"

The Toolbox in ImageReady CS has been reorganized. Many of the less frequently used tools have been grouped inside fly-out menus, and many of the more commonly used tools, which were previously hidden inside fly-out menus, have been placed directly on the Toolbox. ImageReady CS includes two new shape tools: the Tab Rectangle tool and the Pill Rectangle tool, which are labeled B in the illustration. You will learn how to use these new tools in Chapter 7, "*Shapes and Layer Styles.*"

Toolbox Fly-Out Menus

When you see a small arrow on the bottom-right corner of a tool in the Photoshop CS or ImageReady CS Toolbox, it indicates there are hidden tools in fly-out menus. To show the hidden tools, click the arrow, and the additional tool choices will appear to the left or right-hand side of the Toolbox. The following illustrations show the location of the tools, including the fly-out menus, in Photoshop CS and ImageReady CS.

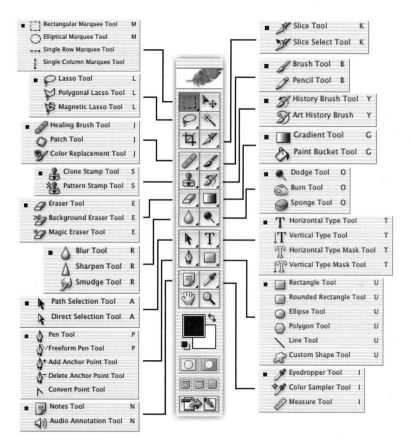

Photoshop CS tool fly-out menus. The letter on the right-hand side of the tool fly-out menu is the shortcut key for the tool. A small arrow on the bottom-right corner of a tool in the Photoshop CS or ImageReady CS Toolbox indicates hidden tools reside in its associated fly-out menu. To access the fly-out menu, click a tool and hold down the mouse button until the fly-out menu appears. Leaving your mouse button depressed, move the cursor over the fly-out menu to make a selection.

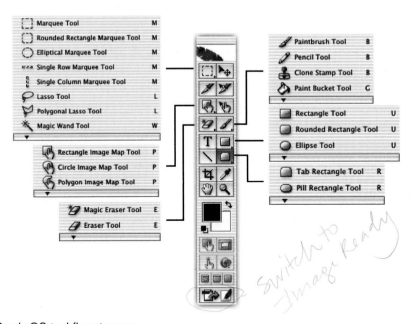

ImageReady CS tool fly-out menus

Jump To Buttons

When you're designing Web graphics, you'll often need to go between Photoshop CS and ImageReady CS. The Jump To button, located at the bottom of the Photoshop CS and ImageReady CS Toolbox, lets you switch quickly between Photoshop CS and ImageReady CS.

Jump To ImageReady CS button in Photoshop CS

Jump To Photoshop CS button in ImageReady CS

When you have an open image and click the Jump To button, the same image reopens in the other program.

Palettes

Photoshop CS and ImageReady CS let you manage the interface through a series of palettes. Each palette is identified by a tab at the top. By default, the palettes are docked together in groups. To make a palette appear at the front of the group, click the palette's tab. To help you customize your workspace so only the palettes you need are visible, Photoshop CS and ImageReady CS let you display each palette individually or as part of a group in any combination.

Some of the palettes in ImageReady CS contain fixed drop-down panels so you can hide and show areas of the palette. This helps reduce the amount of space the palettes take up onscreen. You can expand or contract these panels by clicking the small arrow to the left of the panel name. To expand or contract all of the drop-down panels at once, hold down the **Cmd** (Mac) or **Ctrl** (Windows) key and click any of the arrows in the panel group.

I. [PS/IR] **Docking Palettes in Groups and Individually**

Photoshop CS and ImageReady CS let you reorganize palettes by docking or undocking palettes as custom palette groups or as individual palettes. This is a very convenient thing to do if you find you are working with a unique combination of palettes and you don't want to crowd your workspace with palettes you don't use.

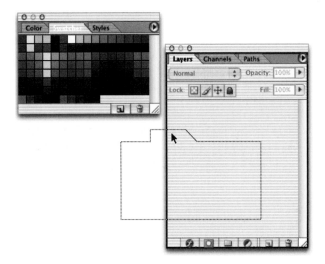

1. In Photoshop CS or ImageReady CS, click the **Swatches** tab (if it's not visible, choose **Window > Swatches**), and drag the **Swatches** palette by its tab into the group of palettes containing the **Layers** palette (if it's not visible, choose **Window > Layers**). As you move the palette, a dotted line will appear around the edges of the **Swatches** palette, and a black line will appear around the edges of the **Layers** palette.

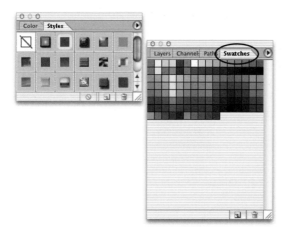

*By dragging the **Swatches** palette by the tab, you can dock it inside another palette group. You will find this helpful when you're using just a few features and you don't want to clutter the screen with lots of individual palettes.*

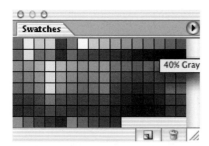

2. You can also create individual palettes, rather than nesting several palettes into a palette group. Drag the **Swatches** palette by its tab out of the **Layers** palette group and drop it anywhere inside the application window. The **Swatches** palette will form its own palette.

2. [PS/IR] _____Docking Palettes Vertically

You can also create vertical palette groups in Photoshop CS and ImageReady CS in addition to the nested palette groups you created in the last exercise.

1. The **Swatches** palette should be on its own right now, if you followed the last exercise. If not, drag the **Swatches** palette by its tab away from the palette group so it forms its own single palette.

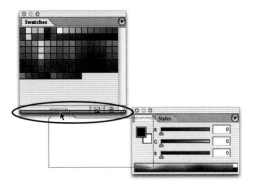

2. Drag the **Color** palette by its tab and position it under **Swatches** palette until a black line appears at the bottom.

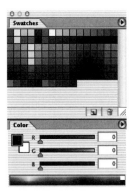

*The **Swatches** and **Color** palettes should now be docked to each other vertically. You will find it helpful to dock palettes vertically if you are using just a few palettes at a time or if you want to see all the contents of palettes you have open.*

NOTE | Returning Palettes to Default Settings

After you have reorganized your palettes, you will often want to return them to the way they were organized when you first opened Photoshop CS or ImageReady CS. The procedure for returning the palettes to default is slightly different in Photoshop CS and ImageReady CS.

In Photoshop CS, choose **Window > Workspace > Reset Palette Locations**.

In ImageReady CS, choose, **Window > Workspace > Default Palette Locations**.

3. [PS] _____Using the Options Bar

The Options bar contains settings for each tool in the Toolbox. The Options bar is context-sensitive, and it changes depending on which tool is selected in the Toolbox. By default, the Options bar is docked to the top of the screen below the application menu. The Options bar is not the only source for tool options. Some tools, such as the Type tool, also have options in palettes. This exercise shows you how to access the Options bar and, when necessary, the additional palettes. The Options bar works the same in Photoshop CS and ImageReady CS, but for this exercise you're going to use Photoshop CS.

1. Choose **File > New**, and click **OK**.

2. Click the **Magic Wand** tool in the **Toolbox**.

*Notice the settings for the **Magic Wand** tool (Selection Type, Tolerance, Anti-aliased, and Contiguous) are visible in the **Options** bar, which is located at the top of the screen.*

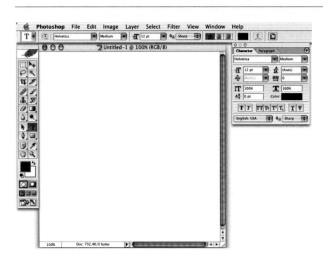

3. Click the **Type** tool in the **Toolbox**.

*The settings for the **Type** tool (Font Family, Font Style, and Font Size) are now visible in the **Options** bar.*

4. Click the **Palette** button on the right-hand side of the **Options** bar.

*This opens **Character** and **Paragraph** palettes. The **Character** and **Paragraph** palettes offer many options for formatting type. In Chapter 6, "Type," you'll learn how to use the type features in Photoshop CS and ImageReady CS to design Web graphics.*

5. Choose **File > Close** to close the file. You don't need to save it.

[PS/IR] _____ Docking Palettes in the Palette Well

In Photoshop CS and ImageReady CS, there's a spot on the right-hand side of the Options bar called the Palette Well, where you can dock one or more palettes. This feature was introduced in Photoshop 7 and is a new feature in ImageReady CS. The Palette Well is useful for keeping frequently used palettes easily accessible and to help keep your workspace uncluttered. For example, you're likely to use the Swatches and the Layers palettes frequently, so you may want to dock them in the Palette Well. There are two ways to dock palettes in the Palette Well. Here's a short exercise to show you how.

Note: You won't be able to see or use the Palette Well in the Options bar unless your screen resolution is set to 1024x768 or higher and you have a big enough screen (set your working area to **Maximize** on Windows). To change your screen resolution so you can see the Palette Well, choose **Apple > System Preferences**. In the **System Preferences** dialog box, double-click the **Display** icon. Change the resolution to 1024 x 768. On Windows, choose **Control Panel > Appearance and Themes > Change the Screen Resolution**, and change the resolution to 1024 x 768 in the **Settings** tab (Windows).

1. Make sure the **Swatches** and the **Layers** palettes are visible. If they are not visible, choose **Window > Swatches** and **Window > Layers**.

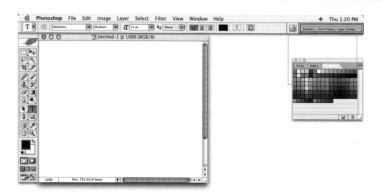

2. Drag the **Swatches** palette by its tab into the **Palette Well** on the right-hand side of the **Options** bar. Release the mouse button when you see a black line appear around the perimeter of the **Palette Well**.

3. Choose **Dock to Palette Well** from the **Layers** palette menu.

*All Photoshop CS and ImageReady CS palettes have a **Dock to Palette Well** command in the palette menus. **Note:** If **Dock to Palette Well** is grayed out in the palette menu, it's because your monitor resolution isn't set high enough to display the **Palette Well** on the far right of your screen. Increase your monitor resolution to at least 1024x768, as explained at the beginning of this exercise.*

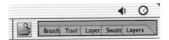

*Now, the **Swatches** palette and the **Layers** palette are docked inside the **Palette Well**, along with the **Brushes**, **Tool Presets**, and **Layer Comps** palettes, which are docked there by default. This makes it easier to access these palettes instead of going to the **Window** menu to find them.*

*If you want to open a palette while it is docked in the **Palette Well**, click its tab, and the corresponding palette will pop up below the **Palette Well**. To undock a palette from the **Palette Well**, drag it by its tab out of the **Palette Well**. You can also remove the palettes you added to the **Palette Well** by restoring your default workspace by choosing **Window > Workspace > Reset All Palette Locations**.*

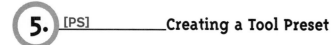

5. [PS] _____Creating a Tool Preset

Photoshop CS lets you save and reuse custom sets of tool options. This comes in handy if you use a tool to complete different kinds of tasks and want to switch easily between the tool options you use for each task.

1. Copy the **chap_02** folder from the **exercise_files** folder on the **H•O•T CD-ROM** to your **Desktop** if you haven't already done so.

2. In Photoshop CS, open **poster.psd** in the **chap_02** folder you copied to your **Desktop**.

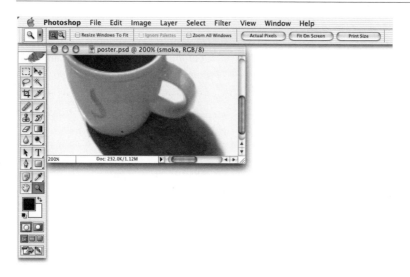

3. Click the **Zoom** tool, and click anywhere in the open image.

Notice the image gets bigger, but the document window remains the same size.

4. In the **Options** bar, check **Resize Windows To Fit**. Make sure the **Zoom** tool is still selected and click inside the image again.

*Notice the document window now expands to fit the magnified image because you checked **Resize Windows To Fit**. This is a useful setup for the **Zoom** tool, and now you'll save it so you can use it again on this or other images.*

5. Click the **Tool Presets** button at the left of the **Options** bar.

*This will open the **Tool Presets** picker. You'll see there are no presets defined yet for the **Zoom** tool, although Photoshop CS ships with presets for some other tools.*

6. Click the **New Tool Preset** icon on the **Tool Presets** picker.

7. In the **New Tool Preset** dialog box, name the preset **Resize Windows To Fit**. Click **OK**.

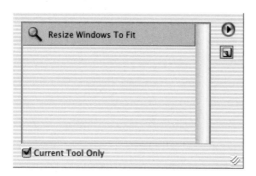

*You can reuse this preset with the **Zoom** tool at any time by choosing **Resize Windows To Fit** from the **Tool Presets** picker or from the **Tool Presets** palette, which is docked in the **Palette Well** by default.*

*If you uncheck **Current Tool Only** in either the **Tool Presets** picker or the **Tool Presets** palette, you'll see a list of all of the tool presets, including the presets that ship with Photoshop CS and the tool presets you create yourself.*

8. Choose **File > Close** to close **poster.psd**. You don't need to save it.

Resetting Tools

The Tool options in the Photoshop CS and ImageReady CS Options bar are "sticky," meaning they remember the most recently-used settings. There's a different procedure in each program for resetting their values back to defaults.

In Photoshop CS, click the **Tool Presets** button at the left of the **Options** bar to open the **Tool Presets** picker. Click the arrow on the top right of the **Tool Presets** picker, and choose **Reset All Tools**. A dialog box will appear asking if you want to reset all tools to default settings. Click **OK**.

In ImageReady CS, click the **Tool Presets** button at the top left of the **Options** bar and choose **Reset All Tools**. A dialog box will appear asking if you want to reset all tools to default settings. Click **OK**.

6. [PS] _____Saving a Custom Workspace

A useful feature in Photoshop CS is the capability to save and reuse a custom configuration of your workspace. In Photoshop CS, you can save all of your open palettes, including those in the Palette Well, exactly where you've left them. Creating custom workspaces can help increase your productivity when you're doing different tasks because you can save a custom workspace that best suits your workflow. The custom workspace feature works the same way in Photoshop CS and ImageReady CS, but for this exercise, you're going to use Photoshop CS.

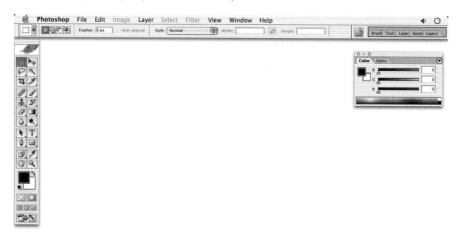

1. Click the **Close** button at the upper-left corner (Mac) or the upper-right corner (Windows) of all the open palette groups except the one containing the **Color** and **Styles** palettes.

If you followed **Exercise 4**, your **Layers** palette and **Swatches** palette will be docked in the **Palette Well** on the **Options** bar. If not, click the **Swatches** and **Layers** tabs and drag them into the **Palette Well**.

2. Choose **Window > Workspace > Save Workspace**.

3. In the **Save Workspace** dialog box, name the workspace **Painting** and click **Save**.

4. Now change things around as much as you like. Choose **Window > Info** to open another palette group; click and drag the **Color** palette to another place on the screen; move the **Layers** palette out of the **Palette Well**.

5. Choose **Window > Workspace > Painting**. Your workspace will immediately return to the saved configuration. Very cool!

Note: Resetting a saved workspace does not restore tool choices or tool options.

Keyboard Shortcuts

Photoshop CS and ImageReady CS have keyboard shortcuts assigned to many common commands. There are many useful keyboard shortcuts in Photoshop CS and ImageReady CS. Here are two important ones:

• The **Tab** key shows or hides all palettes and the Toolbox. To show or hide only the palettes, leaving the Toolbox as is, press **Shift+Tab**.

• To choose a tool quickly, press its shortcut key on your keyboard. To see a tool's shortcut key, move your mouse over the tool in the Toolbox. The shortcut key will be displayed in the tooltip in parentheses.

The following two charts provide the keyboard letter shortcuts to commonly used tools when designing Web graphics in Photoshop CS and ImageReady CS.

Photoshop Shortcut Keys	
Tool	**Shortcut Key**
Eraser	E
Eyedropper	I
Hand	H
Move	V
Switch Background/ Foreground Colors	X
Type	T
Zoom	Z

ImageReady Shortcut Keys	
Tool	**Shortcut Key**
Slice	K
Select Slice	O
Hide/Show Slices	Q

Keys

Customizing Keyboard Shortcuts in Photoshop CS

...tures in Photoshop CS is the capability to customize keyboard shortcuts.
...modify the default keyboard shortcuts or create your own custom sets of key-
...assign new or reassign existing keyboard shortcuts to menu items, tools, and
palette commands. When you're finished, you can save and print a complete list of keyboard shortcuts.
Here is an exercise to show you how.

1. Choose **Edit > Keyboard Shortcuts**.

*Notice the current keyboard shortcut set is **Photoshop Default**. To avoid overwriting the default set,
you'll create your own new set based on the current keyboard shortcuts before making any changes.*

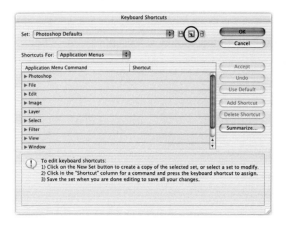

2. Click the **Create New Set** button.

3. In the **Save** dialog box, name your file **web_workflow.kys** and keep the default save location.
Click **Save**.

*Notice the current set is **web_workflow** in the **Keyboard Shortcuts** dialog box. Now you can
begin to make changes without overwriting the default keyboard shortcuts.*

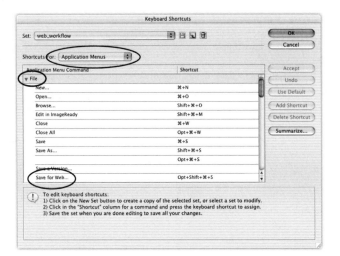

4. In the **Shortcuts For** pop-up menu, choose **Application Menus**. In the **Application Menu Command** list, click the arrow next to **File** to expand the contents of the **File** menu. Scroll down until you can see **Save for Web**.

*One of the commands you're going to be using frequently is **File > Save for Web**. By default, this command is assigned **Option+Shift+Cmd+S** (Mac) or **Alt+Shift+Ctrl+S** (Windows), which are complicated shortcuts to use and a bit difficult to remember. You're going to change them to something simpler.*

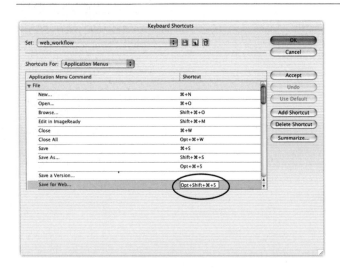

5. In the **Application Menu Command** list, click **Save for Web** to select it. You can now edit the keyboard shortcut for this command.

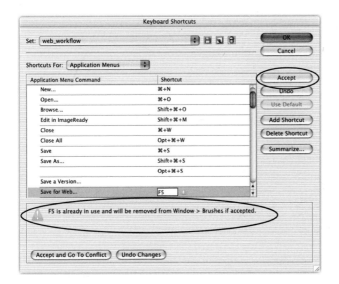

6. Press the **F5** key. A warning message will appear at the bottom of the **Keyboard Shortcuts** dialog box indicating the **F5** key is currently used for **Window > Brushes,** which hides and displays the **Brushes** palette.

*Because most of the available keyboard shortcuts are already being used by other commands in Photoshop CS, you will have to make some compromises about which keyboard shortcuts to keep and which keyboards shortcuts you can live without. In this case, **F5** launches the **Brushes** palette. Since you will not be using the **Brushes** palette very often to create Web graphics, you'll reassign the **F5** keyboard shortcut to the **Save for Web** command. Also, keep in mind this change will only affect the **web_workflow** keyboard shortcuts. You can always return to the default keyboard shortcuts if you want to revert your changes.*

7. Click **Accept** on the right-hand side of the dialog box to assign **F5** to the **File > Save for Web** command.

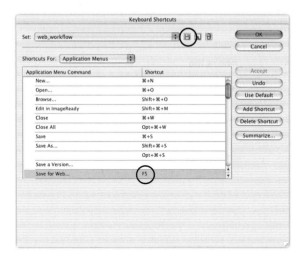

8. Click **Save** to save the changes to the **web_workflow** keyboard shortcut set and click **OK** to close the **Keyboard Shortcuts** dialog box.

9. To test the new **Save for Web** keyboard shortcut, open **poster.psd** from the **chap_02** folder you copied to your **Desktop**. Press the **F5** key.

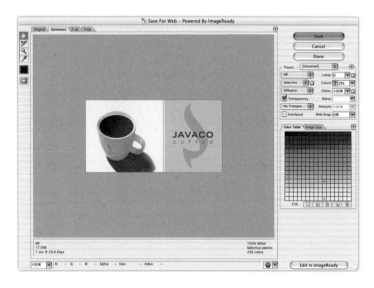

*The **Save For Web** dialog box will open using the customized keyboard shortcut you created.*

10. Click **Cancel** to close the **Save For Web** dialog box. You'll learn all about how to use the **Save for Web** feature in Chapter 4, "*Optimization*."

TIP | Saving and Printing Keyboard Shortcut Sets

One of the great customizable keyboard shortcuts options is the capability to save and print any set of customized keyboard shortcuts. Photoshop CS summarizes the data from keyboard shortcut sets into an HTML file you can save and print for quick reference.

To save and print a keyboard shortcut set, choose **Edit > Keyboard Shortcuts**. Choose the keyboard shortcut set you want to save or print from the **Set** pop-up menu. Click the **Summarize** button on the right-hand side of the dialog box. Type the filename and specify the location where you would like to save the file. Click **Save**.

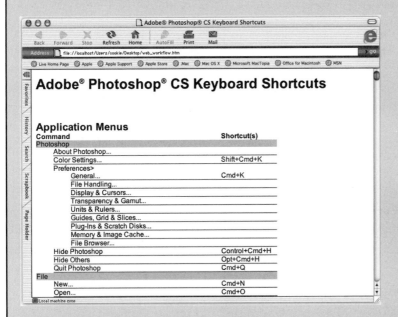

Photoshop CS will automatically launch your default Web browser and display a complete list of keyboard shortcuts. You can print this keyboard shortcut list by choosing **File > Print** in your Web browser.

The File Browser

Photoshop 7 introduced the File Browser, which lets you view and organize folders of images. The File Browser is very useful for organizing any folder of images but is especially useful when organizing source images from a digital camera, which often come into your computer with meaningless names, without image previews, and with the wrong orientation.

A number of enhancements have been made to the File Browser in Photoshop CS, specifically to the interface.

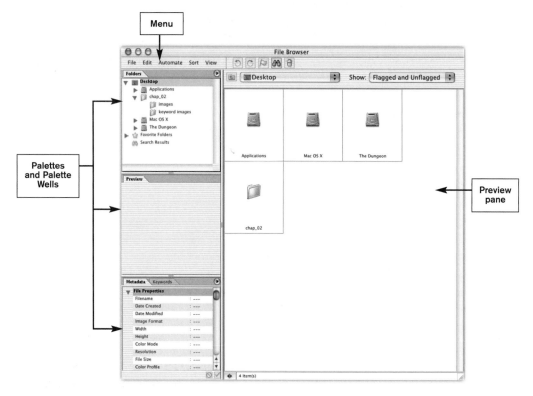

The File Browser in Photoshop CS has its own menu and palette structure, which are shown here. You can customize the palette configuration by dragging the tab of the palette into one of the three Palette Wells to create a single palette or a group of palettes.

In the next two exercises, you'll explore the general features of the File Browser as well as some of the new features in Photoshop CS.

8. [PS] Viewing and Organizing Images in the File Browser

In this exercise, you'll explore some of the basic features of the File Browser, such as navigating and rotating images, as well as some of the new features in Photoshop CS, including arranging images by dragging and dropping and flagging images.

1. To open the **File Browser**, click the **Toggle File Browser** button on the right-hand side of the **Options** bar.

2. Use the **Folders** palette on the top-left side of the **File Browser** to navigate to your **Desktop** by expanding and collapsing the **arrows** (Mac) or the **+** (Windows). The preview pane on the right-hand side of the **File Browser** will display all the files and folders on your **Desktop**, including the **chap_02** folder you copied to your **Desktop** from the **H•O•T CD-ROM** in a previous exercise.

3. In the preview pane of the **File Browser**, double-click the **chap_02** folder. Then double-click the **images** folder inside the **chap_02** folder. Make sure **Flagged and Unflagged** is selected from the **Show** pop-up menu.

*The File **Browser** will display thumbnails of all of the images in the **images** folder.*

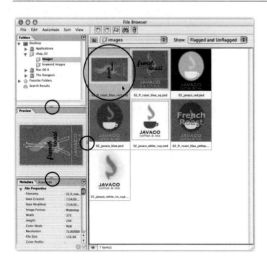

4. Click the image thumbnail at the top left that is rotated 90 degrees counterclockwise.

*Notice the **Preview** palette shows a preview of the selected image, and the **Metadata** palette shows detailed information about the file, such as filename, date created, and date modified. If you want to increase or decrease the size of the **Preview** palette or the **Metadata** palette, drag the horizontal separators between the palettes or the vertical separator between the palettes and the preview pane.*

5. Drag and drop the rotated image between the blue and white Javaco Coffee & Tea images in the second row of the images in the preview pane. As you're dragging the rotated image, a black line will appear between the blue and white Javaco Coffee & Tea images to show where you'll place the image.

*Dragging and dropping to arrange images inside the preview pane is new to Photoshop CS. The **File Browser** remembers the arrangement as a custom view, which is kept until you rearrange the images.*

6. Click the rotated image in the preview pane and click the **Rotate Clockwise** button at the top of the **File Browser**.

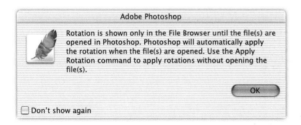

7. A dialog box will appear telling you the image will appear rotated in the **File Browser** until you open it in Photoshop CS. Click **OK**.

*This rotates the selected thumbnail 90 degrees clockwise. To rotate the image counterclockwise, use the **Rotate Counterclockwise** button, which is located to the left of the **Rotate Clockwise** button. You can find additional rotate commands in the **Edit** menu in the **File Browser**. The ability to identify and rotate images is one of the key benefits of the **File Browser**. In earlier versions of Photoshop, it was necessary to open, rotate, and save the image to perform this useful and common operation.*

8. Double-click the thumbnail of the same image to open it in Photoshop CS. The image, which was originally 90 degrees counterclockwise, is automatically rotated to a vertical format because you rotated the thumbnail in the **File Browser**.

*Note: You can now open images from the **File Browser** directly in ImageReady CS by choosing **File > Edit in ImageReady** from the **File Browser** menu. This is a new feature in Photoshop CS.*

9. Close the image in Photoshop CS and return to the **File Browser** by clicking anywhere inside the **File Browser** window.

10. Click the image in the top-left corner of the preview pane and choose **Edit > Flag** from the **File Browser** menu. You will notice a small flag icon in the bottom-right corner of the image preview, which indicates you applied a flag to this image.

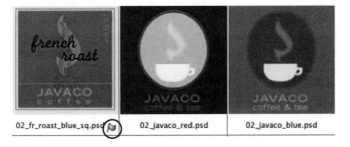

*Flagging and unflagging images is new in Photoshop CS and lets you hide or show designated images inside a folder. For example, you could flag frequently used images in a folder so only those images are displayed in the **File Browser**, even though the unflagged images are still present in the folder. You can choose to display flagged images, unflagged images, or flagged and unflagged images by using the options in the **Show** pop-up menu.*

11. Apply flags to the other two images in the top row of the preview pane by repeating **Step 10**.

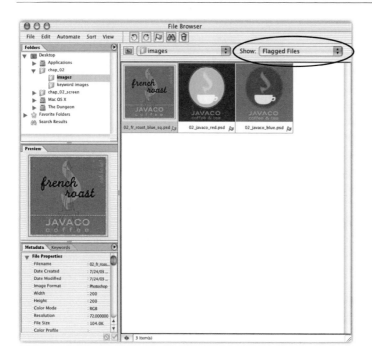

12. Choose **Flagged Files** from the **Show** pop-up menu.

Notice only the files you flagged are visible in the preview pane.

13. Choose **Unflagged Files** from the **Show** pop-up menu.

Notice all the files except those files you flagged are visible in the preview pane.

14. Choose **Flagged and Unflagged** files from the **Show** pop-up menu so all files in the images folder are visible.

15. In the **File Browser**, choose **File > New Folder**. An untitled folder icon will appear in the preview pane.

*The ability to create a folder from within the **File Browser** is very useful because it lets you organize the files on your hard drive from this intuitive and visual interface while you are inside Photoshop CS! The folder you see inside the **File Browser** is real—it will appear on your hard drive, too.*

16. Rename the new folder by clicking the word **untitled** and typing **unflagged images** as the new name.

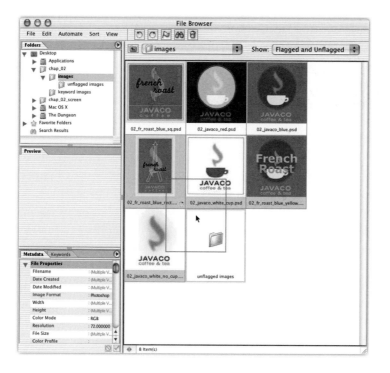

17. In the **File Browser** window, select the unflagged images by holding down the **Shift** key and clicking each image. Drag the selected images into the **unflagged images** folder.

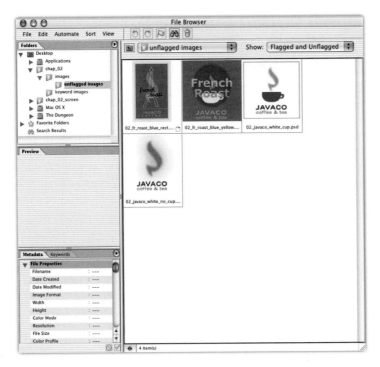

18. Double-click the **unflagged images** folder. You will now see the four images you dragged into this folder in the preview pane.

*Note: If you browse to your **Desktop** and open the **images** folder in the **chap_02** folder, you will see the **unflagged images** folder you just created.*

19. Choose **File > Close File Browser** from the **File Browser** menu.

Assigning Keywords and Searching in the File Browser

One of the great new File Browser features in Photoshop CS is the capability to assign keywords to one or more images using the new Keywords palette. Keywords are search phrases you define to describe your images, and later provide a means to search and locate your images. Once you have assigned keywords to images, you can search for images using the new search feature. Here is an exercise to show you how.

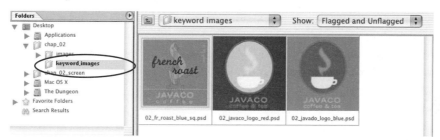

1. Open the **File Browser** from the **Options** bar. Using the **Folders** palette, navigate to the **keyword_images** folder in the **chap_02** folder you copied to your **Desktop**.

2. Click the **Keywords** tab.

Notice there is a list of default keyword sets and a series of keywords nested inside the keyword sets. If any of the keyword sets are expanded, click the arrow to the left of the keyword set name to collapse them.

3. Click the **New Keyword Set** button at the bottom of the **Keywords** palette and name the new keyword set **Javaco**. Press **Return** (Mac) or **Enter** (Windows).

*Notice the list of keyword sets is stored alphabetically in the **Keywords** palette.*

4. Click the **Javaco** keyword set to select it and click the **New Keyword** button on the bottom of the **Keywords** palette. Name the keyword **French Roast**, then press **Return** (Mac) or **Enter** (Windows).

*Notice the **French Roast** keyword is nested inside the **Javaco** keyword set.*

5. Click the **Javaco** keyword set to select it, click the **New Keyword** button, name the keyword **Coffee Cup**, and press **Return** (Mac) or **Enter** (Windows).

*You should now see the keywords **Coffee Cup** and **French Roast** nested alphabetically in the **Javaco** keyword set. Now you can begin assigning these keywords to your images.*

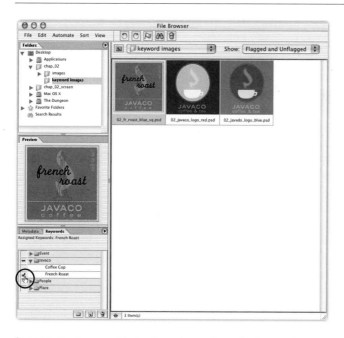

6. Click the image with the **french roast** text in the preview pane. Click in the square next to the **French Roast** keyword in the **Keywords** palette. A black checkmark will appear beside the **French Roast** keyword, and a dash will automatically appear beside the **Javaco** keyword set, indicating the **French Roast** keyword has been assigned to the image.

7. Select the remaining two Javaco Coffee & Tea images by holding down the **Shift** key and clicking each image. Assign the **Coffee Cup** keyword to the images by clicking in the square next to the **Coffee Cup** keyword.

8. A dialog box will appear, indicating you have multiple images selected. Click **Yes** to assign the **Coffee Cup** keyword to both images.

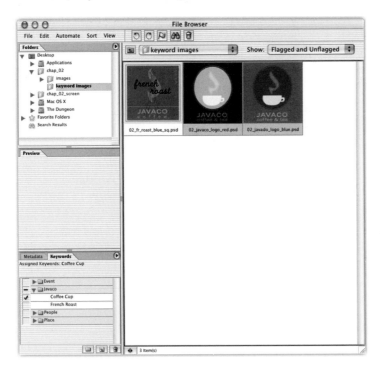

A black checkmark will now appear beside the **Coffee Cup** *keyword, and a dash will automatically appear in the square beside the* **Javaco** *keyword set. Next, you'll use the* **French Roast** *and* **Coffee Cup** *keywords to search in the* **File Browser***.*

9. Click the **Search** button at the top of the **File Browser**.

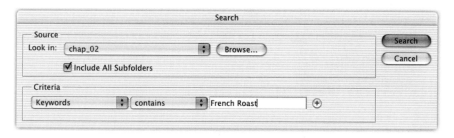

10. In the **Search** dialog box, click the **Browse** button, browse to your **Desktop**, and select the **chap_02** folder. Check **Include All Subfolders**. In the **Criteria** section, choose **Keywords** from the first pop-up menu, choose **contains** from the second pop-up menu, and type **French Roast** in the text field. Click **Search**.

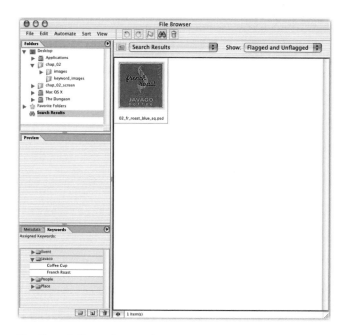

*The **French Roast** image should now be displayed in the preview pane.*

11. Click the **Search** button at the top of the **File Browser**. Click the **Browse** button and browse to the **chap_02** folder on your **Desktop** and check **Include All Subfolders**. In the **Criteria** section, choose **Keywords** from the first pop-up menu, choose **contains** from the second pop-up menu, and type **Coffee Cup** in the text field. Click **Search**.

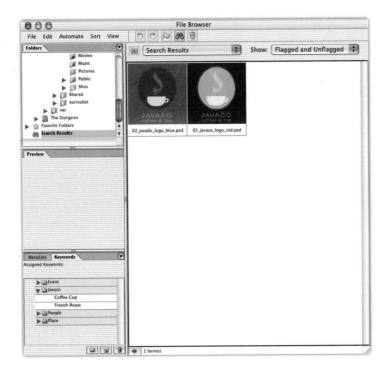

*This time, the **Javaco Coffee & Tea** images should appear inside the preview pane. Pretty cool stuff!*

12. Choose **File > Close File Browser** to close the **File Browser**. Close any open files without saving.

Setting Preferences for the Web

Now that you've learned about the interface in Photoshop CS and ImageReady CS, there is one thing you need to do before you start designing Web graphics. You need to set your preferences for a Web graphics workflow.

There are a number of preference settings in Photoshop CS that help you define your workflow. The only preference that directly impacts whether you are set up properly for a Web graphics workflow is **Units & Rulers**. For a complete list of preferences and their settings, refer to the Photoshop CS User Guide.

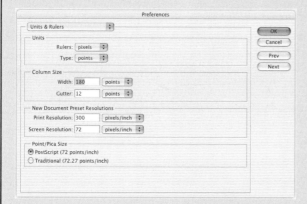

To change **Units & Rulers**, choose **Photoshop > Preferences > Units & Rulers** (Mac) or **Edit > Preferences > Units & Rulers** (Windows). In the **Preferences** dialog box, choose **pixels** from the **Rulers** pop-up menu. Click **OK**.

When you create Web graphics, you measure everything by pixels and sometimes points, not picas, as you would in print.

Note: ImageReady CS is designed specifically for creating Web graphics, so you do not need to set any preferences to prepare for Web work. Units and rulers are set to pixels, and there is no option to change them.

Now that you understand the Photoshop CS and ImageReady CS interfaces, you're ready to begin making some Web graphics. In the next chapter, "Color," you'll learn about choosing and using color in your Web images.

3.
Color

| sRGB for Windows | sRGB and Gamma for Macs |
| The Decline of Web-Safe Color |
| Choosing Web Safe Colors from the Color Picker |
| Loading and Creating Swatches | Recoloring Layered Images |
| Using the Color Replacement Tool | Copy Color as HTML |

chap_03

Photoshop CS/ImageReady CS
H•O•T CD-ROM

Photoshop CS and ImageReady CS offer great tools for working with color. In this chapter, you'll learn useful tips for picking, editing, and changing colors. You'll explore the Color Picker and Swatches palette, then recolor images with the colors you choose. You'll also learn how to recolor images using the new Color Replacement tool in Photoshop CS.

You'll find less emphasis on Web-safe color in this chapter than you may have come to expect in our lynda.com series of books. Today, there's less reason to use to a browser-safe palette, because 8-bit (256-color) computer display systems are practically obsolete. You'll read about the decline of Web-safe color in this chapter, but you'll also discover how to access Web-safe colors when you need them. Along the way, you'll determine how to limit the Color Picker dialog box to Web-safe colors, load a special lynda.com swatch of Web-safe colors, create your own custom color swatches, and copy color values to HTML.

Color Profiles and the Web

Have you ever looked at the same image on two computers and noticed that the colors look different? This very common problem can be caused because there is no calibration standard for screen-based colors.

In the print world, designers use ICC (International Color Consortium) profiles to make sure the colors onscreen look the same when they're printed. ICC profiles are embedded into the image file format and provide additional information about the color characteristics of the image. This color information stays with the file so any device can display or print the file accurately.

Unfortunately, you cannot use ICC profiles when designing Web graphics. First, embedding ICC profiles increases the image size, which negatively impacts how quickly graphics load. In some cases, a color profile can be upwards of 750 KB, which may be larger than an optimized Web graphic. Second, Web browsers can't read color profiles. As a result, any efforts you make to keep colors consistent using ICC profiles will be lost as soon as your graphics hit the Web.

sRGB for Windows

In an effort to standardize how colors are displayed onscreen, Microsoft and Hewlett-Packard developed a new color space called sRGB. The goal of sRGB is to produce a reliable and repeatable method for describing color that can be understood by computer monitors and that picks up one calibration based on an average monitor.

In Photoshop CS, the color settings are set to use sRGB by default. Therefore, you can begin creating Web graphics on Windows without making any changes. Unfortunately, this is not true if you're using a Mac. At the moment, sRGB is a color workspace that is supported natively on Windows systems, and only in certain applications like Photoshop CS on the Mac. If you are on a Mac, please read the following sections that relate to your system.

NOTE | What Is Gamma?

sRGB calls for a standard gamma setting of 2.2. What is gamma, you might ask? The gamma affects the appearance of your computer screen, as it defines a midpoint for gray, meaning that it affects the grays or values between white and black, not the white-point or black-point display. Windows computers ship with a 2.2 gamma setting; Macs use a 1.8 gamma setting. As a result, Web graphics look darker on Windows than they do on Macs. In Photoshop CS and ImageReady CS, there are ways to preview the gamma of a graphic on either platform. Open any graphic inside either program. To preview gamma in Photoshop CS, choose **View > Proof Setup** and select either **Windows RGB** or **Macintosh RGB**. To preview gamma in ImageReady CS, choose **View > Preview** and select either **Standard Macintosh Color** or **Standard Windows Color**.

---

sRGB and Gamma for Macs

If you're using a Mac, you need to consider a few things with respect to color settings before you begin designing Web graphics.

By default, the Photoshop CS color settings are set to Web Graphics Defaults, which uses sRGB and a gamma of 2.2 as its default color setting. On a Mac, this is can be a problem because colors will be different in Photoshop CS than in most other Mac applications, including ImageReady CS (!) and Microsoft Internet Explorer, Safari, and Netscape browsers that don't currently support sRGB! This can be extremely frustrating when you're designing Web graphics on a Mac because your colors will consistently look different, depending on which application you use.

The color workflow is different for Web graphics than it is for print graphics. The great thing about Photoshop CS is that you can change your color settings at any time. This makes it possible to use one color setting for Web color workflow, and another for print color workflow. You'll learn how to change your color settings in Photoshop CS in the sidebar that follows this section.

If you're using a Mac, you can choose to keep the Photoshop CS default color settings so they use sRGB; just be aware your images will appear differently in other applications, including ImageReady CS. If you would prefer that your images look the same in all applications with a 1.8 gamma setting, you can turn off the color settings by following the instructions below.

NOTE | Changing Photoshop CS Color Settings

If you're using a Mac, you may decide to change your Photoshop CS color settings so they no longer use sRGB, which will ensure the colors you choose in Photoshop CS will look the same in ImageReady CS, other graphics applications, HTML editors, and Web browsers that don't use sRGB. Here's how.

Launch Photoshop CS, and choose **Photoshop > Color Settings**.

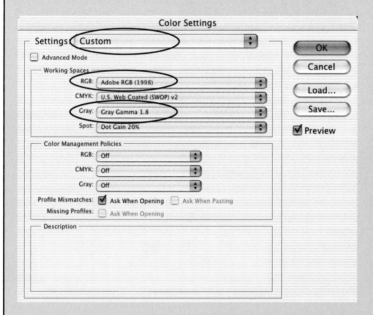

In the **Color Settings** dialog box, change the settings to **RGB: Adobe RGB (1998)** and **Gray: Gray Gamma 1.8**. This will cause the menu called **Settings** to change automatically to **Custom**. Click **OK**.

Note that this change sets the **RGB** working space to **Adobe RGB (1998)**, which leaves the appearance of your monitor set to its defaults as in ImageReady CS, other graphics applications. HTML editors, and Web browsers. The graphics on your screen will appear without any alterations.

NOTE | Setting Gamma on a Mac

If you're using a Mac, you may decide to change your gamma settings to 2.2. If you think your site might have a larger Windows audience, this change may save you from potential unanticipated revisions to lighten up your graphics. Keep in mind that changing your gamma settings will affect all applications, not just Photoshop CS.

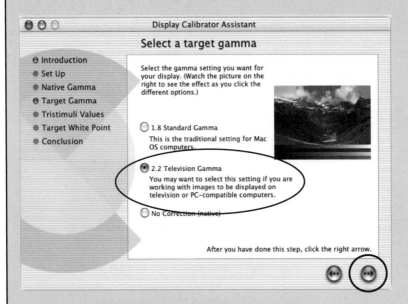

To change your gamma settings, use the calibration utilities built into Mac OS X. In the **Finder**, choose **Go > Applications**. Double-click on the **Utilities** folder, then double-click the **Display Calibrator** to launch the **Display Calibrator Assistant**. Click the forward arrow at the bottom-right corner of the dialog box to navigate to the **Select a target gamma** screen. Choose **2.2 Television Gamma**. Click the forward arrow twice and name your profile **Windows Gamma**. Click **Create**.

Changing your gamma to match Windows is a benefit—it affects all applications, including Photoshop CS, ImageReady CS, other graphics applications, HTML editors, and Web browsers.

> **TIP | Finding Additional Color Management Help**
>
> Photoshop CS ships with additional documentation about color management, which is accessible from the **Welcome Screen**. The **Welcome Screen** appears when you launch the application, or you can open it by choosing **Help > Welcome Screen**. Keep in mind that color management is a complex topic and is primarily used for print design. If you're interested in learning more about color management, be sure to give the additional documentation a read. You can also find more information in the Photoshop CS User Guide.

The Decline of Web-Safe Color

The concept of Web-safe color was introduced when the Web first gained popularity in the mid 1990s. At that time, (back in dark ages!) the majority of computer users owned computers that were only capable of displaying 256 colors or less. These old computers were called 8-bit color systems, because they were limited by hardware constraints to display only 256 colors. Most graphics professionals owned computers that were 24-bit (displayed millions of colors), which at that time cost a lot more money than the average 8-bit consumer computer. For this reason, if a Web designer had a better computer that could display millions of colors, there was a good chance that the better computer could produce colors that would not be accurately portrayed on the more common 8-bit computers in circulation back then.

Hence, the Web-safe palette was born, and was first published and described in Lynda Weinman's book, *Designing Web Graphics* (1996). This palette contains only 216 colors. However, the 216 were special, because these colors could be accurately displayed on the 8-bit computer systems.

The term Web-safe color refers to the use of these special 216 colors. Other terms, such as the Web palette, 216-color palette, Netscape palette, or 6 x 6 x 6 color cube all refer to the same 216 colors. You should limit your color choices to only the browser-safe palette if you think your Web site will be viewed on an 8-bit system. Just a few short years ago, almost all computers had 8-bit video cards. When Web design first emerged as a design medium, it was important for designers to understand Web-safe color and how to create Web graphics in this limited palette. This was no picnic, because the browser-safe palette is not very visually exciting. (It contains mostly highly saturated colors of medium value and not many light or dark colors, nor many muted or tinted tones.)

Good news: In most cases, it is now safe to design for the Web without the browser-safe palette. Today, very few computer users have machines with 8-bit video cards and most users can see any color you design with. If you're unsure about when to use the Web-safe palette, the answer depends on your audience, clients, and maybe even the employer for whom you're designing.

If you're designing Web sites for alternative online publishing devices such as cell phones, PDAs, or Internet appliances, you may still need to use a browser-safe palette. Most of those devices currently display only 8-bit color, and some are still 1-bit (black-and-white) systems.

Some companies still feel it's a badge of Web design honor to work with browser-safe colors, so you might want to know how to use them. As you'll learn in this chapter, the Web palette is built into color picking tools in Photoshop CS and ImageReady CS, so it's easy to create or recolor a Web graphic in browser-safe colors.

Keep in mind there's no harm in using the browser-safe palette. It simply limits your choices to 216 colors. If you don't have a lot of experience or confidence picking colors that work well together, you might find it easier to work with a limited number of color choices. There's no right or wrong about using browser-safe colors as long as you're able to combine them in pleasing and effective ways.

The upside is that the need to stick to a browser-safe palette is on the decline. It may be difficult to let go of the notion that you should design with Web-safe colors, particularly if you've put effort into developing that skill. Try to see it as I do—it's a sign of the great progress that most computers today have better color displays, and a liberating step forward for Web design!

What Happens on an 8-bit System If You Don't Use Web-Safe Colors?

It's useful to know what your site will look like if you don't design with Web-safe colors, and your site is viewed on an 8-bit system. Two problems will occur.

First, the colors you set in the HTML code, such as the colors of page backgrounds, text, and links, will shift in the 8-bit viewer's browser. Unpredictable color shifts can cause text or links to be unreadable against a like-colored background.

Graphic viewed in 24-bit color

Same graphic viewed in 8-bit color

Close-up in 24-bit color   *Close-up in 8-bit color*

The second problem involves color. If you make flat art (such as illustrations or cartoons) with non-Web-safe colors, these colors will appear dithered (made up of tiny dots) when the image is viewed on an 8-bit system. The unwanted dithering is the result of the viewer's 8-bit display system trying to simulate colors it can't display. The previous illustrations demonstrate what that looks like, which shows why you'll want to use Web-safe colors in your flat art Web graphics in the rare event you're designing for an 8-bit audience. However, the opposite is true for photographic content. If you're preparing photographs for the Web, never force them to Web-safe colors. When an 8-bit browser displays photographic images, it converts them to 8-bit on the fly and does a better job than if you'd converted them yourself.

In the next few exercises, you'll learn how to select Web colors when you want them, and how to use the color picking tools Photoshop CS and ImageReady CS offer. You'll also learn how to pull it all together with quick and easy ways to recolor layered artwork.

I. [PS] Choosing Web-Safe Colors from the Color Picker

In early versions of Photoshop, it was difficult to choose a Web-safe color from the Color Picker dialog box without manually typing in Web-safe RGB values. This hassle has been removed since Photoshop 5.5, because the Color Picker dialog box can now be set to display only Web colors.

1. Click on the **foreground color** in the Photoshop CS **Toolbox** to open the **Color Picker** dialog box.

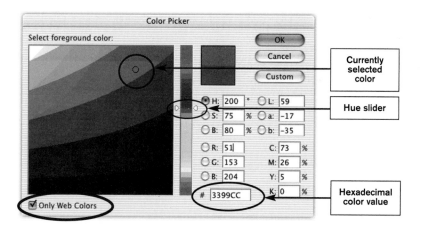

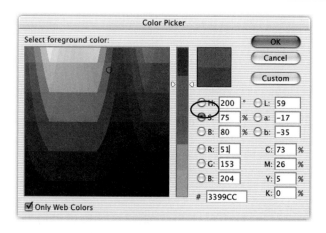

2. Check **Only Web Colors** in the bottom-left corner of the **Color Picker** dialog box.

*Notice the hexadecimal readout at the bottom of the **Color Picker** dialog box. If you move the arrows up the vertical hue slider, you'll see these readout numbers and the colors on the screen change.*

*H, S, and B stand for **Hue**, **Saturation**, and **Brightness**. The **Color Picker** dialog box in the previous screen shot is set to view by hue. All the different radio buttons offer different ways of seeing and picking colors. You may find these different choices help you more quickly find colors that fit together. It's very interesting to see how Web colors spread across the spectrum if you actively move the slider when exploring these different settings of **H, S, B, R, G, B,** or **L, a, b.***

3. Click **S** to view the **Color Picker** by **Saturation**, which is the measure of color intensity. Try moving the vertical slider or clicking on a different color in the rainbow area to view Web-safe colors by **Saturation**. Move the slider arrows up to view more highly saturated Web colors, and down to view the desaturated ones.

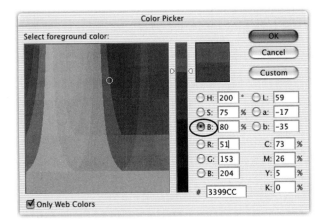

4. Click **B** to view the **Color Picker** by Brightness, which is the measure of light to dark values. To view Web-safe colors by this criterion, try moving the brightness slider or clicking on a different color in the rainbow area. Move the slider arrows up to view brighter Web color values, and down to view darker ones.

*Try clicking on the **R**, **G**, and **B** buttons as well. These stand for **Red**, **Green**, and **Blue**. Click on the **L**, **a**, and **b** buttons next. These stand for **Lightness**, **a Axis** (green to magenta), and **b Axis** (blue to yellow). Aside from the psychedelic color experience, these methods offer some interesting color formations you can use to view or pick Web colors.*

In Photoshop CS, there are often numerous ways to achieve the same goal. Instead of viewing only Web-safe colors, you can view all colors and then snap a non-Web-safe color. This feature is also available in ImageReady CS.

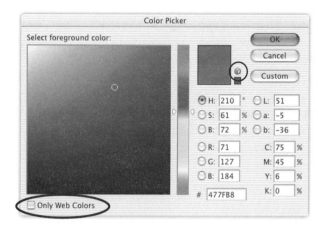

5. Uncheck the **Only Web Colors** box and click on the **H** button to display the **Hues** view. Move and click your cursor around inside the color area on the left. Notice the **cube** icon that appears to the right of the color preview. The cube alerts you when you've selected a non-safe Web color. Click on the **swatch** below the **cube**. The color selection will jump to the closest Web-safe color, and the cube will disappear.

6. Click **OK**, and the Web-safe color you just chose will appear as the **foreground color** in the **Toolbox**.

Note: This feature works identically in ImageReady CS. If you decide to try it out in ImageReady CS now, be sure to return to Photoshop CS for the next exercise.

NOTE | ImageReady CS and Photoshop CS Color Picker Differences

ImageReady CS has a **Color Picker** dialog box almost identical to the Photoshop CS **Color Picker** dialog box. The **Color Picker** dialog box in ImageReady CS lacks some print-oriented features, such as feedback about L.a.b. and CMYK color and out-of-print gamut warnings. That's because Photoshop CS can be used to design for print or the Web; ImageReady CS was developed specifically for designing Web graphics.

TIP | Choosing Web-Safe Colors from the Color Palette

In addition to choosing Web-safe colors from the **Color Picker** dialog box, you can also choose Web-safe colors from the **Color** palette in Photoshop CS and ImageReady CS. You may find it easier to choose colors from the **Color** palette because you can leave it open·at all times instead of reopening and closing the **Color Picker** dialog box. To choose Web-safe colors from the **Color** palette, first make sure the **Color** palette is visible. If it is not, choose **Window > Colors**.

Choose **Web Color Sliders** from the **Color** palette menu.

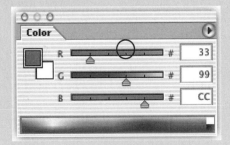

When you use the Web color sliders, the colors will automatically snap to Web-safe colors at the tick marks. If you want to override the Web color sliders, hold down the **Option** key (Mac) or **Alt** key (Windows). As soon as you choose a color that is out of the Web-safe color range, the alert cube will appear to the left of the sliders. You can choose the closest Web-safe color by clicking the swatch below the cube, just as you did using the **Color Picker** dialog box.

Note: In Photoshop CS, you must choose Web-safe colors to view the alert cube. Because ImageReady CS is designed specifically for creating Web graphics, the alert cube is available for all sliders.

2. [PS] Loading Color Swatches

Another way to choose colors in Photoshop CS and ImageReady CS is to use the Swatches palette. Photoshop CS and ImageReady CS ship with a number of prebuilt swatches, including swatches created specifically for designing Web graphics. In addition, you can load swatches created and saved by other Photoshop CS and ImageReady CS users. Here is an exercise to show you how. This exercise takes place in Photoshop CS, but works the same way in ImageReady CS.

1. Make sure the **Swatches** palette is visible. If it is not, choose **Window > Swatches**.

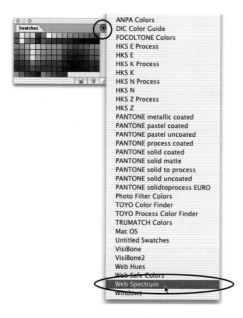

2. Choose **Web Spectrum** from the **Swatches** palette menu.

3. Click **OK** to replace the current swatches with the **Web Spectrum** swatches.

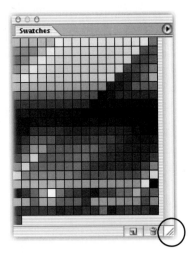

The **Swatches** palette will now be updated with the **Web Spectrum** swatches. Increase the size of the **Swatches** palette so it displays all the colors by dragging the resize handle in the bottom-right corner of the palette. You can choose any color in the **Swatches** palette by clicking it. Note that when you click on a color in the **Swatches** palette to choose it, the foreground color in the **Toolbox** automatically changes to reflect your choice.

Next, you'll learn how to load the **lynda.com** swatch that is included on the **H•O•T CD-ROM**.

Lynda Weinman and Bruce Heavin wrote a book together in 1997 called Coloring Web Graphics, which is now out of print. Bruce developed a series of Web swatches for that book, which he organized aesthetically to make it easier to choose Web-safe colors. One of these swatches is included inside the **chap_03** folder of the **H•O•T CD-ROM** for you to load and use.

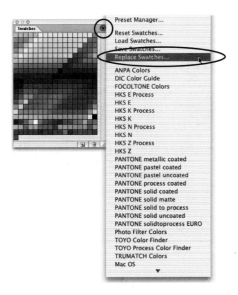

4. Choose **Replace Swatches** from the **Swatches** palette menu.

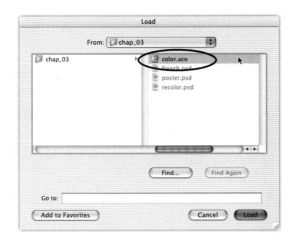

5. Navigate to the **chap_03** folder you copied to your **Desktop** from the **H•O•T CD-ROM** and choose **color.aco**. Click **Load** (or **Open** in ImageReady CS).

*Note: If you choose **Replace Swatches**, you will replace the current swatch with the swatch you are loading. If you choose **Load Swatches**, you will append the current swatch with the colors of the swatch you are loading.*

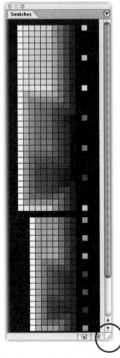

6. Drag the **Swatches** palette window down as far as it will go by using the resize handle in the bottom-right corner of the palette. Then, use the scroll bar to view the entire swatch. This swatch is organized by hue (up and down), by value (right to left), and saturation (up and down).

*Note: Many of the colors are repeated to present an array efficiently organized for color picking. It's nice to see all the hues together. If you want to pick a red, for example, you can view the choices easily. It's also helpful to see all the dark colors and/or colors of equal saturation together. Once you use this swatch set, you will likely never remove it from the **Swatches** palette because it is so useful.*

7. Choose **Reset Swatches** from the **Swatches** palette menu. Click **OK** to replace the **lynda.com** swatch with the default swatch.

3. [PS] _____Creating Custom Swatches

There are going to be times when you have a custom color scheme and you'd rather limit the Swatches palette to contain only those colors. In this exercise, you'll learn to make custom swatches for the Swatches palette two ways—by selecting colors from an existing swatch, and by sampling colors from an image. For this exercise, you'll work in the Preset Manager in Photoshop CS, which is specifically designed to create custom swatches and other application presets. You can also make a custom swatch in ImageReady CS, but it's more tedious because you have work directly in the Swatches palette.

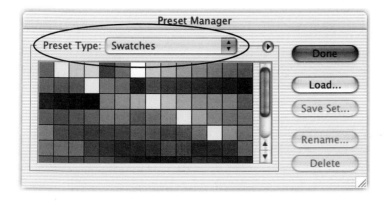

1. Choose **Edit > Preset Manager**. In the **Preset Manager** window, choose **Swatches** from the **Preset Type** pop-up menu.

The **Preset Manager** in Photoshop CS lets you control content libraries, such as swatches, as well as other application presets such as brushes, gradients, styles, and patterns. In this exercise, you'll only learn about swatches. For more information about customizing other content libraries, refer to the Photoshop CS User Guide.

In the ex. on resetting
tools, I didn't under-
stand what it does
for us. b/s it can

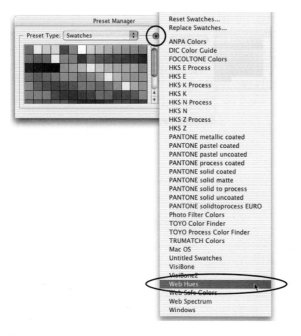

2. Choose **Web Hues** from the **Preset Manager** menu. Click **OK** to replace the current swatch with the **Web Hues** swatch.

*This will replace the currently loaded swatch in the **Preset Manager** (and in the **Swatches** palette) with a swatch that contains all the Web-safe colors. The **Web Hues** swatch is one of a number of prebuilt swatches that ship with Photoshop CS.*

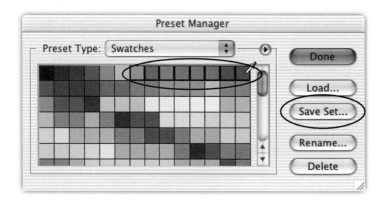

3. Select a few **red** and **orange** colors in the **Web Hues** palette by holding down the **Shift** key and clicking on the colors you want to choose. Click **Save Set**.

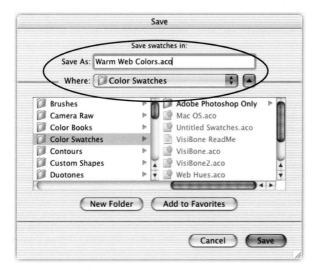

4. In the **Save** dialog box, type the name **Warm Web Colors.aco** in the **Save As** field. Be sure to include the **.aco** extension because it will identify the file as a swatch. In the **Where** pop-up menu, navigate to the **Color Swatches** folder in the **Presets** folder in the **Photoshop CS** application folder. Click **Save**.

5. In the **Preset Manager**, click **Done**.

6. Close and then relaunch Photoshop CS.

*You have to close and reopen Photoshop CS in order to see the new swatch listed in the **Swatches** palette menu.*

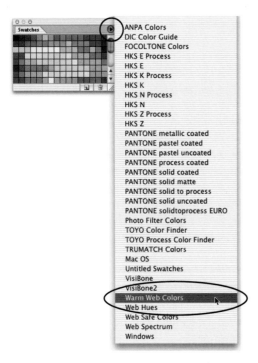

7. Choose **Warm Web Colors** from the **Swatches** palette pop-up menu. You'll see that your custom swatch has been added to the list of swatch presets.

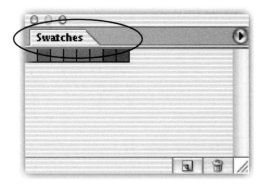

8. Click **OK** to replace the current swatch with the **Warm Web Colors** swatch, which will now open up in the **Swatches** palette.

Next, you'll make a custom swatch from the colors in an existing image. This is a good way to build a collection of pleasing palettes for use in your own images.

9. Open the **french.psd** file from the **chap_03** folder you copied to your **Desktop**.

10. Choose **Preset Manager** from the **Swatches** palette menu.

*The **Preset Manager** opens with your **Warm Web Colors** swatch showing.*

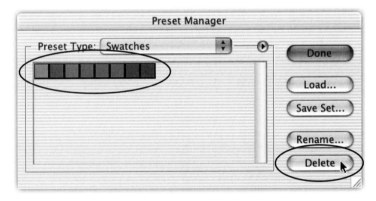

11. Click **Cmd+A** (Mac) or **Ctrl+A** (Windows) to select all the colors in the **Warm Web Colors** swatch in the **Preset Manager**. Click **Delete** to delete all of these colors.

12. Click **Done** to close the **Preset Manager**.

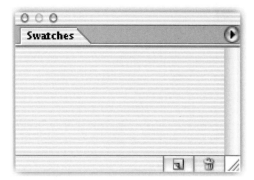

The loaded swatch now displays no colors, leaving you free to create a custom swatch from scratch.

13. Select the **Eyedropper** tool in the **Toolbox**.

14. Click on a color in the open image with the **Eyedropper** tool, then click the **New Color** button at the bottom of the **Swatches** palette.

This will add the color you selected in the image to your custom swatch. Repeat this step until you have all the colors you want in your swatch.

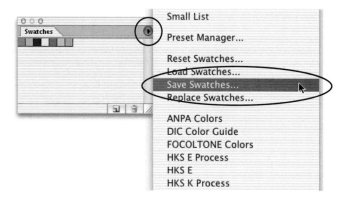

15. Choose **Save Swatches** from the **Swatches** palette menu.

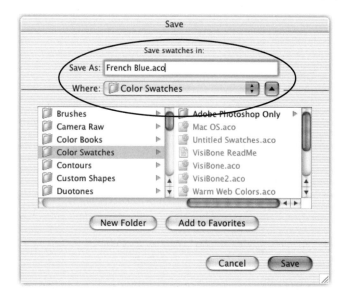

16. Navigate to the **Color Swatches** folder in the **Presets** folder in the **Photoshop CS** application folder, name your new swatch **French Blue.aco**, and click **Save**.

*The next time you launch Photoshop CS, your custom **French Blue** swatch will appear in the list of swatches in the **Swatches** palette menu. You can load that custom swatch and use it to build a new image or recolor an existing image.*

17. Close the image without saving.

[PS] _____**Recoloring Layered Images**

Now that you've learned how to view and pick colors in a variety of different ways, how do you make images using those colors? You could brush or paint with any color at any time. You could also use fill tools. This next exercise focuses on how to recolor an existing Photoshop CS image. It gives you a chance to work with the Lock Transparent Pixels feature, which allows you to easily recolor layered images with any color. Our demonstration takes place in Photoshop CS but will work in a similar fashion in ImageReady CS.

1. Open the lynda.com swatch by choosing **Replace Swatch** from the **Swatches** palette pop-up menu. Navigate to the **chap_03** folder you copied to your **Desktop** and choose **color.aco**. Click **Load**.

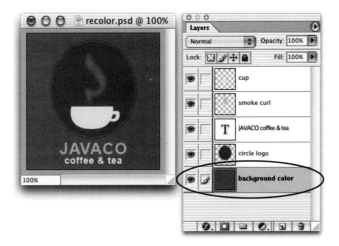

2. Open **recolor.psd** from the **chap_03** folder you copied to your **Desktop**. Make sure the **Layers** palette is visible; if it is not, choose.

*Look at the **Layers** palette (**Window > Layers**), and you'll notice this document is composed of multiple layers. It's helpful to set up your files with separate layers like this and give the layers meaningful names so you can color each layer separately and keep track of it.*

3. Click the **background color** layer at the bottom of the **Layers** palette to select it.

Right now, this image is colored using blues and greens. To change the color scheme to reds and yellows (or any other color choices you'd prefer), you'll be working with one layer at a time, starting with the background color layer.

4. Choose a **dark red** color from the **Swatches** palette.

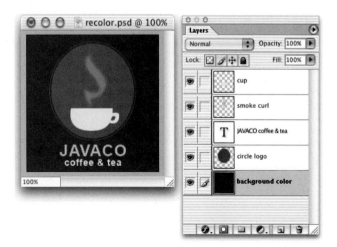

5. To fill the **background color** layer with the dark red color you chose, press **Option+Delete** (Mac), or **Alt+Backspace** or **Alt+Delete** (Windows).

*This is one of my favorite shortcuts for filling a layer with a color, because it is faster than using the menu command, **Edit > Fill**, or the **Paint Bucket** tool.*

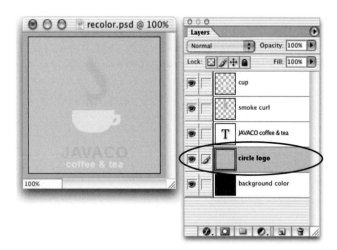

6. Next, select the **circle logo** layer that contains the circle. Pick a **dark yellow** color from the **Swatches** palette, and use the fill shortcut again by pressing **Option+Delete** (Mac), or **Alt+Backspace** or **Alt+Delete** (Windows).

Notice that the entire layer is now filled with this color. In order to recolor the circle, and not the entire contents of the layer, there's a valuable trick you'll learn in the following steps.

7. Undo the fill you just created by using the shortcut key, **Cmd+Z** (Mac) or **Ctrl+Z** (Windows).

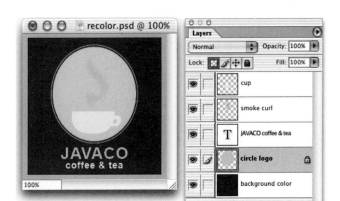

8. Click the **Lock Transparent Pixels** button on the **Layers** palette, and press **Option+Delete** (Mac), or **Alt+Backspace** or **Alt+Delete** (Windows). This time, only the contents of the selected layer fill with yellow.

Tip: *The shortcut key to toggle* **Lock Transparent Pixels** *on or off is the* **/** *(forward slash) key.*

Lock Transparent Pixels *means that Photoshop CS will protect the transparent areas of this layer. When you fill the layer with a new color, Photoshop CS fills only the area of the layer that contains an image and preserves the transparent areas. I can't tell you how many students I've watched try to use the* **Magic Wand** *tool or other selection tools to select shapes on layers in order to fill them. The technique you learned here works much better because it's easier, it fills only areas of the layer that contain pixel information, and it doesn't leave rough edges on color fills.*

9. Next, select the editable type layer (signified by the letter **T** on the layer). Choose an **orange** color from the **Swatches** palette, and press **Option+Delete** (Mac), or **Alt+Backspace** or **Alt+Delete** (Windows).

*Note that the **Lock Transparent Pixels** button is active, even though it's dimmed out. This is the default behavior for an editable type layer.*

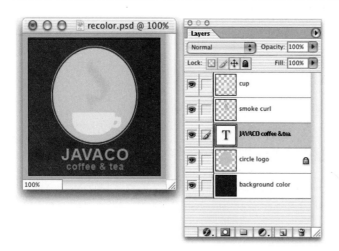

10. Select the **Type** tool from the **Toolbox**. Highlight the words **coffee & tea** in the type layer by clicking and dragging over them.

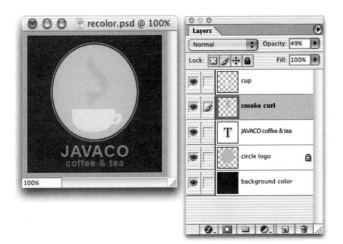

11. Choose a **bright red** color from the **Swatches** palette, and press **Option+Delete** (Mac), or **Alt+Backspace** or **Alt+Delete** (Windows). After you deselect the type by clicking on a different layer, you'll see that only the words **coffee & tea** on the type layer changed color.

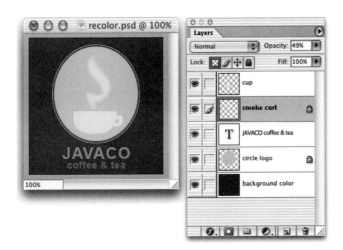

12. Select the **smoke curl** layer. Choose **white** from the **Swatches** palette. Click the **Lock Transparent Pixels** button and use the shortcut keys, **Option+Delete** (Mac), or **Alt+Backspace** or **Alt+Delete** (Windows) to fill with the new color.

*What's really cool about this step is the smoke curl on this layer is slightly blurry. Turning on **Lock Transparent Pixels** is the only way to make a clean selection of a blurry graphic.*

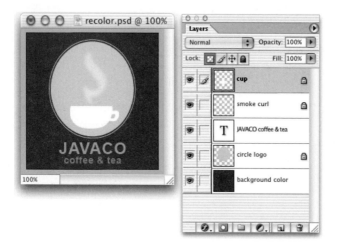

13. Select the **cup** layer. Click the **Lock Transparent Pixels** button and use the shortcut keys, **Option+Delete** (Mac), or **Alt+Backspace** or **Alt+Delete** (Windows) to fill with **white**.

Now all the layers in your image should be recolored from shades of blue and green to shades of red and yellow.

---

14. Close the file without saving.

The skills covered in this exercise will help you recolor layered images as you design Web graphics or any other graphics in Photoshop CS. You'll probably use this technique more than most others in the book.

---

5. [PS] _____Using the Color Replacement Tool

Filling layered images with colors as you did in the last exercise is a great technique if your layers contain only fairly flat colors. If your images have photographic elements, or elements with shaded, textured, or transparent areas, filling with a solid color won't give you the effect you're looking for.

For example, if you're designing a rollover that is photographic in nature or has a lot of texture and shading, and you want to alter the color of the rollover for the Over or Down state, you could recolor the entire image, or a portion of the image, using the Color Replacement tool.

The Color Replacement tool samples the colors in the original image and replaces them with the foreground color while maintaining the texture and shading of the original image. The Color Replacement tool behaves like a brush in that you brush over the areas of the image or layer you wish to recolor.

Here is an exercise to show you how to use the Color Replacement tool in Photoshop CS.

1. In Photoshop CS, open **poster.psd** from the **chap_03** folder you copied to your **Desktop**.

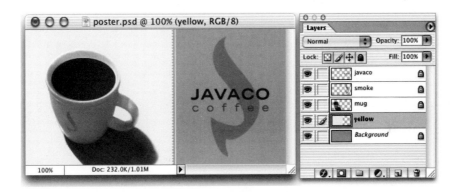

This image is composed of several layers with flat colors, as well as one layer with a photographic object—the mug. The mug, shadow, and background of the left side of the image are made up of yellows, beiges, and browns. You're going to alter the colors of the mug (including the shadow) and background to match the shades of blue in the right side of the image.

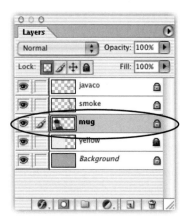

2. In the **Layers** palette, click the **mug** layer to select it.

3. Select the **Eyedropper** tool in the **Toolbox** and click in the **blue background** of the image to change the foreground color.

4. Select the **Color Replacement** tool from the **Healing Brush** fly-out menu by clicking the arrow on the bottom-right corner of the **Healing Brush** tool.

5. Brush over the entire coffee mug, including the shadow to the bottom right of the mug, with the **Color Replacement** tool. If you want to change the size of your brush, use the **[** key to decrease and the **]** key to increase the brush size.

The mug is now shades of blue. Notice that the original tones, shades, highlights, and textures of the coffee mug image have been maintained. Very cool!

Next you're going to recolor the yellow background to match the blue you used for the coffee mug.

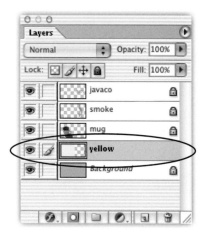

6. In the **Layers** palette, click the **yellow** layer to select it.

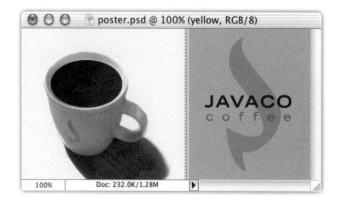

7. Keep the same foreground color you chose in **Step 3**. Now, begin brushing over the **yellow background** with the **Color Replacement** tool.

You'll notice that even though you chose a darker color as the foreground color, the Color Replacement tool identifies that the yellow background is lighter and it applies the blue with the same level of intensity. This is an easy way to recolor graphics with multiple colors based in a completely different color scheme because it preserves the shade and intensity of the original colors.

Alternatively, if you want to recolor the ***poster.psd*** image to match the yellows and beiges on the left side of the image, you can easily do that by sampling the **yellow** from the background and using the **Color Replacement** tool to brush over each of the layers made up of different shades of blue. Using this technique is an easy way to match colors to a new color scheme without having to go through the hassle of choosing new colors that look good together and matching the shading and intensity of the original colors.

Note: The **Color Replacement** tool permanently changes the colors in your image. If you wish to make nondestructive changes and preserve the original image, you may want to use the **Hue/Saturation Adjustment Layers**, which will be covered in Chapter 5, "Layers."

TIP | Using a Wacom Tablet

If you find you're frequently using the Color Replacement tool or any of the other brush tools in Photoshop CS or ImageReady CS, you may want to consider using a Wacom tablet. It gives you the feeling you're painting with a real brush instead of a bar of soap, like when you're using a mouse.

If you create graphics using a computer, a pen tablet will make your workflow faster and easier. You can go from light to dark, thin to thick, or opaque to transparent using the pressure sensitivity of a Wacom tablet. For more information about Wacom tablets, visit Wacom's Web site at **www.wacom.com**.

6. [PS] _____**Copying Color as HTML**

This exercise will be of value to you if you're used to programming your own HTML code or working with an HTML editor. If you don't work with HTML, feel free to skip this one!

If you're making an image in Photoshop CS or ImageReady CS and want to capture a color from that image to place inside your HTML code so you can color a background, link, or other element in HTML to match the image, you can use the Copy Color as HTML feature.

When you specify color in HTML code, as you must for elements like background color, text, and links, you must use values from a different numbering system called the hexadecimal system. In a nutshell, the hexadecimal numbering system is based on 16 digits and uses letters as well as numbers to identify colors. You don't have to worry about knowing any more than that when you're working with Photoshop CS and ImageReady CS. They take care of the math for you.

The Copy Color as HTML feature converts any RGB (red, green, blue) color value (for example, the shade of blue in this example is called 153 153 204 in RGB parlance) to a string of hexadecimal digits (#9999CC in this example). This command also puts the hexadecimal color value into your computer's clipboard so you can paste it as text into other applications—a handy feature if you're writing HTML from scratch and want to place a color value into your code quickly and easily.

1. In Photoshop CS, open **french.psd** from the **chap_03** folder you copied to your **Desktop**.

2. Select the **Eyedropper** tool from the **Toolbox**, then click on a color in the background of the image.

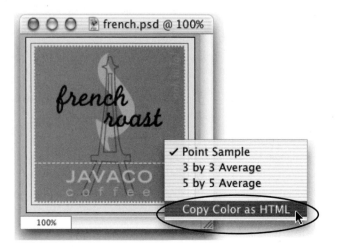

3. Ctrl+click (Mac) or **right-click** (Windows) on a color in a document, and choose **Copy Color as HTML** from the contextual menu.

If you're working in ImageReady CS, first click on a color in the document with the ***Eyedropper*** *tool, then* ***Ctrl+click*** *(Mac) or* ***right-click*** *(Windows) anywhere in the document and choose* ***Copy Foreground Color as HTML***.

Note: *The* ***Eyedropper*** *tool must be selected for this to work in Photoshop CS or ImageReady CS.*

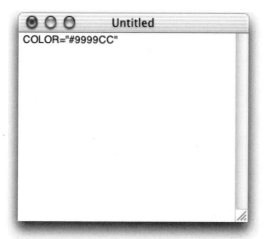

4. Open a text editor or HTML editor and choose **Edit > Paste** or press **Cmd+V** (Mac) or **Ctrl+V** (Windows). When you paste the color into a text editor or HTML program, it will look like this: `COLOR="#9999CC"`.

---

5. Close both files without saving.

Now you know how to use the flexible color-picking features in Photoshop CS and ImageReady CS and how to apply your color choices quickly and efficiently to a layered image. These programs make choosing and using color fun and creative by offering the best color-picking tools around.

In the next chapter, "Optimization," you'll learn how to optimize and save Web graphics.

4.

Optimization

| GIF, JPEG, or Macromedia Flash |
Transparency and Animation	Lossy or Lossless?
What Is Bit Depth?	Photoshop CS JPEG and GIF Options
Saving JPEGs for the Web	Saving GIFs for the Web
Changing Dimensions of a Graphic
Previewing Images in a Web Browser	Previewing and Writing HTML
Exporting Macromedia Flash Files

chap_04

Photoshop CS/ImageReady CS
H•O•T CD-ROM

If you've ever used the Web, you've likely been frustrated by slow-loading Web pages. It's the first design medium where the file size of the graphics translates into how fast someone can view them. Making small Web graphics is an art and a science. Fortunately, Photoshop CS and ImageReady CS are the ideal tools to help you master this craft.

Prepare for a long chapter, because optimization is a fairly complex subject that both Photoshop CS and ImageReady CS handle in great detail. If terms like dither, adaptive palettes, bit depth, JPEG, and GIF are unfamiliar to you, they won't be for long. If you're a pro at optimizing Web graphics, you'll be impressed by the superb optimization capabilities in Photoshop CS and ImageReady CS. The first part of this chapter focuses on optimizing images as JPEGs and GIFs. The last part of the chapter focuses on one of the new enhancements in ImageReady CS—the Export Files as Macromedia Flash feature.

What Affects Speed on the Web?

Unfortunately, just making your file sizes small in Photoshop CS or ImageReady CS does not guarantee fast Web site performance. Here are some other factors that slow down Web sites:

• **Connection speed:** If the connection speed of a Web server is slow, your Web site will be slow.

• **Router problems:** If there are router problems somewhere in the system, your Web site will be slow.

• **Traffic:** If you are using a large Internet service provider, such as AOL, EarthLink, or GeoCities, your Web site may slow down during heavy usage hours due to a high volume of Web traffic. If you're using a small, local Internet service provider, your Web site may be slow because the Internet service provider does not have resources to handle the heaviest traffic periods.

Solutions? Make sure you host your Web site from a fast connection or hire a hosting company that guarantees a fast connection. If you have a serious business site, get a dedicated hosting service instead of a large consumer-based Web service.

If the Web is slow because of router problems, it affects everyone. Such is life. Control the things you can (like file size). The only predictable thing about the Web is that it won't always perform in a predictable manner.

GIF, JPEG, or Macromedia Flash?

GIF stands for **Graphic** Interchange Format and JPEG stands for Joint **Photographic** Experts Group. The words "graphic" and "photographic" are intentionally bolded here to indicate what each file format handles best. It isn't that GIF is better than JPEG or vice-versa. Each compression scheme is best suited for a certain type of image.

• GIFs are best for flat or simple graphic images that incorporate solid areas of color, such as logos, illustrations, cartoons, line art, and so on.

• JPEGs are best for continuous-tone images, such as photographs, glows, gradients, drop shadows, and so on.

Some images don't fall into either category because they are hybrids of line art and continuous-tone graphics. In these cases, you have to experiment with GIF and JPEG to see which gives you the smallest file size and the best image quality. You could also try exporting your files as Macromedia Flash (SWF) files using the new Macromedia Flash Export feature in ImageReady CS.

Macromedia Flash files (SWF) are best for saving vector-based graphics for the Web because the SWF file maintains the vector-based information. (Although ImageReady CS is not a vector-based application, it does have some vector-based functionality such as the shape and type features, which you'll learn about in later chapters.) SWF is also a good format to use if you're trying to optimize an image containing both flat color areas and photographic content because it can compress flat color information and photographic content successfully. The disadvantage of using the SWF format is that viewers must have the Macromedia Flash browser plug-in installed in order to view the file. JPEG and GIF do not require the use of additional plug-ins.

Exporting files to the SWF format is a new feature in ImageReady CS and has two key benefits. First, you can export SWF files, including the required HTML code to make the SWF file work in a Web browser, directly from ImageReady CS and use it successfully on the Web without having to open the file in Macromedia Flash. Second, you can export files created in ImageReady CS, and open and edit them in Macromedia Flash, keeping the vector information intact. In this chapter, you'll learn about the first benefit—exporting SWF files to use on the Web. In Chapter 16, "*Integration*," you'll learn about the second benefit—exporting SWF files to further edit later in Macromedia Flash.

Transparency and Animation

Whether a graphic contains line art or continuous tone is not the sole deciding factor for choosing GIF, JPEG, or SWF. The GIF and SWF formats can do a couple of things the JPEG format cannot, such as transparency and animation. If you're looking for specific information about saving files as transparent GIFs, animated GIFs, or animated SWFs, you can refer to Chapter 9, "*Transparent GIFs*," or Chapter 13, "*Animated GIFs and Flash*." In the meantime, I've provided a brief explanation of these terms in this chapter because their capabilities may factor into your optimization strategy.

Transparency and Animation Terms	
Term	**Description**
Transparency	All digital image files are rectangular. The shape of your Photoshop CS document window is always square or rectangular, and even if an image inside is not in that shape, the file itself is defined by the rectangular boundaries. What if you have a button design that is circular and intended to be viewed on a colored or patterned background? In such a case, you use transparent pixels to mask out parts of the image, leaving a shape that appears circular in a Web browser. If you want to use transparent images on the Web, you can choose one of two file formats: GIF or SWF.

continues on next page

Transparency and Animation Terms *continued*	
Term	**Description**
GIF transparency	The GIF file format supports 1-bit masking, which means the image can be turned off in specified areas, making it possible to create graphics that appear irregularly shaped. Because the file format supports only 1-bit transparency, there are no degrees of opacity except on or off (visibility or no visibility for each pixel). For more information, check out Chapter 9, "*Transparent GIFs.*"
Macromedia Flash transparency	Like the GIF format, SWF also supports masking, but of much higher quality. SWF supports 32-bit masking, whereas GIF supports 1-bit masking. The process for exporting SWF files with transparency is identical to exporting SWF files without transparency, which you'll learn about later in this chapter.
Animation	Animations are a series of still images (called frames) that appear to be moving. When you work with animations, you can control how fast and how many times the animation plays. ImageReady CS lets you save animations in two different formats: animated GIFs and SWF.
GIF animation	A single GIF file can contain multiple images and display them in a slideshow fashion. GIF files that contain multiple images are called "animated GIFs." For more information on how the GIF file format supports animation, check out Chapter 13, "*Animated GIFs and Flash.*"
Macromedia Flash animation	Macromedia Flash (SWF) files offer the ability to create more complex animations than animated GIFs. SWF files are also powerful enough that you can create Web buttons or free-form interfaces for Web site navigation, including sound and animation. Although you can't take advantage of all the features of Macromedia Flash in ImageReady CS, the ability to export files as SWFs is a huge benefit. Once you've exported files as SWFs, you can open and edit the files directly in Macromedia Flash. Exporting SWF files is one of the key new features in ImageReady CS. For more information, check out Chapter 13, "*Animated GIFs and Flash.*"

Lossy or Lossless?

There are two categories of file compression—lossy and lossless. Lossy file compression reduces file size by discarding visual information. Lossless file compression reduces file size without throwing away visual information. JPEG is a lossy compression method. Traditionally, GIF was a lossless method, but in Photoshop CS and ImageReady CS, you can add lossiness to GIF compression to reduce file size. When you work with SWF files, you can also choose lossy (JPEG) or lossless (Lossless-8 or Lossless-32) compression.

WARNING | Don't Recompress a Compressed Image

Recompressing a JPEG or a lossy GIF can erode the image quality because you throw away visual information each time you apply lossy compression. The result can be visible, unwanted compression artifacts, which cause the image to look distressed. If you need to make a change to an image that's already been compressed as a JPEG or lossy GIF, find the original, uncompressed version of the image, make your changes, and compress the file as a fresh JPEG or lossy GIF to maintain the image's quality. This is one reason you should always save the original PSD (Photoshop Document format) files you create in Photoshop CS or ImageReady CS.

How Can You Make Small JPEGs?

Here is a handy chart that shows what can be done to improve compression of an image using the JPEG format. You'll practice these techniques later in the chapter.

JPEG Compression	
What To Do	**Why Do It**
Start with an image that has tonal qualities, such as a photograph, continuous tone graphic, or an image that incorporates effects like glows, drop shadows, and so on.	The JPEG file format looks for the type of data it is best at compressing: areas of low contrast, subtle variation, and slight tonal shifts. It can't compress areas of solid color effectively, and it doesn't work well for flat, graphic-style artwork.
Add blur	The JPEG format compresses blurry images effectively. Adding a little blur to a JPEG can decrease its file size.
	continues on next page

JPEG Compression *continued*	
What To Do	**Why Do It**
Add more JPEG compression	The more JPEG compression you add, the smaller the file size. Too much JPEG compression can cause unwanted compression artifacts. It's your job to find the balance between making the file small and making it look good.
Decrease the saturation	The JPEG format has an easier time compressing images with low color saturation than images with highly saturated colors. Decreasing saturation usually results in a smaller-sized JPEG.
Decrease the contrast	The JPEG format favors low-contrast images. Decreasing the contrast in an image usually results in a smaller-sized JPEG.
Use an alpha channel	Compressing different areas of a single image with two different levels of JPEG compression sometimes lowers the overall file size of the image. The two areas are delineated by an alpha channel. You'll learn how to do this later in the chapter.

How Can You Make Small GIFs?

The principles for making a small GIF are almost opposite to those you'd use to make a small JPEG. The GIF file format works best on areas of solid color—and that's why it's best for line art, logos, illustrations, and cartoons.

NOTE | Recompressing GIFs

Compression artifacts are not an issue with GIFs (as long as they don't use lossy compression, which you'll learn about later in this chapter) as they are with JPEGs. You can recompress a GIF with no ill compression effects, though it's sometimes preferable to begin with a clean original PSD, PICT, or BMP than to recompress an already compressed GIF. For example, if you recompressed a GIF that had been set to six colors, you wouldn't be able to introduce any more colors even if you wanted to. You would have more latitude with your choices if you instead compressed a GIF from the original image source.

GIF Compression	
What To Do	**Why Do It**
Start with an image that has large areas of solid color	The GIF file format looks for patterns in artwork, such as large runs of a single color in a horizontal, vertical, or diagonal direction. Note: Areas of color change cause increased file sizes.
Reduce the number of colors	Reducing the number of colors in a GIF image reduces the file size. At some point during the color-reduction process, the image won't look right, and that's when you'll have to go back and add in more colors. The objective is to find that exact threshold where the image looks good but contains the fewest number of colors.
Reduce the amount of dithering	Dithering is a process that adds different-colored pixels in close proximity to each other to simulate secondary colors or smooth gradations of color. A dithered image often looks noisy or has scattered pixels. Some images must contain dithering to look good, but it's best to use the least amount of dithering possible to keep the image size small.
Add lossy compression	Adding a small amount of lossy compression to a GIF will often reduce its file size.
Add an alpha channel	Use an alpha channel to weigh the choice of colors and the amount of dither applied to different areas of a GIF during compression. You can also apply these techniques to a type or vector layer. You'll see how this works when you learn about weighted GIF optimization later in the chapter.

What Is Bit Depth?

Bit depth refers to the number of colors in an image. GIF is an 8-bit file format and JPEG is a 24-bit file format. You don't need to memorize these numbers, but if you ever need to refer to a chart that lists bit depth, you can use the following:

Bit-Depth Chart	
32-bit	16.7 million colors plus an 8-bit alpha channel
24-bit	16.7 million colors
16-bit	65.6 thousand colors
8-bit	256 colors
7-bit	128 colors
6-bit	64 colors
5-bit	32 colors
4-bit	16 colors
3-bit	8 colors
2-bit	4 colors
1-bit	2 colors

Photoshop CS JPEG and GIF Options

In the upcoming exercises, you'll use the Save For Web feature in Photoshop CS to prepare images for compression as GIFs and JPEGs. When you open the Save For Web window, you'll see lots of options in the GIF and JPEG settings area. Here's a quick reference guide to help you understand the different settings. You'll try out the majority of these settings in the exercises that follow. You'll also find similar settings in the ImageReady CS Optimize palette, as you'll learn shortly.

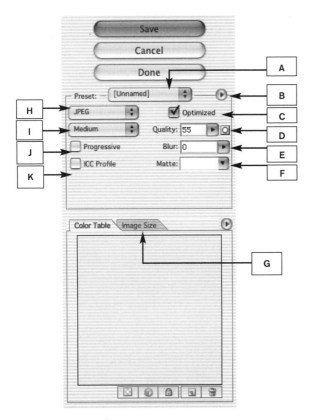

	JPEG Options	
A	**Preset pop-up menu**	Choose from preset compression values, including settings that ship with Photoshop CS and your own custom settings.
B	**Optimize menu**	Save and load custom settings for the Preset pop-up menu (A).
C	**Optimized check box**	Turn on the Optimized setting. Keep in mind that turning on Optimized will make the smallest possible JPEG images.
D	**Quality slider**	Set the compression quality. You can manually type in the value or use the slider and drag to the desired value. Click the alpha channel button beside the Quality pop-up menu to access the Modify Quality Setting dialog box, which lets you use alpha channels to modify the quality in different parts of the image.

continues on next page

		JPEG Options *continued*
E	**Blur slider**	Choose a blur value. JPEGs compress better when they are slightly blurry than when they are sharp images. You can manually type in the value or use the slider and drag to the desired value. I prefer using the slider because it's easier to make small incremental changes to the blur, which helps prevent the image from appearing too blurry.
F	**Matte pop-up menu**	Set a matte color to replace the transparency when an image is saved as a JPEG. This is important when you begin with an image that is against a transparent background. Later in this chapter, you'll learn how to set the Matte color for a JPEG.
G	**Image Size tab**	Change the physical dimensions of an image by adjusting the pixel or percent values.
H	**Optimized File Format pop-up menu**	Apply JPEG, GIF, or PNG compression to an image.
I↔D	**Compression Quality pop-up menu**	Choose a preset quality value for a JPEG image. You can use one of the presets or enter values into the Quality setting (D).
J	**Progressive check box**	Turn on the Progressive setting. Keep in mind that progressive JPEGs, like interlaced GIFs, appear chunky and come into focus as they download.
K	**ICC Profile check box**	Turn on ICC (International Color Consortium) profiles. Keep in mind that ICC profiles work with some printing devices but not with Web browsers. They add file size to a compressed image. I don't recommend using them for Web images at present. However, there might come a day when browsers recognize ICC profiles.

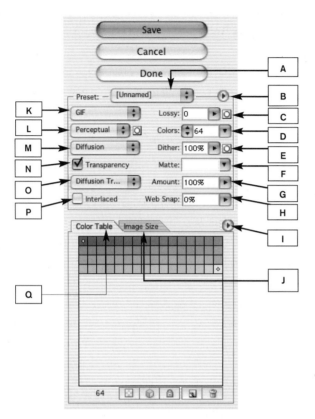

	GIF Options	
A	**Preset pop-up menu**	Choose from preset compression values, including settings that ship with Photoshop CS and your own custom settings.
B	**Optimize menu**	Save and load custom settings for the Settings menu (A).
C	**Lossy slider**	Add lossy compression to your GIF images. I often find that small values of lossy compression decrease the file size of a GIF. This works best on continuous-tone GIF files such as photographs. The alpha channel symbol to the right of the lossy pop-up menu allows access to the Modify Lossiness Setting dialog box, which lets you use alpha channels to vary lossy compression in different parts of the image.

continues on next page

		GIF Options *continued*
D	**Colors pop-up menu**	Reduce the number of colors in a GIF image to decrease file size. The trick is to find the perfect combination of the fewest colors for the best-looking image.
E	**Dither slider**	Choose the amount of dither. Adding dither to a GIF always increases file size, but it is sometimes necessary for the image color to look best. The alpha channel button beside the Dither pop-up menu allows access to the Modify Dither dialog box, which lets you use alpha channels to vary the amount of dither in different parts of an image.
F	**Matte pop-up menu**	Change the matte color of an image with transparent areas to blend the image into a Web page background. You'll get a chance to do this in Chapter 9, "*Transparent GIFs*."
G	**Transparency Dither Amount slider**	Set the amount of dither to partially transparent pixels on the edges of a transparent GIF. Transparency dither sometimes helps blend an image with a patterned Web page background.
H	**Web Snap slider**	Set a threshold to quickly "snap" non-Web-safe colors to Web-safe colors. I recommend changing colors to Web-safe colors individually instead of using the Web Snap slider so you can maintain control over which colors shift.
I	**Color Palette menu**	Sort the colors in your Color palette, load and save Color palettes, and create new colors in your Color palette.
J	**Image Size tab**	Change the physical dimensions of an image by adjusting the pixel or percent values.
K	**Optimized File Format pop-up menu**	Apply JPEG, GIF, or PNG compression to an image.

continues on next page

		GIF Options *continued*
L	**Color Reduction Palette pop-up menu**	Choose the best color palette to compress your GIF images. The Adobe engineers give you a lot of options for using different palettes to best compress your GIF images. You'll try them out in several upcoming exercises. The alpha channel button beside the Color Reduction Palette pop-up menu allows access to the Modify Color Reduction dialog box, which lets you use alpha channels to influence the palette applied to different parts of an image.
M	**Dither Algorithm pop-up menu**	Choose different dither options. Dither algorithm is just a fancy way of saying there are a few types of dithering options. You'll try them out in this chapter.
N	**Transparency check box**	Turn on Transparency to make transparent GIF images. You might find the check box is grayed out, which likely means your image doesn't contain any transparent areas. You'll learn all about how to make perfect transparent GIFs in Chapter 9, *"Transparent GIFs."*
O	**Transparency Dither Algorithm pop-up menu**	Choose which type of dithering to apply to partially transparent edges of a transparent GIF to help blend it with a Web page background. You'll try out this technique in Chapter 9, *"Transparent GIFs."*
P	**Interlaced check box**	Turn on Interlaced to create interlaced GIFs. Interlaced images will look chunky until they finish downloading. Interlaced GIFs work on all Web browsers, so you don't have to worry about compatibility issues. I suggest you don't use interlacing on images with text because it can be frustrating to wait for an image to appear in focus when you have to read it. If you're ever going to use interlacing, it might be on graphics that contain no text; but the truth is, I don't ever use interlacing because I don't like the way it looks. To each his or her own!
Q	**Color Table tab**	View the colors being assigned to a GIF image. You'll explore this feature later in the chapter.

Macromedia Flash Export Options

One of the key new features in ImageReady CS is the ability to export images as Macromedia Flash (SWF) files. When you open the Macromedia Flash Export dialog box (available from the File > Export menu), you'll see a number of controls. Here is a handy chart to help you understand all the options. Note: The Export as Macromedia Flash feature is only available in ImageReady CS.

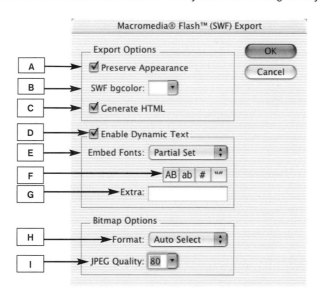

Macromedia Flash Export Options		
A	**Preserve Appearance check box**	Keeps the appearance of the ImageReady CS file. In some cases, vector-based type and shape layers will be rasterized. If you do not turn on the Preserve Appearance option, type and shape layers will be maintained as vector layers; however, layer effects will be dropped from all vector-based layers.
B	**SWF bgcolor pop-up menu**	Lets you choose a background color you want the SWF file to appear over when you view the file.
C	**Generate HTML check box**	Saves HTML code as well as the SWF file.

continues on next page

	Macromedia Flash Export Options *continued*	
D	**Enable Dynamic Text check box**	Lets you specify which type characters you want to embed into the file (for images containing vector text). You can choose from None, Full Set, or Partial Set. If you plan to use the image on the Web directly after exporting it from ImageReady CS, use the Dynamic Text feature. If you plan to import the file into Macromedia Flash before using the image on the Web, it's best to set up text variables directly in Macromedia Flash.
E	**Embed Fonts pop-up menu**	Lets you embed fonts used in the image in the SWF file. You can choose None, Full Set, or Partial Set.
F	**All Uppercase, All Lowercase, All Numbers, and All Punctuation buttons (available only when Partial Set is selected from the Embed Fonts pop-up menu)**	Lets you embed all uppercase, lowercase, numbers, or punctuation characters if you choose Partial Set from the Embed Fonts pop-up menu.
G	**Extra field (available only when Partial Set is selected from the Embed Fonts pop-up menu)**	Lets you specify additional fonts you want to embed when you choose Partial Set from the Embed Fonts pop-up menu.
H	**Format pop-up menu**	Lets you choose one of the following formats: AutoSelect, Lossless-8, Lossless-32, or JPEG. If you're exporting a graphic image, use one of the lossless formats. If you're exporting a photograph, use the JPEG format.
I	**JPEG Quality pop-up menu (available JPEG is selected from the Format pop-up menu or when AutoSelect is selected from the Format pop-up menu and uses JPEG as the format)**	Lets you specify the quality of an image that is being exported using the JPEG format.

I. 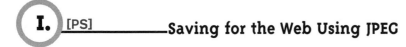 [PS] _____Saving for the Web Using JPEG

This first exercise walks you through saving a JPEG. It introduces you to the Save For Web feature in Photoshop CS, which gives you control over so many options that once you master its nuances, you'll be able to make the smallest possible Web graphics.

1. Copy the **chap_04** folder to your hard drive from the **H•O•T CD-ROM**, if you haven't already done so.

2. Open **javapress.psd** from the **chap_04** folder you copied to your **Desktop**.

3. Choose **File > Save For Web**.

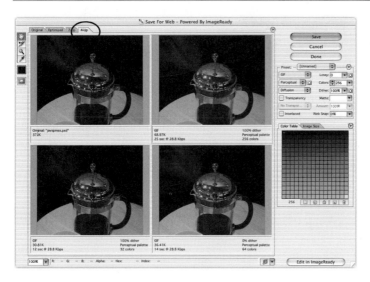

4. Click the **4-Up** tab in the **Save For Web** window. The multiple previews in this tab let you compare different compression settings.

Notice the upper-left tab has the term "Original" in it? This lets you compare the original, uncompressed image to the other previews, which show how the image would look with different combinations of compression settings.

*If you have already used the **Save For Web** window, your version of Photoshop CS might default to different compression settings than you see here. That's because the **Save For Web** window memorizes whatever compression settings you used when you last saved an optimized image. If that's the case, don't worry; you'll learn what settings to input in the following steps.*

5. Click the top-right image preview. You'll see a blue border around the preview, indicating that it is the active preview.

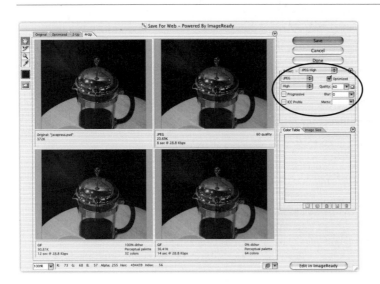

6. Choose **JPEG** from the **File Format** pop-up menu. Choose **High** from the **Compression Quality** pop-up menu to set the quality of the selected preview to **60**.

Notice that the JPEG is better looking than any of the other GIF previews? This illustrates that continuous-tone images, such as photographs, always compress better as JPEGs than as GIFs.

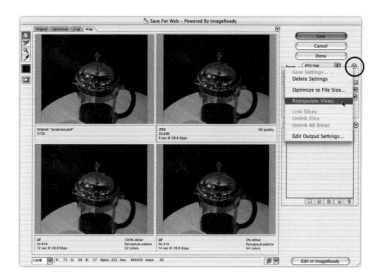

7. Choose **Repopulate Views** from the **Optimize** menu. This will change the other two previews in the bottom frames of the **Save For Web** window to the same file format as the selected preview (**JPEG** in this case).

*Notice the readout below each preview? It tells you the JPEG quality and file size of each preview. Photoshop CS estimates how long this graphic will take to load over a slow connection. Note this is a theoretical estimate of speed; it may not be accurate due to other factors, such as server speed. Your readouts may also have different numbers than those cited in this example; Photoshop CS remembers the compression levels from the last time you used the **Save For Web** window with JPEG settings.*

Judging from the relative image quality and file sizes of all the previews in this example, it looks like the best choice for the JPEG compression quality is between 60 and 30. The higher the compression quality, the larger the file size will be. The lower the quality setting, the more artifacts you'll see. Every image you optimize will have a different balance of quality versus size.

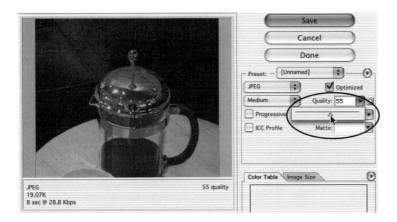

8. With the top-right preview selected, decrease the compression quality to **55** using the **Quality** slider. **Note:** You must release the slider for the results of the new setting to take effect.

*The slider is useful because it lets you experiment easily with settings between the default numbers in the **Compression Quality** presets.*

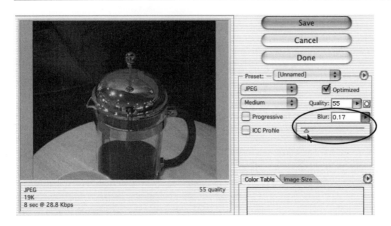

9. Using the **Blur** slider, increase the blur slightly to **0.17** or so.

Adding blur will lower the file size, but it will also affect the crispness of the image. The goal is to make the image smaller but have it look good. You should now see a slight savings in file size. Avoid adding too much blur or you will adversely affect the quality of the image.

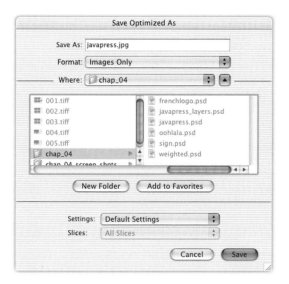

10. When you are satisfied with your optimization settings, click **Save** to open the **Save Optimized As** dialog box.

The program automatically adds a .jpg file extension to the file name for you. It also generates a file name based on the name of the original image, which you can change easily.

11. Navigate to the **chap_04** folder on your hard drive and click **Save**.

Notice that the original, uncompressed javapress.psd file remains open in Photoshop CS. You haven't altered the original image. When you choose Save For Web, Photoshop CS saves an optimized copy of the file on your hard drive and does not modify the original file.

12. Close the original **javapress.psd** image without saving.

2. [PS] _____ Selective JPEG Optimization with Alpha Channels

An alpha channel is a type of mask that Photoshop CS stores in the Channels palette. If you create an alpha channel and store it with an image, you can compress the masked area of the image with a different JPEG quality setting than the unmasked part of the image. This selective optimization technique helps reduce the overall file size of a JPEG. The following exercise shows you how to do it in Photoshop CS. You can do the same thing in ImageReady CS using the controls in the Optimize palette, except that you'd have to create the alpha channel in Photoshop CS before bringing the image into ImageReady CS, because you can't create alpha channels in ImageReady CS.

1. Open **javapress_layers.psd** from the **chap_04** folder on your hard drive.

This is the same image you used in the last exercise, except that the table, mug, and coffee press are on a separate layer from the background, which will make it easier for you to create a perfect mask.

2. Hold down the **Cmd** key (Mac) or **Ctrl** key (Windows) and click the **table** layer in the **Layers** palette. The cursor will change to a hand with a rectangle and a selection marquee will appear around the contents of the table layer.

This is my favorite shortcut for creating a perfect selection around imagery on a layer. It's much better than using the **Magic Wand** tool or any of the other selection tools in Photoshop CS, because it always gives you a perfect selection. Any time you have a layer with content and transparency, this is the best method for making a selection. However, if you are working with an image that does not have transparent layers, you can use any of the selection tools in Photoshop CS to create a selection and then use the optimization technique taught in this exercise.

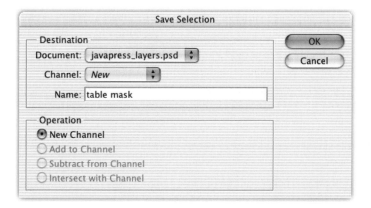

3. Choose **Select > Save Selection** to open the **Save Selection** dialog box. In the **Name** field, type **table mask**, and click **OK**.

That's all there is to turning an ordinary selection into a mask that's stored in an alpha channel!

---

4. Press **Cmd+D** (Mac) or **Ctrl+D** (Windows) to deselect the contents of the **table** layer.

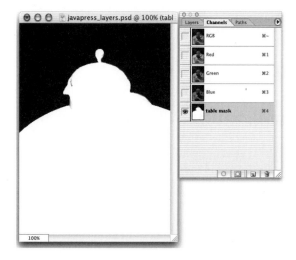

*If you want to see the mask you just created, click the **Channels** palette tab, which is next to the **Layers** palette. In the **Channels** palette, click the **table mask** alpha channel to display the grayscale mask in the document window. If you notice any substantial holes in the mask, you can set the fore- ground color in the **Toolbox** to **white** or **black**, and use a **Brush** tool to touch up those areas. When you're done viewing the mask, click the **RGB** channel in the **Channels** palette and return to the **Layers** palette. This step is optional. You do not have to view the alpha channel for it to work; it's simply a suggestion if you've never worked with alpha channels before.*

---

5. Choose **File > Save For Web**. In the **Save For Web** window, click the **2-Up** tab so you can see more of the image preview than in the **4-Up** tab. Choose **JPEG** from the **File Format** pop-up menu. Set the **Quality** slider as low as possible but without noticeable artifacts on the most important items in the image—the coffee press and other foreground items.

*Hint: Try setting the **Quality** slider to **55**. With the entire image compressed at 55%, the file size will be approximately 19.14K.*

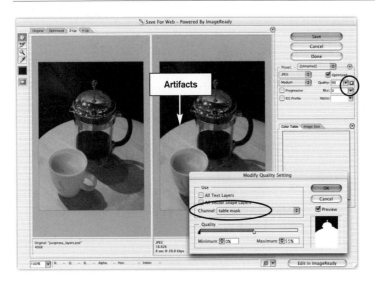

6. Click the **alpha channel** button to the right of the **Quality** slider to open the **Modify Quality Setting** dialog box. In the **Channel** pop-up menu, choose **table mask**.

*Notice the black and white preview of your alpha mask and the two sliders in the **Quality** area. The white slider (on the right) sets the level of quality for the content that is inside the white alpha channel (the table, the coffee press, and the cup). The black slider sets the level of quality for the content that is outside the white alpha channel.*

7. Leave the **white** slider set to its default of **55%**. In the preview image, notice the artifacts around the outer edge of the table (shown in the previous illustration). This area is covered by the black area of the alpha channel.

8. Increase the **black** slider to **30%** to eliminate the artifacts. Click **OK**.

*With the white and black sliders set to their defaults, 55% and 0% respectively, the overall size of the file (reported at the bottom left of the preview window) is less than it was when you had the quality of the entire image set to 55, back in **Step 6**. As you move the black slider to the right, increasing the quality of the image covered by the black part of the alpha channel to 30, the file size increases slightly, but it's still less than when the quality of the entire image was set to 55.*

In this example, applying relatively high compression (low quality) to the area outside the white alpha channel, without sacrificing the higher quality necessary for the more important areas inside the mask, resulted in a small reduction in overall file size. The amount of file size you can save with this technique varies from image to image and mask to mask. In most cases, it's worth experimenting with this technique to see if you can lower file size while applying optimal compression to different areas of an image.

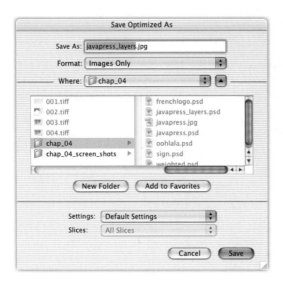

9. Click **Save** in the **Save For Web** window. In the **Save Optimized As** dialog box, save this image as **javapress_layers.jpg** in the **chap_04** folder. Click **Save**.

10. Close the **javapress_layers.psd** file without saving.

3. [PS] _____ Saving for Web Using GIF

Optimizing an image as a GIF is more complex than optimizing an image as a JPEG because there are so many more GIF settings that affect file size. The next few exercises will show you the key settings for optimizing a GIF: lowering the number of colors, adjusting the dither options, and choosing a palette.

1. Open **frenchlogo.psd** from the **chap_04** folder you copied to your **Desktop** and choose **File > Save For Web**.

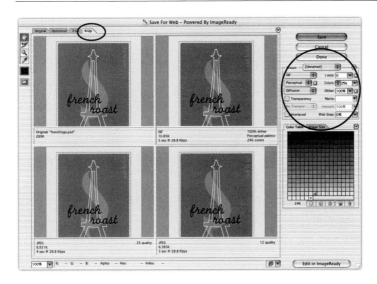

2. Click the **4-Up** tab in the **Save For Web** window. Click the top-right preview. Choose **GIF** from the **File Format** pop-up menu. Change any of the settings on the right side of your **Save For Web** window that do not match those in the illustration here (**GIF**, **Perceptual**, **Diffusion**, **Lossy: 0**, **Colors: 256**, **Dither: 100%**).

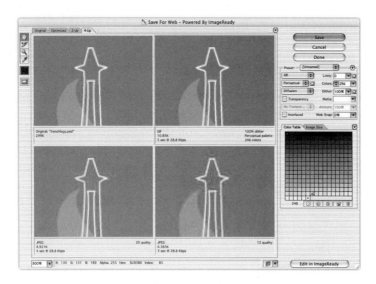

3. Choose the **Zoom** tool from the **Save For Web** toolbox on the left side of the **Save For Web** window. Click twice in the top-right preview to change the magnification in all the views to 300%. Select the **Hand** tool from the **Save For Web** toolbox. Click and drag inside any of the preview panes to move the image to match the illustration here.

Notice that the two JPEG previews on the bottom contain artifacts that make them look distressed, but the GIF preview on the top right looks more like the original image on the top left. As we mentioned before, flat graphics such as this one are better suited for GIF, not JPEG.

4. Choose **100%** from the **Zoom Level** pop-up menu to return all the previews to normal size.

No one will ever see your Web images at anything other than 100%, so don't fuss too much with images at a high magnification. I asked you to zoom in so you could see the artifacts I was describing, but when you're actually optimizing an image, it's best to judge image quality at 100% magnification.

5. Click the JPEG preview at the bottom left, and then click back on the GIF preview on the top right, keeping your eye on the settings at the far right of the **Save For Web** window. As you switch from JPEG to GIF, notice that the optimization settings in this context-sensitive window change, and that there are more and different options available for GIF than for JPEG.

*Notice that when a preview is set to GIF, the **Color Table** is visible, but when it's set to JPEG, there is not. That's because the GIF file format supports a maximum of 256 colors. All the colors in the original image have to be converted (this process is sometimes called "mapped") to a limited palette of colors, which you'll learn to select in the next exercise. The Color Table displays the colors in the currently selected palette to which this GIF preview is mapped. The JPEG format supports millions of colors, so a JPEG doesn't need to map to a limited palette.*

6. Click the top-right preview. Choose **Repopulate Views** from the **Optimize** menu. This changes all the views to the same format as the selected preview—GIF.

*You can choose **Repopulate Views** whenever you want to see variations on one compression format.*

7. Leave this file open in the **Save For Web** window for the next exercise.

*Note: If you click **Cancel**, the **Save For Web** window will not remember all of these settings. If you have to take a break and can't leave the **Save For Web** window open, click **Done** to save these settings so they appear the next time you open any image in the **Save For Web** window.*

4. [PS] _____Choosing the Right Color Reduction Palette

The Color Reduction Palette settings for the GIF file format are the most difficult optimization controls to understand. This exercise is designed to shed light on these mysterious settings and help you get through the hardest part of optimizing a GIF file.

1. The image **frenchlogo.psd** should be open in the **Save For Web** window from the previous exercise. Make sure the top-right preview is selected. Click the **2-Up** tab.

You'll see the original image on the left and a single preview on the right (although the pictures of the screens that follow include only the preview so you can see the optimization settings in detail, too).

2. With the preview on the right selected, change the **Color Reduction Palette** setting from **Perceptual** to **Selective**, then **Adaptive**, and then **Restrictive (Web)**, to see the effect these settings have on the file size and appearance of the selected preview.

Perceptual   *Selective*

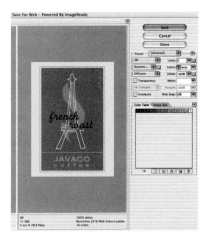

Adaptive   *Restrictive (Web)*

*Notice the **Color Table**, file size, and image appearance are almost identical when set to **Perceptual**,
Selective, and **Adaptive**. That's because all three of these palettes are derived from the colors in the
image, each by means of a slightly different algorithm. The **Restrictive** (or **Web**) palette has fewer colors and doesn't look very good. That's because the **Restrictive** palette is independent of the colors in
any image and tries to force the colors in an image into a set palette. For this reason, I almost always
use the **Adaptive**, **Perceptual**, or **Selective** palettes instead of the **Restrictive** palette.*

3. Once you've looked at all these palette choices, choose **Perceptual** from the **Color Reduction
Palette** pop-up menu, choose **Diffusion** from the **Dither Algorithm** pop-up menu, set the **Dither** slider
to **100%**, and choose **256** from the **Colors** pop-up menu. There's nothing magical about these particular settings. They're just the settings you should return to so your settings match those in the rest of
these GIF optimization exercises.

4. Leave the **Save For Web** window open and move to the next exercise. If you have to quit
Photoshop CS right now and start the next exercise later, be sure to click **Done** so the next time you
open the **Save For Web** window your last settings will be saved.

NOTE | When to Use Which Color Reduction Palette

Use either the Adaptive, Selective, or Perceptual palette whenever you're optimizing a GIF. Each will result in a GIF file that contains colors similar to those in the original image. To choose between them, apply each of the three palettes to an image preview, as you did in the previous exercise. Choose the palette with a relatively small file size and an image whose color and appearance are as close to the original image as possible.

The only time to use the Restrictive palette is if you need a quick-and-dirty way to convert an image with non-Web-safe colors to one with Web-safe colors. As mentioned before, the disadvantage of using the Restrictive palette is that it has no relationship to the original image, which might adversely affect your optimized image. If you do have to convert to Web-safe colors, we suggest you do so selectively, as described in the following note.

NOTE | Changing Selected Colors in a Palette to Web-Safe Colors

If you must convert a non-Web-safe image to a Web-safe one, I recommend you change only those colors that fill large, solid-color areas of your image. This will eliminate the most noticeable dithering in an 8-bit browser, while keeping the GIF as true as possible to the colors in the original image. Avoid the Web palette or the Snap to Web slider because both are wholesale solutions that don't let you control which colors will be changed to Web-safe colors. Instead, do the following:

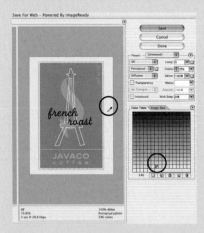

Choose the **Eyedropper** tool from the **Save For Web** toolbox. Click the color in the image preview you want to change. The corresponding color swatch will become highlighted in the **Color Table** on the bottom right.

continues on next page

NOTE | Changing Selected Colors in a Palette to Web-Safe Colors *continued*

Click the **Shift to Web-safe Color** icon (the cube) at the bottom of the **Color Table**. This shifts the color in the image preview to the nearest Web-safe color from the palette you chose.

The color swatch in the Color Table now contains two small icons. The diamond indicates that the swatch is a Web-safe color, and the square indicates that it's locked. The lock means this color will be retained in the Color Table even if you reduce the number of colors in the image. You'll learn how the lock works in **Exercise 6**.

If you don't like the Web-safe color that was chosen for you, and you want to change to a different color, double-click the highlighted color swatch in the **Color Table** to open the **Color Picker** dialog box, which will let you choose a different Web-safe color.

5. [PS] _____ Reducing Colors

Minimizing the number of colors in a GIF is the most significant thing you can do to reduce GIF file size. Your goal is to reduce the number of colors until you arrive at the fewest colors that are necessary to keep the image looking good. This exercise shows how to reduce colors using the Photoshop CS Save For Web feature.

1. The file **frenchlogo.psd** should still be open in the **Save For Web** window from the last exercise. Make sure the top-right preview is selected and the optimization settings for the preview are the same as they were at the end of the last exercise (**GIF**, **Perceptual**, **Colors: 256**, **Diffusion**, **Dither: 100%**).

Notice that although the number in the **Colors** field is set to 256, the note at the bottom of the selected preview tells you there are only 246 colors in the optimized image. That's because this particular image was originally made with less than 256 colors. The 256 in the **Colors** field is the maximum number of colors you can map in an image using this setting.

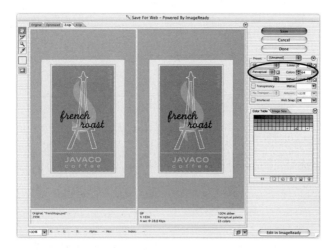

2. With the **Color Reduction Palette** set to **Perceptual** from the previous exercise, change the number of colors from **256** to **64** using the **Colors** pop-up menu. You'll see the file size get smaller right away. Compare this preview to the original, and you'll see the preview still looks great. Try smaller values until the image stops looking good.

I'm satisfied with this image at 32 colors, which results in a file size of about 8.1K. When I tried reducing the colors to 16, the edges of the text looked too rough for my taste. I still think this image size can be reduced slightly.

3. With the number of colors set to **32**, move the **Dither** slider to **0%**.

Notice that the file size is now slightly smaller—about 7.922K. Different types of images realize different amounts of file saving with dithering set to zero, but lowering or omitting dither almost always results in some file savings.

4. Click **Save** to save the GIF in the **Save Optimized As** dialog box, and close the original **frenchlogo.psd** without saving.

NOTE | What Is Dither?

When you limit the number of colors available in the Color Table, you might make it impossible to reproduce some of the colors from the original image in the GIF image preview. Photoshop CS takes two colors that are in your Color Table and places small dots of each right next to one another to try to simulate the original color. Photoshop CS offers three patterns of dither dots— diffusion, pattern, and noise—which differ mainly in the way the dither dots are arranged. You can apply any of these to an image preview by choosing one from the Dither Algorithm pop-up menu. The Diffusion dither offers the opportunity to regulate the amount of dither applied by using the Dither slider as you did in this exercise.

In most cases, your best bet is to avoid dither, because it adds to file size and makes the image appear dotted. However, if your image has a large area of gradient, glow, or shadow, adding dither can sometimes improve its appearance. Try each of the dither patterns and the Dither slider to see if changing the dither improves the appearance of the image without increasing the file size significantly.

6. [PS] ————Locking Colors

One of the great features of Photoshop CS and ImageReady CS is the capability to influence which colors are included in a GIF, even when you greatly reduce the number of colors in the Color Table.

1. Open **oohlala.psd** from the **chap_04** folder you copied to your **Desktop**. Choose **File > Save For Web**.

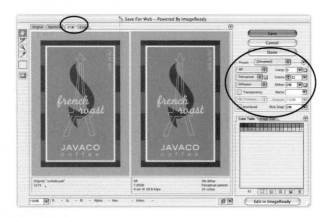

2. Click the **2-Up** tab and change the settings to **GIF**, **Perceptual**, **Diffusion**, **Lossy: 0**, **Colors: 32**, **Dither: 0%**. You may already see these settings, because they are same settings you used at the end of the last exercise.

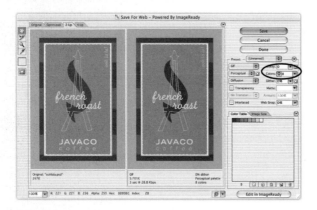

3. Reduce the number of colors to **8** in the **Colors** pop-up menu. Notice that this causes some of the central colors to change in the preview.

Some unanticipated colors changed in the preview because Photoshop CS decided which colors to throw away without your input.

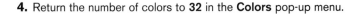

4. Return the number of colors to **32** in the **Colors** pop-up menu.

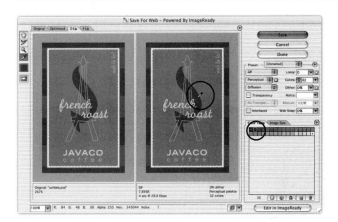

5. Using the **Eyedropper** tool, click the **purple** color in the steam graphic. Its corresponding color swatch in the **Color Table** will be highlighted.

6. Click the **Lock** symbol at the bottom of the **Color Table** to lock the color.

Once the color has been locked, a small, white square will appear in the bottom-right corner of the color swatch.

7. Go through the image with the **Eyedropper** tool and lock all the colors you want to preserve.

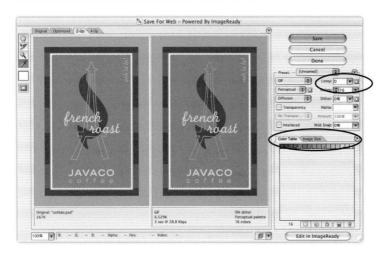

8. Once you have all the colors locked, reduce the colors to **16** using the **Colors** pop-up menu.

*This time, all the important colors in the image were preserved. Locking colors is a very useful feature in the **Save For Web** window.*

9. Leave the file open in the **Save For Web** window for the next exercise.

7. [PS] _____Changing the Dimensions of a Graphic

There is only one more thing you can do to make this image smaller: change the dimensions. The cool thing is that you can change the dimensions directly inside the Save For Web window. It's convenient, and it also leaves the original image untouched, resizing only the optimized version.

1. With **oohlala.psd** still open in the **Save For Web** window from the previous exercise, click the **Image Size** tab.

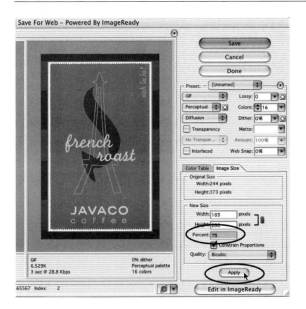

2. In the **Percent** field, type **75**. Click **Apply** and watch the file size and image dimensions decrease.

3. In the **Save Optimized As** dialog box, click **Save** to save the GIF. Close the original **oohlala.psd** file without saving.

In this exercise, you decreased the GIF to 75% without changing the size of the original image.

8. [PS] ———————— Selective GIF Optimization with Alpha Channels

Earlier, you learned how to selectively optimize parts of a JPEG using alpha channels. You can also apply selective optimization to GIF files by using alpha channels, which enables you to control color reduction, dither, and lossy compression. Photoshop CS can automatically create an alpha channel based on the content of all type layers or vector shape layers in your image. This exercise will show you how to create an automatic alpha channel based on a type layer, and how you can selectively optimize color reduction, dither, and the amount of lossy compression.

> ## NOTE | When to Use Selective GIF Optimization
>
> The purpose of selective GIF optimization is to apply different levels of compression to two differ-ent parts of an image. The objective is to protect important areas of an image from degradation by giving it higher quality while letting the other parts have inferior quality. This reduces file size and lets the important part of the image look as good as possible.

1. Open **weighted.psd** from the **chap_04** folder you copied to your **Desktop**. In the **Layers** palette, notice that this file has one type layer, which contains the words "French Roast."

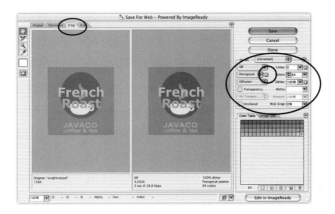

2. Choose **File > Save For Web**. Click the **2-Up** tab and choose **GIF** from the **File Format** pop-up menu. Choose a **Perceptual** palette, **Diffusion**, **Dither: 100%**, and **64** colors, as shown here.

---

3. Click the **alpha channel** button next to the **Color Reduction Palette** pop-up menu to open the **Modify Color Reduction** dialog box.

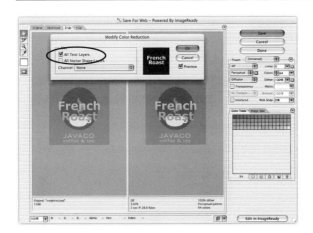

4. Turn on **All Text Layers** in the **Modify Color Reduction** dialog box, keeping an eye on the colors in the **Color Table** as you do.

Notice the colors in the Color Table change to different shades of yellow. The Color Table is now weighted toward the yellow colors in the Type layer, rather than uniformly representing all the colors in the image. Notice also there's a white mask over the words "French Roast" in the Modify Color Reduction dialog box. Photoshop CS automatically creates a mask when you enable All Text Layers. The white area of the mask determines which part of the image has the most influence over the selection of colors in the Color Table.

---

5. Turn off **All Text Layers** in the **Modify Color Reduction** dialog box to remove the alpha channel and balance the **Color Table** with the colors in the image. Now you'll see more blues in the **Color Table**, which represent the areas without text in the image. Click **OK** to close the **Modify Color Reduction** dialog box.

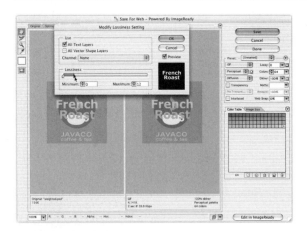

6. Click the **alpha channel** button beside the **Lossy** slider to open the **Modify Lossiness Setting** dialog box. Turn on **All Text Layers** to create a white alpha channel defined by the words "French Roast," which are the contents of the type layer.

7. Adjust the **white** and **black Lossiness** sliders to apply a different amount of lossy compression to the text than to the rest of the image. Leave the **white** slider at **0** and move the **black** slider to the left until the nontext area in the preview looks good to you (try around **12**). Click **OK**.

The white slider controls the amount of lossiness applied to the text in the white area of the alpha channel. The black slider controls the amount of lossiness applied to the rest of the image, which is in the black area of the alpha channel.

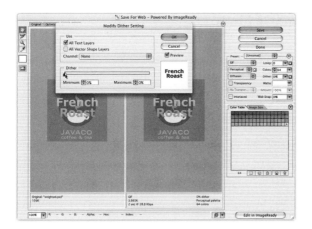

8. Click the **alpha channel** button next to the **Dither** slider to open the **Modify Dither Setting** dialog box. Turn on **All Text Layers**.

*You could use the sliders to apply different amounts of dither to the text and nontext areas of the image. However, there's no reason to do that in this case because no area of the image stands to benefit from dithering. So either push both sliders all the way to **0%** in the **Modify Dither Setting** dialog box and click **OK**, or close this dialog box and move the **Dither** slider to **0%**.*

*Using the techniques in this exercise, you decreased the size of the original **weighted.psd** file from 156K to 3.86K.*

9. Leave **weighted.psd** open in the **Save For Web** window for the next exercise.

9. [PS] _____Previewing Images in a Web Browser

You can preview your images in a Web browser when you're using the Save For Web feature in Photoshop CS.

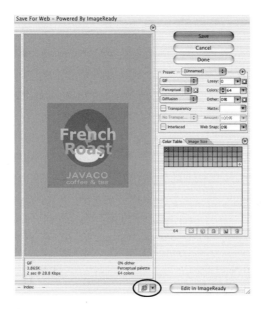

1. With **weighted.psd** still open in the **Save For Web** window, click the **Preview in Browser** icon to preview the optimized image in your default Web browser, or choose a different Web browser from the **Select Browser** pop-up menu.

*Note: The highlighted preview in the **Save For Web** window will be displayed in the Web browser.*

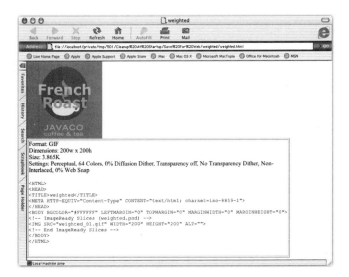

*The information and HTML code in the **Preview Browser** window is temporary and used for preview purposes only. If you want to use HTML code that Photoshop CS generates, you must save an HTML file when you save an image. You'll learn to do this in future exercises.*

---

2. Return to Photoshop CS and click **Save** in the **Save For Web** window to open the **Save Optimized As** dialog box and save this image as **weighted.gif** in the **chap_04** folder.

---

3. Close the **weighted.psd** image without saving.

ImageReady CS Palettes and Preference Settings

The following exercises show you how to perform some of the same optimization tasks in ImageReady CS that you just learned in Photoshop CS, so you'll know how to optimize in both applications.

You might wonder why you would optimize a graphic in ImageReady CS when you can optimize it in Photoshop CS. There are two reasons. First, if you're already working in ImageReady CS, it's more convenient to optimize there. I find I do lots of optimizing in ImageReady CS because I'm often using the program to perform Web-oriented tasks that I can't do in Photoshop CS, such as making rollovers or animations. Second, it's easier to make changes to the original image while you're optimizing images in ImageReady CS because you do not have to exit the Save For Web window like you do in Photoshop CS. In ImageReady CS, there is no separate Save For Web window, so you can access the original version of the image at any time.

Don't worry about the results being different in these two programs; the underlying code is identical. In fact, you probably noticed the title bar of the Save For Web window reads "Powered by ImageReady."

The only true differences are in the two interfaces. In Photoshop CS, the optimization settings are contained in the Save For Web window. In ImageReady CS, the optimization settings are contained in a series of palettes.

To prepare for optimizing in ImageReady CS, we suggest you dock your **Optimize** and **Color Table** palettes together vertically, as you learned in Chapter 2, "*Interface*." If you don't see either of these palettes on your screen, choose **Window > Optimize** or **Window > Color Table**.

Before you begin, you should also change one ImageReady CS optimization preference:

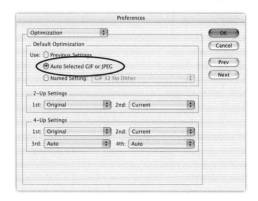

Choose **ImageReady > Preferences > Optimization** (Mac) or **Edit > Preferences > Optimization** (Windows). In the **Preferences** dialog box, change the **Default Optimization** setting to **Auto Selected GIF or JPEG**.

This instructs ImageReady CS to make a best guess as to which type of compression format (GIF or JPEG) to use for each image. You can override its guess, but why not have ImageReady CS offer a starting point?

IO. [IR] ——————Optimizing a JPEG in ImageReady CS

Everything in this exercise should be pretty familiar to you. The optimization process is almost identical in ImageReady CS and Photoshop CS. We'll show you a few new tricks along the way that you can try in either application.

1. Make sure you are in ImageReady CS. Open **sign.psd** from the **chap_04** folder on your hard drive.

*Notice that the image opens in the main document window, which has four tabs: **Original**, **Optimized**, **2-Up**, and **4-Up**.*

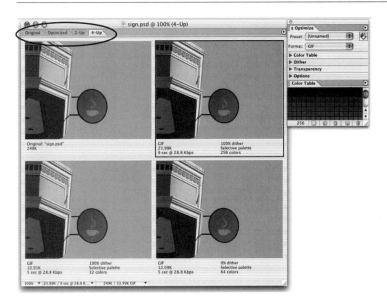

2. Click the **4-Up** tab so the image appears in four small preview windows.

3. Position the **Optimize** palette where you want it onscreen. (It should bring the **Color Table** palette with it if you docked the two palettes vertically as suggested.)

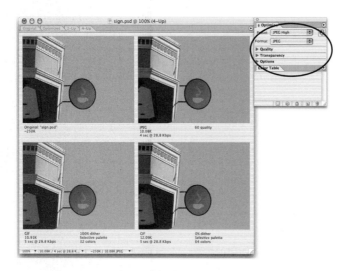

4. Click the top-right preview. In the **Optimize** palette, choose **JPEG** from the **File Format** pop-up menu.

*Notice that the sections in the **Optimize** palette changed to **Quality**, **Transparency**, and **Options**. The **Optimize** palette is context-sensitive, and the controls in it change depending on which file format you choose from the **File Format** pop-up menu.*

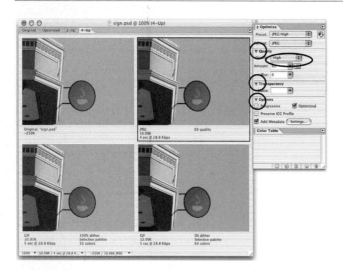

5. Expand the **Quality**, **Transparency**, and **Options** sections of the **Optimize** palette—you'll need to access the controls in these sections of the exercise.

6. Choose **High** from the **Quality** pop-up menu.

7. Choose **Repopulate Views** from the **Optimize** palette menu to set all of the previews to JPEG.

JPEG is the best format to use for the image, which has photographic elements and a continuous-tone gradient. The image will look better and be smaller when optimized as a JPEG.

8. Try all the things you learned in the Photoshop CS section of this chapter. Change the **Quality** setting, add **Blur**, and see what makes the smallest file size.

Most of these settings are identical to the ones in Photoshop CS.

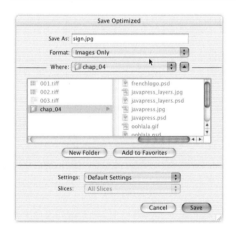

9. When you're ready to save the JPEG, choose **File > Save Optimized**. The **Save Optimized** dialog box will appear with the file name **sign.jpg**. Leave the other settings at their defaults for now. Save the optimized file and leave **sign.psd** open for the next exercise.

*Whenever you want to save a file for the Web, choose **Save Optimized** or **Save Optimized As**. Whenever you want to save the original PSD file, choose **Save** or **Save As**.*

II. [IR] _____Using a Matte Color on a JPEG in ImageReady CS

One major difference between Photoshop CS and ImageReady CS is that you can edit images more easily in ImageReady CS during the optimization process. To edit an image in Photoshop CS, you must exit the Save For Web window and return to the Photoshop CS image-editing environment. In ImageReady CS, you can edit the image whenever you want.

It's best to work with the Original tab chosen in the document window. Otherwise, ImageReady CS will try to optimize the graphic while you're working, which can take a long time. In this exercise, you will edit the image by erasing the background and inserting a new color using the Matte feature.

1. With **sign.psd** open from the previous exercise, click the **Original** tab in the document window. This will cause the **4-Up** view to collapse into a single view of the original image.

2. In the **Layers** palette, click the **Visibility** icon (the eye) beside the layer named **sky** to turn off the visibility of that layer. (If the **Layers** palette is not open, choose **Window > Layers**.) A checkerboard pattern will appear behind the sign, indicating that the background is transparent.

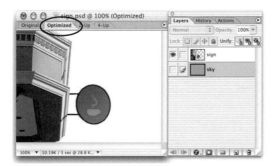

3. Click the **Optimized** tab in the document window.

Notice that the checkerboard background disappeared and turned white? That's because the JPEG format doesn't support transparency. ImageReady CS replaces transparent pixels with a solid (matte) color in the JPEG preview. You didn't specify a matte color, so ImageReady CS defaulted to white. You'll learn how to assign a different matte color in the next few steps.

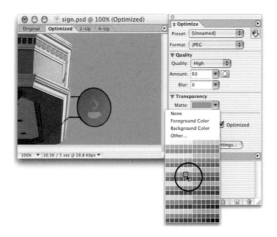

4. Expand the **Transparency** section of the **Optimize** palette. (If the **Optimize** palette is turned off, choose **Window > Optimize**.) In the **Matte** pop-up menu, choose a **light brown** color.

The image background of the image will now be filled with the color you chose.

*If you click back on the **Original** tab, you'll see the matte color disappear. The matte color exists only in the JPEG format. You have not permanently altered the file except to turn off the visibility of the sky layer.*

5. Keep the file open for the next exercise.

I2. [IR] _____Previewing and Writing HTML in ImageReady CS

If you're an experienced Photoshop CS user, you might be wondering why you would use the Matte color to insert a background color into a JPEG. You could have easily made a new layer in ImageReady CS, filled it with color, and achieved the same result. Here's the advantage: if you use the Matte feature, ImageReady CS can write this same color into the background of an HTML page so the image blends into the background. It's a way to fake transparency in a JPEG, which doesn't support real transparency. This exercise will show you how to set the background color of a Web page to match the Matte color in ImageReady CS.

Warning: There are times when the JPEG Matte color will not perfectly match an HTML background color. If this happens to you, it would be better to create a transparent GIF, which you will learn about in Chapter 9, "*Transparent GIFs*."

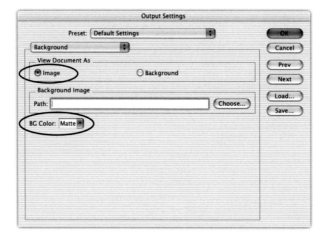

1. With **sign.psd** still open from the last exercise, choose **File > Output Settings > Background**. In the **Output Settings** dialog box, set **View Document As** to **Image** and choose **Matte** from the **BG Color** pop-up menu. Click **OK**.

2. Choose **File > Preview In** and select the browser of your choice.

Notice that ImageReady CS creates a preview in the browser and puts a white box below the image that displays temporary HTML code. You can select, copy, and paste this code into an HTML editor. Better yet, you can have ImageReady CS write a full HTML file for you. You'll learn to do that next.

3. Return to ImageReady CS and choose **File > Save Optimized As**.

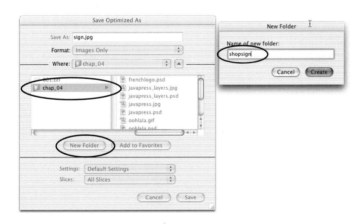

4. In the **Save Optimized As** dialog box, create a new folder in the **chap_04** folder by clicking **New Folder** (Mac) or the yellow **Create New Folder** button (Windows). Name the folder **shopsign** and click **Create** (Mac) or **OK** (Windows). **Note**: If you're using Windows, open the new folder **shopsign** after you create it.

A separate folder is not required, but it helps to keep your files organized.

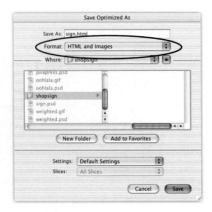

5. In the **Save Optimized As** window, keep the default name **sign.html**, choose **HTML and Images** from the **Format** (Mac) or **Save as type** (Windows) pop-up menu, and click **Save**.

6. Look on your hard drive for the **shopsign folder.**

*Notice there are two items there—an HTML file called **sign.html** and a folder labeled **images** that contains the **sign_01.jpg** image.*

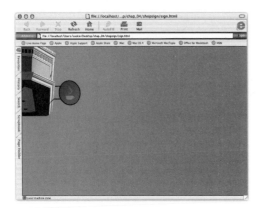

7. Double-click **sign.html**. You'll see the page open in your Web browser without the white information box you originally saw in the preview.

You can open this file in any HTML editor or upload it directly to the Web. If you want to make formatting changes, such as centering the image or adding a headline at the top, you can add these elements in an HTML editor.

8. Return to ImageReady CS and choose **File > Save** to save the original PSD file with its changes, then close the file.

I3. [IR] _____Exporting Images as Macromedia Flash

One of the key enhancements to ImageReady CS is the Macromedia Flash Export feature, which lets you export images as Macromedia Flash (SWF) files directly from ImageReady CS. Once you save files in the SWF format, you can use them directly on the Web, or you can open and edit the files in Macromedia Flash. In this exercise, you'll learn how to export an image as a SWF. **Note**: The Export to Macromedia Flash feature is only available in ImageReady CS.

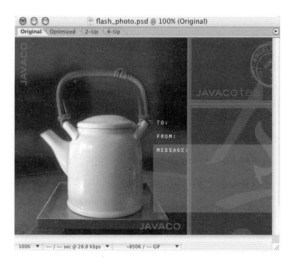

1. Open **flash_photo.psd** from the **chap_04** folder you copied to your **Desktop**.

2. Choose **File > Export > Macromedia Flash SWF**. The **Macromedia Flash Export** dialog box opens automatically.

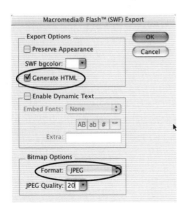

3. In the **Macromedia Flash Export** dialog box, turn on the **Generate HTML** option and choose **JPEG** from the **Format** pop-up menu. Because the image is largely made up of photographic content, it's best to choose **JPEG** from the **Format** pop-up menu for this example. Type **20** in the **JPEG Quality** field. Make sure the **Preserve Transparency** and **Enable Dynamic Text** options are turned off as shown in the illustration above. Click **OK**.

Note: For the purpose of this exercise, I wanted to create a SWF file as small as possible so it can be viewed quickly on the Web. If you plan to export the file as a SWF and open it in Macromedia Flash to do some additional work with the file, make sure you increase the quality setting to the maximum so you don't compromise the quality of the file during the export process. When you're finished making changes to the file in Macromedia Flash, you can optimize it directly from there, which will ensure the best quality optimization.

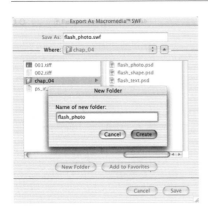

4. In the **Export as Macromedia Flash** dialog box, navigate to the **chap_04** you copied to your **Desktop**. Click the **New Folder** button. In the **New Folder** dialog box, type **flash_photo** and click **Create** (Mac) or **OK** (Windows). Leave the file name as the default—**flash_photo.swf**. Click **Save**.

5. Browse to the **flash_photo** folder in the **chap_04** folder you copied to your **Desktop**. Notice the folder contains two files: **flash_photo.html** and **flash_photo.swf**.

6. Double-click the **flash_photo.html** file to preview it in your default Web browser. It's that easy to export SWF files from ImageReady CS!

Note: Depending on what you want to do with the file, you don't always have to save the HTML code. In this case, I saved the HTML code to show you how the exported SWF file would look in a Web browser. If you prefer, you can create the HTML code in an HTML editor, such as Adobe GoLive or Macromedia Dreamweaver. This exercise teaches you how to export a static graphic as a SWF file. In Chapter 13, "Animated GIFs and Flash," you'll learn how to export an animation as a Macromedia Flash file.

7. Return to ImageReady CS. Save and close the file.

You should congratulate yourself for doing so much in this chapter! Knowing how to optimize images is one of the most valuable skills a Web designer can have, and it is well worth the time and effort you put in here.

5.
Layers

| Using Layers | Using Linked Layers |
| Using Layer Sets | Using Layer Comps |
| Working with Multiple Layers in ImageReady CS |
Exporting Layers as Files	Creating Solid Color Layers
Creating Gradient Layers	Creating Pattern Layers
Using Adjustment Layers	Using Clipping Groups

chap_05

Photoshop CS/ImageReady CS
H•O•T CD-ROM

Understanding layers is one of the most important cornerstones of mastering Photoshop CS. When you use layers, you are able to separate elements of your image so they can be edited individually. With layers, you can isolate image areas and apply special effects, or change the image's location, color, or opacity without affecting the contents of the other layers. Photoshop CS offers an amazing new feature called **Layer Comps**, which lets you store any combination of layer visibility, position, or blending options. Layers are powerful, yet complex. The exercises in this chapter will help you become comfortable with common layering tasks.

options → new layer
new layer → icon

What Are Layers?

When layers were introduced to Photoshop in 1996, they revolutionized the way designers created, edited, and saved their work. Prior to layers, pixels in an image would be canceled out if other pixels were placed on top of them. This changed when layers came along.

Separating areas of an image into layers allows you to have stacks and stacks of images on individual layers that can be changed or moved without altering the pixels in the image areas above or below. As long as you don't "flatten" your layers, each layer remains independent of the others so you can make infinite changes.

Although layers were originally introduced to Photoshop to help designers edit specific areas of images, they have grown more powerful with each new version. Now, layers not only isolate areas or elements of an image, but they can contain layer masks, patterns, gradients, solid fills, and vector shapes. Plus, in Photoshop CS, you can use the new Layer Comps feature to save different configurations of visibility, position, and blending all within the same file! These concepts might seem a bit abstract now, but the following exercises will make them come to life for you.

I. [PS] _____Using Layers

In this exercise you'll learn about the stacking order of layers, how to alter the stacking order, how to rename a layer, how to change the Background layer from fixed to editable, and how to create new layers.

Note: Everything you learn in this chapter is applicable in ImageReady CS.

1. In Photoshop CS, open **shop.psd** from the **chap_05** folder you copied to your **Desktop** from the **H•O•T CD-ROM**.

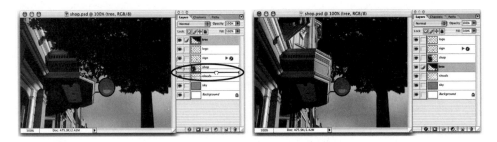

2. In the **Layers** palette, drag and drop the **tree** layer below the **shop** layer. As you drag, the cursor will change to a closed fist icon. Drop the type layer when you see a **double line** under the **shop** layer.

You just changed the stacking order of the layers. When you change stacking order, you don't touch the image at all; you just move the layers around.

The tree should appear behind the coffee shop. Notice the stacking order goes from the background to the foreground as you move from the bottom of the **Layers** palette to the top.

3. Click the **clouds** layer in the **Layers** palette and drag it to the top of the layer stack (above the **logo** layer).

In the image, the clouds look out of place in front of the tree. In the next step, you'll learn how to fix this problem by making the clouds layer invisible.

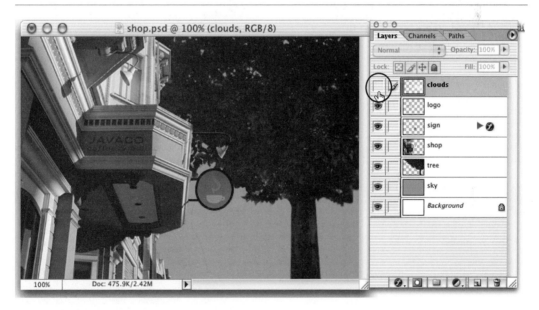

4. In the **Layers** palette, click the **Visibility** icon (the Eye) on the **clouds** layer to turn the layer visibility off.

*Notice you no longer see the contents of the clouds layer in your document window. Clicking the **Eye** icon toggles the visibility of a layer on and off.*

5. Click the **Background** layer and try moving it above the **clouds** layer.

*Did you notice the **Background** layer cannot be moved? A background layer, which is generated automatically when you create a new document with a non-transparent background, has different properties than a layer. You can't move it unless you convert it to a layer, which you'll do in the next step.*

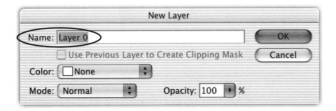

6. Double-click the **Background** layer to open the **New Layer** dialog box. Leave the default name **Layer 0** in the **Name** field and click **OK**.

7. Move **Layer 0** above the **sky** layer just like you did with the **tree** layer in **Step 2**.

8. When you're working with layered images, it's important to keep your layers organized with descriptive names so you know what's on each layer. **Layer 0** isn't a terribly descriptive name for the white layer. To rename it, double-click the layer name in the **Layers** palette. A bounding box will appear around the words **Layer 0**. Type a new name—**white**—and press **Return** (Mac) or **Enter** (Windows).

*Be careful to double-click directly on the layer name. If you click anywhere else on the layer, you'll inadvertently open the **Layer Style** dialog box and you won't be able to rename the layer.*

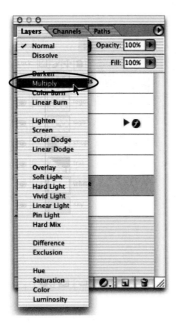

9. With the **white** layer selected, click the **Layer Blending Mode** pop-up menu (which is set to **Normal** by default) and choose **Multiply**.

*Layer-blending modes control the way the color and tone of pixels on a selected layer interact with pixels on the layers below. The **Multiply** mode blends layers to produce a darker color, turning the white sky to blue in this case.*

*There are 23 layer-blending modes in Photoshop CS, including a new layer-blending mode called **Hard Mix**. Experiment with layer-blending modes on different images. It's the best way to get a sense of what each one does. For a description of each layer-blending mode, refer to the Photoshop CS User Guide.*

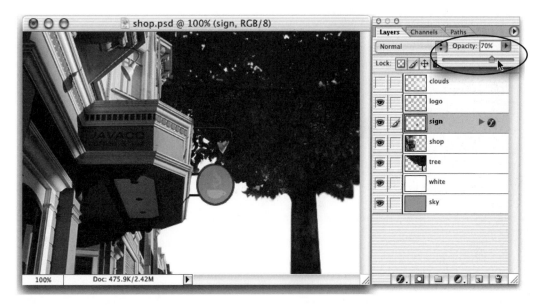

10. Click the **sign** layer to select it and lower the **Opacity** slider to **70%**. Notice the contents of this layer—the sign and the black border around it—are less opaque (more see-through). The sign border looks unnaturally faded, so return the **Opacity** slider to **100%**.

Lowering the opacity of a layer makes the image on the layer more transparent, so the layers beneath show through. The sign on this layer is artwork. The black border is a special effect called a stroke layer style. You'll learn about layer styles in Chapter 7, "Shapes and Layer Styles." For now, remember the Opacity slider affects everything on a layer, including layer styles.

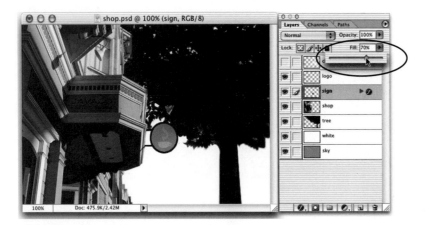

11. With the **sign** layer still selected, lower the **Fill** slider to **70%**. Notice the sign becomes less opaque, but the black border around the sign, which is a layer style, does not.

*The **Fill** slider, unlike the **Opacity** slider, does not affect everything on a layer. It makes the artwork on a layer less opaque, but does not affect any layer styles on the layer. The **Fill** slider is useful when you want the interior of an object to contain a different opacity than its stroke or outline.*

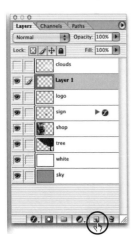

12. Click the **logo** layer to select it and click the **New Layer** icon at the bottom of the **Layers** palette.

*Notice a new empty layer appears in the **Layers** palette just above the **logo** layer, but nothing has changed inside the document window.*

When you add a new layer, it is empty and transparent by default. Next, you'll draw on the empty layer. The benefit to drawing on this layer, instead of drawing on any of the other layers, is it can be isolated on its own—turned on or off, opacity lowered or raised, reordered, etc.

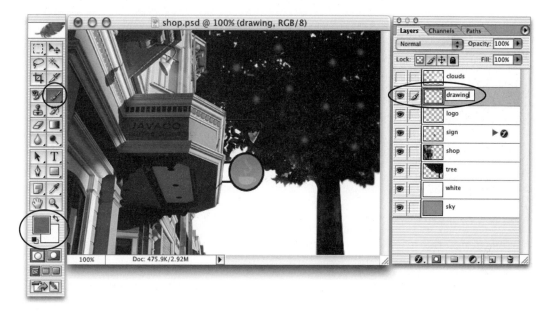

13. Click **Layer 1** to select it. Choose the **Brush** tool from the **Toolbox**, choose a color, and draw dots on the tree. Rename **Layer 1** as **drawing**, using the technique you learned in **Step 8**.

The benefit to drawing on this new empty layer is you can turn it off or delete it if you don't like what you draw.

14. Experiment more with the techniques you just learned. Turn the visibility on and off, move layers around, reduce opacity and fill opacity, and rename layers.

The more you play with the layers in this image, the more you'll understand layers.

15. Close and save the file.

NOTE | Flattening Photoshop Files

In Photoshop CS, the term "flattened" means the layers have been compressed into a single layer. There are times when you might want to flatten a Photoshop CS file—to send it to a client, or to make the file size smaller. If you need to flatten a file, save a non-flattened version as well as a flattened version. You never know when you will need access to the layered file.

In Photoshop CS, you can flatten all the layers or just flatten specific layers to simplify a complex layered file.

To flatten an image or specific layers, choose one of the following items from the **Layers** palette menu:

Merge Down: Combines (flattens) the selected layer and the layer directly below it. **Note:** You must select a layer that is positioned above other layers in the Layers palette before you can use **Merge Down**.

Merge Visible: Combines all visible layers (with Eye icons turned on). This is a great way to flatten layers that aren't next to each other in the **Layers** palette.

Merge Linked: Combines linked layers to one another, which you'll learn about in **Exercise 3**. This is another great way to flatten layers that aren't next to each other in the **Layers** palette. **Note: Merge Linked** will be grayed out unless you select a linked layer.

Flatten Image: Combines all layers into a single layer.

2. [PS] Moving Layers

In the last exercise, you learned to move the stacking order of layers up and down, but what if you want to move a layer's position? This next exercise will teach you how to move layers.

1. In **Photoshop CS**, open **moving.psd** from the **chap_05** folder on your **Desktop**.

*Notice there are four buttons in the image, which are represented by eight layers of button artwork and text in the **Layers** palette.*

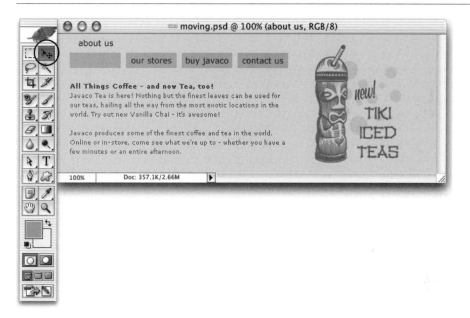

2. Select the **Move** tool from the **Toolbox** or use the keyboard shortcut by pressing the letter V. It's worth memorizing the keyboard shortcut for the **Move** tool. You'll use often in Photoshop CS.

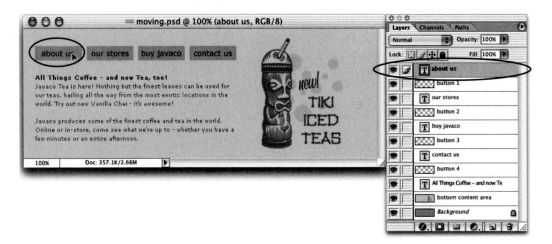

3. Click the **about us** layer in the **Layers** palette to select it. With the **about us** layer selected, click and drag inside the document window. The contents of the layer, in this case the words **about us**, should move as you move the layer.

You've just hit one of the biggest hurdles in Photoshop CS. You must select a layer before you can move it. This is a difficult concept for most new users because there is a disconnect between wanting to move a piece of an image and having to think first about which layer to move. Photoshop CS can help you with this concept if you instruct it to automatically select layers, as you'll learn to do in the next step.

4. Make sure the **Move** tool is still selected in the **Toolbox**. Turn on the **Auto Select Layer** checkbox in the **Options** bar.

5. With the **Move** tool selected in the **Toolbox**, click on different areas of your image. Watch the currently selected layer in the **Layers** palette change automatically.

*Using the **Auto Select Layer** option is easier than selecting layers manually in the **Layers** palette.*

If you click on an area where two or more layers overlap, Photoshop CS selects the topmost layer.

6. With the **Move** tool selected in the **Toolbox**, turn off the **Auto Select Layer** checkbox in the **Options** bar.

7. Keep **moving.psd** open for the next exercise.

3. [PS] _____Moving Linked Layers

In the last exercise, you learned how to move layers individually. When you're working in Photoshop CS, you'll often want to move more than one layer at the same time. The next exercise will show you how to link layers so you can do just that.

1. If you followed the last exercise, you will have **moving.psd** open. If not, open it from the **chap_05** folder you copied to your **Desktop**. In the **Layers** palette, click the **about us** layer to select it.

2. Click inside the **Link** region, which is located between the layer thumbnail and the visibility icon, on all the layers except the three layers (**All Things Coffee**, **bottom content area**, and **background**) at the bottom of the layer stack.

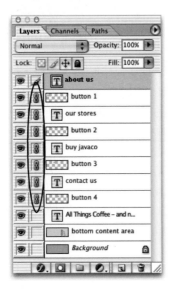

*Notice your active layer (the **about us** layer) has a **Paint Brush** icon instead of a **Link** icon. This means all the other layers are linked to the about us layer.*

3. With the **about us** layer selected in the **Layers** palette and the **Move** tool selected in the **Toolbox**, click and drag on your screen.

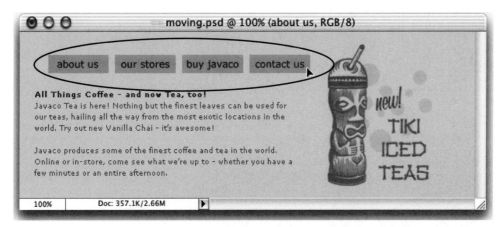

Notice all the linked layers move together. Pretty cool!

4. Click in the **Link** region of the **button 1** layer. Then drag down through the **Link** regions of the linked layers to remove the **Link** icon. This unlinks the layers.

Tip: It's smart to unlink layers when you're done. Otherwise, you might inadvertently affect more than one layer when you're working on another task.

5. Close and save the file.

The next exercise will show you how to easily align linked layers.

4. [PS] Aligning Linked Layers

The Link feature in Photoshop CS is useful for more than just moving more than one layer at the same time. You can align linked layers to the left, center, or right, and distribute distances between layers easily.

1. Open **align.psd** from the **chap_05** folder you copied to your **Desktop** from the **H•O•T** **CD-ROM**.

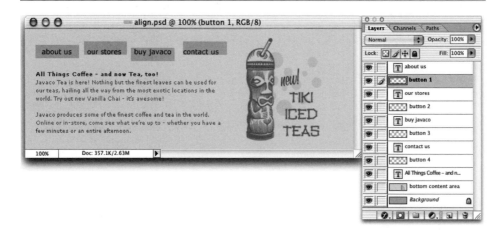

2. First, you'll align the navigation buttons by their top edges. Select the **button 1** layer in the **Layers** palette.

*You'll see a **Paint Brush** icon in the **Link** region confirming this is your active layer.*

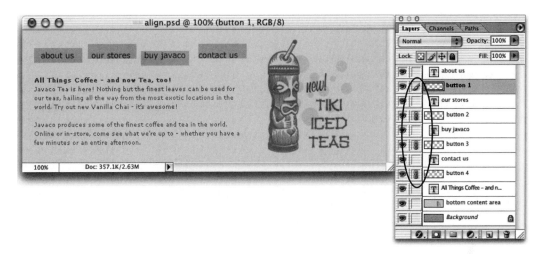

3. In the **Layers** palette, click in the **Link** region of layers **button 2**, **button 3**, and **button 4** to link the buttons together.

4. With the **Move** tool selected in the **Toolbox**, click the **Align top edges** button on the **Options** bar to align the buttons horizontally. You'll see the buttons line up horizontally at the top.

5. Click the **Distribute horizontal centers** button on the **Options** bar to evenly space the buttons horizontally.

*With the **Move** tool selected, you can move these four perfectly aligned and spaced buttons around and they'll stay linked this way.*

6. Now you'll align the text inside the buttons. First, unlink the layers you linked to the **button 1** layer in the preceding steps.

7. Click the **button 2** layer to select it, then link the **our stores** layer to it.

8. With the **Move** tool selected in the **Toolbox**, click the **Align horizontal centers** button on the **Options** bar. The words **our stores** will be centered on the second button. Repeat these steps to center the **about us**, **buy javaco**, and **contact us** text layers to their respective buttons. This shows how linking relationships can be changed any time to achieve different kinds of alignment results.

*Hint: Select the button first, then link the text to it before you align. Alignment is always based on the selected layer as the starting point, as indicated by the **Paint Brush** icon. If you select the text first and link the button layer to the text, the button will move instead.*

9. Close and save the file.

What Are Layer Sets?

A layer set is a group of layers stored inside a folder in the Layers palette. Layer sets keep your layers organized if you have lots of layers in an image. Specifically, layer sets are extremely helpful if you have several layers that make up a single design element. For example, if you create a Web button with one layer for the button shape and one layer for the type, you can put both layers into a layer set so you can make changes to both layers at the same time.

Putting layers in a layer set also lets you change the visibility, opacity, layer blending mode, and position of multiple layers at once. You can also group layer sets in a meaningful way and minimize the stack of layers in the Layers palette. You'll work with layer sets in the upcoming exercise. The following chart summarizes what you can do with layer sets versus individual layers.

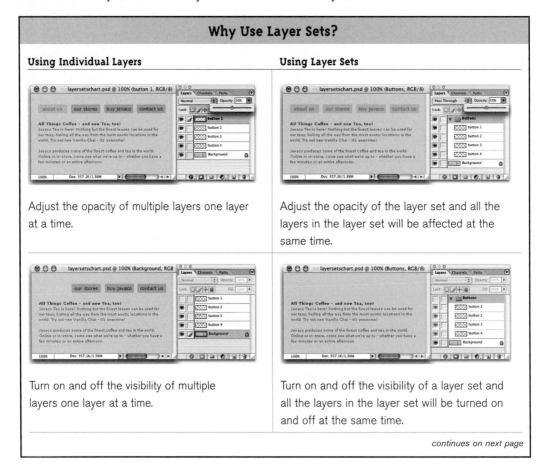

Why Use Layer Sets?	
Using Individual Layers	**Using Layer Sets**
Adjust the opacity of multiple layers one layer at a time.	Adjust the opacity of the layer set and all the layers in the layer set will be affected at the same time.
Turn on and off the visibility of multiple layers one layer at a time.	Turn on and off the visibility of a layer set and all the layers in the layer set will be turned on and off at the same time.

continues on next page

Why Use Layer Sets? *continued*

Using Individual Layers

Using Layer Sets

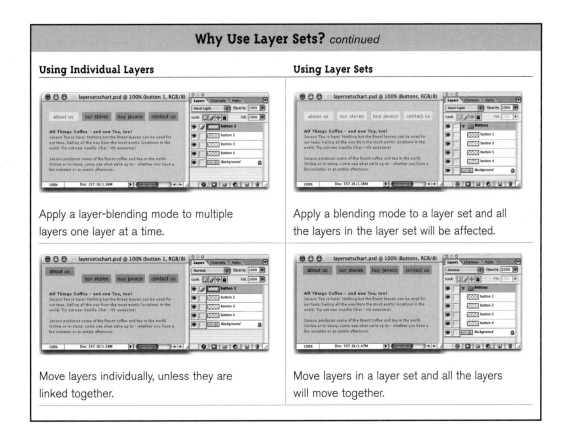

Apply a layer-blending mode to multiple layers one layer at a time.

Apply a blending mode to a layer set and all the layers in the layer set will be affected.

Move layers individually, unless they are linked together.

Move layers in a layer set and all the layers will move together.

5. [PS] _____Using Layer Sets

In this exercise, you'll practice creating layer sets, adding layers to layer sets, and changing the opacity, visibility, position, alignment, and blending mode of layers in a layer set. The benefit of putting layers into layer sets is that you can make changes to multiple layers at the same time and shorten the layer stack in the Layers palette.

1. Open **layersets.psd** from the **chap_05** folder you copied to your **Desktop**.

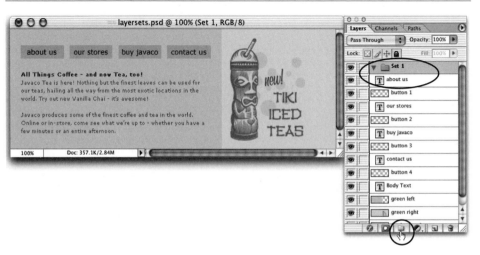

2. In the **Layers** palette, select the **about us** layer. Click the **New Set** icon at the bottom of the **Layers** palette. A folder called **Set 1** will appear above the selected layer.

Tip: *Before you create a new layer set, click on one of the layers you plan to put into the layer set. This ensures the layer set will be created right above the layer, which makes it easier to drag the appropriate layers into the layer set.*

3. Click and drag the **about us** layer into the **Set 1** layer set.

*As you drag the **about us** layer into **Set 1**, your cursor will change to a closed fist, and the **Set 1** folder icon will open when you move the cursor over the layer set.*

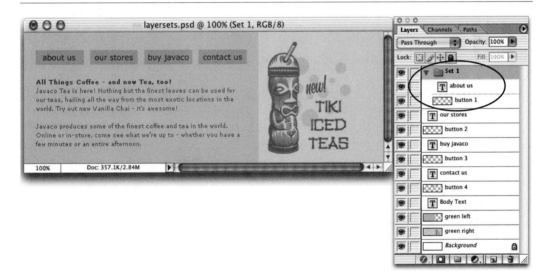

4. Click and drag the **button 1** layer into the **Set 1** layer set.

Tip: *You can move the stacking order of layers in a layer set just like you can with any other layer.*

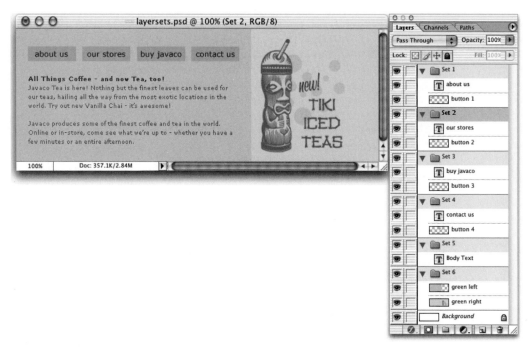

5. Click the **New Set** icon at the bottom of the **Layers** palette five more times to create a total of six layer sets. Move the o**ur stores** and **button 2** layers into **Set 2**, the **buy javaco** and **button 3** layers into **Set 3**, the **contact us** and **button 4** layers into **Set 4**, **Body Text** into **Set 5**, and **green left** and **green right** into **Set 6**.

Note: Another unique property of a background layer is that it cannot be moved into a layer set. Try it and you'll see.

You just created individual layer sets for each of the Web buttons. This is beneficial because now you can make changes to the shape and the type layers, which together make the Web buttons, at the same time. Next, you'll learn to rename layer sets and change the color of layer set entries in the **Layers** *palette so you can identify layer sets easily.*

6. Click the arrow beside layer sets **1** through **5** to collapse the layer sets and hide their contents.

This makes the **Layers** *palette shorter and more manageable, especially when you have lots of layers in an image.*

Tip: You can shorten the **Layers** *palette by clicking on the bottom-right corner and dragging.*

7. Double-click **Set 6** in the **Layers** palette, and rename **Set 6** to **green background** to give it a more meaningful name.

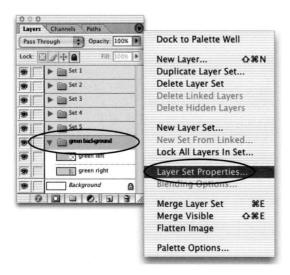

8. Click the **green background** layer set to select it. Choose **Layer Set Properties** from the **Layers** palette menu.

9. In the **Layer Set Properties** dialog box, choose **Green** from the **Color** pop-up menu. Click **OK**.

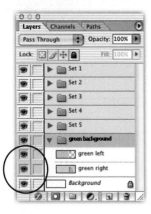

*The **green background** layer set and each of its nested layers in the **Layers** palette are now marked with green. This is a great way to identify and organize layer sets.*

10. Collapse the **green background** layer set by clicking the arrow beside the **green background** layer set.

11. Expand **Set 1** so you can see the layers inside the layer set. Click **Set 1** to select it. Choose the **Move** tool from the **Toolbox**. Click and drag inside the document to move the **about us** button and text.

*Using the **Move** tool with a layer set selected in the **Layers** palette lets you move all the layers in a layer set at the same time. This is an excellent way to keep design elements such as Web buttons, which contain more than one layer, organized and it can be easier than linking layers if you have several layers in a file.*

Note: *If you're having trouble with this step, take a look at the **Auto Select Layer** option in the **Options** bar. It has to be unchecked when you're working with layer sets.*

Next, you'll link the layer sets together so you can move multiple layer sets at the same time.

12. Select **Set 1** in the **Layers** palette. Click the link region next to **Set 2**, **Set 3**, **Set 4**, and **Set 5** so they are linked to **Set 1**. Select the **Move** tool in the **Toolbox**. Click and drag the layers inside the document window.

Notice that all the layers inside the layers sets move together. This is a very helpful way to move several layers at the same time. The ability to link layer sets saves you time linking individual layers.

Next you'll learn to align layers in layer sets.

13. Unlink the layer sets you linked in the last step by clicking inside the link regions beside the layer sets.

14. Select **Set 2** in the **Layers** palette. Click in the **Link** region next to **Set 1**. Click the **Align top edges** button in the **Options** bar to align **Set 1** (the **about us** button and text you moved in the last step) to **Set 2**.

*Notice there are active **Link** icons next to **Set 1** and **Set 2**, but the **Link** icons next to the individual layers are grayed out. That's because aligning layer sets to each other is a separate operation from aligning layers to one another.*

Next, you'll align the layers inside the layer sets, which shows you can still align individual layers even if they are contained inside layer sets.

15. Expand **Sets 2**, **3**, and **4** in the Layers palette. Select the **buy javaco** layer. Click in the **Link** regions next to the **about us**, **our stores**, and **contact us** layers. Click the **Align vertical centers** button on the **Options** bar to align the type layers to one another.

The ability to link and align individual layers in a layer set is very helpful because it gives you the flexibility of working with individual layers plus the added organizational benefits of working with layer sets. In this case, the shape part of the Web buttons were already aligned but the text wasn't aligned consistently across the buttons. Linking and aligning the type layers individually provide the ability to align the type without affecting the shape.

16. Unlink the layers and collapse all the layers sets except **Set 1.**

Most of the operations you'll do on layer sets will work the same whether the arrows on the layer sets are expanded or collapsed. I've asked you to collapse them to shorten the layer stack.

Next, you'll learn how to turn off visibility, change opacity, and change layer-blending modes for layer sets.

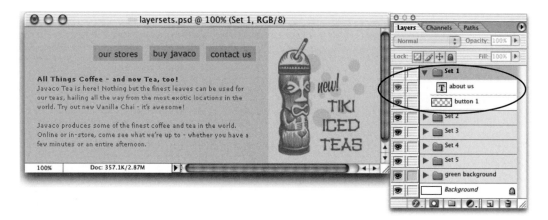

17. Turn off the visibility for **Set 1** in the **Layers** palette and you'll see both the **about us** button and text disappear. Click again to make **Set 1** visible. Layer sets are useful for turning on and off the visibility of multiple layers at the same time.

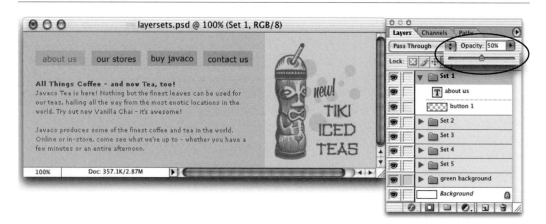

18. With **Set 1** selected, change the **Opacity** slider to **50%**. This will affect the opacity of both layers in **Set 1**. Change the **Opacity** back to **100%**.

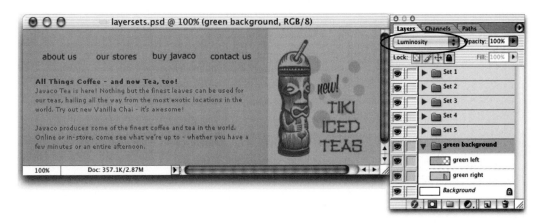

19. Expand the **green background** layer set, and then click to select it. Choose **Luminosity** from the **Layer Blending Mode** pop-up menu.

*This changes how the whole layer set interacts with the layer below, which is the white background. (The **Luminosity** blending mode blends the **green background** layer set and the **Background** layer, creating a range of grays.) If you click on the **green left** or **green right** layer, you'll see each has its own blending mode—**Normal**. Layers in a layer set blend together first, using their own blending modes. The result of the blend is then blended with the layers below the layer set, using the blending mode assigned to the layer set.*

*Note: The default blending mode for a layer set is **pass through**, which means only the blending mode of the layers nested in the layer set has an effect.*

---

20. Close and save the file.

NOTE | Nesting Layer Sets

One of the new features in Photoshop CS is the ability to nest layer sets inside layer sets up to a maximum of five levels. This new feature makes it even easier to keep your layers organized. For example, if you are designing a Web site, you can create a layer set for the entire site, then create layer sets for each of the individual pages. Since Web pages are made up of several elements, which are typically contained in separate layers, this is an excellent way for you to keep you layers organized.

To create nested layer sets, click a layer set to select it and then click the **New Layer Set** button at the bottom of the **Layers** palette. A new layer set will be created inside the layer set you selected.

[IR] _____ Working with Multiple Layers in ImageReady CS

ImageReady CS has a new object-based interface that lets you select multiple layers in the Layers palette. Once you have multiple layers selected, you can execute several commands over the layers such as moving, aligning, nesting, merging, and duplicating. Many of the same tasks you can accomplish with links or layer sets can also be achieved by selecting multiple layers. This is just a case of there being three ways to do the same thing. Which method should you choose? Whichever is most convenient! Here's an exercise that shows you how work with multiple layers in ImageReady CS.

1. Open **multiple.psd** from the **chap_05** folder you copied to your **Desktop**.

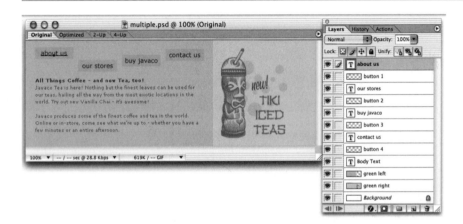

2. Click the **about us** layer to select it. Hold down the **Shift** key and click the **button 4** layer.

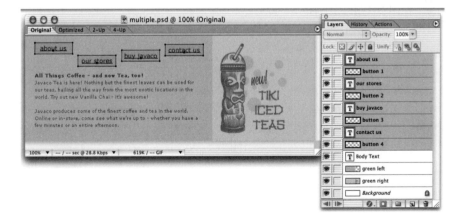

All the layers between **about us** and **button 4** should now be selected.

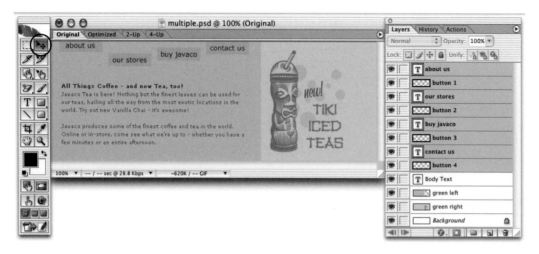

3. Keep the layers selected in the **Layers** palette. Choose the **Move** tool from the **Toolbox**. Click and drag inside the document window.

*Notice all the layers move together because they are selected in the **Layers** palette. This technique achieves the same result as linking layers, which you learned in **Exercise 3**. Why would you select multiple layers instead of linking layers to achieve the same result? Selecting multiple layers is more temporary than linking layers. Once you click off the selected layers, they won't be selected anymore. When you link layers, you can leave them linked until you've finished doing more than one task. Selecting multiple layers is useful because it's fast and easy.*

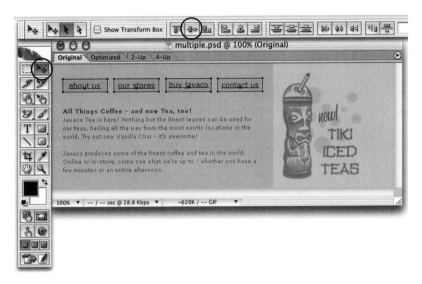

4. With the **Move** tool selected in the **Toolbox**, click the **Align vertical centers** button on the **Options** bar.

Notice the four buttons, including the type, are now aligned.

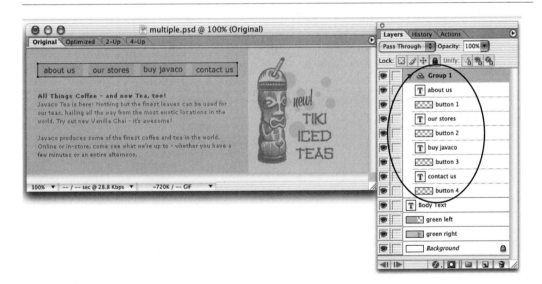

5. With the layers still selected in the **Layers** palette, press **Cmd+G** (Mac) or **Ctrl+G** (Windows).

Notice the selected layers are automatically grouped together in a group called Group 1. This is a great way to group layer sets quickly. **Note:** *"Group" is another name for a layer set, which you learned about earlier in this chapter.*

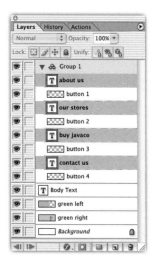

6. In the **Group 1** layer set, click the **about us** layer to select it. Hold down the **Cmd** (Mac) or **Ctrl** (Windows) key and click each of the following layers: **our stores**, **buy javaco**, and **contact us**.

*You should now have four layers selected inside the **Group 1** layer set.*

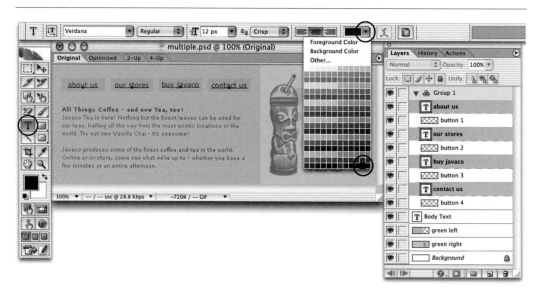

7. Click the **Type Tool** in the **Toolbox**. On the **Options** bar, choose a different color from the **Color** pop-up menu.

Notice the colors of all four type layers changed to the color you selected. You'll learn more about type in Chapter 6, "Type." For now, remember you can change the type settings for selected type layers in ImageReady CS.

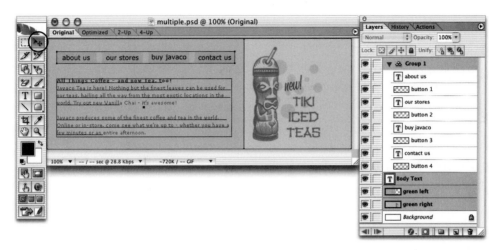

8. Choose the **Move** tool from the Toolbox. Type **Cmd+A** (Mac) or **Ctrl+A** (Windows) to select all layers and layer sets.

*The **Group 1** layer set, **body text**, **green left**, and **green right** layers should be selected in the **Layers** palette.*

*Tip: To deselect all layers, type **Cmd+D** (Mac) or **Ctrl+D** (Windows).*

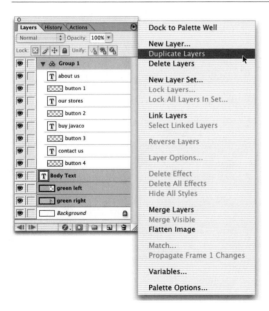

9. Choose **Duplicate Layers** from the **Layers** palette menu.

*You should now see copies of **Group 1**, **body text**, **green left**, and **green right** above the original layers.*

10. The layers you just copied using the **Duplicate Layer** command should still be selected. If not, click **Group 1,** hold down the **Shift** key and click on each copied layer to select it as shown in the illustration above.

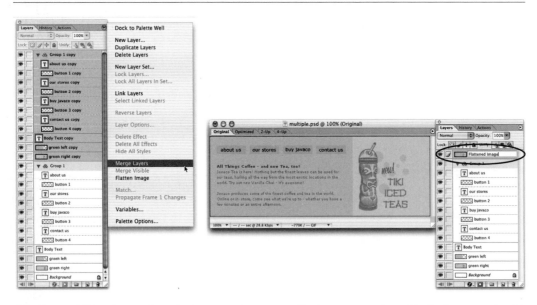

11. Choose **Merge Layers** from the **Layers** palette menu. The layers you selected in the last step should now be combined into a single layer. Double-click the layer name and rename it to **Flattened Image**.

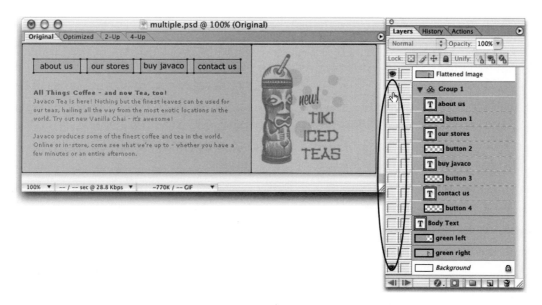

12. In the **Layers** palette, click **Group 1** to select it. Hold down the **Shift** key and select each of the following layers: **body text**, **green left**, and **green right**. Turn off the **Visibility** icon beside **Group 1**.

Notice the visibility is automatically turned off beside each of the layers you selected.

*Tip: Duplicating and merging layers is a great technique if you need to create a flattened image for a client but you want to keep the original layered file. You can also use the **Export Layers as Files** feature to save the flattened layer as a separate image. You'll learn how to use the **Export Layers as Files** feature in the next exercise.*

13. Close and save the file.

MOVIE | Multiple Selections

To learn more about **multiple layer selections** and what can be done with them, check out **m_layer_select.mov** in the **movies** folder on the **H•O•T CD-ROM**.

Comparing Linked Layers, Layer Sets and Multiple Layers

Now that you've learned about linking, working with layer sets, and selecting multiple layers, you may be wondering what you can do with and when to use each method for working with layers. Here's a brief chart to show you:

Comparing Linked Layers, Layer Sets, and Multiple Layers			
Task	**Linked Layers**	**Layer Sets**	**Select Multiple Layers (ImageReady CS only)**
Moving Layers	You can move one or more linked layers at the same time.	You can move layers inside a layer set at the same time when the layer set is selected in the Layers palette.	You can move one or more layers at the same time when you select multiple layers in the Layers palette.
Aligning Layers	You can align linked layers.	You cannot align layers inside a layer set when the layer set is selected in the layers palette (unless you link or multiple select the individual layers in the layer set).	You can align layers when you select multiple layers in the Layers palette.
Creating Layer Sets	You can create a layer set from linked layers.		You can create layer sets when you select multiple groups in the Layers palette.
Duplicating Layers	You can duplicate the selected layer but not the layers that are linked to it.	You can duplicate the entire contents of a layer set.	You can duplicate one or more layers when you select multiple layers in the Layers palette.
Deleting Layers	You can delete linked layers.	You can delete the layer set, the contents of a layer set, or the layer set and its contents.	You can delete one or more layers when you select multiple layers in the Layers palette.

continues on next page

Comparing Linked Layers, Layer Sets, and Multiple Layers *continued*			
Task	**Linked Layers**	**Layer Sets**	**Select Multiple Layers (ImageReady CS only)**
Linking Layers		You can link the layers in a layer set.	You can link one or more layers when you select multiple layers in the Layers palette.
Merging Layers	You cannot merge linked layers.	You can merge the layers in a layer set into a single layer.	You can merge one or more layers when you select multiple layers in the Layers palette.
Locking Layers	You can lock the selected layer but not the layers that are linked to it.	You can lock all the layers in a layer set at the same time.	You can lock one or more layers when you select multiple layers in the Layers palette.
Modifying Type Settings	You can modify the font settings of the selected layer but not the layers that are linked to it.	You cannot modify the font settings of a layer set unless you select the individual layer(s).	You can modify type settings for one or more layers when you select multiple layers in the Layers palette.

What Are Layer Comps?

One of the great additions to Photoshop CS and ImageReady CS is the Layer Comps feature. Layer Comps let you save different configurations of layer visibility, position, and blending all within the same file! This makes it easy to work with different variations of an image without having to save multiple files. For example, if you're creating an image for clients and you want to show them different variations such as color or type, you can save a series of layer comps with the different variations all in the same Photoshop CS file. Likewise, you can quickly create a series of Web pages from a master page design and save each Web page as a layer comp in the original file.

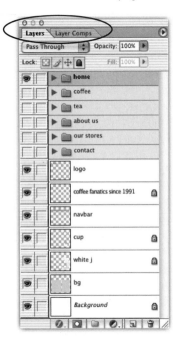

Before you begin using Layer Comps in Photoshop CS, I suggest you dock the **Layers** and **Layer Comps** palettes together, as you learned in Chapter 2, "*Interface*." If you don't see the **Layers** or **Layer Comps** palettes onscreen or in the **Palette Well**, choose **Window > Layers** or **Window > Layer Comps**.

7. [PS] _____ Using Layer Comps

In this exercise, you'll learn how to use the Layer Comps feature to save different layer configurations in a Photoshop CS file. It works the same way for ImageReady CS.

1. Open **layercomps.psd** from the **chap_05** folder you copied to your **Desktop**.

*In the document window, you'll see the basic elements for the Javaco Web site. In the **Layers** palette, you'll see six layer sets (one for each of the following pages: **home**, **coffee**, **tea**, **about us**, **our stores**, **contact**) and six individual layers, which make up the basic elements of the Web site you see in the document window.*

The first layer comp you'll save is the current configuration on your screen—the basic site elements.

2. Click the **Layer Comps** tab. Click the **Create New Layer Comp** button at the bottom of the **Layer Comps** palette.

*The **New Layer Comp** dialog box opens automatically.*

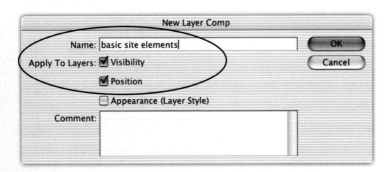

3. In the **New Layer Comp** dialog box, type **basic site elements** in the name field. Turn on **Visibility** and **Position**. Click **OK**.

*You should now see **basic site elements** in the **Layer Comps** palette.*

*The **basic site elements** layer comp will remember the visibility and position of the current layer configuration in the **Layers** palette.*

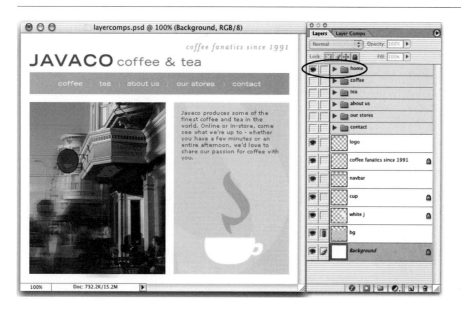

4. Click the **Layers** tab. Turn on the visibility of the **home** layer set.

You should now see the home page of the Javaco Web site in the document window.

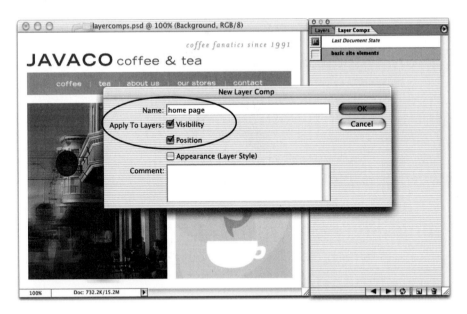

5. Click the **Layer Comps** tab. Click the **Create New Layer Comp** button at the bottom of the **Layer Comps** palette. In the **New Layer Comp** dialog box, type the name **home page** in the name field and make sure the **Visibility** and **Position** options are turned on. Click **OK**.

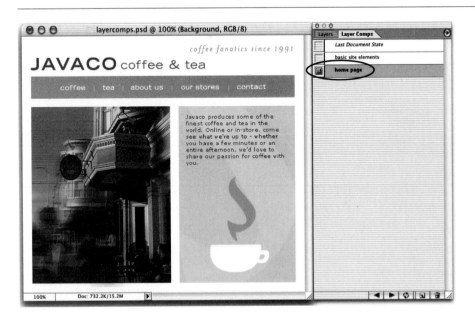

*You should now see **home page** in the **Layer Comps** palette.*

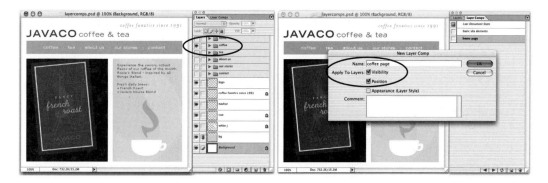

6. Click the **Layers** palette tab. Turn off the visibility of the **home** layer set. Turn on the visibility of the **coffee** layer set. Click the **Layer Comps** tab. Click the **Create New Layer Comp** button at the bottom of the **Layer Comps** palette. In the **New Layer Comp** dialog box, type the name **coffee page** in the **name field** and make sure the **Visibility** and **Position** options are turned on. Click **OK**.

7. Repeat the instructions in **Step 6** to create layer comps for the **tea**, **about us**, **our stores**, and **contact** layer sets.

8. In the **Layer Comps** palette, turn on the **Layer Comp** button beside the **tea page** layer comp.

The contents of the document window will change to the tea page of the Javaco Web site. Pretty cool!

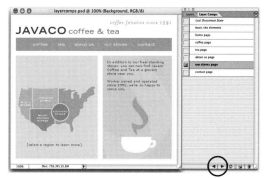

9. Click the **Previous** and **Next** buttons at the bottom of the **Layer Comps** palette to view the layer comps you saved.

*This is a great way to create a series of Web pages inside a single document. It's also an easy way to deliver a complex Photoshop CS document to a client. You could instruct them to click the different layers comps in the **Layer Comps** palette to view different visual ideas (or comps, as they're called in professional circles of graphic and Web design.) The client doesn't have to manage layers or know much about how the document was constructed and won't be touching the layers in the **Layers** palette, which is a good thing, especially if he/she doesn't know Photoshop CS!*

10. Save and close the file. The Layer Comps you created will automatically be saved in the file.

 MOVIE | Layer Comps

To learn more about **layer comps**, check out **layer_comps.mov** in the **movies** folder on the **H•O•T CD-ROM**.

8. [IR] _____Exporting Layers as Files

If you design entire Web pages in Photoshop CS or ImageReady CS, you'll often want to save the contents of layers as individual files. ImageReady CS has a fabulous new feature called Export Layers as Files, which lets you save individual layers or layer sets as separate files quickly and easily. You can specify one format for all layers or a different format for each layer. Plus, you can apply different optimization settings to suit each layer. Here's an exercise to show you how.

1. Open **export.psd** from the **chap_05** folder you copied to your **Desktop**.

*In the **Layers** palette, you'll see a layer set called **site_elements** and three separate layers called **shop**, **text**, and **nav**. In the following steps, you'll export the layers and layer set into individual files.*

2. Click **File > Export > Layers as Files**.

*The **Export Layers as Files** dialog box opens automatically.*

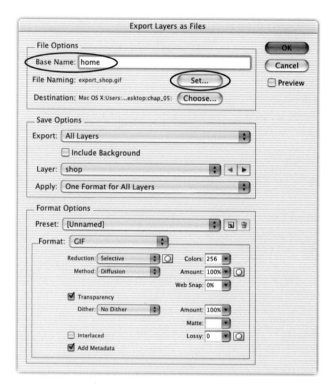

3. In the **Base Name** field, type **home**. Click the **Set** button to open the **Layer File Naming** dialog box.

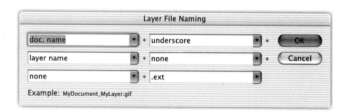

4. In the **Layer File Naming** dialog box, choose **doc. name + underscore**, **layer name + none**, and **none + .ext** as shown in the illustration above. Click **OK**.

*The settings you apply in the **Layer File Naming** dialog box ensure your file names are consistent and save you from naming each file manually. Based on these settings, your file names will begin with the word **home**, followed by an **underscore**, followed by the **layer name**, followed by the **file extension**. Here is an example: **home_shop.jpg**.*

Tip: If you have file or layer names made up of more than one word, make sure you separate the words with an underscore or remove the spaces. ImageReady CS will leave the spaces in the final saved file name, which can cause you problems down the road.

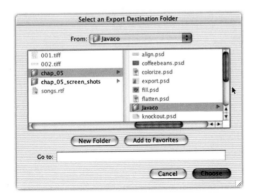

5. Click the **Choose** button to open the **Set an Export Destination Folder** dialog box (Mac) or the **Browse for Folder** dialog box (Windows). Choose the **Javaco** folder inside the **chap_05** folder you copied to your **Desktop**.

Your files will be automatically saved in the Javaco folder inside the chap_05 folder.

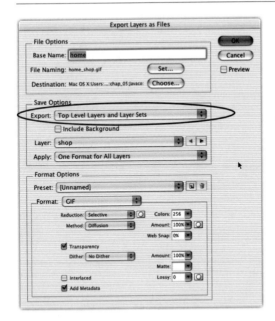

6. Choose **Top Level Layers and Layer Sets** from the **Export** pop-up menu.

*This setting lets you save the **shop**, **text**, and **nav** layers as individual files and also lets you save the contents of the **site_elements** layer set as a single file.*

*Tip: If you want to save the contents of a layer set as individual files, you can choose **All Layers** instead of **Top Level Layers** and **Layer Sets** from the **Export** pop-up menu.*

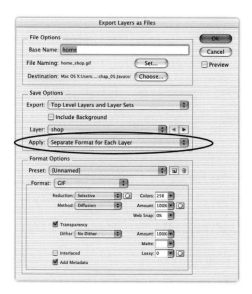

7. Choose **Separate Format for Each Layer** from the **Apply** pop-up menu.

*This setting lets you save different layers with different file formats. In this case, the **shop** layer is photographic and you'll want to save it as a JPEG. The other layers are text layers or layers with simple colors that you'll want to save as GIFs.*

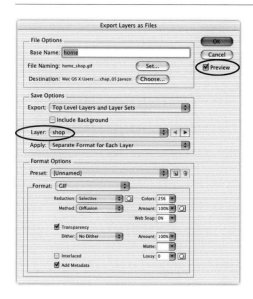

8. Choose **shop** from the **Layer** pop-up menu. Turn on the **Preview** option so you can preview the optimization settings.

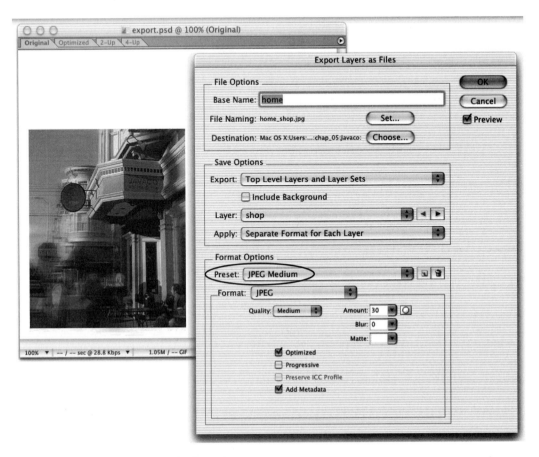

9. Choose **JPEG Medium** from the **Preset** pop-up menu.

Note: In this exercise, you'll use the optimization presets in ImageReady CS from the **Export Layers as Files** dialog box. For more information about optimizing images for the Web, refer to Chapter 4, "Optimization."

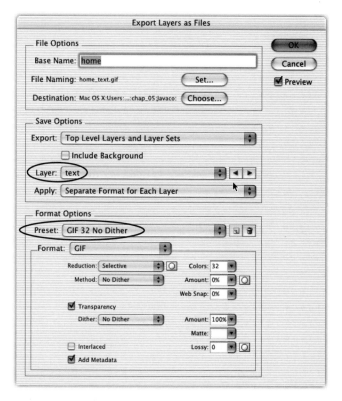

10. Choose **text** from the **Layers** pop-up menu and choose **GIF 32 No Dither** in the **Presets** pop-up menu.

11. Choose **nav** from the **Layers** pop-up menu and choose **GIF 32 No Dither** in the **Presets** pop-up menu.

12. Choose **site_elements** from the **Layers** pop-up menu and choose **GIF 32 No Dither** in the **Presets** pop-up menu.

13. Choose **background** from the **Layers** pop-up menu and choose **GIF 32 No Dither** in the **Presets** pop-up menu.

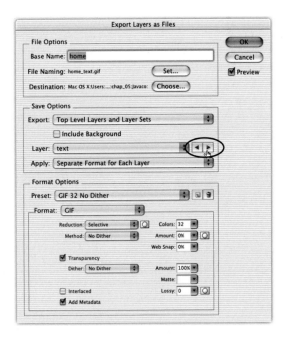

14. Use the **Previous** and **Next** buttons beside the **Layers** pop-up menu to browse through each layer and layer set and make sure the settings are to your liking. When you're satisfied with the settings, click **OK**.

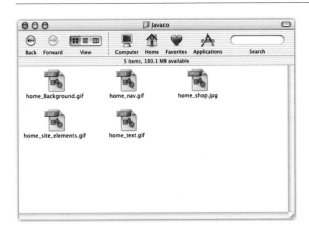

15. Browse to your **Desktop**. Double-click the **chap_05** folder to open it and double-click the **Javaco** folder to open it. You should see the following files in the **Javaco** folder: **home_Background.gif**, **home_shop.jpg**, **home_site_elements.gif**, **home_text.gif**, and **home_nav.gif**.

This is a very cool new feature in ImageReady CS!

TIP | Exporting Layers as Macromedia Flash Files

In addition to exporting layers as GIFs and JPEGs, you can also export layers as Macromedia Flash (SWF) files.

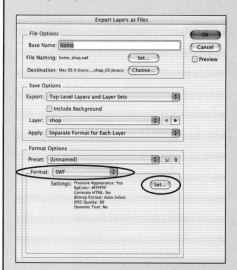

To export layers as Macromedia Flash files, choose **SWF** from the **Format** pop-up menu in the **Format Options** section of the **Export Layers as Files** dialog box.

If you want to change the settings, click the **Set** button to open the **Macromedia Flash Export** dialog box. For more information about how to export images as Macromedia Flash files, refer to Chapter 4, "*Optimization.*"

16. Save and close **export.psd**.

NOTE | Understanding the Export Layers Options

The Export Layers dialog box has a number of different options and you may be wondering what they're all for. Here is a brief chart that outlines the options in the Export Layers dialog box:

Export Layers Options	
Base Name	Lets you choose the common name each file will have. For example, if type home in the Base Name field, all the files you save will contain the word home.
File Naming	Lets you choose a convention for naming your files. There are a number of different conventions you can use to name your files such as layer name, document name, date, etc.
Destination	Lets you choose where you want to save the files.
Export: All Layers	Lets you export all the layers in the Layers palette to individual files.
Export: Top Level Layers and Layer Sets	Lets you export first-level layers and layer sets. For example, if you have a file with layer 1, layer 2, and layer set 1, you will end up with three files—one for layer 1, one for layer 2, and one for layer set 1. The contents of layer set 1 will be exported into a single file.
Export: Selected Layers	Lets you export selected layers in the Layers palette to individual files.
Include Background	Lets you include the background with a layer when you export the file.
Apply: One Format for All Layers	Lets you use the same file format for all layers you want to export.
Apply: Separate Format for Each Layer	Lets you use different file formats for each layer you want to export.
Save Options	Lets you specify optimization settings for each image. These settings are similar to the settings in the Optimize palette.

TIP | Exporting Selected Layers as Files

In Exercise 7, you learned to select multiple layers in ImageReady CS using the Shift and Cmd (Mac), or Ctrl (Windows) keys.

You can export selected layers as separate files. Here's how:

Select the layers or layer sets you want to export in the **Layers** palette.

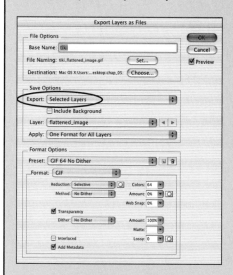

Choose **File > Export > Layers as Files**. Choose **Selected Layers** in the **Export** pop-up menu. Set the **File Options** and **Format Options** to your liking and click **OK**. You'll now have a file with the selected layers. Pretty cool!

What Are Fill Layers?

Fill layers let you apply solid colors, gradients, or patterns to a layer without permanently modifying the original image. If you decide you want to remove a Fill layer, you can do so easily because it doesn't make permanent changes. The next three exercises will show you how to add Fill layers to your images.

9. [PS] _____Creating Solid Color Layers

This exercise will show you how to create a Solid Color layer in Photoshop CS, which is useful for changing backgrounds on images. You can't create Solid Color layers in ImageReady CS, but ImageReady CS will recognize Solid Color layers created in Photoshop CS.

1. Open **fill.psd** from the **chap_05** folder you copied to your **Desktop**.

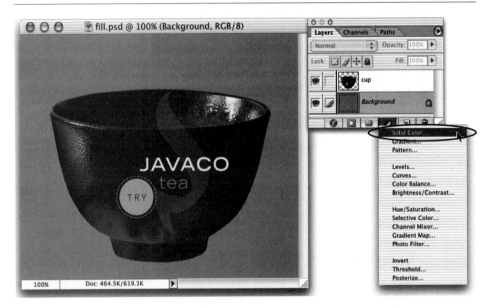

2. Click the **Background** layer to select it. Choose **Solid Color** from the **Create new fill or adjustment layer** pop-up menu at the bottom of the **Layers** palette.

*Notice the **Color Picker** dialog box opens automatically.*

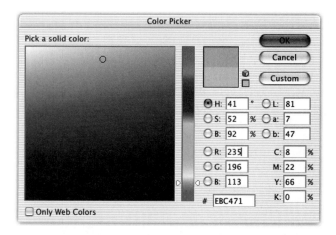

3. Choose a color in the **Color Picker** dialog box and click **OK**.

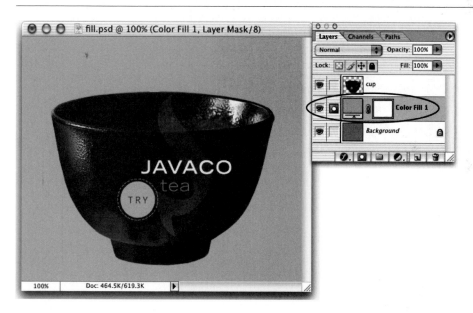

*Notice a new layer, **Color Fill 1**, has been added to the **Layers** palette and it has two thumbnails. The thumbnail on the left is a layer thumbnail showing the **Solid Color** layer. The thumbnail on the right is a layer mask thumbnail. When you create a solid color layer, Photoshop CS automatically creates a layer mask as well. You can see the solid color fill through the layer mask because the layer mask is set to white.*

Solid Color *layers give you the flexibility to change color quickly. The next step will show you how easy it is to change the color of a **Solid Color** layer.*

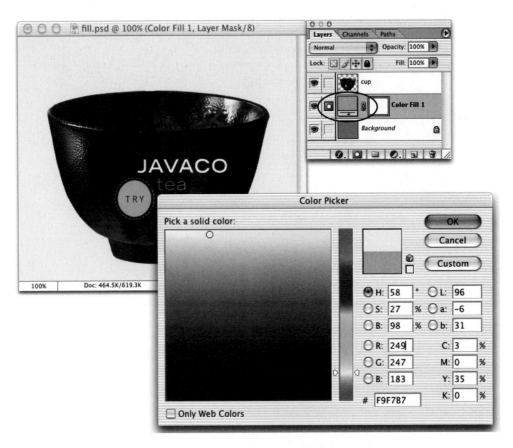

4. In the **Layers** palette, double-click the **Solid Color** layer thumbnail to open the **Color Picker** dialog box. Choose a new color in the **Color Picker** dialog box. In the document window, you'll see a live preview of the color you selected. Click **OK**.

5. Leave this image open for the next exercise.

10. [PS] _____Creating Gradient Layers

Next, you'll create a Gradient layer. Gradient layers are one of several ways to create a gradient in Photoshop CS. The advantage of using a Gradient layer is that it's quick to use and very flexible if you want to change the colors or the blend. Like Solid Color layers, Gradient layers cannot be created in ImageReady CS, but ImageReady CS will recognize Gradient layers created in Photoshop CS.

1. In the **Layers** palette, select the **Color Fill 1** layer you created in the last exercise. Selecting the **Color Fill 1** layer first ensures the **Gradient** layer will appear above the **Fill 1** layer in the stacking order.

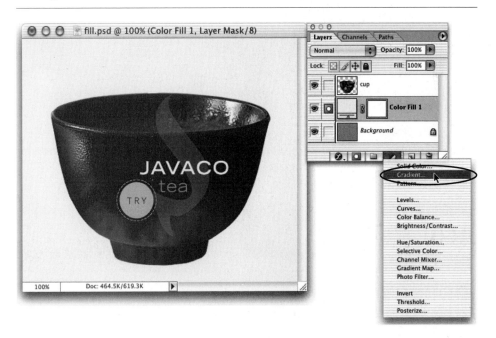

2. Choose **Gradient** from the **Create new fill or adjustment layer** pop-up menu at the bottom of the **Layers** palette.

Notice the **Gradient Fill** dialog box opens automatically.

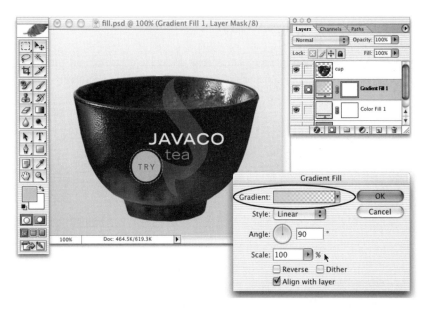

*Your gradient may look different from the one in this illustration, depending on the gradient you last used. The gradient you see here is the **Foreground to Transparent** (transparent lets the layer beneath the gradient show through). Notice the live preview in the document window.*

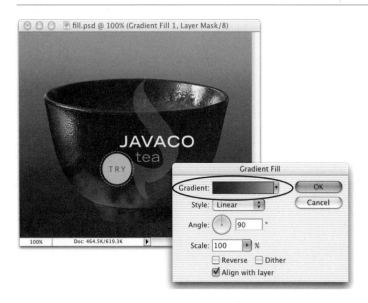

3. Open the **Gradient Picker**. Click on some of the **Gradient Presets** to preview different gradients in your image. Choose a gradient and click inside the **Gradient Fill** dialog box to close the **Gradient Picker**.

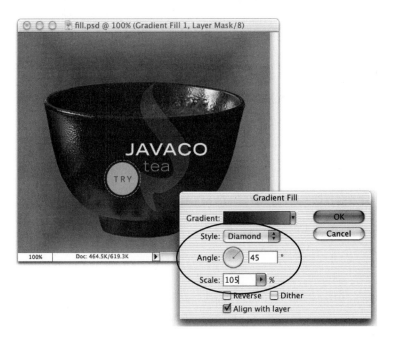

4. Change the **Style**, **Angle**, and **Scale** options in the **Gradient Fill** dialog box to see how these controls change the appearance of the gradient. When you're finished, click **OK**.

*What if you don't like the **Gradient Presets** and you want to make your own custom gradient? You'll learn how in the following steps.*

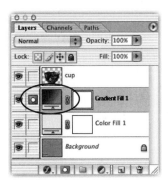

5. In the **Layers** palette, double-click the **Gradient Fill 1** thumbnail to re-open the **Gradient Fill** dialog box.

*Like the **Solid Color** layer, the **Gradient Fill** layer also has two thumbnails: a gradient thumbnail and a layer mask thumbnail.*

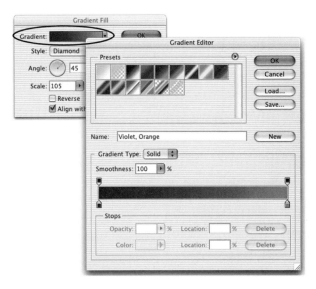

6. In the **Gradient Fill** dialog box, click inside the **Gradient Bar** to open the **Gradient Editor** dialog box.

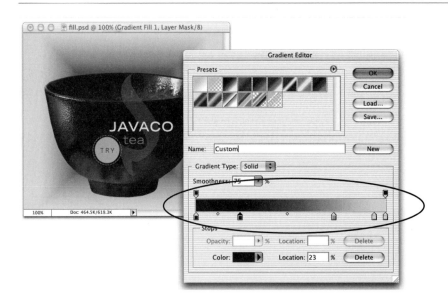

7. Experiment with changing and moving the colors on the **Gradient Bar** in the **Gradient Editor** dialog box.

*The **Color Stops** under the **Gradient Bar** control the colors in the gradient. Click on one of the **Color Stops** and move your mouse into the image to sample a color for the **Stop**. Double-click one of the **Color Stops** to open the **Color Picker**, and choose a color for the **Stop**. **Omit a Color Stop** by clicking and dragging it off the gradient bar. Add a **Color Stop** by clicking just beneath the **Gradient Bar**.*

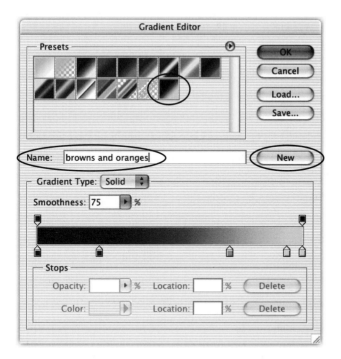

8. When you're satisfied with the custom gradient, click in the **Name** field, type a name for the new gradient, and click **New**. You'll see your new gradient in the **Presets** library at the top of the **Gradient Editor** dialog box.

9. Click **OK** in the **Gradient Editor**, and click **OK** in the **Gradient Fill** dialog box.

10. Leave the file open for the next exercise.

II. [PS] _____Creating Pattern Layers

Pattern layers let you fill a layer with…you guessed it, a pattern! This exercise introduces you to Pattern layers. In Chapter 8, "*Background Images*," you'll learn more about patterns, including how to make a seamless pattern tile for a Web page. Pattern layers cannot be created in ImageReady CS, but ImageReady CS will recognize Pattern layers created in Photoshop CS.

1. In the **Layers** palette, select the **Gradient Fill 1** layer you created in the last exercise. Selecting the **Gradient Fill 1** layer first ensures the **Pattern** layer will appear above the **Gradient Fill 1** layer in the stacking order.

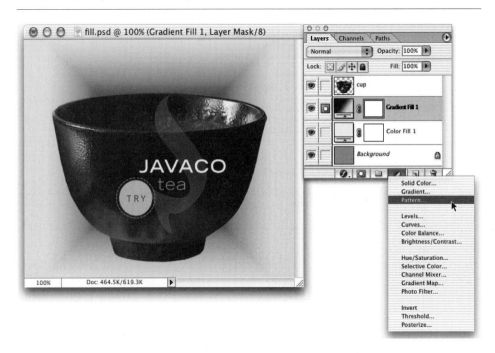

2. Choose **Pattern** from the **Create new fill or adjustment layer** pop-up menu at the bottom of the **Layers** palette.

*Notice the **Pattern Fill** dialog box opens automatically.*

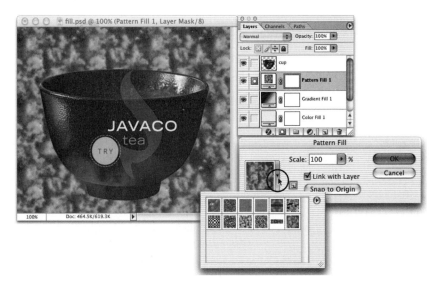

3. Open the **Pattern Picker**.

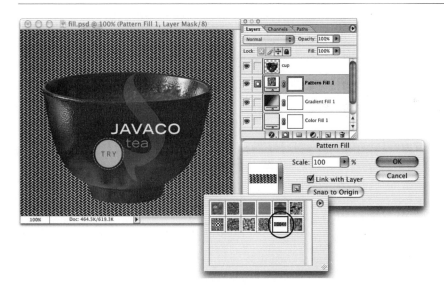

4. Click the patterns in the **Pattern Picker** until you find one you like. Click **OK**.

Chances are, you're wondering if you can create custom patterns. The answer is yes. You'll learn about creating custom patterns in Chapter 8, "Background Images."

5. You're finished learning about fill layers. Save and close the file.

NOTE | Pattern Features and When to Use Them

You may be wondering when to use a Pattern layer and when to use other pattern features, such as the Pattern Maker and the offset filter. Here's a small chart to help you.

Pattern Features	
Pattern Feature	**When to Use It**
Pattern layer	Use a Pattern layer when you want to fill the entire background of a layered image with a pattern, as you learned to do in the above exercise. You might use such an image in the foreground on a Web page. A Pattern layer becomes part of the image and can't be separated and reused to create a repeating background image in HTML. You'll learn about background images in Chapter 8, "*Background Images.*"
Pattern Maker	Use the Pattern Maker to generate custom patterns you can insert into a Pattern layer. This feature isn't covered in this book, but you can refer to the *Photoshop CS User Guide* if you want to make custom patterns.
Offset filter	Use the offset filter when you're making small tiles that will repeat themselves over and over in the background of a Web page. The offset filter helps arrange patterns so tiles appear seamless when the patterns repeat. It may sound confusing here, but you'll learn how to create seamless patterns in Chapter 8, "*Background Images.*"

What Are Adjustment Layers?

Adjustment layers let you make tonal and color changes without permanently modifying the image. When you use an adjustment layer, the changes you make are contained on a separate layer and they affect all the layers below. If you change your mind about the changes you make to an image using adjustment layers, you can modify or delete them.

12. [PS] _____ Using Adjustment Layers

Using adjustment layers is a great way to change contrast, hue, or color balance levels in an image. You'll learn how in this exercise. Adjustment layers cannot be created in ImageReady CS, but ImageReady CS will recognize adjustment layers created in Photoshop CS.

1. Open **colorize.psd** from the **chap_05** folder you copied to your **Desktop**.

2. Click the **tea collage** layer to select it. Choose **Hue/Saturation** from the **Create new fill or adjustment layer** pop-up menu at the bottom of the **Layers** palette.

*Notice the **Hue/Saturation** dialog box opens automatically.*

3. In the **Hue/Saturation** dialog box, turn on the **Colorize** option.

*The image is now tinted with different hues of the foreground color (in this case, green). Experiment with the **Hue**, **Saturation**, and **Lightness** sliders to change the effect. When you're satisfied with the result, click **OK**.*

*Notice the new **Hue/Saturation 1** layer in the **Layers** palette? You can re-open the **Hue/Saturation** dialog box by double-clicking the **Hue/Saturation** layer thumbnail.*

4. Click the **Hue/Saturation 1** layer to select it. Choose **Color Balance** from the **Create new fill or adjustment layer** pop-up menu at the bottom of the **Layers** palette.

*Notice the **Color Balance** dialog box opens automatically.*

5. In the **Color Balance** dialog box, experiment with the different settings. When you're satisfied, click **OK**.

*Try applying other adjustment layers such as **Levels**, **Curves**, **Brightness/Contrast**, **Posterize**, etc. Remember, because adjustment layers are nondestructive, you can modify them, turn them off, or delete them if you don't like the changes you made. This is a great advantage of nondestructive editing!*

6. Close and save the file.

I3. [PS] _____ Using Clipping Groups

Have you ever seen type that contains a photographic image inside the letters? The next exercise shows you how to accomplish this effect using clipping groups in Photoshop CS or ImageReady CS. For this exercise you'll use Photoshop CS, but it works the same way in ImageReady CS.

1. Open **coffeebeans.psd** from the **chap_05** folder you copied to your **Desktop**.

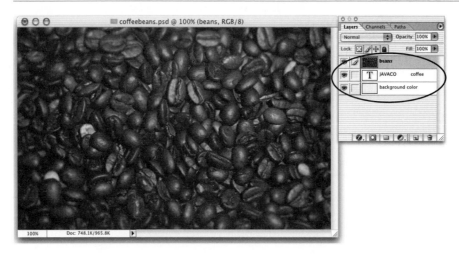

2. In the **Layers** palette, click the **beans** layer to select it. Drag and drop the **beans** layer to move it above the **JAVACO coffee** layer.

You should no longer see the type in the image.

3. Hold down the **Option** (Mac) or **Alt** (Windows) key and move your cursor over the dividing line between the **JAVACO coffee** and the **beans** layers.

*The cursor will change from the **hand** icon to the **clipping group** icon.*

4. Click the line and the coffee beans image will appear inside the type.

*Notice an arrow on the left side of the **beans** layer thumbnail? This arrow indicates a clipping group has been applied to the **beans** layer.*

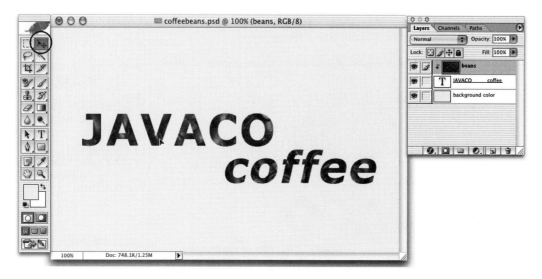

5. With the **beans** layer selected in the **Layers** palette and the **Move** tool selected in the **Toolbox**, click inside the document window to move the **beans** layer independently from the type. Position the **beans** layer wherever you like.

6. If you want to move the type and the image together, select the **beans** layer and click the **Link** region (circled above) in the type layer. Now if you use the **Move** tool, both layers will move together.

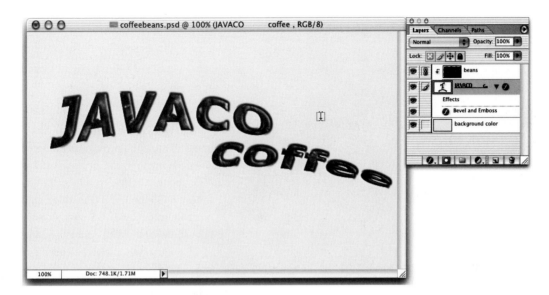

Because the type is editable, you can still change the font, the size, or the style even though you applied a clipping group. Here I warped the type layer and applied a bevel and emboss layer style. You'll learn about these special effects in Chapter 6, "Type."

MOVIE | clippinggroup.mov

To learn more about **clipping groups**, check out **clippinggroup.mov** in the **movies** folder on the **H•O•T CD-ROM**.

You've just finished another long chapter. Now that you've seen how powerful layers can be, put them to work and boost your creativity and productivity as you create Web graphics in Photoshop CS and ImageReady CS.

*In the next chapter, you'll learn how to use another important feature—the **Type** tool!*

6.

Type

| Comparing Type in Photoshop CS and ImageReady CS |
| Using the Type Options Bar |
| Using the Character and Paragraph Palettes |
| Checking Spelling | Finding and Replacing Type |
| Warping Type | Creating Type on a Path |
| Rasterizing and Transforming Type |

chap_06

Photoshop CS/ImageReady CS
H•O•T CD-ROM

Working with type on the Web can be frustrating because HTML affords very little typographic control. Many Web designers avoid the limitations of HTML type by embedding text in GIF or JPEG files. Photoshop CS and ImageReady CS offer incredible tools for creating, formatting, and editing type, making it easy to create typographic imagery for the Web.

In this chapter, you'll learn to create and format type for the Web using the Options bar and the Character and Paragraph palettes in Photoshop CS and ImageReady CS. You'll also learn to edit type using the spell checking and find-and-replace features. Plus you'll learn some fun typographic techniques such as warping type, and a new feature in Photoshop CS and ImageReady CS– creating type on a path.

Comparing Type in Photoshop CS and ImageReady CS

Photoshop CS and ImageReady CS handle type the same way. In both programs, you enter vector-based type directly into the document window. Vector-based type is defined mathematically rather than by pixels. As a result, type layers remain editable, which means you can scale, rotate, skew, or warp type without degrading its appearance.

The only noticeable difference between the type features in the two applications is the presence of the layer edge marker in ImageReady CS, which automatically places a thin blue line around the edges of all selected layers, including type layers.

In ImageReady CS, a tiny blue line appears around layers, including type layers.

*To make the blue line disappear, click off the type layer in the **Layers** palette and choose **View** >* ***Show** > **Layer Edges**. Keep in mind the layer edge marker is used for all layers, so if you turn it off, it will affect all layers, not just type layers.*

Another key difference between the type features in Photoshop CS and ImageReady CS is the capability to edit type on multiple layers. In Photoshop CS, you can only edit one type layer at a time. One of the great new features in ImageReady CS is the ability to select and edit multiple type layers at the same time. Editing type on multiple layers is extremely helpful if you're creating a series of buttons and you want to apply the same formatting changes to all the buttons at the same time.

*To select multiple layers, hold down the **Shift**, **Cmd** (Mac), or **Ctrl** (Windows) keys and click the layers you want to select.*

*Adjust the type properties in the **Options** bar. Notice all the type layers update with the changes you've made.*

The Type Options Bar

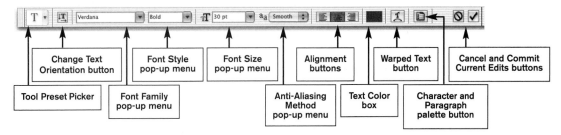

The Options bar contains many type formatting controls. This chart briefly describes each control.

Type Options Bar Controls	
Feature	**Function**
Tool Preset Picker	Provides access to create and select tool presets
Change Text Orientation button	Toggles between the Horizontal Type tool and the Vertical Type tool
Font Family pop-up menu	Changes the font
Font Style pop-up menu	Changes the font style
Font Size pop-up menu	Changes the font size
Anti-Aliasing Method pop-up menu	Changes the anti-aliasing method, such as smooth or crisp
Alignment buttons (Left, Center, Right)	Aligns text to the left, center, or right
Text Color box	Opens the Color Picker dialog box, which lets you choose a font color
Warped Text button	Opens the Warp Text dialog box, which lets you warp your text in different ways, such as Arc, Flag, Twist, and so on
Character and Paragraph palette button	Toggles the Character and Paragraph palettes on and off
Cancel Current Edits button	Cancels edits and returns type to the last state
Commit Current Edits button	Commits edits when you've finished formatting type

I. [PS] _____Using the Type Options Bar

The next few exercises will show you how to create and format type in Photoshop CS using the Type tool, the Options bar, and the Character and Paragraph palettes. You'll use Photoshop CS for these exercises but the type features work the same way in ImageReady CS.

1. Copy the **chap_06** folder from the **H•O•T CD-ROM** to your **Desktop**.

2. In Photoshop CS, open **coupon.psd** from the **chap_06** folder.

*In the **Layers** palette, you'll see a layer with a **T** icon, which means it is an editable, vector-based type layer. There is another layer, labeled **javaco**, which contains type but has no **T** icon. The javaco type was originally created as a type layer but was rasterized, which means the type was converted to pixels. You'll learn how and why to rasterize type layers later in this chapter.*

***Note:** The type in **coupon.psd** was created using the Verdana font, which is easy to read on the Web and ships with current Windows and Mac operating systems. If you don't have Verdana installed on your computer, Photoshop CS will automatically substitute other fonts. You can download Verdana for free from the Microsoft Web site (**http://www.microsoft.com/typography/fonts/default.asp**).*

3. Click the **javaco** layer to select it and click the **Lock All** button at the top of the **Layers** palette.

*Lock All is helpful when you don't want to accidentally move or edit a layer. When you click the **Lock All** button, you'll see a dark gray lock icon in the javaco layer. Notice the **Background** layer already has a light gray lock icon, which means it is partially locked. One of the special characteristics of a **Background** layer is that it can't be moved.*

4. Click the **Horizontal Type** tool in the **Toolbox** to select it. Notice the **Options** bar changes to display type controls.

5. On the **Options** bar, choose **Verdana** from the **Font Family** pop-up menu, choose **Bold** from the **Font Style** pop-up menu, and choose **30 pt** from the **Font Size** pop-up menu to set the font settings for the type you're about to create.

6. Click inside the document window. Be careful not to click too close to the type—you don't want to type into the type layer that's already there! Type the words **1 Free Coffee**.

*In the **Layers** palette, Photoshop CS automatically creates a separate layer for the new type.*

7. Select the **Move** tool in the **Toolbox**. Click and drag inside the document window to move the type layer you just created to the middle of the image.

8. With the **1 Free Coffee** layer selected in the **Layers** palette, select the **Horizontal Type** tool from the **Toolbox**. Click in the **Font Color** box on the **Options** bar to open the **Color Picker** dialog box. Choose a **dark blue** or **purple**, and click **OK**.

*The type on the **1 Free Coffee** layer should now be a dark blue or purple.*

You can also change the color of selected text on a type layer. You'll learn how in the next steps.

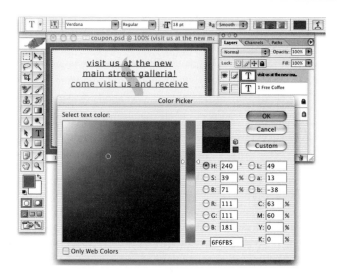

9. With the **Horizontal Type** tool selected, click and drag your cursor across the phrase **come visit us and receive**, which is part of another type layer. Click in the **Font Color** box on the **Options** bar to open the **Color Picker** dialog box. Choose a **medium blue** or **purple** and click **OK**.

*Note: Even though you have the type selected, when you open the **Color Picker** dialog box, you can't see the highlight. Photoshop CS automatically hides the highlight when the **Color Picker** dialog box is open so you can accurately preview the color before you make your final selection.*

Notice you changed only the color on selected type, not the entire type layer as you did in the previous example.

10. Press **Cmd+H** (Mac) or **Ctrl+H** (Windows) to remove the highlight from the selected text. Choose **14 pt** from the **Font Size** pop-up menu on the **Options** bar.

Notice the type is still selected even though you can't see it because the highlighting is hidden.

---

11. Click the **Commit Current Edits** button (the check mark) on the **Options** bar to accept the changes you made to the selected type.

*Note: You have to accept or cancel type edits and move out of type editing mode before you can perform other operations in Photoshop CS. There are lots of ways to accept a type edit other than clicking the **Commit Current Edits** button on the **Options** bar. You can click on another layer in the **Layers** palette, select a different tool in the **Toolbox**, click another palette, choose a menu command, or press **Return** (Mac) or **Enter** (Windows). If you want to cancel type edits, click the **Cancel Current Edits** button on the **Options** bar.*

12. With the **Horizontal Type** tool selected in the **Toolbox**, click the **visit us** type layer. Choose **None** from the **Anti-Aliasing Method** pop-up menu.

Notice the edges of the text now appear jagged.

*Note: When you change the color of the type, you must highlight the type first. When you change the anti-aliasing method, you don't have to highlight the type as long as the layer you want to modify is selected in the **Layers** palette.*

13. Choose **Smooth** from the **Anti-Aliasing Method** pop-up menu.

Tip: None and Sharp are the best anti-aliasing methods if you're creating type smaller than 14 pt. If you're using type larger than 14 pt, use Crisp, Strong, or Smooth.

14. Save **coupon.psd** and keep it open for the next exercise.

NOTE | What Is Anti-Aliasing?

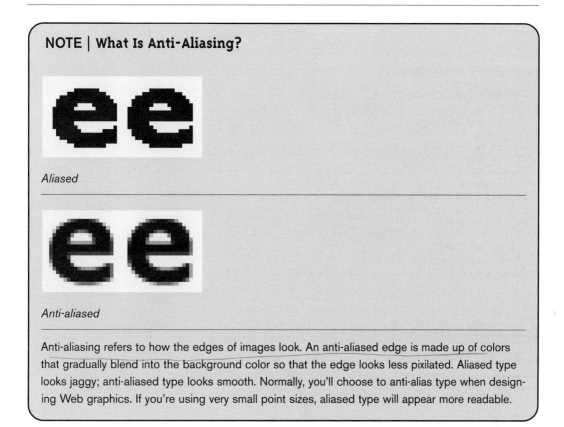

Aliased

Anti-aliased

Anti-aliasing refers to how the edges of images look. An anti-aliased edge is made up of colors that gradually blend into the background color so that the edge looks less pixilated. Aliased type looks jaggy; anti-aliased type looks smooth. Normally, you'll choose to anti-alias type when designing Web graphics. If you're using very small point sizes, aliased type will appear more readable.

The Character Palette

The Character palette contains many type formatting controls. This chart briefly describes each control.

Character Palette Controls	
Feature	**Function**
Font Family pop-up menu	Changes the font
Font Size pop-up menu	Changes the font size
Kerning pop-up menu	Adjusts the spacing between characters
Vertical Scale field	Distorts type by scaling it on a vertical axis
Baseline field	Adjusts the baseline of type to create subscript or superscript
Faux Bold, Faux Italic buttons	Applies faux styles to fonts that don't have bold or italic styles
All Caps button	Applies uppercase
Small Caps button	Applies small caps
Superscript	Applies superscript
Subscript	Applies subscript
Underline button	Underlines characters

continues on next page

Character Palette Controls *continued*	
Feature	Function
Strikethrough button	Puts a horizontal line through characters
Language pop-up menu	Changes the dictionary referenced by the spell checker
Font Style pop-up menu	Changes the font style, such as bold or italic
Leading pop-up menu	Adjusts the amount of space between lines of type
Tracking pop-up menu	Adjusts the amount of space equally between selected characters in a word or paragraph
Horizontal Scale field	Distorts type by scaling it on a horizontal axis
Text Color box	Changes the color of a selected character, word, or line of type Anti-Aliasing
Method pop-up menu	Blends and smoothes edges

2. [PS] _____Using the Character Palette

In the last exercise, you learned to edit type with the Options bar. In this exercise, you'll learn to edit type using the Character palette. Although some of the controls are the same as those in the Options bar, there are many controls available only on the Character palette. You'll work with some of the exclusive Character palette controls in this exercise.

1. With the **Horizontal Type** tool selected, click the **Character** and **Paragraph** palettes button on the **Options** bar to display the **Character** palette and **Paragraph** palette.

2. With the **Horizontal Type** tool selected, position the cursor and click between the letter **a** and the **exclamation point** in the word **galleria!**

The insertion cursor should now be visible.

3. Hold down the **Option** (Mac) or **Alt** (Windows) key and press the right- or left-arrow key.

Notice the space between the characters expands and contracts? Adjusting the space between characters is known as kerning.

*You can also adjust kerning in the **Character** palette by choosing a value from the **Kerning** pop-up menu. Choose **200** from the **Kerning** pop-up menu so your document and **Character** palette match the illustration here.*

4. With the **Horizontal Type** tool selected, highlight the third line of type in the image—**come visit us and receive**. Choose **200** from the **Tracking** pop-up menu on the **Character** palette.

Notice the space between the selected characters expands. Kerning affects the space between two characters. Tracking affects the space between selected characters.

5. With the type still highlighted, choose **30** from the **Leading** pop-up menu.

Notice the selected line of type moves down so there is more vertical space between it and the preceding line of type. Leading affects the space between lines of type. The term "leading" refers to the days of typesetting, when typesetters used pieces of lead to physically separate lines of type.

6. Click the **Commit Current Edits** button in the **Options** bar to accept the edits to the highlighted type.

7. With the **Horizontal Type** tool selected, highlight the word **new**. In the **Character** palette, click the **Faux Bold** and **Faux Italic** buttons.

Faux Bold *and* ***Faux Italic*** *let you apply italic and bold effects to fonts that don't otherwise include those styles. (Even though Verdana does have bold and italic font styles, I wanted to show you where these controls are located.)*

8. In the **Layers** palette, click the **1 Free Coffee** layer to select it.

Selecting a different layer in the ***Layers*** *palette has the same effect as clicking the* ***Commit Current Edits*** *button in the* ***Options*** *bar—it accepts the type edits you made on the previously selected type layer.*

9. With the **Horizontal Type** tool selected, highlight the word **Free** and click the **All Caps** button on the **Character** palette.

You just converted the characters to uppercase letters.

*Experiment with the other buttons and settings on the **Character** palette. For example, try the **Baseline** control, which allows you to move one or more characters above or below the baseline to create a superscript or a footnote. When you're done, click the **Commit Current Edits** or **Cancel Current Edits** button on the **Options** bar.*

10. Save and close the file.

NOTE | Simulating HTML Type with System Layout

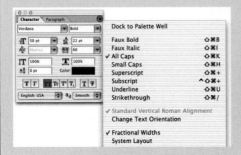

You'll find more type settings in the Character palette menu.

visit us at the *new*

main street galleria!

Default 12 pt. type

visit us at the *new*

main street galleria!

12 pt. type with System Layout on, simulating HTML type

For example, the System Layout option is useful when you're mocking up a Web page and you plan to include HTML type. Choosing **System Layout** from the **Character** palette menu modifies a type layer so it looks like HTML type. Using the System Layout option helps you visualize how a Web page will look with HTML type.

The Paragraph Palette

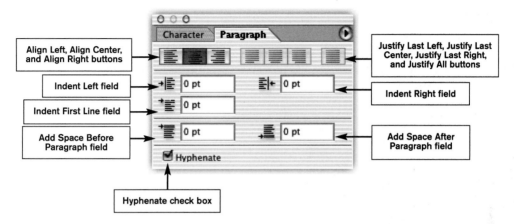

Align Left, Align Center, and Align Right buttons

Indent Left field

Indent First Line field

Add Space Before Paragraph field

Justify Last Left, Justify Last Center, Justify Last Right, and Justify All buttons

Indent Right field

Add Space After Paragraph field

Hyphenate check box

The Paragraph palette contains many controls for formatting paragraph type. This chart briefly describes the controls.

Paragraph Palette Controls	
Feature	**Function**
Alignment buttons (Left, Center, Right)	Aligns paragraph type to the left, center, or right
Justification buttons (Last Left, Last Centered, Last Right, Justify All)	Justifies paragraph type
Indent fields (Indent Left Margin, Indent Right Margin, Indent First Line)	Indents paragraph type
Add Space buttons (Before Paragraph, After Paragraph)	Adds space between paragraphs
Hyphenate check box	Determines if words can be hyphenated over a line break

3. [PS] _____Creating Paragraph Type

Paragraph type is defined by a bounding box and is designed for creating, formatting, and editing type with one or more paragraphs. It allows you to rotate, scale, or skew an entire paragraph of type at once. You can also reshape paragraph type, controlling how it flows, aligns, justifies, and indents inside its bounding box. The Paragraph palette contains settings that let you format paragraph type. You'll use these controls in this exercise.

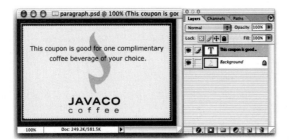

1. Open **paragraph.psd** from the **chap_06** folder you copied to your **Desktop**.

This image contains character type and is identical to the type you've been working with in the last exercises. Before you begin, you need to convert the point type to paragraph type so you can format the entire paragraph.

2. Click the type layer in the **Layers** palette to select it. Then choose **Layer > Type > Convert to Paragraph Text**.

3. With the **Horizontal Type** tool selected in the **Toolbox**, click on the type. You'll see a bounding box appear around the outside of the type.

*This is how you convert point type to paragraph type. You can also create paragraph type from scratch by selecting the **Horizontal** or **Vertical Type** tools from the **Toolbox**, clicking and dragging inside an image to make a bounding box, and typing inside the box. You'll learn to create paragraph type using this technique later in the exercise.*

4. Position the mouse over the top-right corner of the bounding box until you see a diagonal arrow appear. Click and drag the arrow to reshape the bounding box.

Notice the flow of the type automatically adjusts to fit the new shape of the bounding box.

Note: *If you see a cross in the bottom-right corner of the bounding box, it means the box is too small to contain the type. Click and drag to expand the box.*

5. Position the mouse outside the bottom-right corner of the bounding box. You'll see the cursor change to a rotate symbol. Click and drag to rotate the type and the bounding box.

6. Hold down the **Cmd** key (Mac) or the **Ctrl** key (Windows) and drag the corner of the bounding box.

Notice the type sizes and positions itself automatically inside the bounding box.

7. Select the **Move** tool in the **Toolbox**. Click the type and reposition it onscreen.

*Note: By clicking the **Move** tool in the **Toolbox**, you automatically committed the current edits.*

*Now that you've reshaped and transformed the paragraph type, you'll practice formatting it using options in the **Paragraph** palette.*

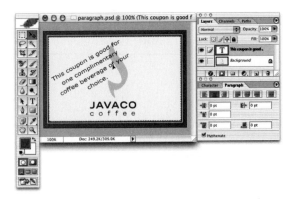

8. With the **Horizontal Type** tool selected in the **Toolbox** and the type layer selected in the **Layers** palette, click the **Align Left** button on the **Paragraph** palette to align the type to the left edge of its bounding box. (The bounding box is currently invisible.)

*Try some of the other controls on the **Paragraph** palette, such as indenting and justification.*

In the next step, you'll create paragraph type from scratch.

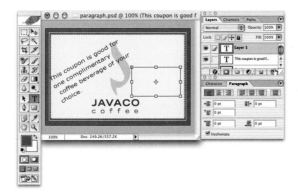

9. With the **Horizontal Type** tool selected from the **Toolbox**, click and drag in the image to create a new bounding box.

10. Type the following: **Try our espresso, cafe au lait, or specialty drinks**.

Your type will appear inside (and become constrained by) the shape of the bounding box.

11. Reshape the bounding box as you did in **Step 4**. Experiment with rotating, moving, and aligning the type as you did in previous steps.

12. Save and close the file.

*Note: You can create and edit Paragraph text in ImageReady CS, too. If you don't see the bounding box in ImageReady CS, choose **View > Show > Text Selection**.*

4. [PS] _____Checking Spelling

The spell checking feature, which you'll learn to use in this exercise, is extremely helpful if you're creating type in your images. ImageReady CS does not have the spell checking feature. If you need to check spelling when you're creating type in ImageReady CS, use the **Jump to** button on the **Toolbox** to open the image in Photoshop CS.

1. Open **spell.psd** from the **chap_06** folder you copied to your **Desktop**.

2. Choose **Edit > Check Spelling**.

*The **Check Spelling** dialog box opens automatically. By default, Photoshop CS will check spelling on all type layers. If you want to limit spell checking to the selected layer, turn off the **Check All Layers** option at the bottom of the **Check Spelling** dialog box.*

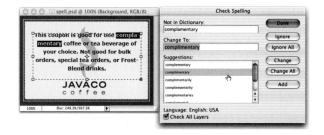

3. The spell checker identifies **complamentary** as a misspelled word, offers a preferred spelling, and suggests other spellings. Click to select the word **complimentary** in the **Suggestions** area of the **Check Spelling** dialog box. Click **Change**.

"Complamentary" is automatically changed to "complimentary."

4. The spell checker stops on the name **FrostBlend** because it is not in the **English: USA** dictionary that ships with Photoshop CS. Click **Ignore** to leave this word spelled as is in the image.

*Alternatively, you can click **Add** to add this word to the active dictionary so that it won't be identified as misspelled again.*

*Photoshop CS ships with dictionaries in various languages. You can change the spell checker's active dictionary by choosing a language from the **Language** pop-up menu at the bottom of the **Character** palette.*

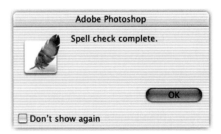

5. Click **OK** to acknowledge that spell checking is complete and to close the **Check Spelling** dialog box.

6. Keep the file open for the next exercise.

5. [PS] ——————Finding and Replacing Type

Photoshop CS also offers a **Find and Replace** feature, which is helpful if you want to change all the instances of a word in the same file. Here's a short exercise to show you how it works.

1. If you followed the last exercise, **spell.psd** should already be open. If not, open **spell.psd** from the **chap_06 folder** you copied to your **Desktop**.

2. Choose **Edit** > **Find and Replace Text**.

*The **Find and Replace Text** dialog box opens automatically.*

3. In the **Find What** field, type **tea**. In the **Change To** field, type **juice**.

4. Click **Find Next** to identify the first instance of the word **tea** in the image.

5. Click **Change** to change that instance of **tea** to **juice**.

6. Click **Done** to close the **Find and Replace Text** dialog box.

7. Save and close the image.

6. [PS] _____Creating Warped Type

Warping lets you distort type to create different shapes, such as arc, twist, or wave. You probably won't use warped type very often when you're creating Web graphics but here is a fun exercise to show you how.

1. Open **banner.psd** from the **chap_06** folder you copied to your **Desktop**.

2. Select the **Horizontal Type** tool in the **Toolbox**. Click to select the **FrostBlend** layer in the **Layers** palette.

3. Click the **Warp Text** button on the **Options** bar.

The **Warp Text** dialog box opens automatically.

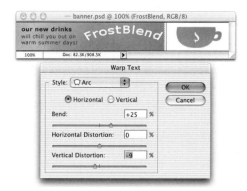

4. Choose **Arc** from the **Style** pop-up menu in the **Warp Text** dialog box. Adjust the **Bend**, **Horizontal Distortion**, and **Vertical Distortion** sliders to distort the type.

5. Experiment with the other styles and adjust the sliders to see different warp effects. When you're satisfied with your changes, click **OK**.

Warped type can be edited and undone after the file is saved. If you change the type, it keeps the warp effect. Have fun with this tool, but use it sparingly in your designs because too much warped text can result in visual overload!

6. Save and close the file.

7. [PS] _____Creating Type on a Path

One of the new features in Photoshop CS is the capability to create fully editable type on an open or closed path. Just as you won't use warped type too frequently, you probably won't use type on a path very often either when you're designing Web graphics. But it's still fun to learn how to use this new feature. You can't create type on a path in ImageReady CS, but ImageReady CS will recognize type on a path that was created in Photoshop CS.

1. Open **path.psd** from the **chap_06** folder you copied to your **Desktop**.

2. Select the **Ellipse** tool from the **Toolbox**. Click the **Paths** button on the **Options** bar.

It's important to select the **Paths** button because it tells Photoshop CS to create a path of an ellipse containing no visual properties. When you finish with the file, the path is still there, but it's invisible.

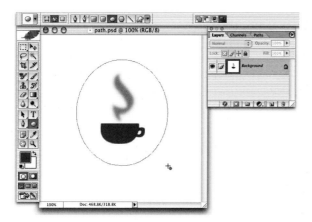

3. Click and drag to create a closed, elliptical path around the coffee cup and steam in the **path.psd** image.

4. Select the **Horizontal Type** tool in the **Toolbox**. On the **Options** bar, choose **Verdana** from the **Font Family** pop-up menu, choose **Regular** from the **Font Style** pop-up menu, choose **18 pt** from the **Font Size** pop-up menu, choose **Smooth** from the **Anti-Aliasing Method** pop-up menu, and click the **Align Center** button.

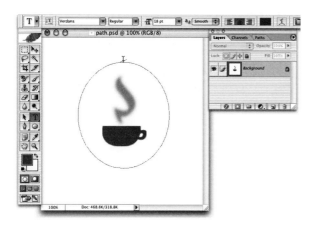

5. Position your cursor at the top of the path until the **Path Type** cursor appears.

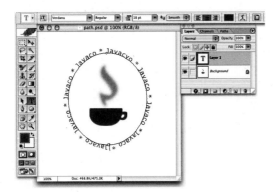

6. With the **Path Type** cursor visible, click the top of the path and type the following: **Javaco * Javaco * Javaco * Javaco * Javaco * Javaco * Javaco * Javaco ***.

*Notice the type spaces evenly around the path you created in **Step 3**. This is an automatic feature of the Type on Path feature in Photoshop CS. Pretty cool!*

7. In the **Layers** palette, click the **Background** to hide the path so you can see the type you created.

*If you want to adjust the font, size, or tracking, select the type layer. Click and drag to highlight the text and make the changes on the **Options** bar or in the **Character** palette.*

Next you'll create type on an open path.

8. In the **Layers** palette, turn off the **Visibility** icon of the **Javaco** type layer you just created and click the **Background** to select it.

9. Select the **Freeform Pen** tool in the **Toolbox**. Click the **Paths** button on the **Options** bar.

10. With the **Freeform Pen** tool selected in the **Toolbox**, click and drag to create a wavy line anywhere inside the image.

11. Select the **Horizontal Type** tool in the **Toolbox**. Position your cursor over the left edge of the path until you see the **Path Type** cursor.

12. With the **Path Type** cursor visible, click and type the following: **Javaco Coffee and Tea**.

The type will follow the path you created with the Freeform Pen tool. Pretty cool!

13. In the **Layers** palette, click the **Background** to hide the path so you can see the type you created.

*You can adjust the positioning of the type on the path by selecting the **Path Selection** tool in the **Toolbox** and dragging the nodes to different locations on the path. You can also highlight the type with the **Horizontal Type** tool selected in the **Toolbox** and change the type settings in the **Options** bar or in the **Character** palette.*

14. Save and close the file.

NOTE | Warping Type on a Path

You can combine type on a path with warped type to create many interesting type effects. Once you've created type on a path, select the **Horizontal Type** tool in the **Toolbox** and click the **Warped Text** button on the **Options** bar.

This illustration shows the type you created on a closed path in the last exercise with **Shell Upper** style applied in the **Warp Text** dialog box.

This illustration shows the type you created on an open path in the last exercise with the **Wave** style applied in the **Warp Text** dialog box.

8. [IR] _____ Rasterizing Type

Working with vector-based type in Photoshop CS and ImageReady CS gives you the flexibility to edit your type without degrading the quality of the type with each edit.

There are situations when you may want to convert vector-based type layers to pixel-based layers. For example, you may want to apply Filter effects, distort type, or apply brush strokes using the Brush tool. Or, you may want to share a file with someone who doesn't own the font you've chosen. In all of these cases, you'll want to rasterize type layers. Rasterizing converts editable, vector-based type to a pixel-based image of the type. Here's an exercise to show you how. For this exercise, you're going to use ImageReady CS, but it works the same way in Photoshop CS.

1. In ImageReady CS, open **rasterize.psd** from the **chap_06** folder you copied to your **Desktop**.

2. Click to select the **click me** type layer in the **Layers** palette. Choose **Duplicate Layer** from the **Layers** palette menu.

*Notice a type layer named **click me copy** was automatically created in the **Layers** palette.*

3. Click the **Visibility** icon to turn off the visibility of the **click me** layer. Select the **click me copy** layer.

It's wise to make a copy of any type layer you're going to rasterize, because once a type layer is rasterized it can no longer be edited. This way you'll have an editable type layer in case you have to make any changes.

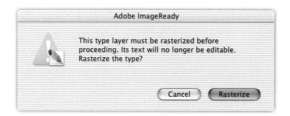

4. Choose **Filter > Blur > Gaussian Blur**. A dialog box will appear asking if you want to rasterize the type layer. Click **Rasterize** (Mac) or **Yes** (Windows).

*Rasterizing a type layer converts the editable vector-based type to non-editable pixel-based type. The type is no longer editable with the type controls but you can edit it as you would regular layers. For example, you can apply filter effects, paint inside the type with the **Brush** tool, or distort the shape of type as you'll do in the next exercise.*

NOTE | Rasterizing Type Manually

When you apply a filter to a type layer, Photoshop CS and ImageReady CS automatically rasterize the type layer for you as you've seen in this exercise. If you're rasterizing a type layer for another reason, such as sharing the file with a user who doesn't have a particular font, you'll have to rasterize the type layer manually.

To rasterize a type layer, select the type layer you want to rasterize in the **Layers** palette and choose **Layer > Rasterize > Type**. The type layer will be automatically converted to a regular layer, as shown in the illustration here.

5. In the **Gaussian Blur** dialog box, increase or decrease the **Radius** slider to your liking. Make sure the **Preview** option is turned on so you can preview the changes to the image. When you're satisfied with the changes, click **OK**.

6. Choose **File > Save As**. In the **Save As** dialog box, name the file **rasterize2.psd** and save it in the **chap_06** folder. Click **Save**.

7. Close the file, and leave ImageReady CS open for the next exercise.

*Note: This exercise works identically in Photoshop CS. Saving the file as **rasterize2.psd** saves a copy with your changes and leaves the original **rasterize.psd** untouched so you can try this exercise in Photoshop CS.*

9. [IR] _____Transforming Type

When you're working with type, you'll often want to resize, rotate, skew, or distort it. In previous exercises, you learned how to change the font size, how to rotate and transform paragraph type, and how to distort type using the Warp feature. There are alternate ways to achieve these effects using Transform commands. Here's an exercise to show you how. You'll use ImageReady CS, but it works the same way in Photoshop CS.

1. Open **sale.psd** from the **chap_06** folder you copied to your **Desktop**.

2. Click the **SALE** type layer to select it.

3. Press **Cmd+T** (Mac) or **Ctrl+T** (Windows) to put the type into **Free Transform** mode. A bounding box will appear around the type in the image.

**Free Transform** means freedom of movement. When you put a layer into **Free Transform** mode, you can rotate, scale, skew, distort, and adjust the perspective by any value.

4. Click and drag the top-middle or bottom-middle anchor point to change the height of the type. Click and drag the left-middle or right-middle anchor point to change the width of the type. When you're satisfied with the changes, click the **Commit Transform** button on the **Options** bar.

The following chart describes your options when you manipulate objects in **Free Transform** *mode.*

Using Free Transform Mode	
Feature	**Function**
Stretch Vertically	Click and drag a top or bottom anchor point.
Stretch Horizontally	Click and drag a left or right anchor point.
Scale Uniformly	Hold down the Shift key and click and drag a corner point.
Rotate	Position your cursor outside one of the corner anchor points. When the cursor turns into a rotate symbol, click and drag.

Don't be afraid to increase the size of type when you're in **Free Transform** *mode. Because the type is vector-based, it won't become pixilated as you increase the size. Unless you've rasterized the type, increasing the size will keep the edges crisp. You can transform rasterized type using the* **Free Transform** *feature, but the edges will appear fuzzy if you significantly increase the size.*

5. You can also access a number of **Free Transform** controls on the **Options** bar. Select the **SALE** layer in the **Layers** palette. Press **Cmd+T** (Mac) or **Ctrl+T** (Windows) to transform the type layer. Type values into the fields on the **Options** bar as shown in this illustration. Click the **Commit Transform** button on the **Options** bar.

6. To change the distortion or perspective, you must rasterize the type first. Choose **Layer > Rasterize > Type**. Choose **Edit > Transform > Distort** or **Edit > Transform Perspective**. Click and drag the anchor points to change the distortion or perspective of the type. When you're satisfied with the changes, click the **Commit Transform** button on the **Options** bar.

7. Save and close the file.

You've mastered how to create, format, and edit type in Photoshop CS and ImageReady CS!

In the next chapter, you'll learn about shapes and layer styles.

7.

Shapes and Layer Styles

| Comparing Bitmap Images and Vector Graphics |
About Shape Tools	About Shapes	About Shape Layers
Using Shape Tools and Shape Layers	About Layer Styles
Creating Layer Styles	Saving Custom Layer Styles
Applying Layer Styles from the Styles Palette

chap_07

Photoshop CS/ImageReady CS
H•O•T CD-ROM

Creating buttons is one of the most common tasks in a Web graphics workflow. The shape tools, shape layers, and layer styles make it extremely easy to create buttons with unique shapes and special effects.

The shape tools in Photoshop CS and ImageReady CS are vector-based, not pixel-based. You can use the shape tools to make buttons with crisp edges that remain scalable and editable in a layered Photoshop CS file. Drawing with the shape tools automatically creates a special kind of layer called a shape layer. In this chapter, you'll learn to use shape tools and shape layers to create a navigation bar with Web buttons.

Layer styles offer special effects to make your buttons unique. A layer style can be a simple effect such as a drop shadow or bevel, or it can be a combination of different styles. In this chapter, you'll see that layer styles are easy to use and fun to explore.

Comparing Bitmap Images and Vector Graphics

This chapter introduces you to shapes, shape tools, and shape layers, which are vector-based features in Photoshop CS and ImageReady CS. Before you begin the exercises, take a minute to understand the differences between "bitmap" and "vector."

For many versions, Photoshop was exclusively an application that let you create and edit bitmap images. In Photoshop 6, vector-based objects, including shapes, paths, and type, were introduced.

Bitmap images are made up of a series of pixels with each pixel assigned a specific color and location. Vector objects are defined by mathematical instructions. For example, a bitmap circle is composed of pixels arranged in a circular shape on an invisible grid. A vector circle is composed of mathematical instructions such as "radius=100." You may have worked with vector drawing programs such as Adobe Illustrator, CorelDRAW, Macromedia FreeHand, or Macromedia Flash.

This behind-the-scenes explanation helps you understand the differences between the terms "bitmap" and "vector." But you're probably wondering how and when you should use a bitmap image versus a vector graphic. Here's a chart to help you out.

Bitmap Images Versus Vector Graphics		
	Bitmap Images	**Vector Graphics**
When to use	Bitmap images are best for continuous tone images such as photographs, glows, soft edges, and blurs.	Vector graphics are best for flat, graphical content such as shapes, type, and objects that require sharp edges.
How to create	Create a bitmap image using the painting tools or fill commands.	Create vector graphics with the shape tools, pen tools, or type tools.
How to edit	Bitmap images are edited by modifying individual pixels.	Vector graphics are edited by manipulating points and handles around an object.

About Shape Tools

The shape tools were introduced in Photoshop 6. Since then, a few new shapes have been introduced. Here's a chart that describes the shape tools in Photoshop CS and ImageReady CS.

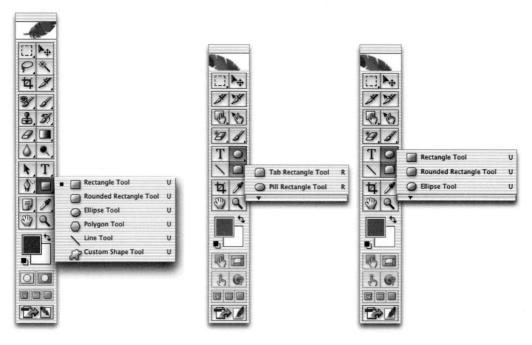

The shape tools in Photoshop CS   The shape tools in ImageReady CS

Photoshop CS and ImageReady CS Shape Tools

Shape Tool Name	Functionality	Example
Rectangle tool	Draws squares and rectangles.	
Rounded Rectangle tool	Draws squares and rectangles with rounded corners. You can adjust the radius of the rounded corners on the Options bar.	
Ellipse tool	Draws ellipses and circles.	
Polygon tool (available in Photoshop CS only)	Draws multisided shapes, including stars. You can set the number of sides on the Options bar.	
Line tool (available in Photoshop CS only)	Draws straight lines and arrows.	
Custom Shape tool (available in Photoshop CS only)	Draws with prebuilt shapes accessible from the Options bar. You can create and save custom shapes.	
Tab Rectangle tool (available in ImageReady CS only)	Draws tabs with rounded corners at the top. You can adjust the radius of the rounded corners on the Options bar.	
Pill Rectangle tool (available in ImageReady CS only)	Draws rectangles or squares with rounded ends. You can adjust the radius of the ends on the Options bar.	

About Shapes

In Photoshop CS and ImageReady CS, shapes are defined as individual objects. Therefore, you can select, edit, and move shapes individually even if they are on the same layer. Shapes are defined by smooth outlines called paths, which can be modified after shapes have been drawn. Shapes have a number of attributes, such as fill color and fill style, which you can change at any time using the controls on the Options bar. Because shapes are vector-based, you can resize them without degrading the quality of the image or making the edges fuzzy.

Keep in mind, when you save images in a file format other than the native Photoshop CS file format, shapes and shape layers are automatically rasterized (converted to pixels) and you lose the vector properties. Remember, you should always save copies of your layered images in the native Photoshop CS file format in case you need to make changes to the images later.

About Shape Layers

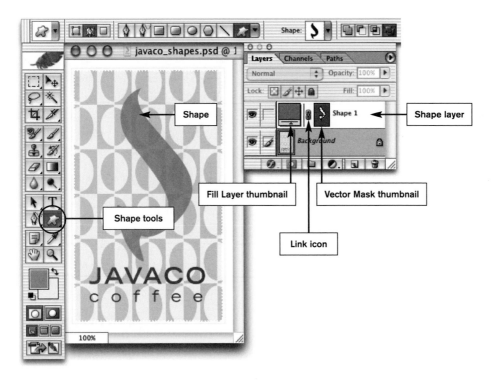

When you draw a shape with the shape tool, a shape layer is automatically created in the Layers palette. Shape layers are made up of three components: a fill layer, a vector mask, and a link. Here are descriptions of each.

- **Fill layer:** Fill layers contain information about the fill color and fill style. By default, fill layers are solid color fills and they pick up the Foreground Color in the Toolbox. You can change the solid color fill to a gradient fill or pattern fill. The left thumbnail on a shape layer represents the fill layer.

- **Vector mask:** Vector masks are black and white images that hide and reveal the contents of fill layers. Vector masks contain a path, which is an outline of the shape. They mask (or hide) any part of the fill layer that appears outside the path. Paths are vector-based, which gives them smooth edges and allows them to be resized without degrading the quality of the shape. The right thumbnail on a shape layer represents a vector mask.

- **Link:** By default, fill layers and vector masks are linked so you can move them together. There may be times when you want to move the fill layer independent of the vector mask. For example, if a fill layer contains a pattern, you may want to unlink the vector mask so you can reposition the fill layer and see a different part of the pattern inside the shape. The Link icon is located between the fill layer thumbnail and the vector mask thumbnail on a shape layer.

I. [PS] _____Using Shape Tools and Shape Layers

Now that you've read about shapes, shape tools, and shape layers, it's time to try them out! In this exercise, you'll learn to create and edit shapes.

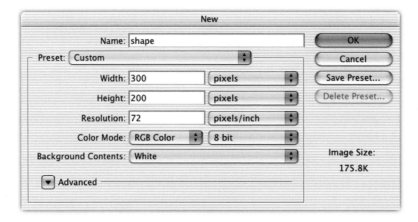

1. Choose **File > New**. In the **New** dialog box, adjust the settings to match the illustration here. Click **OK**.

*Note: If you set **Width** and **Height** to **pixels**, it doesn't matter what number you type in the **Resolution** field. The **Resolution** field, which measures pixels per inch, is only relevant for print work created in inches. When you're designing Web graphics, measure your images by pixels and keep the **Resolution** set at **72** because that's the way it will display on the Web.*

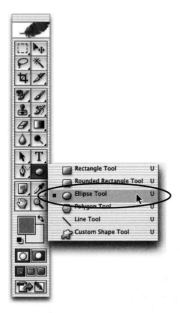

2. Select the **Ellipse** tool from the **Toolbox.**

*Notice the **Options** bar displays an icon for each of the shape tools. You can use these buttons to quickly switch between shape tools.*

*Notice the **Pen** tool and the **Freeform Pen** tool are also located on the **Options** bar. You can use the pen tools to draw vector shapes from scratch. However, it's often quicker and easier to start with one of the shapes in Photoshop CS and modify it, which you'll learn to do in this exercise.*

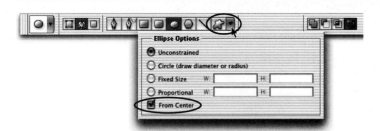

3. On the **Options** bar, open the **Geometry Options** box. The **Geometry Options** box is context-sensitive based on the shape tool you have currently selected. In the **Ellipse Options** box, turn on the **From Center** option. Click anywhere outside the **Ellipse Options** box to close it.

*The **From Center** option allows you to draw an ellipse from the center out, which you may find easier than drawing from the edge of the ellipse.*

4. On the **Options** bar, click the **Shape Layers** button.

*Note: If the **Paths** or **Fill Pixels** buttons are selected in the **Options** bar instead of the **Shape Layers** button, you will not create a new shape layer when you draw with the shape tools.*

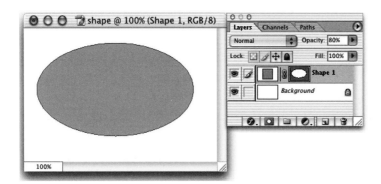

5. Click and drag inside the middle of the document window to draw an ellipse.

You control the shape and size of the shape while your mouse is pressed down.

*Notice a shape layer called **Shape 1** was automatically created in the **Layers** palette. **Shape 1** has three components: a fill layer, a vector mask, and a link.*

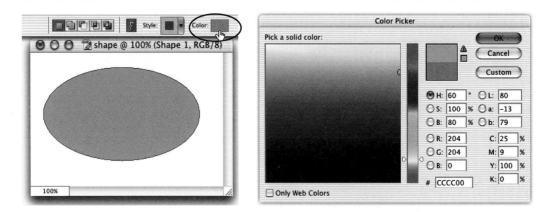

6. Click the **Color** box on the **Options** bar to open the **Color Picker** dialog box. Choose a bright, **olive green** color. Click **OK**.

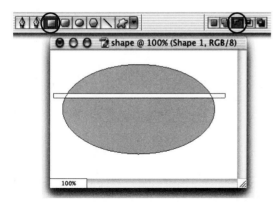

7. Select the **Rectangle Shape** tool on the **Options** bar. Click the **Subtract from shape area** button on the **Options** bar. Click and drag in the document window to create a narrow rectangular shape that cuts through the ellipse horizontally.

*The **Subtract from shape area** option allows you to use the **Rectangle Shape** tool to cut out a piece of the ellipse shape on the same layer. There are several options on the **Options** bar that allow you to combine multiple shapes on a single layer.*

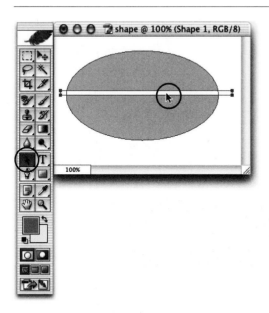

8. Select the **Path Selection** tool (the black arrow) in the **Toolbox**. Click the rectangle to select it. Click and drag to move the rectangle to the vertical center of the ellipse.

You can move shapes independently on a shape layer because they are vector-based.

9. Select the **Direct Selection** tool (the white arrow) from the **Toolbox**.

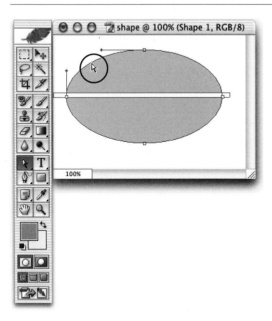

10. Click the black outline of the ellipse. You'll see small square anchor points and handles for editing the shape.

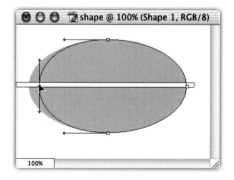 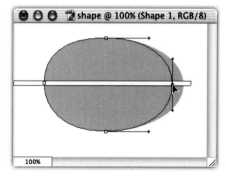

11. Click the anchor point on the left side of the ellipse and move it slightly toward the center to adjust the shape. Repeat the same steps on the right side of the ellipse, squeezing the shape toward its center.

The ellipse should now be slightly rounder and fatter, as shown in the illustrations.

You just edited the path, which changed the shape of the vector mask. Because shapes are vector-based, you can change the path as much as you want without affecting the quality of the edges.

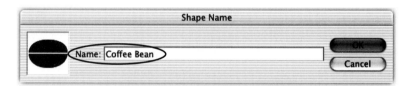

12. With the shape still selected, choose **Edit > Define Custom Shape**. In the **Shape Name** dialog box, type **Coffee Bean** in the **Name** field. Click **OK**.

*The **Coffee Bean** shape will now appear in the **Custom Shapes Picker** so you can use it in other images. You'll learn more about custom shapes at the end of this exercise.*

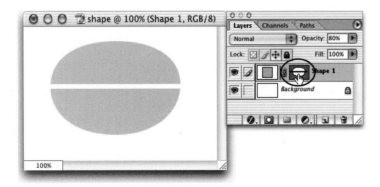

13. Click the vector mask thumbnail on the **Shape 1** layer to hide the shape outline (the path) in the document window.

Now you can see the shape without the distraction of the outline. Notice the shape has very smooth edges.

---

14. Save and close the file.

Images created with the shape tools in Photoshop CS offer more flexibility than images created with bitmap-based tools. Shapes are ideal for creating Web graphics such as buttons and icons because they can be recolored, resized, and reshaped and still keep their crisp edges.

Shapes work similarly in ImageReady CS but with a few limitations. For example, ImageReady CS does not have the Polygon, Line, or Custom Shape tools. In addition, ImageReady CS does not provide options for combining multiple shapes on a layer.

NOTE | Custom Shapes

The Custom Shapes tool in Photoshop CS lets you use preset custom shapes in your images and create and save custom shapes as you did in the last exercise. Photoshop CS ships with hundreds of preset custom shapes. The custom shapes are stored in libraries, which you can access from the Custom Shapes Picker on the Options bar.

Open the **Custom Shapes Picker** and you'll see the **Coffee Bean** shape you saved in the last exercise.

To view all the preset custom shapes in Photoshop CS, choose **All** from the **Custom Shapes Picker** menu as shown here. Click **OK** to replace the current shape library with the **All** library.

Click and drag the bottom-right corner of the **Custom Shapes Picker** so you can see the variety of custom shapes that ship with Photoshop CS.

If you want to experiment with these custom shapes, click **File > New** to open a new image. Choose a shape in the **Custom Shapes Picker**. Click and drag inside the document window with the custom shape. When you're finished, close the file.

About Layer Styles

Next, you'll learn to apply different effects to shapes using layer styles in Photoshop CS. You can use layer styles to apply shadows, glows, bevels, textures, patterns, gradients, colors, and stroked outlines to shapes. With layer styles, the creative possibilities are endless!

Here is handy chart that shows the different layer styles in Photoshop CS and ImageReady CS.

Photoshop CS and ImageReady CS Layer Styles		
Layer Style Name	**Functionality**	**Example**
Drop Shadow	Adds a shadow behind the edges of a layer	
Inner Shadow	Adds a shadow inside the edges of a layer, which makes the layer appear recessed	
Outer Glow	Adds a glow to the outside edges of a layer	french roast
Inner Glow	Adds a glow to the inside edges of a layer	french roast
Bevel and Emboss	Adds a beveled edge or an embossed edge to the edges of a layer	french roast
Satin	Adds shading to the inside of a layer, which results in a satiny appearance	french roast
Color Overlay	Fills the layer will solid color	french roast
Gradient Overlay	Fills the layer with a gradient	french roast
Pattern Overlay	Fills the layer with a pattern	french roast
Stroke	Outlines the layer with a color, gradient, or pattern	french roast

The beauty of layer styles is that they are non-destructive, which means you can apply and edit as many layer styles as you want without affecting the original image. Plus, if you create a layer style you like, you can save the layer style and apply it to other layers or files.

2. [PS]_____Creating Layer Styles

Photoshop CS includes a number of different layer styles you can apply to shapes to create unique Web buttons. Here's an exercise to show you how. For the next three exercises, you'll use Photoshop CS, but layer styles work the same way in ImageReady CS.

1. Open **button.psd** from the **chap_07** folder you copied to your **Desktop**.

You'll see a replica of the button you created in the last exercise with a type layer called french roast.

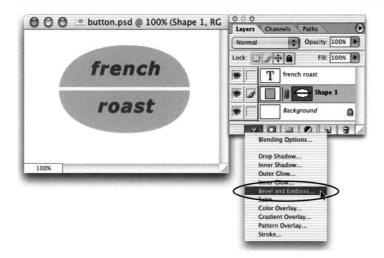

2. Click the **Shape 1** layer in the **Layers** palette to select it. Choose **Bevel and Emboss** from the **Add a layer style** pop-up menu at the bottom of the **Layers** palette.

The Layer Style dialog box opens automatically.

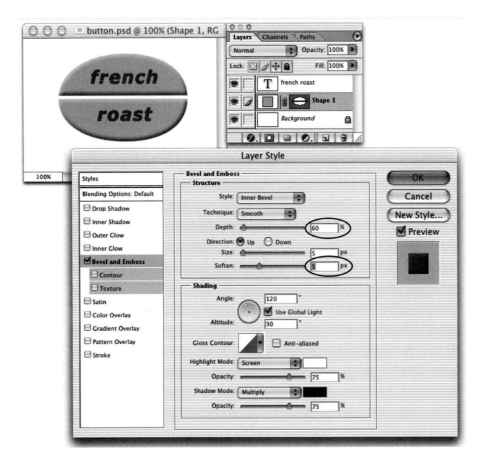

3. In the **Layer Style** dialog box, decrease the **Depth** to **60%** and increase the **Soften** to **5 px**.

Next, you'll change the color of the shadow.

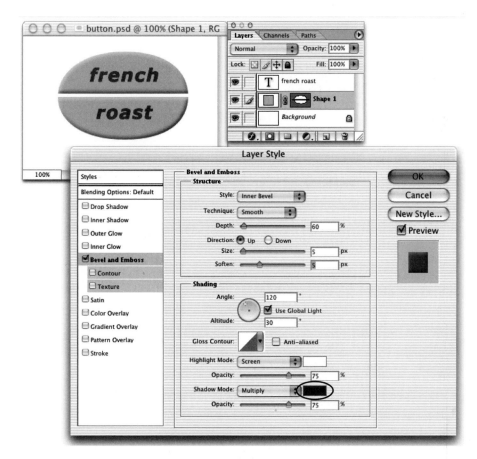

4. Click the **Color** box beside the **Shadow Mode** pop-up menu to open the **Color Picker** dialog box. Choose a dark **green** to change the color of the shadow from the default **black**. Changing the shadow color will make the bevel look more realistic. Click **OK** to close the **Color Picker** dialog box.

*Do not click **OK** in the **Layer Style** dialog box yet; you'll need it open for the next step.*

5. Experiment with some of the other settings. When you're finished, match the settings to those in the illustration in **Step 4**. Click **OK** to close the **Layer Style** dialog box.

*Your image will automatically update with the changes you made in the **Layer Style** dialog box. As you explore the settings, you'll see terms that may be new to you such as **Choke**, **Contour**, and **Jitter**. For more information about some of these terms, refer to the chart at the end of this exercise.*

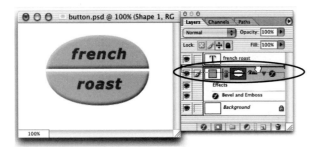

6. In the **Layers** palette, drag and drop the **Bevel and Emboss** layer style between the **Shape 1** and **french roast** layers.

The text now appears beveled, just like the button! You can copy any layer style to another layer by dragging. You can also move multiple layer styles at once. This is much easier than applying new layer styles each time.

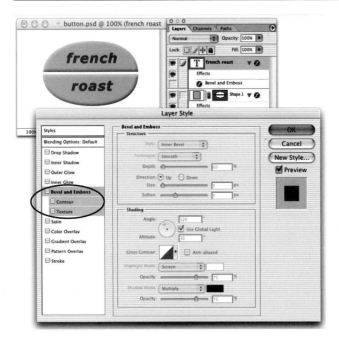

7. Double-click the **Bevel and Emboss** layer style on the **french roast** type layer to open the **Layer Style** dialog box. Turn off the **Bevel and Emboss** layer style on the left side of the **Layer Style** dialog box. This turns off the visibility of the **Bevel and Emboss** layer without discarding the layer style.

*You can turn on the visibility of the **Bevel and Emboss** layer style by turning on the **Visibility** icon in the **Layers** palette.*

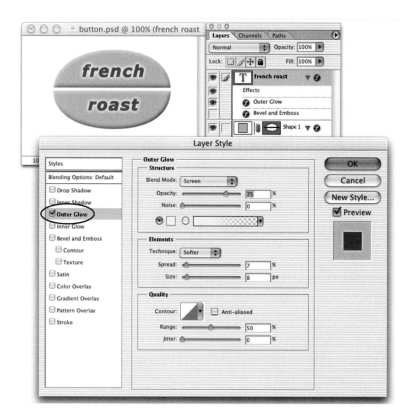

8. Click **Outer Glow** to turn on the **Outer Glow** option in the **Layer Style** dialog box. The contents of the **Layer Style** dialog box will change to show the controls for the **Outer Glow** layer style. Change the **Spread** to **7%** and change the **Size** to **8%** to make the glow more visible. When you're satisfied with the changes, click **OK**.

*You'll see a new **Outer Glow** layer style on the **french roast** layer in the **Layers** palette.*

*Note: You have to click the name of a layer style in the **Layer Style** dialog box to highlight it before you can edit the settings. Turning on the check box beside the layer style name only activates the effect. You can create new layer styles from the **Layer Style** dialog box as you did here or from the **Add a layer style** pop-up menu at the bottom of the **Layers** palette.*

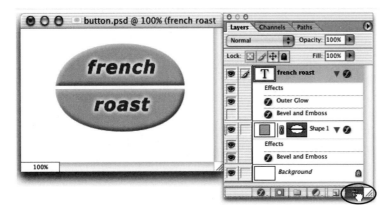

9. You no longer need the **Bevel and Emboss** layer style. To discard it, click and drag it to the **Trash** icon at the bottom of the **Layers** palette.

*If you want to discard all the layer styles on a layer, drag the word **Effects** to the **Trash** icon at the bottom of the **Layers** palette and the layer styles below it will be deleted.*

TIP | Turning Off the Visibility of Layer Styles

Like you can with layers, you can turn on and off the visibility of layer styles to show or hide the effect you applied. Turning off the visibility means you no longer see the layer style, but it's still part of the image should you decide you want to use it.

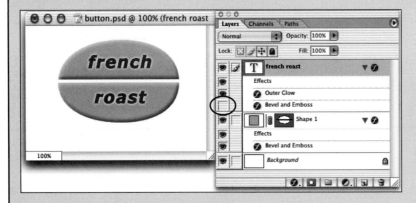

To turn off the visibility of a layer style, turn off the **Visibility** icon (the eye) in the **Layers** palette.

---

10. Save the file as **mybuttonstyles.psd** in the **chap_07** folder on your **Desktop** and leave it open for the next exercise.

NOTE | The Layer Style Dialog Box

The settings in the Layer Styles dialog box are context-sensitive based on the layer style you have selected. There are a number of terms in the Layer Style dialog box that may be foreign to you, such as Spread, Contour, or better yet—Gloss Contour! Here's a handy chart describing some of the complex terms in the Layer Style dialog box.

Layer Style Terms	
Term	**Definition**
Blend Mode	Determines how the layer style blends with underlying layers. Uses the standard Photoshop CS blending modes, such as Multiply, Screen, and so on.
Opacity	Changes the opacity of the layer style.
Color	Specifies the color of the layer style, such as drop shadow or glow.
Angle	Determines the lighting angle.
Spread/Choke	Determines the intensity of the layer styles, such as glows or strokes. Spread increases the flow outward to increase the size. Choke decreases the flow inward to decrease the size.
Noise	Adds dithering to soften edges.
Contour	Sculpts the ridges, valleys, and bumps in some layer styles, such as bevel and emboss.
Anti-Alias	Affects how the edges blend with underlying layers.
Depth	Affects the dimensional appearance.
Gloss Contour	Adds a glossy, metal-like appearance to bevel and emboss.
Gradient	Applies a gradient from the Gradient Editor.
Highlight or Shadow Mode	Determines the blending mode of a highlight or shadow using standard Photoshop CS blending modes, such as Multiply, Screen, and so on.
Jitter	Varies the color and opacity of a gradient.
Layer Knocks Out	Controls the visibility of the drop shadow or invisibility of a semi-transparent layer.
Drop Shadow	Controls the visibility of the drop shadow or invisibility of a semi-transparent layer.
Soften	Blurs the layer style.

3. [PS] _____Saving Custom Layer Styles

When you're working with layer styles, you'll often find a combination of settings you like and want to apply to other layers. In Photoshop CS, it's easy to save a custom layer style. Here's an exercise to show you how.

1. The file you saved in the last exercise, **mybuttonstyles.psd**, should still be open. If it's not, open the prebuilt **buttonstyles.psd** from the **chap_07** folder you copied to your **Desktop**.

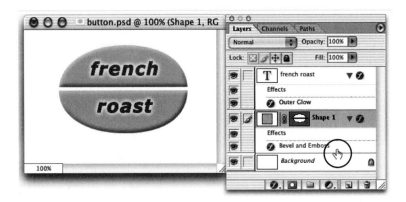

2. Double-click the **Bevel and Emboss** layer style on the **Shape 1** layer in the **Layers** palette to open the **Layer Style** dialog box.

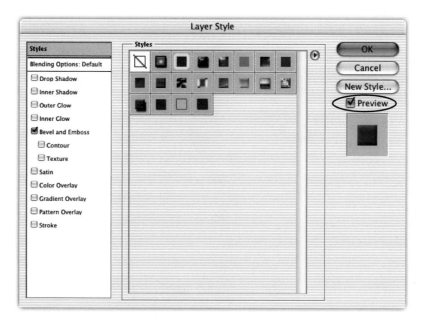

3. Click the **Styles** header on the left side of the **Layer Style** dialog box. You'll see a collection of style thumbnails in the **Styles** panel of the **Layer Styles** dialog box. Make sure the **Preview** option is turned on so you can see a thumbnail preview of the layer style you created in the last exercise. Click the **New Style** button.

4. In the **New Style** dialog box, turn on the **Include Layer Effects** option. Type **French Roast Button** in the **Name** field. Click **OK**.

*A thumbnail of the new layer style will appear in the **Styles** panel of the **Layer Style** dialog box. Move your cursor over the thumbnail and you'll see the name **French Roast Button**.*

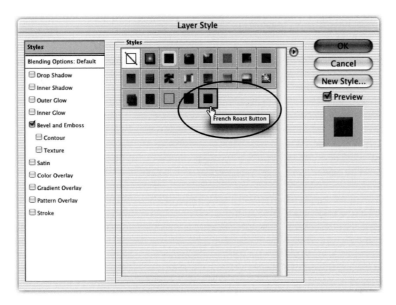

Notice the thumbnail for the new layer style is gray. It contains only the **Bevel and Emboss** layer style, which is colorless (unlike some other layer styles such as **Color Overlay** and **Gradient Overlay**). You can apply the **French Roast Button** style to any graphic without changing the color.

5. Click **OK** to close the **Layer Style** dialog box.

6. Choose **Window > Styles** to open the **Styles** palette. Drag the window by the bottom-right corner to make it larger.

You'll see a thumbnail of the layer style you just created! Position your mouse over the thumbnail and you'll see the name **French Roast Button**.

Next, you'll learn to create a custom layer style from the **Styles** palette.

7. Select the **french roast** type layer in the **Layers** palette. Click the **New Style** button at the bottom of the **Styles** palette. In the **New Style** dialog box, type **French Roast Type**. Click **OK**.

*In the **Styles** palette, you'll see a thumbnail of the new **French Roast Type** layer style you just created. The thumbnail is gray with a pale yellow glow because it contains the **Outer Glow** layer style. The **French Roast Type** layer style does not contain information about color or font, so you can apply it to any graphic, not just type.*

8. Close the file. You don't need to save the file because you haven't made any changes to it since the last exercise.

TIP | Accessing Layer Styles from the Layers Palette

In this exercise, you learned to access layer styles by double-clicking an existing layer style to open the Layer Styles dialog box and by using the controls in the Styles palette. You can also access layer styles directly from the Layers palette. Here's how:

At the bottom of the **Layers** palette, click the **Layer Styles** pop-up menu and choose a layer style. When you choose a style, the **Layer Styles** dialog box will open automatically. You can apply layer styles and create your own custom layer styles directly from **Layer Styles** dialog box.

[PS] _____ **Applying Custom Layer Styles from the Styles Palette**

Now that you've created, applied, and saved custom layer styles, it's easy to apply those layer styles to other buttons to quickly create a collection of buttons with a consistent appearance.

1. Open **navbar.psd** from the **chap_07** folder you copied to your **Desktop**.

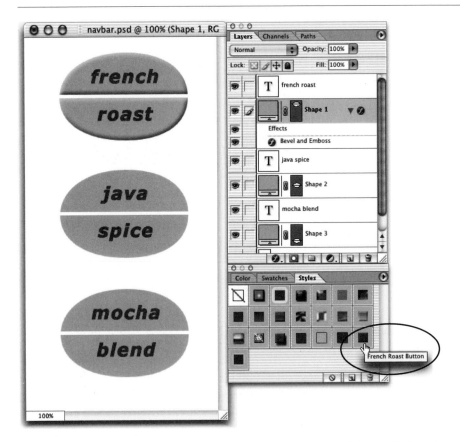

2. Select the **Shape 1 layer** in the **Layers** palette. Click the **French Roast Button** thumbnail in the **Styles** palette.

A **Bevel and Emboss** layer style should be applied to the **Shape 1** layer. Now that you've applied the layer style using the **Styles** palette, you can apply the same style to the other shape layers by dragging.

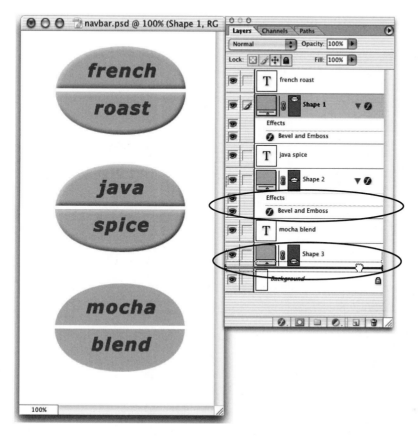

3. Drag the **Bevel and Emboss** layer style and drop it below the **Shape 2** layer in the **Layers** palette. Drag the **Bevel and Emboss** layer style and drop it below the **Shape 3** layer in the **Layers** palette.

*All three buttons should now have the **Bevel and Emboss** layer style applied. This is a simple and fast way to make buttons look consistent. Now you'll do the same for the type.*

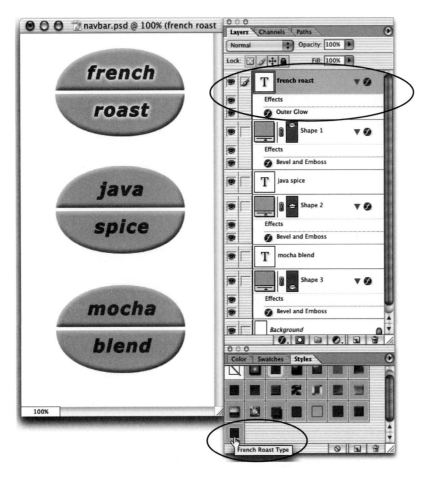

4. Select the **french roast** type layer in the **Layers** palette. Click the **French Roast Type** thumbnail in the **Styles** palette.

*Now that you've applied the layer style using the **Styles** palette, you can apply the same style to the other type layers by dragging.*

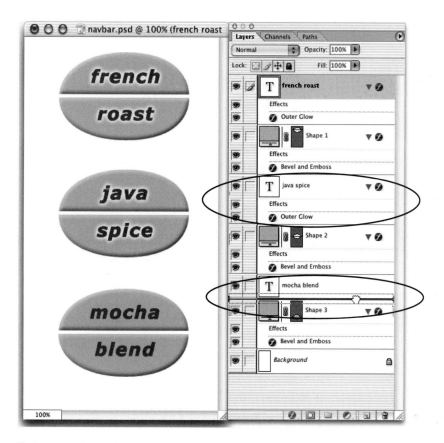

5. Drag the **Outer Glow** layer style and drop it below the **java spice** type layer in the **Layers** palette. Drag the **Outer Glow** layer style and drop it below the **mocha blend** type layer in the **Layers** palette.

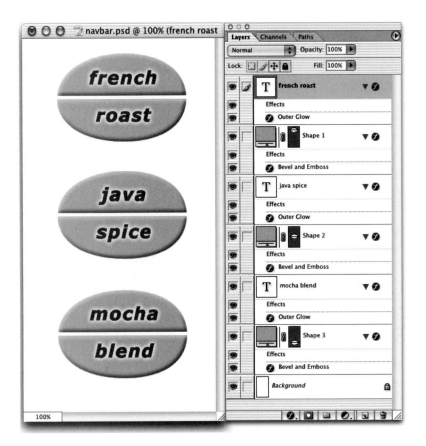

6. Save and close the file.

TIP | Deleting Styles from the Styles Palette

When you're working with layer styles in Photoshop CS or ImageReady CS, you'll often want to delete a layer style you applied.

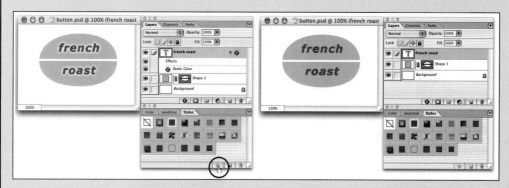

You can drag the layer style to the **Trash** icon on the **Layers** palette, as you learned in previous exercises, or you can use the **Clear Style** button on the **Styles** palette.

Congrats, you've finished another chapter! Now you know how to use shapes and layer styles in Photoshop CS to create Web buttons.

In the next chapter, you'll learn how to create different kinds of background images for your Web pages.

8.

Background Images

| What is a Background Image? | About Image Sizes |
| Defining, Previewing, Resizing, and Saving Background Images |
| Creating Symmetrical and Non-Symmetrical Background Images |
| Creating Seamless Background Images from Photographs |
| Creating Full-Screen Graphic and Photographic Background Images |
| Using Directional Tiles to Create Background Images |

chap_08

Photoshop CS/ImageReady CS
H•O•T CD-ROM

Designing for HTML is challenging because standard HTML is capable of displaying only two layers—a background layer and a foreground layer. In most graphics applications, including Photoshop CS, ImageReady CS, Adobe Illustrator, and Macromedia FreeHand, you can work with an unlimited number of layers. Because HTML restricts you to only two layers, knowing how to create a variety of appearances for the background layer is extremely important. This chapter will show you techniques for creating background images for Web pages.

One way to get around the two-layer limitation of HTML is to use style sheets instead of standard HTML. However, this book is about designing Web graphics, not about writing code or using a Web page editor, so this chapter focuses on the challenges of and solutions for making effective background images that work with standard HTML.

There are two core issues to think about when you're making a background image: the speed at which it will load, which you learned about in Chapter 4, "*Optimization*," and its appearance, which you'll learn about in this chapter.

What Is a Background Image?

Background images appear on the background layer of a Web page. Background images are made up of a series of tiles that repeat to make up an entire background image. By default, background images repeat to fill the size of the active Web browser window. The number of times a background tile repeats depends on the size of the original image and the size of the active Web browser window. As a result, background images often appear differently on different monitors. The challenge in designing background images is to prepare a graphic that can look different from monitor to monitor and still look good. Not easy! This chapter will provide techniques to help you design background images.

Regardless of how many times a background tile repeats in a Web browser window, it downloads only once to the viewer's computer. Each time the tile appears on a Web page, it is recalled from the cache in the viewer's computer, rather than being downloaded again and again. As a designer, you can get a lot of mileage from a background tile. If you create a tile with a small file size, you can fill an entire Web browser window in very little time.

HTML allows you to use a single background image and multiple foreground images. As a result, you can put other images on top of a background layer. If you want an illustration, a photograph, text, or any other image to float on top of a background image, you must identify the background image as an HTML background, which you'll learn to do in this chapter.

What differentiates background images from regular images in HTML code is the **BODY** tag. Understanding HTML for a tiled background is simple. Here's an example of the HTML required to create a tiled background from a simple image (*small.jpg* in this case).

```
<html>
<body background="small.jpg">
</body>
</html>
```

NOTE | Vocabulary: Background Tile and Tiling

In this chapter, you'll run into the terms "tiling" and "background tile." Tiling refers to the horizontal and vertical repetition of an HTML background image in a Web browser when the image is smaller than the Web browser window. Background tile is used interchangeably with the term "background image" to mean a GIF or JPEG that repeats in an HTML background.

TIP | Design Tips for Readability

When you're creating background images, it's important to pay attention to your color choices. Try to use either all dark colors or all light colors. If you combine darks and lights in a single background image, your background might look great on its own, but your viewers may have problems reading the type.

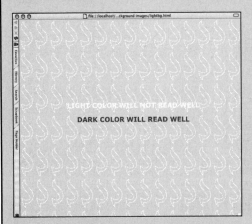

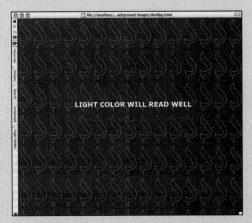

Light background   *Dark background*

If you're wondering how to pick colors for backgrounds in relation to foreground type, here are some basic guidelines:

- If you're using a light background, use dark type.

- If you're using a dark background, use light type.

- Avoid using a medium value for a background image, because neither light nor dark type will read well on top of it.

- Avoid using contrasting values in a background image, because it will make type very difficult to read.

About Background Image Sizes

You can use graphics of any dimension for background images. The size of a background tile will determine the number of times it will repeat inside a Web browser window.

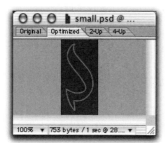

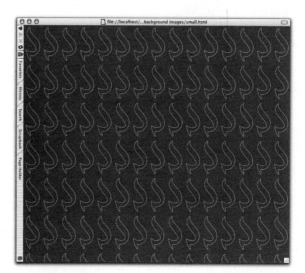

Small

Result in Web browser

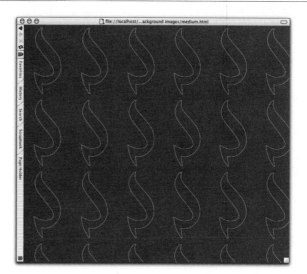

Medium

Result in Web browser

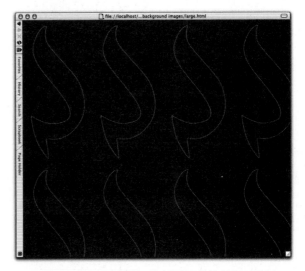

Large   *Result in Web browser*

As you can see in these examples, a background tile with larger dimensions repeats less than a smaller background tile. For example, a background tile measuring 40 × 40 pixels will repeat 192 times (16 times across and 12 times down) in a 640 × 480 Web browser window. A background tile measuring 320 × 240 pixels will repeat four times (two times across and two times down) in a 640 × 480 Web browser window. You can also create extra-large background images so they repeat only once in a standard-size Web browser window. Before you decide which size to make the background tile, you need to decide what kind of effect you want to create.

Enlarging the dimensions of a background tile will increase its file size. If you create a 50K background tile, it's going to increase the size of your Web page by 50 KB, which will increase the time it takes to load. A rough formula for determining load time is as follows: 1K equals 1 second. Although this formula isn't scientifically accurate, it's what many designers use as a rough guideline when designing Web graphics. Therefore, it's just as important to practice good optimization skills when creating background images as it is with other types of images.

I. [IR] ____Defining, Previewing, and Resizing Background Images

Once you've created or opened an image, you can use the Output Settings in ImageReady CS to specify a background image. Once you've done this, you can use the Preview in Browser feature in ImageReady CS to see how the image will look in a Web browser as a tiled background.

In this exercise, you'll learn to define images as background images, preview background images in a Web browser, and resize background images. For this exercise, you'll use ImageReady CS. You can create background images in Photoshop CS in the Save For Web window, but it's easier to make background images in ImageReady CS because the output and preview controls are easier to access.

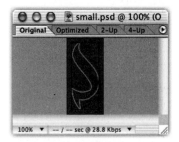

1. In ImageReady CS, open **small.psd** from the **chap_08** folder you copied to your **Desktop**.

*First, you'll define the image as an HTML background in the **Output Settings** dialog box. Defining the image as a background tells ImageReady CS to output the image as a tiled background image instead of a single foreground image.*

2. Choose **File > Output Settings > Background**.

*The **Output Settings** dialog box opens automatically with the options for **Background** already selected.*

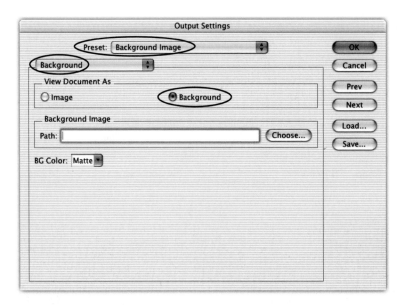

3. In the **Output Settings** dialog box, choose **Background Image** from the **Preset** pop-up menu and choose the **View Document As: Background** option to identify the image as an HTML background. Click **OK**.

4. Click the **Preview In Default Browser** button in the **Toolbox** to open your default Web browser.

*If you want to preview the image in a different Web browser, choose **File > Preview In > Other Browser** and navigate to where the Web browser is installed on your computer.*

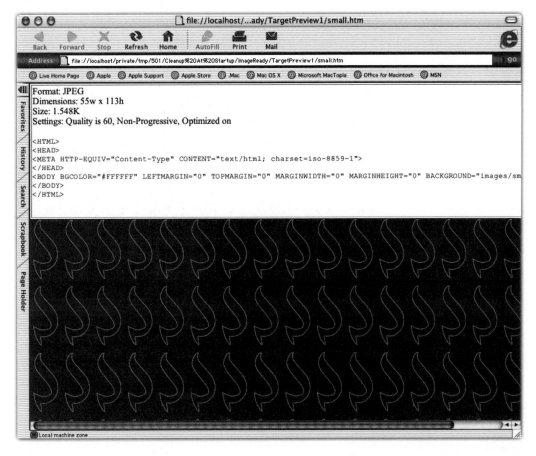

ImageReady CS automatically launches the selected Web browser (if it isn't already open) and displays a preview of the image as a repeating background image.

Notice the preview includes a white text box containing information about how the image was optimized, as well as the HTML used to define this image as a background. In the next exercise, you'll learn to save HTML files without the text box.

Next, you'll change the size of the image so you can learn how changing the sizes of images affects the appearance of background images in a Web browser.

5. Close the Web browser window and return to ImageReady CS.

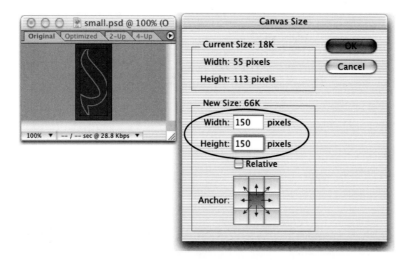

6. Choose **Image > Canvas Size**. Change the canvas size to **150 pixels** by **150 pixels**. Make sure the **center square** in the **Anchor** diagram is selected and that **Relative** is unchecked, as shown in the illustration. Click **OK**.

You'll see the size of the canvas is larger but the javaco smoke graphic is the same size. Notice the new pixels you added to the image are transparent.

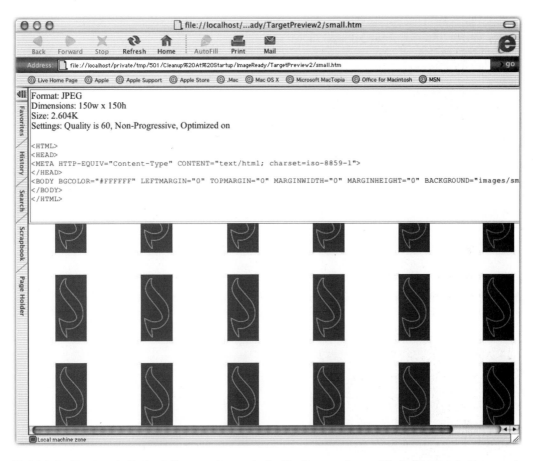

7. Click the **Preview in Default Browser** button in the **Toolbox** or choose **File > Preview in Browser > Other Browser** to choose a different Web browser so you can preview how the change in dimensions affects the appearance of the tiled background.

Notice the transparent areas of the canvas appear white in the Web browser. ImageReady CS substitutes white for any transparent pixels in an image unless you specify otherwise. If you want to change the color of the transparent pixels, you'll need to fill them with another color.

8. Close the Web browser and return to ImageReady CS.

9. Select the **Eyedropper** tool in the **Toolbox**. Click the dark **purple** in the image to sample the color.

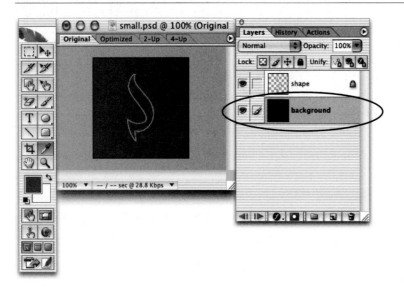

10. In the **Layers** palette, click the **background** layer to select it. Press **Option+Delete** (Mac) or **Alt+Backspace** (Windows) to fill the **background** layer with dark **purple**.

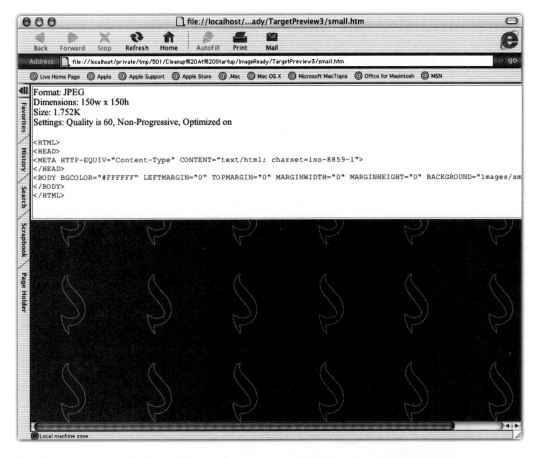

11. Click the **Preview in Default Browser** button in the **Toolbox** or choose **File > Preview in Browser > Other Browser** to choose a different Web browser so you can preview how this change affects the background image.

Notice the areas that were white in the last preview are now dark purple, and the background image is perfectly tiled.

12. Close the Web browser and return to ImageReady CS.

13. Save the changes and leave the image open for the next exercise.

The capability to preview background images quickly and easily in ImageReady CS is a great feature because it allows you to try different dimensions, color treatments, or other imaging techniques before you choose the final design for your background image.

2. [IR] _____Saving Background Images

In order for a background image to work properly in a Web browser, you must do two things:

- Save the image as an optimized JPEG or GIF.

- Save the HTML code that tells the Web browser the image is a background tile.

Fortunately, ImageReady CS makes this process easy by letting you save both the image and the required HTML in a single step. Alternately, you could save the optimized image without HTML, open the image in an HTML editor, and code the image as a background tile.

In this exercise, you'll learn to save a background image and the required HTML code so you can use the image as a background tile for a Web page.

1. With **small.psd** open from the last exercise, click the **Optimized** tab in the document window.

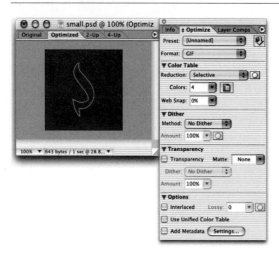

2. Match the settings in the **Optimize** palette to those shown here.

Note: Because the image is composed of flat colors, it's going to look and compress best as a GIF.

3. Choose **File > Save Optimized**.

*The **Save Optimized** dialog box opens automatically.*

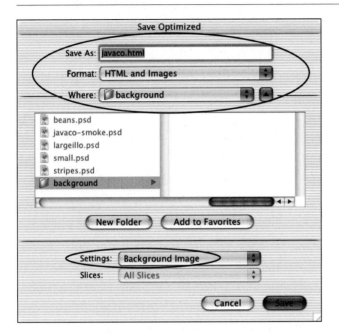

4. In the **Save Optimized** dialog box, create a new folder called **background** in the **chap_08** folder by clicking the **New Folder** button (Mac) or the **Create New Folder** button (Windows). Type the name **javaco.html** in the **Save As** field. Choose **HTML and Images** from the **Format** pop-up menu (Mac) or **Save as type** pop-up menu (Windows). Click **Save**.

*Tip: You can define images as background images from the **Save Optimized** dialog box by choosing **Background Image** from the **Settings** pop-up menu. Because you defined the image as a background image in the last exercise in the **Output Settings** dialog box, **Background Image** was already selected in the **Settings** pop-up menu. If you know you want to save an image as a background image, being able to specify **Background Image** in the **Save Optimized** dialog box will save you an extra step. For more information about the **Save** options in ImageReady CS, refer to the chart at the end of this exercise.*

NOTE | Saving HTML from ImageReady CS

Some designers do not use the HTML file that ImageReady CS generates for background images because they prefer to use an HTML editor such as Adobe GoLive or Macromedia Dreamweaver to assemble Web pages. Using a dedicated HTML editor allows more precise control over place- ment of foreground images on top of the background. Whether you use ImageReady CS or an HTML editor to create HTML is up to you. Just remember that saving an image and the HTML from ImageReady CS is a great way to view the background image without the white preview text read- out and eliminates the need to use another application during the design process.

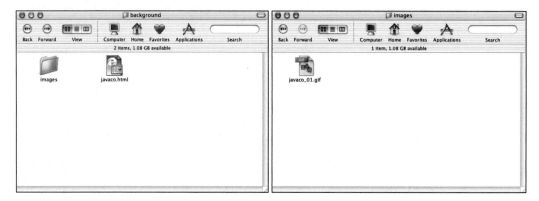

5. Browse to the **chap_08** folder on your **Desktop** and open the **background** folder.

*Notice a folder called **images**, which contains an image called **javaco_01.gif**, and a file called **javaco.html** (which contains the **<body background>** tag that identifies the GIF as a background image). Because you defined the image as a background image in the last exercise, ImageReady CS automatically saved the required HTML code when you saved the file.*

Next, you'll check out the final results by opening the HTML file in a Web browser.

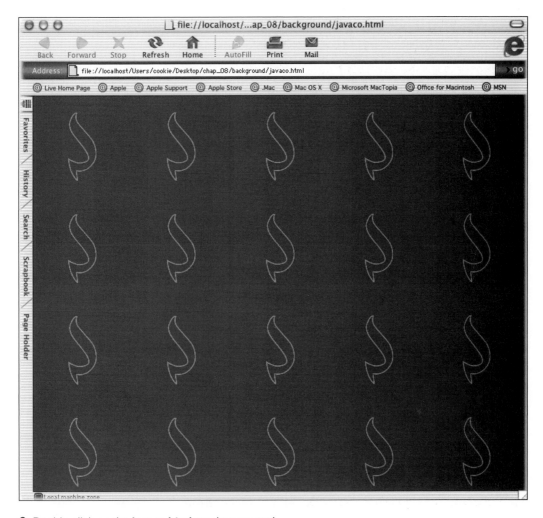

6. Double-click on the **javaco.html** you just created.

*The file will open automatically in your default Web browser. If you prefer to view the file in a different Web browser, launch the Web browser, choose **File > Open**, and navigate to the **javaco.html** file on your computer.*

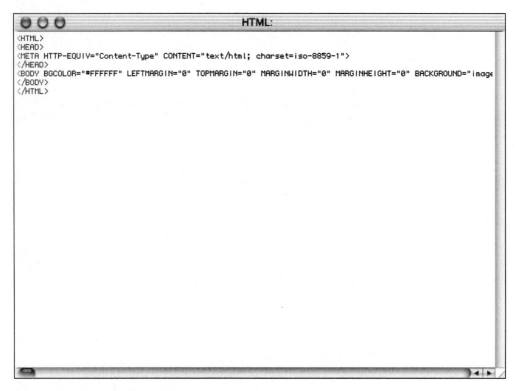

7. Choose **View > Source** (Internet Explorer) or **View > Page Source** (Netscape Navigator) to view the HTML code ImageReady CS generated.

8. Return to ImageReady CS. Save and close the file.

ImageReady CS Save Options

There are many different Save options in ImageReady CS. Here's a handy chart to help you understand:

ImageReady CS Save Options	
Function	**Result**
Save Optimized	Saves the file with its current optimization settings and current file name.
Save Optimized As	Saves the file with its current optimization settings and lets you change the file name. It overwrites an old file if you save it with the same file name.
Update HTML	Allows you to overwrite HTML that ImageReady CS generated. You will get to use this feature in Chapter 16, *"Integration with Other Programs."*
Save	Saves the file as a Photoshop file (PSD).
Save As	Saves the file as a Photoshop file (PSD) and lets you change the file name. It overwrites an old file if you save it with the same file name.
Export Original	Lets you save (export) your images to other file formats, such as Photoshop (PSD), BMP, PCX, PICT, Pixar, QuickTime Movie, Targa, and TIFF.

3. [IR] _____ Creating Symmetrical Background Images

The background images you created in the last two exercises produced patterns with very linear repetitions. In the following exercises, you'll learn how to use the **Offset** filter in ImageReady CS to create the illusion of a seamless (nonrepeating) background image.

In this exercise, you'll create a seamless, symmetrical background using the javaco smoke graphic and the Offset filter. For this exercise, you'll use ImageReady CS, but you can achieve the same results in Photoshop CS.

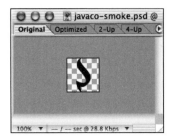

1. Open **javaco-smoke.psd** from the **chap_08** folder you copied to your **Desktop**.

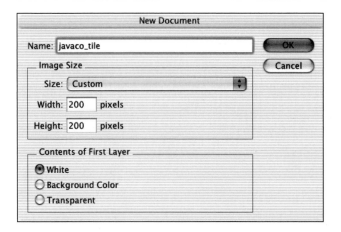

2. Choose **File > New**. In the **New Document** dialog box, type **javaco_tile** in the **Name** field, **200** in the **Width** field, and **200** in the **Height** field. Select **White** in the **Contents of First Layer** section. Click **OK**.

It's important to make the canvas larger than the graphic you plan to use for the seamless tile. The relationship between the tile size you're creating and the size of the graphic determines the spacing of the graphic on the background tile. In this case, the javaco smoke graphic is 50 × 50 pixels, so a 200 × 200–pixel file should do the trick.

3. Click inside the document window of the **javaco-smoke.psd** image to make it the active document. Press **Cmd+A** (Mac) or **Ctrl+A** (Windows) to select the entire image.

4. Press **Cmd+C** (Mac) or **Ctrl+C** (Windows) to copy the graphic to the clipboard. Click inside the document window of the new image, **javaco_tile.psd**, to make it active. Press **Cmd+V** (Mac) or **Ctrl+V** (Windows) to paste the graphic into the new document.

*The logo appears in the center of the image. When you paste an element into a document, ImageReady CS centers it automatically. With the graphic in place, you're ready to start creating a seamless tile using the **Offset** filter.*

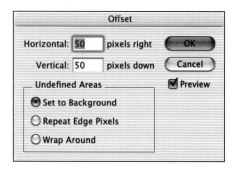

5. Choose **Filter > Other > Offset**. In the **Offset** dialog box, match the settings to the illustration shown here. Click **OK**.

*Because you're making a symmetrical repeating tile, you want to keep the **Horizontal** and **Vertical** settings the same.*

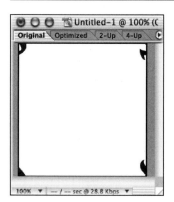 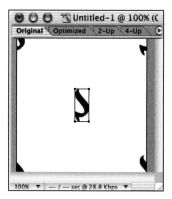

6. The graphic should look like it's split into four quarters, which are positioned at the four corners of the tile. Press **Cmd+V** (Mac) or **Ctrl+V** (Windows) to paste another copy of the logo into the center of the image.

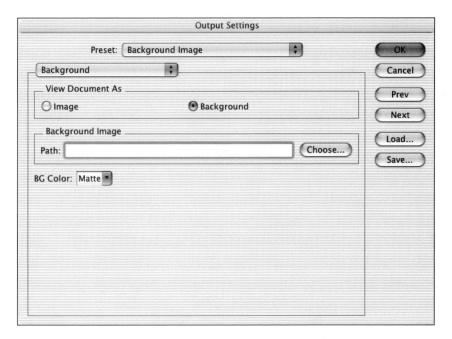

7. Choose **File > Output Settings > Background** to define the image as a background image. Match the settings in the **Output Settings** dialog box with the illustration shown here. Click **OK**.

Now you're ready to preview the seamless background tile in a Web browser.

8. Click the **Preview in Default Browser** button in the **Toolbox**.

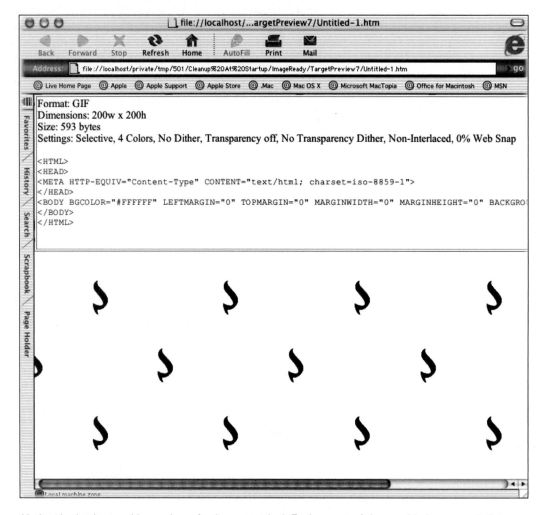

*Notice the background image is perfectly symmetrical. Each repeat of the graphic is an equal distance from the others because you started with a square image, pasted the graphics into the center of the document, and set both the **Horizontal** and **Vertical** offset values to 50 percent.*

In the next exercise, you'll learn to create nonsymmetrical effects by adjusting the offset percentages.

9. When you're finished, save and close the file.

NOTE | Using the Offset Filter in Photoshop CS

If you want to use the Offset filter in Photoshop CS, you can access it by choosing **Filter > Other > Offset**.

There are two disadvantages to creating background images in Photoshop CS: images cannot be identified as HTML backgrounds, and images cannot be previewed in a Web browser directly from the application. To perform either of these operations, you must have the **Save For Web** window open, which involves extra steps.

[IR] _____Creating Non-Symmetrical Background Images

In the last exercise, you created a seamless, symmetrical background image using an existing graphic. In this exercise, you'll use the brush tools to design and create a seamless, non-symmetrical background image.

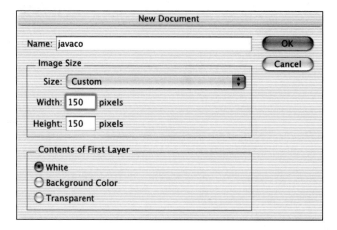

1. In ImageReady CS, choose **File > New**. In the **New Document** dialog box, type **javaco** in the **Name** field, **150** in the **Width** field, and **150** in the **Height** field. Set the **Contents of First Layer** to **White**. Click **OK**.

Next, you'll choose a color for the background.

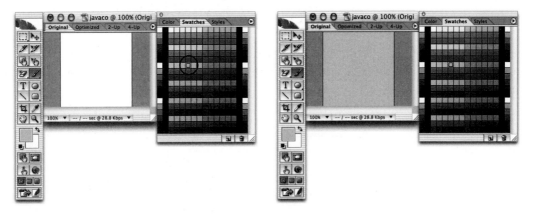

2. In the **Swatches** palette, choose a light **green**. Press **Option+Delete** (Mac) or **Alt+Backspace** (Windows) to fill the background with the color you chose.

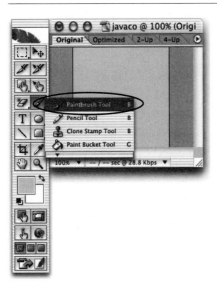

3. Select the **Paintbrush** tool from the **Toolbox**.

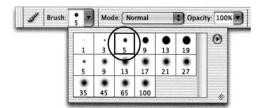

4. Open the **Brush Picker** on the **Options** bar and choose a brush.

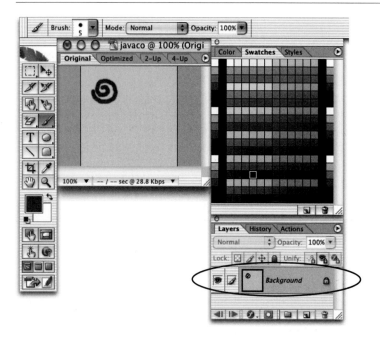

5. Choose a color from the **Swatches** palette. Make sure the **Background** layer is selected in the **Layers** palette. Begin drawing in the top-left corner of the **Background** layer of the image. Make sure your drawing does not touch the edge of the canvas—you want to leave some space between your drawing and the edge of the canvas.

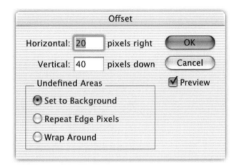

6. Choose **Filter > Other > Offset**. In the **Offset** dialog box, type **20** in the **Horizontal** field and **40** in the **Vertical** field. Choose **Set to Background** in the **Undefined Areas** section of the **Offset** dialog box. Click **OK**.

*In the last exercise, you set the offset values to 50 × 50 in the **Offset** dialog box, which let you create a perfectly symmetrical seamless tile. In this exercise, you'll create a non-symmetrical background, which is why you chose irregular values in the **Offset** dialog box. Because you want this background to appear more organic, it's better to use irregular numeric values so the offset is less predictable.*

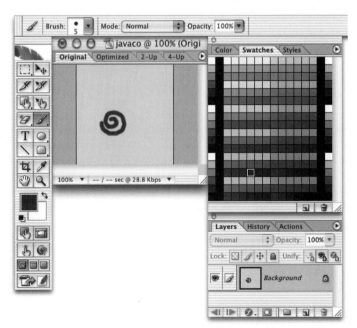

*The **Offset** filter shifts your original image to the right and down, leaving more room to add additional drawings.*

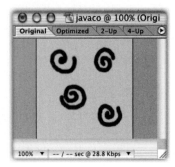

7. Continue to draw inside the blank areas of the image.

Make sure your drawings don't touch the edges of the image.

8. Press **Cmd+F** (Mac) or **Ctrl+F** (Windows) to apply the **Offset** filter again.

Note: This keyboard shortcut will reapply whichever filter you last applied. This will shift the pixels again and wrap them around the image, opening up some blank areas on the canvas.

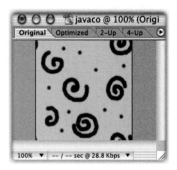

9. Continue to draw, filling in the blank areas of the image without touching the edges of your canvas. The goal is to create an image where there is no large unfilled area.

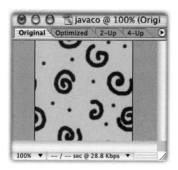

10. Press **Cmd+F** (Mac) or **Ctrl+F** (Windows) to apply the **Offset** filter again. Continue to apply the **Offset** filter until there are no large unfilled areas and you are satisfied with the results.

Next, you'll identify the image as a background image.

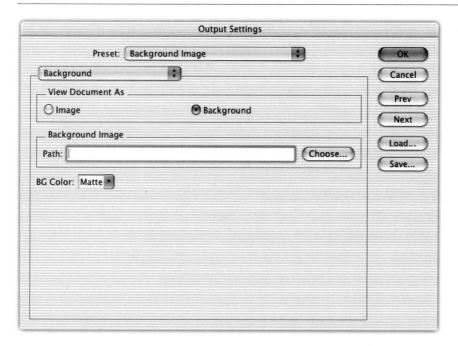

11. Choose **File > Output Settings > Background**. In the **Output Settings** dialog box, choose **Background Image** from the **Preset** pop-up menu and select the **View Document As: Background** option to identify the image as an HTML background. Click **OK**.

Next, you'll preview the background in a Web browser.

12. Click the **Preview in Default Browser** button in the **Toolbox**.

Notice it's hard to see the repeats in the background image? The power of this technique is the ability to create seamless, non-symmetrical backgrounds.

Note: *Don't worry if your compression settings are different from those shown in the previous illustration. ImageReady CS remembers the last settings used, which is the reason the settings in the illustration may be different from yours.*

13. Return to ImageReady CS. Save and close the file.

TIP | Accessing the Offset Filter in ImageReady CS

You may have noticed there are three ways to access the Offset filter in ImageReady CS. Here's a chart to explain the differences.

Accessing the Offset Filter in ImageReady CS	
Option	**Result**
Filter > Other > Offset	Lets you access the Offset filter so you can apply it to an image. Use this option when you are applying the Offset filter for the first time or when you want to create new offset settings.
Filter > Offset	Lets you access the Offset filter dialog box so you can change the settings.
Filter > Apply Offset	Lets you access the Offset filter when you want to reapply the offset with the same settings as the last time you used it.

 MOVIE | offset.mov

To learn more about how to use the **Offset filter** to create seamless backgrounds, check out **offset.mov** in the **movies** folder on the **H•O•T CD-ROM**.

5. [IR] _____Creating Seamless Backgrounds from Photographs

In the last two exercises, you created seamless background images using flat, graphical elements. What if you want to create a background using a photograph? The **Tile Maker** filter in ImageReady CS lets you create perfect, seamless backgrounds from photographs.

The Tile Maker filter overlaps and blends the edges of a photograph, which creates a convincing seamless pattern. Consider this technique if you're looking for ways to incorporate photographic backgrounds into your Web pages but you want to keep the file size down.

The Tile Maker filter works best on abstract photographs because they are least likely to show easily discernible, repeating patterns. This exercise works only in ImageReady CS. Photoshop CS does not have the Tile Maker filter.

1. In ImageReady CS, open **beans.psd** from the **chap_08** folder you copied to your **Desktop**. Click the **Optimized** tab in the document window.

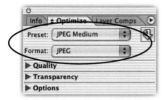

2. In the **Optimize** palette, choose **JPEG Medium** from the **Preset** pop-up menu. The **Format** pop-up menu will change to **JPEG** automatically.

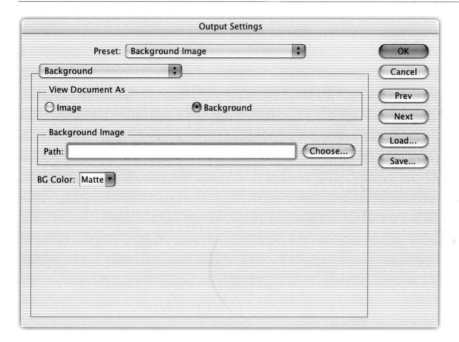

3. Choose **File > Output Settings > Background**. In the **Output Settings** dialog box, choose **Background Image** from the **Preset** pop-up menu and choose the **View Document As: Background** option to identify the image as an HTML background. Click **OK**.

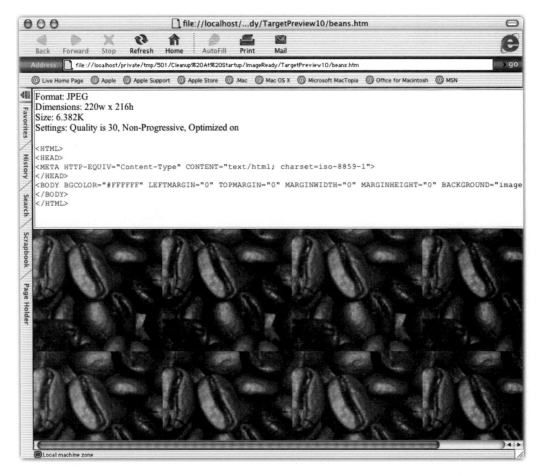

4. Click the **Preview in Default Browser** button in the **Toolbox**.

*Notice the obvious repeats in the pattern from the edges and seams of the source image? The **Tile Maker** filter will transform this into a seamless pattern in a snap!*

5. Return to ImageReady CS. Choose **Filter > Other > Tile Maker**.

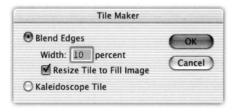

6. In the **Tile Maker** dialog box, choose **Blend Edges**, type **10** in the **Width** field, and turn on the **Resize Tile to Fill Image** option. Click **OK**.

*Tip: Choosing the **Kaleidoscope Tile** option can give you some beautiful abstract effects. You might want to experiment with it later.*

*Here's how the image will look after you apply the **Tile Maker** filter. You can see it's a little magnified.*

Next, you'll preview the image in a Web browser.

7. Click the **Preview in Default Browser** button in the **Toolbox**.

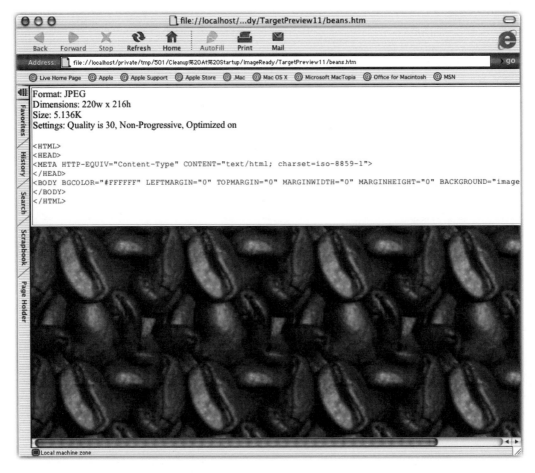

Notice the background appears softer and the edge blending has hidden the sharp edges where the coffee beans run off the background tile.

*Tip: If you want to preview just the background without the HTML information box displayed, save an HTML file by choosing **File > Save Optimized.** In the **Save Optimized** dialog box, choose **Save HTML and Images** from the **Format** pop-up menu (Mac) or **Save as type** pop-up menu (Windows). If you need a refresher on saving and previewing, revisit **Exercise 2**.*

Although this image is attractive and has no visible seams, it contains too much contrast to work effectively as a background image. Next, you'll modify the brightness and the hue of the image so it will work more effectively as a background image.

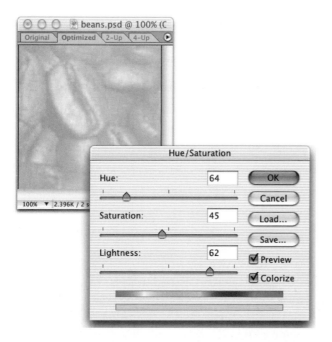

8. Return to ImageReady CS. Choose **Image > Adjustments > Hue/Saturation**. In the **Hue/Saturation** dialog box, adjust the settings until you're satisfied with the result. In this example, I significantly increased the lightness so the image would appear faded with lighter colors to make the background image appear more subtle and to decrease the file size when optimizing. When you're finished, click **OK**.

*Tip: Turning on the **Colorize** option makes the image appear monochromatic rather than full color. You can uncheck it to turn it off if you want to retain the natural colors of the image.*

Next, you'll preview the results in a Web browser.

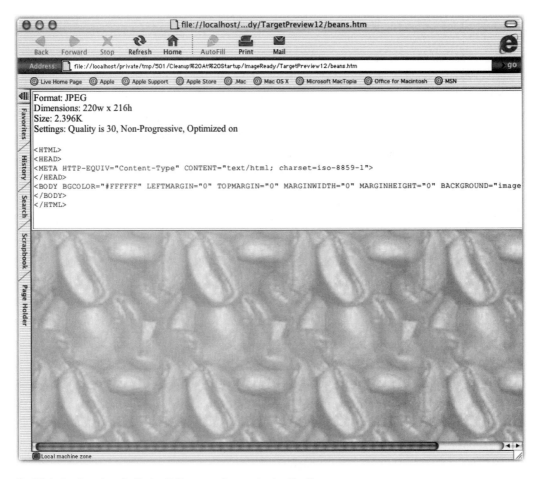

9. Click the **Preview in Default Browser** button in the **Toolbox**.

In this example, the background image is much lighter and type will be more readable when placed over it.

10. Close and save the file.

6. [IR] _____ **Creating Full-Screen Graphic Background Images**

Using a full-screen graphic as a background image can produce an impressive effect. If optimized properly, you can create a full-screen graphic background that loads quickly. The key to creating fast-loading background images is to limit your colors and use large areas of flat color.

The challenge in designing full-screen graphic backgrounds is considering the different screen resolutions your viewers will be using when they view your Web site, and creating background images that look good at each resolution. If you design a background image at 800 × 600, and your Web page is viewed at 1024 × 768, the Web browser will automatically repeat (or tile) the background image to fill the entire browser window, which probably won't look good.

Before you begin designing background images, consider the highest screen resolution your viewers will be using. Then, use this same size to design your background images. From there, you can rework your image to make it look good at lower resolutions.

This exercise will show you a helpful technique for viewing background images at different resolutions. For this exercise, you'll use ImageReady CS, but you can achieve the same result using Photoshop CS.

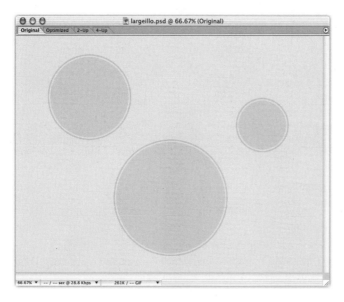

1. In ImageReady CS, open **largeillo.psd** from the **chap_08** folder you copied to your **Desktop**.

It's a big file—1024 × 768 pixels—but when optimized as a GIF with four colors, its file size is less than 4K. Images with large areas of solid colors optimize unbelievably well. You don't have to worry too much about download speed, but you do need to worry about how the image will look at different resolutions.

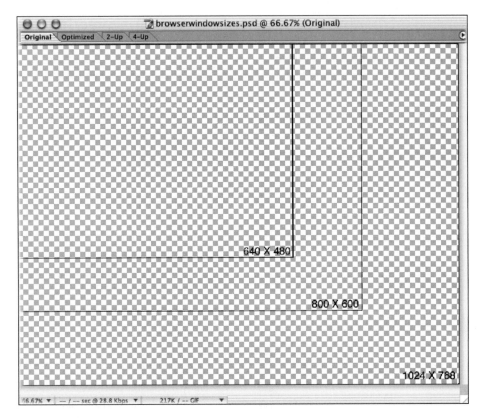

2. Open **browserwindowsizes.psd** from the **chap_08** folder you copied to your **Desktop**.

You can use this file to help you create full-screen background images. It helps you understand how the image will look at different resolutions. For example, a viewer whose system is set to 640 × 480 pixels will see only a portion of the background image and any foreground elements you place on top of it that fit within the box marked 640 × 480.

Sound a bit confusing? Follow the next few steps and you'll understand.

---

3. Select the **Move** tool from the **Toolbox**. In the **browserwindowsizes.psd** file, select the **screen resolutions** layer in the **Layers** palette.

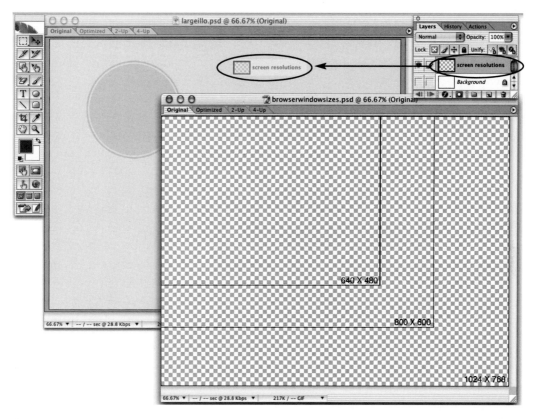

4. Drag and drop the **screen resolutions** layer from the **Layers** palette in the **browserwindowsizes.psd** file anywhere inside the **largeillo.psd** document window. As you're dragging, you'll see a shadow of the **screen resolutions** layer below the fist icon.

*When you drag and drop the layer, you'll see the **screen resolutions** layer appear in the **Layers** palette of the **largeillo.psd** file. Make sure the **screen resolution** layer is at the top of the layer stack. If it's not, click and drag it to the top.*

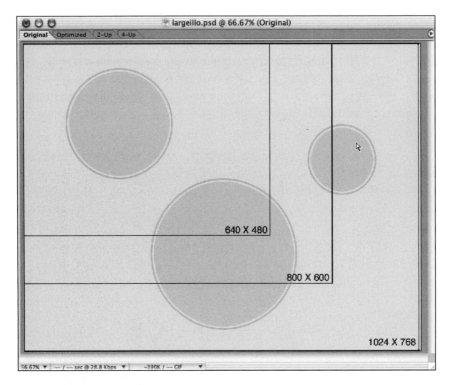

5. Click the **screen resolutions** layer in the **Layers** palette to select it. Using the **Move** tool and the arrow keys on your keyboard, align the top-left corners of the **screen resolutions** layer and the **Background** layer. Since these are large images, you might want to zoom in to fine-tune the alignment.

Now you can see how the background image will appear at 640 × 480, 800 × 600, and 1024 × 768. Using an overlay like this one will save you the time-consuming task of previewing the image at different resolutions while you're designing the background image.

6. Close both files.

This exercise showed you how to give careful consideration to resolution when designing full-screen graphic backgrounds. The overlay provided helps you visualize how a background will look at different resolutions. Feel free to use this overlay when you're designing your own large background images.

 MOVIE | dragginglayer.mov

To learn more about dragging layers from one document into another, check out the **dragginglayer.mov** movie in the **movies** folder on the **H•O•T CD-ROM**.

7. [IR]_____Creating Full-Screen Photographic Background Images

Full-screen backgrounds are not limited to flat color graphics like the one used in the last exercise. If you optimize a large photograph carefully, you can use it as a full-screen background. The key is to compress the photograph so it's small enough to download at a reasonable speed. This exercise will show you some of the optimization options for creating photographic background images. For this exercise, you'll use ImageReady CS, but it works similarly in Photoshop CS.

1. In ImageReady CS, open **largephoto.psd** from the **chap_08** folder you copied to your **Desktop**. Click the **Optimized** tab in the document window.

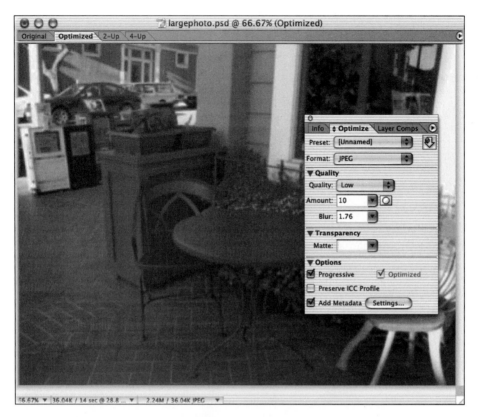

2. In the **Optimize** palette, choose **JPEG** from the **Format** pop-up menu. Choose **Low** from the **Quality** pop-up menu. Increase the **Blur** to **1.76**. Turn on the **Progressive** option.

With these settings, I was able to reduce the image size to 28K.

There are a few other ways to make a photograph smaller. In the next step, you'll reduce the hue and saturation using the image adjustment controls in ImageReady CS. Not only will this change reduce the file size, it will offer the added benefit of making text easier to read when placed on top of the photographic background.

3. Click the **Original** tab in the document window.

*If you're in the **Optimized** tab, it will take longer to make changes to the image because ImageReady CS will try to optimize the image each time you make a change.*

4. Choose **Image > Adjustments > Hue/Saturation**. Adjust the settings to match the illustration here or experiment with the settings until you're happy with the result. When you're finished, click **OK**.

5. Click the **Optimized** tab in the document windows. Check the **File Size Information** field at the bottom of the document window to see if the file size got smaller. In this example, changing the hue and saturation reduced the file size by half—from about 30K to about 15K.

Next, you'll define the image as a background image.

6. Choose **File > Output Settings > Background**. In the **Output Settings** dialog box, choose **Background Image** from the **Preset** pop-up menu and choose the **View Document As: Background** option to identify the image as an HTML background. Click **OK.**

7. Click the **Preview in Default Browser** button in the **Toolbox.**

8. Save and close the file.

8. [IR] Using Directional Tiles to Create Background Images

A wonderful trick that's widely used in Web design is to make directional tiles—graphics that are narrow and tall or short and wide so they can expand to full-screen images when repeated as background images. You can create the illusion of a large, full-screen graphic background with a tiny tile. Because the original image is so small, you get maximum effect for minimal download time. In this example, the optimized file size is 580 bytes, which is a very small file size for a background image.

In this exercise, you'll work with a small file to create a vertically striped background image. You'll use ImageReady CS, but it works similarly in Photoshop CS.

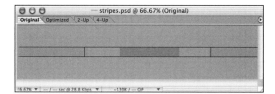

1. Open **stripes.psd** from the **chap_08** folder you copied to your **Desktop**.

2. Choose **File > Output Settings > Background**. In the **Output Settings** dialog box, choose **Background Image** from the **Preset** pop-up menu and choose the **View Document As: Background** option to identify the image as an HTML background. Click **OK**.

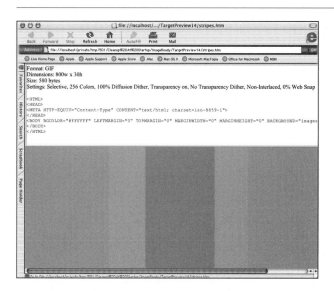

3. Click the **Preview in Default Browser** button in the **Toolbox**.

Notice the effect of the long, thin tile—a background image composed of vertical stripes.

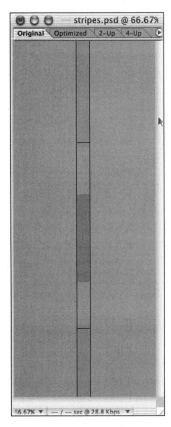

4. Return to ImageReady CS. Choose **Image > Rotate Canvas > 90°CW** to rotate the image 90 degrees clockwise.

*CW stands for clockwise, which means it rotates the image to the right. **CCW** stands for counterclockwise, which means it rotates the image to the left.*

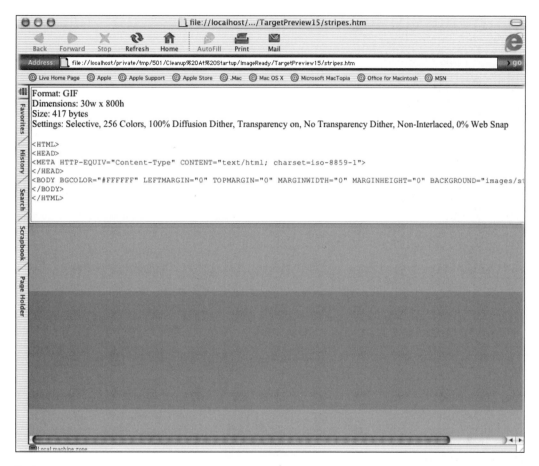

5. Click the **Preview in Default Browser** button in the **Toolbox**.

Notice the effect of the tall, narrow tile—a background image composed of horizontal stripes.

You should now have an idea of how directional tiles work. Try filling the image with a different color scheme or select and fill a new area to create a new stripe. Now that you know how images repeat inside Web browsers, the sky's the limit!

6. Save and close the file.

You've finished another chapter! With the techniques you've learned here, you can design unique, yet functional background images for any Web page!

9.

Transparent GIFs

| Understanding the Limitations of GIF Transparency |

| Understanding GIFs, Masks, and Transparency |

| Understanding Offset Problems in Browsers |

| Creating and Previewing GIF Transparency |

| Working with Transparent GIFs | Diffusion Transparency Dither |

| Saving Transparent Images |

chap_09

Photoshop CS/ImageReady CS
H•O•T CD-ROM

By default, all computer-generated graphics are rectangular or square. As a result, most images you see on the Web are rectangular, causing many sites to look similar. Fortunately, you can work around the rectangular limitation by creating transparent GIFs. You'll learn several techniques for creating transparent GIFs in this chapter.

Currently, GIF is the only file format in wide use for the Web that supports transparency. Unfortunately, GIF transparency settings are limited and can produce an unwanted halo around graphics. As you'll see in this chapter, both Photoshop CS and ImageReady CS have excellent tools for countering the inherent transparency problems in the GIF file format.

Understanding the Limitations of GIF Transparency

When you create graphics in Photoshop CS or ImageReady CS with soft edges such as drop shadows, glows, feathered edges, or anti-aliased edges, you're using 8-bit (or 256-level) transparency. This functionality lets the programs display different levels of partially transparent pixels at the edges of graphics. As a result, edges appear smooth with 8-bit transparency, making nonrectangular graphics look natural.

Photoshop CS anti-aliased edge   *Photoshop CS glow*

Photoshop CS and ImageReady CS use up to 256 levels of transparency. As a result, anti-aliased edges, glows, and other soft edges appear smooth and natural.

Unfortunately, the GIF file format only supports 1-bit masking instead of the sophisticated 8-bit transparency native to Photoshop CS and ImageReady CS. One-bit masking does not support partially transparent pixels, which means pixels in a GIF are either fully transparent or fully opaque (either on or off). The 1-bit masking limitation causes an unattractive halo (sometimes called a fringe or matte) of colored pixels. You'll learn how to fix this problem in the following exercises.

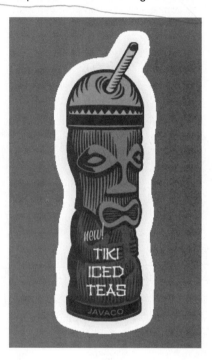

GIF anti-aliased edge   *GIF glow edge*

The GIF file format is limited to 1-bit masking. Notice the halos around the edges of the transparent GIFs in these illustrations when they are displayed against a colored HTML background. In this chapter, you'll learn why this happens and how to fix it.

What Is Anti-Aliasing?

The term "anti-alias" describes the edge of a graphic that blends into a surrounding color. The advantage of anti-aliasing is that it hides the otherwise jagged nature of color transitions in computer-generated graphics. Most graphics programs offer the capability to anti-alias. Photoshop CS and ImageReady CS include an anti-aliasing option for most of the creation tools, including the selection tools, the Type tool, the shape tools, the brushes, and the erasers.

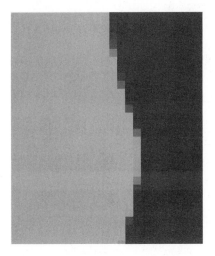

An anti-aliased edge

A blurry graphic uses anti-aliasing, too

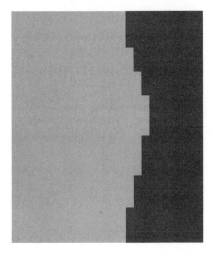

An aliased edge

Recognizing Transparent Layers

One way to create transparent GIF files in Photoshop CS or ImageReady CS is to create your graphic on (or convert it to) a transparent layer. How can you tell if your graphic is using transparent layers? The checkerboard pattern in Photoshop CS or ImageReady CS is the visual cue that lets you identify transparent pixels.

In Photoshop CS and ImageReady CS, the checkerboard pattern in the background of your images means your images are on a transparent layer. If you have other layers turned on that prevent you from seeing the checkerboard background, you must turn them off before you save the image as a transparent GIF.

Understanding GIFs, Masks, and Transparency

In this chapter, there will be references to a number of different terms such as GIFs, masks, and transparency. Here's a chart to help you understand what the terms mean.

Terminology	
Term	**Definition**
GIF	GIF stands for **G**raphic **I**nterchange **F**ormat. GIFs are one of the two main graphic file formats you can use when designing Web graphics. (JPEG is the other.) GIFs are best used for flat or simple graphic images that incorporate solid areas of color, such as logos, illustrations, cartoons, and line art. Because GIFs support transparency (JPEGs do not), GIF is the format to use if you want to include transparent areas in your Web graphics. You can turn on GIF transparency in the Save For Web window in Photoshop CS and in the Optimize palette in ImageReady CS.
Masks	Masks hide the visibility of specific areas of an image. In a transparent GIF image, the mask hides the transparent areas. The mask is invisible to the end user.
Transparent	Transparent means you can "see through" pixels to images or layers below. In Photoshop CS and ImageReady CS, transparent areas are defined by a checkerboard background. When you add graphics to a transparent layer in Photoshop CS or ImageReady CS, the program automatically creates an invisible mask called a transparency channel. The transparency channel, or mask, hides and shows transparent areas in an image.
Transparent GIF	Transparent GIFs include an invisible mask that hides and shows transparent areas of the image in a Web browser. As a result, you can create images that have the illusion of being a shape other than a rectangle or a square.

Understanding Offset Problems in Browsers

You might be wondering, why fuss with this transparency stuff? Couldn't you just incorporate the background image into the foreground image and position it over the same background layer? If you're designing a Web site with a flat, single-color background, it is possible to use that technique. Unfortunately, if your background image is made from a pattern or a photograph, your foreground image will not line up correctly with the background image. Due to constraints of HTML, foreground and background images don't line up in browsers, and as a result, you end up with unwanted offset, as shown in the following illustration.

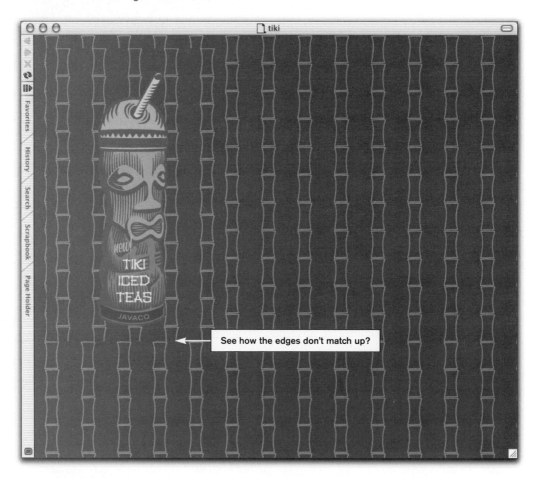

You can't forgo making a foreground GIF transparent, because if you just place the foreground and background images together, they don't necessarily line up in browsers. Note the offset in this image.

I. [IR] _____ Creating and Previewing GIF Transparency

In this exercise, you'll learn how to create transparent GIFs and how to preview the results in a Web browser. You can create transparent GIF files in both Photoshop CS and ImageReady CS. I've chosen to show this process in ImageReady CS because it's easier to define background and foreground images and preview the results in a Web browser than in Photoshop CS. In Exercise 7, you'll learn how to achieve the same result in Photoshop CS.

1. In ImageReady CS, open **tiki.psd** from the **chap_09** folder you copied to your **Desktop** from the **H•O•T CD-ROM**. Click the **Optimized** tab.

2. Make sure the **Optimize** and **Color Table** palettes are visible, as shown here. If not, choose **Window > Optimize** and/or **Window > Color Table**. In the **Optimize** palette, adjust the settings to match the illustration here. Make sure you turn on the **Transparency** option—this option defines your image as transparent when you save it as a GIF.

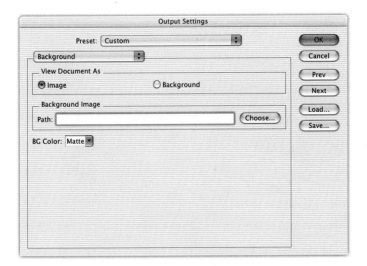

3. Choose **File > Output Settings > Background**. In the **Output Settings** dialog box, choose **Custom** from the **Preset** pop-up menu and select **Image** in the **View Document As** section.

This tells ImageReady CS you want to preview the image as a foreground image, not a background.

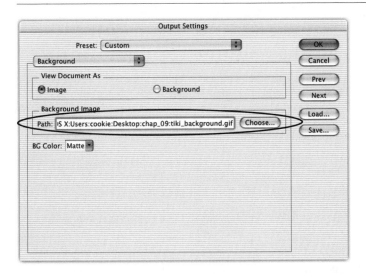

4. Click the **Choose** button in the **Output Settings** dialog box. Navigate to the **chap_09** folder you copied to your **Desktop**. Choose **tiki_background.gif** and click **Open**. The path to the background image should appear in the **Background Image** section of the **Output Settings** dialog box. Click **OK**.

*This process tells ImageReady CS you want **tiki_background.gif** to appear as the background image behind the transparent **tiki.psd** foreground image.*

5. Click the **Preview in Default Browser** button in the **Toolbox.**

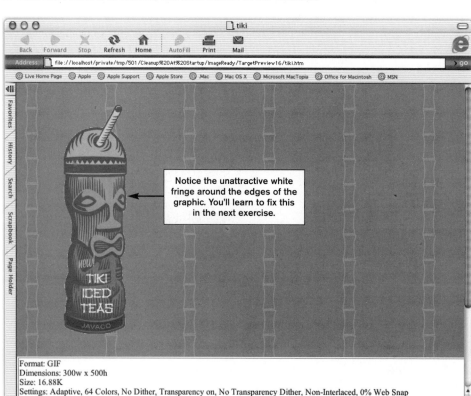

*Your default Web browser will open automatically and you'll see the transparent **tiki.psd** image on top of the **tiki_background.gif** image.*

*You can see the transparency settings are working, but notice the white fringe around the edges of the **tiki.psd** image. In the next exercise, you'll learn to eliminate that white fringe.*

*Tip: The white HTML text box always appears when you're previewing images. If you want to see the Web page without the white HTML text box, choose **File > Save Optimized As**. In the **Save Optimized As** dialog box, choose **HTML and Images** from the **Format** pop-up menu, specify a file name, and choose the location where you want to save the file. Click **Save**. Browse to where you saved the file and double-click to open it in your default Web browser. For more information about saving background images, refer to Chapter 8, "Background Images."*

6. Return to ImageReady CS and leave the file open for the next exercise.

2. [IR] _____Fixing the Edges of Transparent GIFs

In the last exercise, you learned to create a transparent GIF using the transparency controls in the Optimize palette. When you previewed the image over a patterned background, a white fringe or halo appeared around the outside edges of the image. In this exercise, you'll learn how to eliminate the unwanted halo so the edges around the image look crisp and clean.

1. If you followed the last exercise, **tiki.psd** should still be open in ImageReady CS. Open **tiki_background.gif** in the **chap_09** folder you copied to your **Desktop**.

_You should now have two images open in ImageReady CS: **tiki.psd** and **tiki_background.gif**._

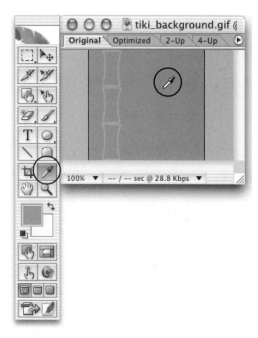

2. Select the **Eyedropper** tool from the **Toolbox**. Click the **green** background in **tiki_background.gif** to sample color and to change the **Foreground Color** swatch in the **Toolbox**.

Now that you've sampled the color, you'll specify it as the matte color for your transparent GIF, which will eliminate the white fringe around the edges.

3. Switch to the **tiki.psd** image. If it's hidden behind other windows on your screen, choose **Window > Documents > tiki.psd**. Click the **Optimized** tab.

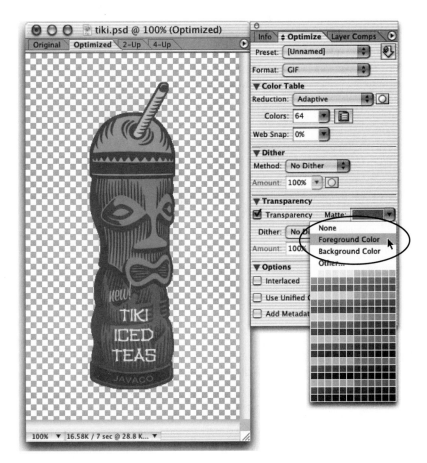

4. Choose **Foreground Color** from the **Matte** pop-up menu in the **Transparency** section of the **Optimize** palette, as shown in the illustration here.

*The color you selected from the background image should now appear in the **Matte** field of the **Transparency** section of the **Optimize** palette.*

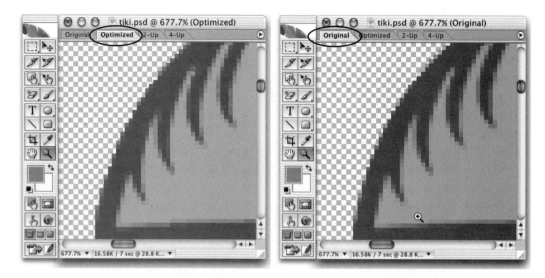

5. Choose the **Zoom** tool from the **Toolbox**. Zoom in on the edges of the **tiki.psd** file and look closely at the edges. You should see the green under the anti-aliased edge of the graphic. Toggle between the **Optimized** tab and the **Original** tab to see the change you made.

Notice in the original image, the edges are white, and in the optimized image, the edges are green. This will help blend the image into the background, and it will eliminate the white fringe.

6. When you're finished observing the changes, double-click the **Zoom** tool in the **Toolbox** to reset the zoom level to **100%**.

7. Click the **Preview in Default Browser** button in the **Toolbox**.

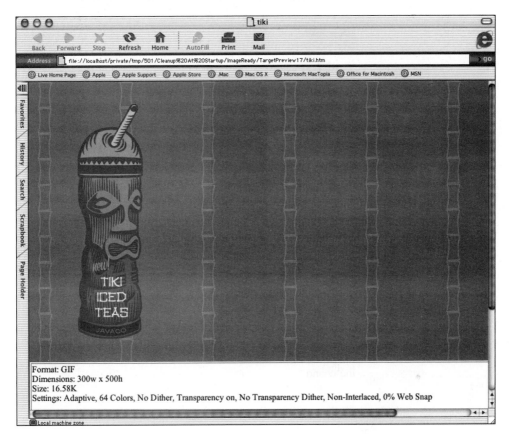

The background image is still set from the last exercise. In the Web browser, you'll see the **tiki.psd** *image as the foreground and* **tiki_background.gif** *as the background. Unlike the last exercise, you won't see a distracting white halo around the edges of the* **tiki.psd** *image. Instead,* **tiki.psd** *has a green matte around the edge that blends in with the background. With a fine-toothed background pattern like this, even though the background is busy, the matte color produces a crisp, clean edge.*

8. Return to ImageReady CS. Leave **tiki.psd** open for the next exercise. Close **tiki_background.gif**.

MOVIE | setting_mattecolor.mov

To learn more about setting matte color, check out **setting_mattecolor.mov** inside the **movies** folder on the **H•O•T CD-ROM**.

3. [IR]   Adding a Drop Shadow to Transparent GIFs

Changing the matte color to match the color in the background image eliminated the white fringe on a simple, anti-aliased foreground image. What if the edge of your foreground image contains a very soft edge, such as a drop shadow or a glow? As you'll see in this exercise, the matching technique you just learned can camouflage even a soft drop shadow or glow, as long as you place it over a certain kind of background image—one that has a fine-toothed pattern (as opposed to a pattern with big bold elements).

1. With **tiki.psd** still open in ImageReady CS from the last exercise, click the **Original** tab.

*Tip: It's important to switch back to the **Original** tab. Otherwise, ImageReady CS tries to optimize the graphic as you're editing, which makes the editing process unnecessarily slow. Also, when the **Original** tab is active, it's possible to perform editing tasks such as using brush, shape, and type tools, which are not available when the **Optimized** tab is active.*

2. In the **Layers** palette, choose **Drop Shadow** from the **Layer Styles** pop-up menu. Click **OK** in the **Layer Styles** dialog box. You don't need to make any changes to the default drop shadow settings.

*You'll see a slight, black drop shadow around the edges of the **tiki.psd** image.*

3. Click the **Optimized** tab. You'll see a green border around the image, which is a result of the matte color you applied in the last exercise.

Notice you can still see the edges of the drop shadow clearly against the matte. Although the image looks strange with the green matte, it will look just fine against the background image in a Web browser, which you'll get to preview in the next step.

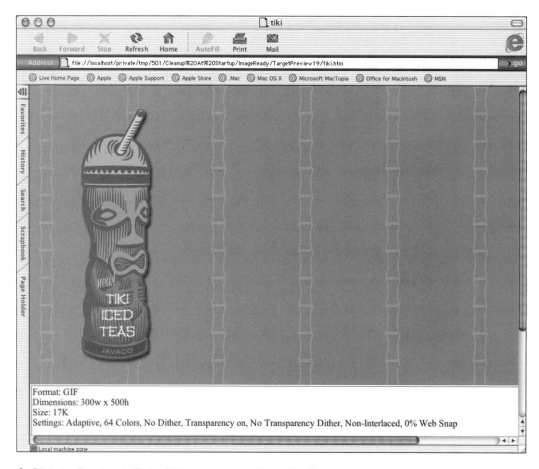

4. Click the **Preview in Default Browser** button in the **Toolbox**.

Notice the integrity of the black drop shadow is still intact. If you look closely, you can see small areas of the green matte. Regardless, it sure beats having unwanted colored edges around the entire image, and it maintains the soft edges of the drop shadow.

5. Return to ImageReady CS. Leave the file open for the next exercise.

4. [IR] _____Working with Transparent GIFs on Broad Backgrounds

Applying a matte color that matches the background image worked in the last two exercises because the background image had a very simple, fine-toothed pattern with little color variation. As a result, you were able to apply a matte color to the edges of the image to hide the white halo caused by anti-aliased images, and you were able to maintain the integrity of the drop shadow against the background. Unfortunately, matching the matte color to the background will not work if you have a broadly patterned background that uses several colors. This exercise will show you a workaround to use when creating transparent GIFs for broadly patterned backgrounds.

1. With **tiki.psd** open from the last exercise, choose **File > Output Settings > Background**. Choose **Custom** from the **Preset** pop-up menu and select **Image** in the **View Document As** section of the **Output Settings** dialog box. Click the **Choose** button and browse to the **chap_09** folder you copied to your **Desktop**. Choose **tiki_broad_background.gif** and click **Open**. Click **OK** in the **Output Settings** dialog box.

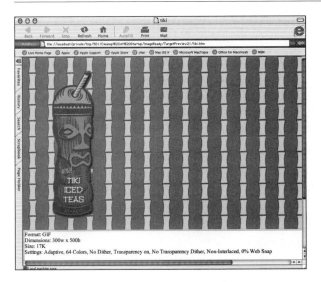

2. Click the **Preview in Default Browser** button in the **Toolbox**. The result is not pretty!

Unfortunately, matching the matte to the background image will not work in this case because the pattern in the background image is too broad and the color changes are too extreme. In this case, you can see the green matte in the yellow areas of the background. If you change the matte color to yellow, the yellow will stand out against the green areas of the background. In a case like this, the best solution is to remove the matte, the soft edges created by the drop shadow layer style, and the anti-aliasing of the graphic. You'll end up with a hard-edged, aliased, nonmatted image, which you'll create in the next few steps.

3. Return to ImageReady CS. Click the **Original** tab. In the **Layers** palette, turn off the visibility of the **Drop Shadow** layer style you created in the last exercise.

4. Choose **None** from the **Matte** pop-up menu in the **Transparency** section of the **Optimize** palette.

*This will remove all the anti-aliasing from the outside edges of the image. The great thing about using the **Matte: None** feature is that it removes anti-aliasing from the outer edges of the graphic but keeps any anti-aliasing that exists in the interior of the image (such as the anti-aliasing around the blue section).*

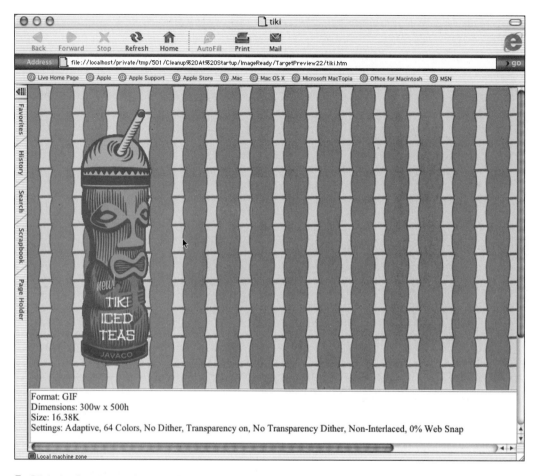

Format: GIF
Dimensions: 300w x 500h
Size: 16.38K
Settings: Adaptive, 64 Colors, No Dither, Transparency on, No Transparency Dither, Non-Interlaced, 0% Web Snap

5. Click the **Preview in Default Browser** button in the **Toolbox**.

Notice the green matte and the anti-aliasing have been removed, which means there is no white fringe around the edges of the image.

6. Return to ImageReady CS. Keep **tiki.psd** open. You'll need it for **Exercise 6**.

5. [IR] _____Diffusion Transparency Dither

In the last exercise, you set the matte color to None to remove anti-aliasing from the image, which eliminated the white fringe on a broad background. You're probably wondering what to do if you want to use a drop shadow or a glow with a broad background. You could apply **Diffusion Transparency Dither**, which you'll learn about in this exercise. This odd-sounding term is useful when working with broad backgrounds and glows because it helps maintain the look of the drop shadow or glow while working within the limitations of 1-bit GIF transparency. Not everyone likes the effect Diffusion Transparency Dither creates, but it's worth learning about so you know all the options available when creating transparent GIFs.

1. Open **tikiglow.psd** from the **chap_09** folder you copied to your **Desktop**.

Notice the glow around the edges? ***Diffusion Transparency Dither*** *works only with images that contain a soft edge.*

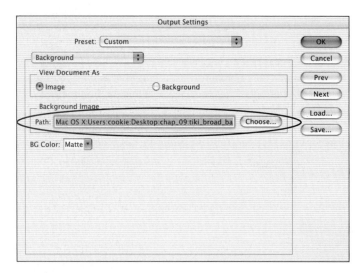

2. Choose **File > Output Settings > Background**. Choose **Custom** from the **Preset** pop-up menu and select **Image** in the **View Document As** section of the **Output Settings** dialog box. Click the **Choose** button and browse to the **chap_09** folder you copied to your **Desktop**. Choose **tiki_broad_background.gif** and click **Open**. Click **OK** in the **Output Settings** dialog box.

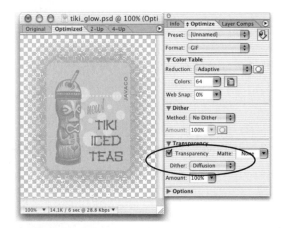

3. Click the **Optimized** tab. Match the settings in the **Optimize** palette to the settings shown in the illustration here. Make sure the **Transparency** option is turned on. Choose **Diffusion** from the **Dither** pop-up menu in the **Transparency** section of the **Optimize** palette.

Notice the glow around the image looks very pixilated. Some designers like this effect, and some designers don't. The best way to decide if you like it is to preview the image with the background in a Web browser.

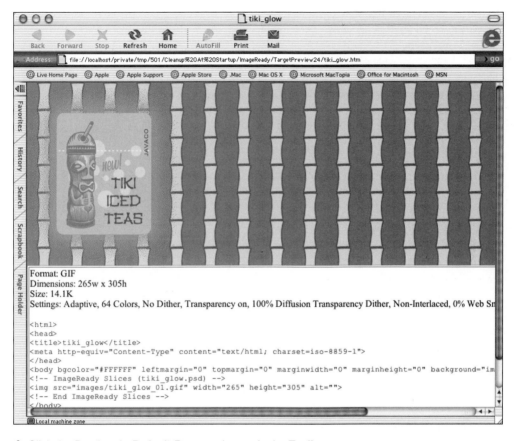

4. Click the **Preview in Default Browser** button in the **Toolbox**.

Although you can see the background through the transparent areas of the image, the glow appears very pixilated. Because GIF transparency is on or off, it can't produce smooth transitions like the transitions you can create in Photoshop CS or ImageReady CS. This is a limitation of the GIF file format, not a limitation of ImageReady CS or Photoshop CS. The best way maintain the integrity of drop shadows or glows is to use a simple, fine-toothed background and apply a matte color that matches the background.

It's important to keep this limitation in mind when you're designing Web pages. If you really want the look of drop shadows on your foreground images, make sure you design a background that showcases the drop shadow effectively. Likewise, if you really want the look of a broadly patterned background, make sure the foreground images can stand on their own without drop shadows or glows.

5. Return to ImageReady CS. Close the file without saving your changes.

NOTE | What Does Dither Mean?

At this point you've probably noticed a few references to the term "dither" in the Photoshop CS and ImageReady CS interface. Dither reduces smooth color transitions so they can be represented by fewer colors. Unfortunately, it always results in the appearance of dots or individual pixels.

On the Optimize palette in ImageReady CS, there are two different locations for dither settings.

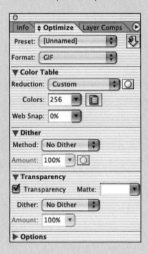

The **Dither Method** in the **Dither** section of the **Optimize** palette sets dithering to the picture itself. The **Dither Method** in the **Transparency** section of the **Optimize** palette sets dithering to the edge of the picture.

In both cases, you can choose one of three options from the pop-up menu: **Diffusion**, **Noise**, or **Pattern**. **Diffusion** matches dots to the contents of the image. For example, the dots in a glow or drop shadow will gradually taper off when set to **Diffusion**. **Noise** creates a random texture of dots. **Pattern** creates an obvious patterned series of dots. Feel free to experiment with these different options. Most designers prefer to use the **Diffusion** setting because it produces the most natural-looking results.

6. [IR] _____Saving Transparent Images in ImageReady CS

In the last few exercises, you learned how to create and troubleshoot transparent GIFs for different backgrounds. Next you'll learn how to save a transparent GIF with its corresponding background image using the **Save Optimized As** feature in ImageReady CS. In Exercise 7, you'll learn how to save transparent GIFs from Photoshop CS.

1. You should have **tiki.psd** open from **Exercise 5**. Click the **tiki.psd** file to make it the active image. If it's hidden behind other windows on your screen, choose **Window > Documents > tiki.psd**.

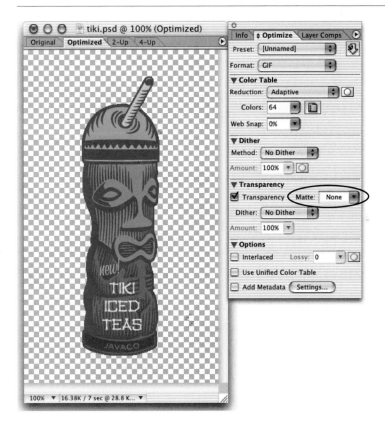

2. Click the **Optimized** tab. Match the settings in the **Optimize** palette to the illustration shown here. For this exercise, assume the image is going to appear against a broad background and choose **None** from the **Matte** pop-up menu.

3. Choose **File > Save Optimized As**. The **Save Optimized As** dialog box opens automatically.

*Notice ImageReady CS automatically keeps the file name the same and changes the file extension to the appropriate format (the file extension is dependent upon the option you choose from the **Format** pop-up menu).*

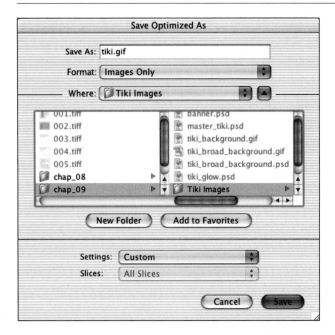

4. In the **Save Optimized As** dialog box, choose **Images Only** from the **Format** pop-up menu (Mac) or the **Save as type** pop-up menu (Windows). Navigate to the **chap_09** folder on your **Desktop**. Click the **New Folder** button and create a new folder called **Tiki Images**. Click **Create**. In the **Save Optimized As** dialog box, make sure the **Tiki Images** folder is selected. Click **Save**.

*Note: Choosing **Images Only** saves the foreground and background images. If you want to save the required HTML code as well as the images, choose **HTML and Images** from the **Format** pop-up menu. Choosing to save the HTML depends on whether you want to build your Web page using ImageReady CS or whether you prefer to build pages using an HTML editor such as Adobe GoLive or Macromedia Dreamweaver.*

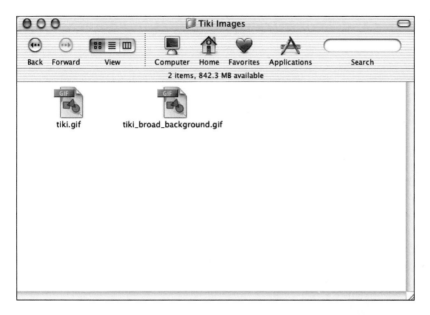

5. Browse to the **Tiki Images** folder in the **chap_09** folder on your **Desktop**.

*In the **Tiki Images** folder, you'll notice both the foreground image (**tiki.gif**) and the background image (**tiki_broad_background.gif**) saved automatically. One of the benefits of using the **Save Optimized As** command in ImageReady CS is the capability to save both foreground and background images at the same time.*

6. Close the **tiki.psd** file. You don't need to save the changes.

7. [PS] Creating and Saving Transparent GIFs in Photoshop CS

In this chapter, you've learned to create, troubleshoot, and save transparent GIFs in ImageReady CS. There are going to be times when you'll want to create transparent GIFs in Photoshop CS instead of ImageReady CS. In this exercise, you'll learn to set a matte color (to avoid the white fringe around transparent images) and create and save transparent GIFs in Photoshop CS.

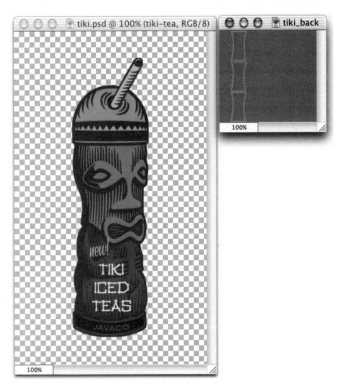

1. In Photoshop CS, open **tiki.psd** and **tiki_background.gif** from the **chap_09** folder you copied to your **Desktop**.

2. Click **tiki_background.gif** to make it the active image. Choose **File > Save For Web**.

*First, you'll sample color from **tiki_background.gif** so you can specify it as the matte color for **tiki.psd**.*

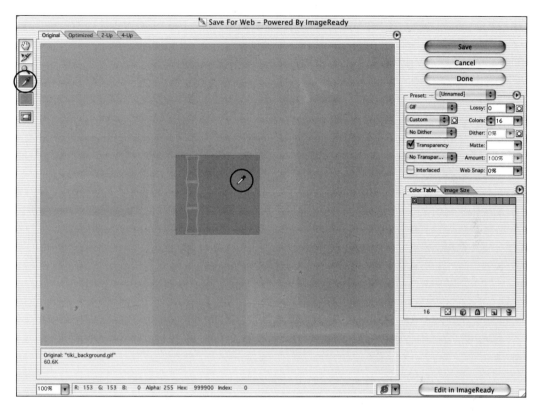

3. Select the **Eyedropper** tool in the **Save For Web** window. Click the **green** background of **tiki_background.gif** to sample color. Click **Cancel**.

The purpose of this step was to sample color from the background image.

*Note: Unlike in ImageReady CS, you must sample color in the **Save For Web** interface, not in the main Photoshop CS interface. This is one of the reasons I prefer to create transparent GIFs in ImageReady CS rather than Photoshop CS.*

---

4. Click **tiki.psd** to make it the active image. If it's hidden behind other windows on your screen, choose **Window > Documents > tiki.psd**.

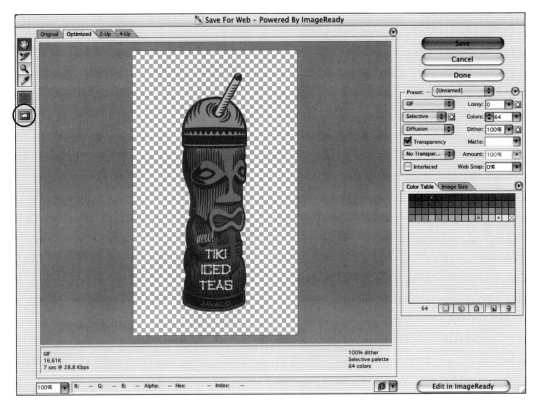

5. Choose **File > Save For Web**.

*Notice the green you sampled in **Step 3** is still in the color well?*

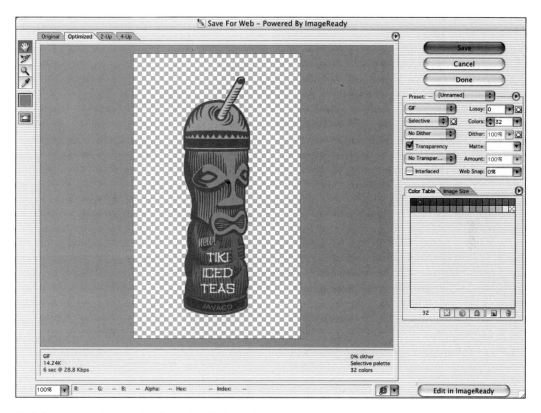

6. Adjust the settings in the **Save For Web** window to match the settings shown in the illustration here: **GIF**, **Selective**, **No Dither**, **Colors: 32**.

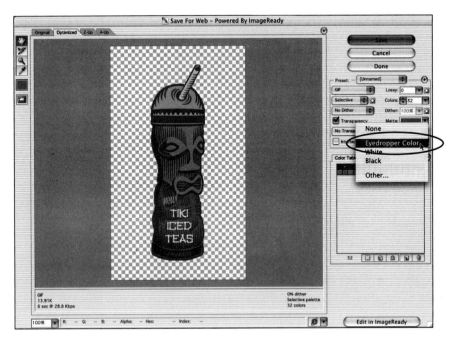

7. Choose **Eyedropper Color** from the **Matte** pop-up menu.

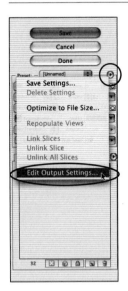

8. In the **Save For Web** window, choose **Edit Output Settings** in the **Optimize** menu.

*The **Output Settings** dialog box will open automatically.*

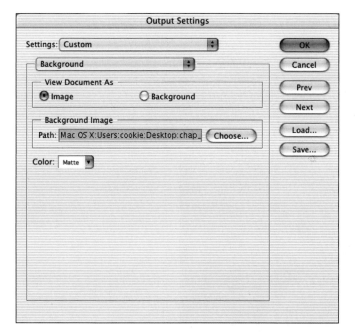

9. In the **Output Settings** dialog box, choose **Custom** from the **Settings** pop-up menu. Choose **Background** in the pop-up menu below the **Settings** pop-up menu.

*When you choose **Background**, the contents of the **Output Settings** dialog box change, and it appears identical to the **Output Settings** dialog box you used in ImageReady CS.*

10. Select **Image** in the **View Document As** section of the **Output Settings** dialog box. Click the **Choose** button. Navigate to the **chap_09** folder you copied to your **Desktop** and choose **tiki_broad_background.gif**. Click **Open**. Choose **Matte** in the **Color** pop-up menu. Click **OK**.

*Specifying **tiki_broad_background.gif** in the **Path** field tells Photoshop CS you want the **tiki.psd** image to be viewed in the foreground over top of the **tiki_broad_background.gif** image.*

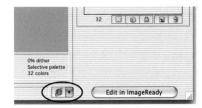

11. In the **Save For Web** window, choose a Web browser from the **Select Browser** pop-up menu.

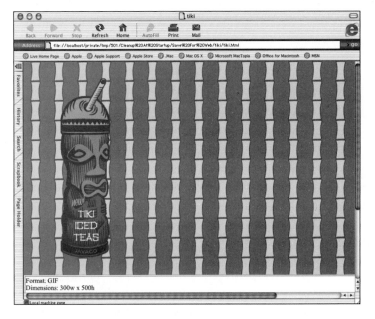

In the Web browser, you'll see the transparent GIF on top of the background image you specified in the last step.

12. Return to the **Save For Web** dialog box. Click **Save**.

*The **Save Optimized As** dialog box opens automatically.*

13. In the **Save Optimized As** dialog box, choose **HTML and Images** from the **Format** pop-up menu (Mac) or the **Save as type** pop-up menu (Windows). Change the **Save As** field to **tiki2.html**. Navigate to the **chap_09** folder you copied to your **Desktop** and click **Save**.

*If you'd rather create the HTML code in an HTML editor, choose **Images Only** from the **Format** pop-up menu and change the **Save As** field to **tiki2.gif**.*

14. Close the file. You don't need to save your changes to the Photoshop CS file.

8. [PS]   Creating Transparent GIFs from Non-Transparent Images

Throughout this chapter, you've worked with **tiki.psd**, which was created in Photoshop CS using transparent layers. Because the image contained transparent layers, it was easy to create and save it as a transparent GIF. But what if you're working with an image that doesn't have transparent layers, and you want to create a transparent GIF? How would you define which areas of the image you want to be transparent? In this exercise, you'll learn to use the **Map Transparency** option in Photoshop CS to help you define transparent areas. Unfortunately, this technique is only available in Photoshop CS.

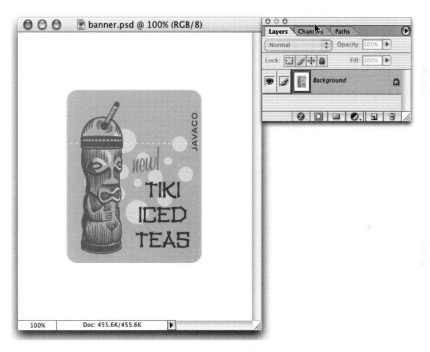

1. In Photoshop CS, open **banner.psd** from the **chap_09** folder you copied to your **Desktop**.

Notice there are no transparent areas in the image (indicated by a checkerboard pattern).

2. Choose **File > Save For Web**. Choose **GIF** from the **File Format** pop-up menu. Turn the **Transparency** option on and off and watch the results in the preview section of the **Save For Web** window.

Notice that nothing happens. Because this file does not have transparent layers, Photoshop CS doesn't know which part of the image should be transparent in the optimized GIF. In order to create transparent GIFs, your images must contain transparent layers. In the next few steps, you'll learn how to instruct Photoshop CS to convert regular pixels to transparent pixels.

3. Match the settings in the **Save For Web** window to the settings shown in the illustration here: **GIF**, **Selective**, **Colors: 16**, **No Dither**.

Next, you'll tell Photoshop CS which areas you want to appear transparent.

4. Turn on the **Transparency** option. Select the **Eyedropper** tool in the **Save For Web** window and click the **white** background.

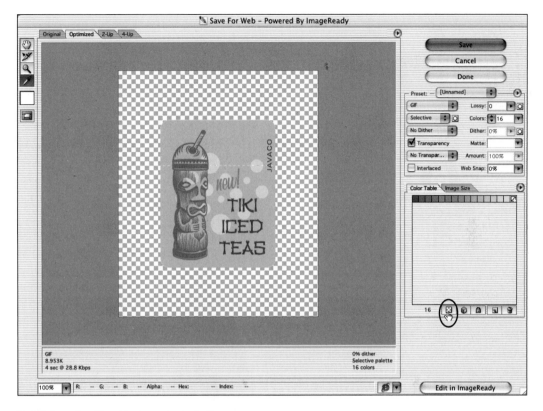

5. Click on the **Map Transparency** button.

*Notice the areas that were previously white are now a checkerboard pattern, which indicates transparency. Photoshop CS converts the color you selected with the **Eyedropper** tool to transparent pixels.*

This feature is very useful when you must work with an image that doesn't have a transparent layer. Unfortunately, the feature is only available in Photoshop CS.

---

6. Click **Done** in the **Save For Web** window and save the optimized file. Close the Photoshop CS file without saving it.

You've finished another complex chapter! Now you're ready to create transparent GIFs against a variety of backgrounds in ImageReady CS or Photoshop CS!

10.

Slicing

| Creating User and Layer-Based Slices |
Editing Slices	Renaming, Optimizing, and Saving Slices
Applying Alt Text to Slices	Assigning URLs to Slices
Using Slices Sets	Working with Slices and Layer Comps

chap_10

Photoshop CS/ImageReady CS
H•O•T CD-ROM

Slicing allows you to cut a single image into multiple images so they can be reassembled in an HTML table. Wondering why you would ever do that? There are two reasons: first, you can optimize different parts of an image with different compression settings and file formats in order to reduce the file size; second, you can use slices to create rollovers. In this chapter, you'll learn slicing basics. In Chapter 11, "*Rollovers*," you'll apply your knowledge of slicing to create rollovers.

At first glance, slicing looks very simple, but it can be deceptively complex. Although it's easy to cut images into slices, managing the resulting images takes practice and an understanding of HTML. In this chapter, you'll learn about different types of slicing, how to create and edit slices, how to optimize and save slices (including the required HTML code) and how to work with the new slice sets feature in ImageReady CS.

About Slices

Slices let you divide a single large image into a number of smaller images. The smaller images are then reassembled using an HTML table to look like the original image. When you slice an image, you can apply different optimization settings to each slice, which decreases download time and maintains the highest quality. Here is an example:

The **coming_soon.psd** image can be sliced effectively into four sections: the top green section, the javaco section, the photographic section, and the bottom green section. Because the top and bottom slices are made up of single colors, you can optimize these slices as GIFs and set the Color Table to 2, colors which will make downloading faster. You can optimize the javaco section as a GIF but increase the color table to 8 colors. You can optimize the photograph as a JPEG (even though the other three slices are GIFs) because it will optimize better as a JPEG than as a GIF. The result will be higher quality optimization and faster download time.

When you slice and save images in Photoshop CS or ImageReady CS, the program creates one image for each slice along with the required HTML table code to reassemble the images in their exact formations. The HTML table code allows Web browsers to assemble the images seamlessly and consistently so they look like a single image.

In the following exercises, you'll learn how to use the slicing tools and options in ImageReady CS. You can slice images in Photoshop CS, but I find it easier to slice images in ImageReady CS because it has a number of slicing features unavailable in Photoshop CS. Plus, it's easier to access the slicing options in the Toolbox, Web Content palette, and Slice palette in ImageReady CS rather than the Save For Web window in Photoshop CS. For these reasons, you'll use ImageReady CS for all the exercises in this chapter.

About Slice Types

Before you begin creating slices, it's important to understand the four different types of slices, which are represented by four different icons that appear when you slice a document. Here is a chart to explain them:

Slice Types	
User slice	You can create user slices with the Slice tool or from guides or selections. User slices are the most flexible because they offer the following editing capabilities: move, duplicate, combine, divide, resize, delete, arrange, align, and distribute. You can also apply different optimization settings to user slices in the same image.
Layer-based slice	You can create layer-based slices from the contents of a specific layer. If you move or edit the contents of a layer, the layer-based slice will update automatically to reflect the changes. Layer-based slices offer limited editing capabilities. To achieve the flexibility of user slices, you can promote layer-based slices to user slices.
Auto slice	Photoshop CS and ImageReady CS create auto slices automatically when you create or edit user slices or layer-based slices. If you define a single slice in an image, a series of auto slices will automatically be generated to fill up the remainder of the image. If you add to or edit the user or layer-based slices, the auto slices will automatically update. Auto slices offer no editing capabilities. To achieve the flexibility of user slices, you can promote auto slices to user slices.
Sub slice	Sub slices are a form of auto slices that appear automatically when you create three or more overlapping slices. Sub slices are regenerated automatically each time you create, edit, or modify slices in an image. Sub slices offer no editing capabilities. To achieve the flexibility of user slices, you can promote sub slices to user slices.

About Slice Lines, Slice Numbers, Slice Symbols, and Slice Colors

In addition to understanding the slice types in Photoshop CS and ImageReady CS, it's helpful to understand the visual components that identify slices. Each slice you create will have four key visual components: a series of slice lines, a slice number, a slice symbol, and a slice color. Here is a chart to help you understand:

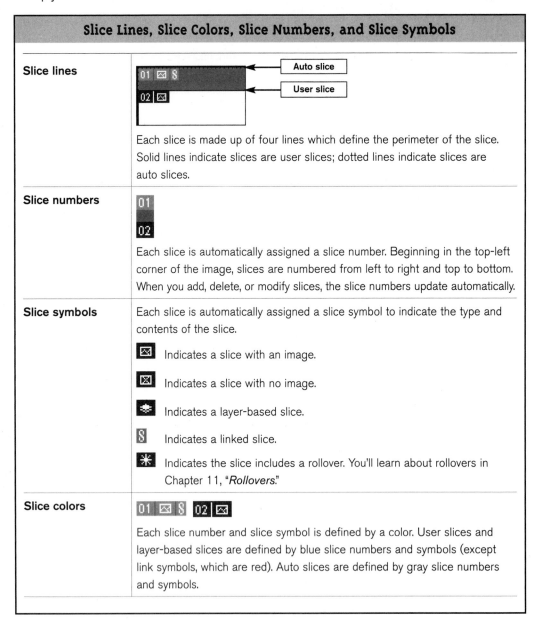

Slice Lines, Slice Colors, Slice Numbers, and Slice Symbols	
Slice lines	Each slice is made up of four lines which define the perimeter of the slice. Solid lines indicate slices are user slices; dotted lines indicate slices are auto slices.
Slice numbers	Each slice is automatically assigned a slice number. Beginning in the top-left corner of the image, slices are numbered from left to right and top to bottom. When you add, delete, or modify slices, the slice numbers update automatically.
Slice symbols	Each slice is automatically assigned a slice symbol to indicate the type and contents of the slice. Indicates a slice with an image. Indicates a slice with no image. Indicates a layer-based slice. Indicates a linked slice. Indicates the slice includes a rollover. You'll learn about rollovers in Chapter 11, "*Rollovers.*"
Slice colors	Each slice number and slice symbol is defined by a color. User slices and layer-based slices are defined by blue slice numbers and symbols (except link symbols, which are red). Auto slices are defined by gray slice numbers and symbols.

About the Web Content and Slice Palettes

When you're working with slices in ImageReady CS, you'll need to access the Web Content and Slice palettes. Here is an overview of the palettes and their roles in the slicing process.

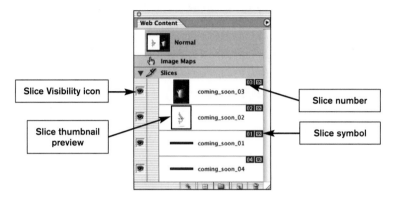

The Web Content palette lets you preview user slices in an image. Similar to the Layers palette, the Web content palette displays a thumbnail preview of the slice, the slice name, and lets you turn on and off the visibility of a slice. The Web Content palette also displays the slice number, slice symbol, and information about rollovers and image maps (which you'll learn about in later chapters).

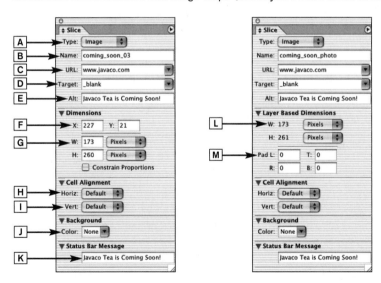

The Slice palette lets you specify slice options, which control how slices and slice data appear in a Web browser. The Slice palette is context-sensitive and changes depending on the currently selected slice. The Slice palette is divided into sections: Slice, Dimensions (for user slices), Layer Based Dimensions (for layer-based slices) Cell Alignment, Background, and Status Bar Message. Here's a handy chart to help you understand the controls in the Slice palette.

	Slice Palette Controls	
A	**Type pop-up menu**	Choose one of the following slice content types for the currently selected slice: **image**, **no image**, or **table**.
B	**Name field**	Specify a name for the currently selected slice.
C	**URL field pop-up menu**	Specify a URL you want the currently selected slice to link to.
D	**Target field pop-up menu**	Choose one of the following target types when you specify a URL for the slice: **_blank**, **_self**, **_parent**, or **_top**.
E	**Alt field**	Specify the text you want viewers to see when images are turned off in a Web browser.
F	**X and Y Coordinates**	Specify the left edge (X) and top edge (Y) of a slice.
G	**Width and Height fields**	Specify the width and height of a slice in either pixels or percents.
H	**Horizontal Cell Alignment pop-up menu**	Choose one of the following options: **Left**, **Right**, **Center**, or **Default**.
I	**Vertical Cell Alignment pop-up menu**	Choose one of the following options: **Top**, **Baseline**, **Middle**, **Bottom**, or **Default**.
J	**Background Color pop-up menu**	Choose a background color for transparent sections of the slice.
K	**Status Bar Message field**	Specify the message you want to appear in the status bar of the Web browser when you position your mouse over a slice.
L	**Layer Width and Height pop-up menus** (available for layer-based slices only)	View or edit size information for the currently selected layer-based slice.
M	**Slice Outset fields** (available for layer-based slices only)	Specify the slice size for layer-based slices. For example, if your layer-based slice is 100 × 100 pixels, and you want the slice to be 10 pixels larger than the layer, you can specify 5 pixels in the **Left**, **Right**, **Top**, and **Bottom** fields, and the slice will increase to 110 × 110 pixels.

I. [IR] _____Creating User Slices

In this exercise, you'll learn how to use the Slice tool to create user slices, how to identify auto slices, and how to promote auto slices to user slices. You'll also learn how to resize, delete, and turn on and off the visibility of slices.

1. In **ImageReady CS**, open **coming_soon.psd** from the **chap_10** folder you copied to your **Desktop** from the **H•O•T CD-ROM**. Make sure the **Web Content** palette is visible. If it's not, choose **Window > Web Content** to make it visible.

*The **Web Content** palette makes it easier to see the slices you create.*

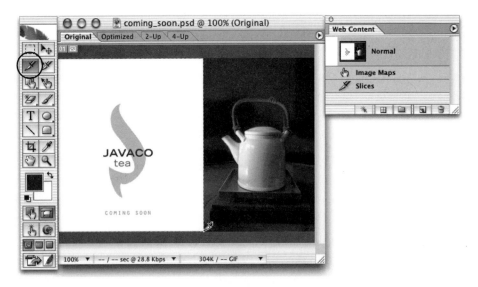

2. Select the **Slice** tool from the **Toolbox**. Click and drag to select the **white** section of the image.

Take a look at the document window. Notice the user slice you created has a blue icon. Notice three other slices with gray icons were created automatically. The slice you created is called a user slice because you (the user) defined it. The other slices are called auto slices. ImageReady CS automatically creates auto slices for the undefined areas so the entire image is divided into slices.

*In the document window, notice each slice has a number. Are you wondering why the first slice you created is labeled **Slice 02**? ImageReady CS keeps track of all slices, including user, layer-based, auto, and sub slices by assigning a number to each slice. Slices are numbered from left to right and top to bottom starting in the top-left corner.*

*Take a look at the **Web Content** palette. Notice only one slice appears in the **Web Content** palette, even though there are four slices in the image that are visible in the document window? The **Web Content** palette shows only user slices and layer-based slices. In this example, there is only one slice in the **Web Content** palette—the user slice you just created with the **Slice** tool. The **Web Content** palette is where you set rollovers and animation options to user slices and layer-based slices, which you'll learn about in future chapters.*

NOTE | Resizing User Slices

If you create a slice with the Slice tool, you can resize the slice easily. Here's how:

With the **Slice** tool selected in the **Toolbox**, position your mouse over one of the nodes on the perimeter of the slice. You'll notice the cursor change from the **Slice** tool icon to the resize icon. When the cursor changes to the resize icon, click and drag to resize the slice.

You can only resize user slices. You cannot resize auto slices, layer-based slices, or sub slices.

3. With the **Slice** tool selected in the **Toolbox**, click and drag over the **teapot** section of the image.

You should now have two user slices and two auto slices.

*Next, you'll learn to promote the auto slices to user slices. Because user slices offer more flexibility, you'll often want all slices in an image to be user slices. Converting auto slices to user slices is a quick and easy way to create user slices because it saves you manually selecting areas of the image with the **Slice** tool.*

NOTE | Deleting Slices

When you create a user slice or a layer-based slice, you can delete it easily. Here's how:

Select the **Slice Select** tool in the **Toolbox**. Click to select the slice you want to delete. Press the **Delete** (Mac) or **Backspace** (Windows) key or choose **Slices > Delete Slices**. The slice will disappear. Sometimes, an auto slice will take its place, depending on how the image is sliced. If you deleted the slice, choose **Edit > Undo** so you're ready for the next step in the exercise.

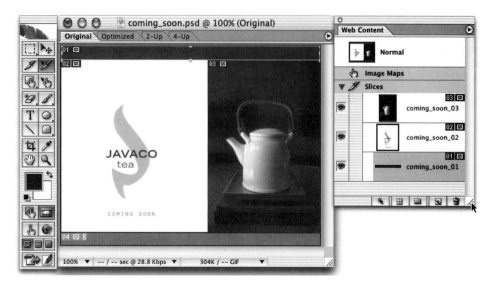

4. With the **Slice Select** tool selected in the **Toolbox**, click anywhere inside the **Slice 01** auto slice to select it. Choose **Slices > Promote to User Slice**.

*Notice the gray slice number and slice symbols are now blue, indicating **Slice 01** is now a user slice.*

5. With the **Slice Select** tool selected in the **Toolbox**, click anywhere inside the **Slice 04** auto slice to select it. Choose **Slices > Promote to User Slice**.

*There should now be four user slices in the **coming_soon.psd** image. Take a look at the **Web Content** palette to see how the slice names, symbols, and thumbnails are displayed. The slice names are created automatically based on the original file name (**coming_soon.psd**) and the slice number. You can change the name of slices, which you'll learn to do in an upcoming exercise.*

You might be wondering if you can turn off the slices so you can see the image without the interference of slice borders and icons. You'll learn how in the next step.

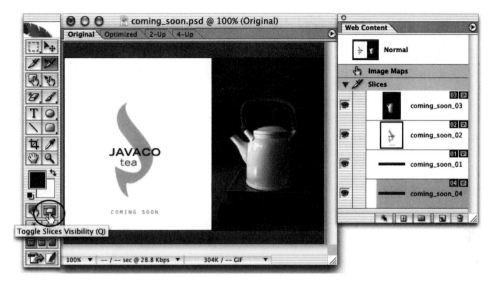

6. Click the **Toggle Slices Visibility** button on the **Toolbox** or press the shortcut key (**Q**).

Now you can see the image without the slice lines, numbers, and symbols.

7. Save and close the file.

NOTE | Slice Preferences

ImageReady CS lets you snap slices to the edges of other slices. You'll find this helps align slices and avoid overlap. Snapping is turned on by default. If it's not turned on, choose **View > Snap To > Slices**.

 MOVIE | slicing.mov

To learn more about slicing images, check out **slicing.mov** from the **movies** folder on the **H•O•T CD-ROM**.

2. [IR] _____Creating Layer-Based Slices

In the last exercise, you learned how to create user slices with the Slice tool and how to promote auto slices to user slices. In this exercise, you'll learn how to create layer-based slices.

Layer-based slices are a great way to slice images containing several layers because they create slices the same size as the layer. As a result, you don't have to resize slices to ensure they exactly match the dimensions of the layer. In addition, if you change the contents of a layer or move a layer, the slice updates automatically. This great feature of layer-based slices will save you time from reslicing images if you need to make changes to your Web graphics. You can also move layer-based slices, which you can't do with user slices. Plus, if you decide you want to promote a layer-based slice to a user slice, you can do so easily.

1. Open **our_stores.psd** from the **chap_10** folder you copied to your **Desktop**.

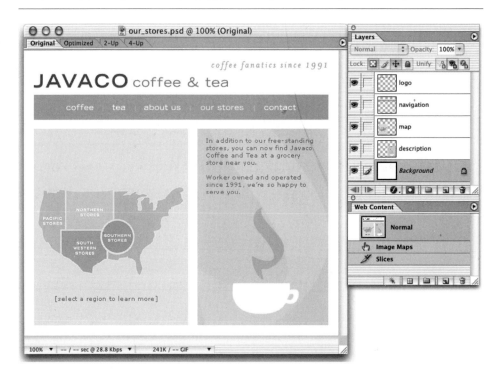

2. Make sure the **Layers** palette and the **Web Content** palette are visible. If they aren't, choose **Window > Layers** and **Window > Web Content**.

Notice the image is made up of four layers, excluding the background. In the next few steps, you'll create layer-based slices from each layer.

3. In the **Layers** palette, click the **description** layer to select it. Choose **Layer > New Layer Based Slice**.

*Notice a layer-based slice is created as well as four auto slices. The slice symbol indicates **Slice 03** is a layer-based slice.*

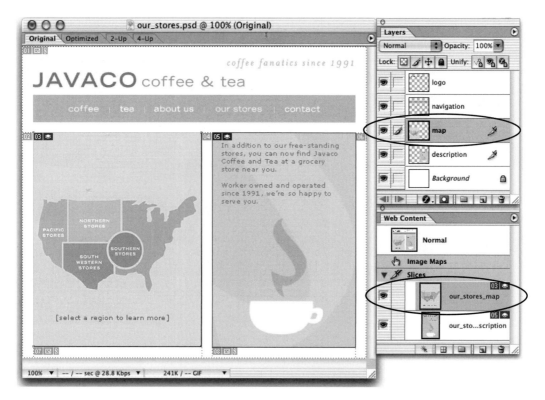

4. Click the **map** layer in the **Layers** palette to select it. Choose **Layer > New Layer Based Slice**.

Notice there are now eight slices in total—two layer-based slices and six auto slices.

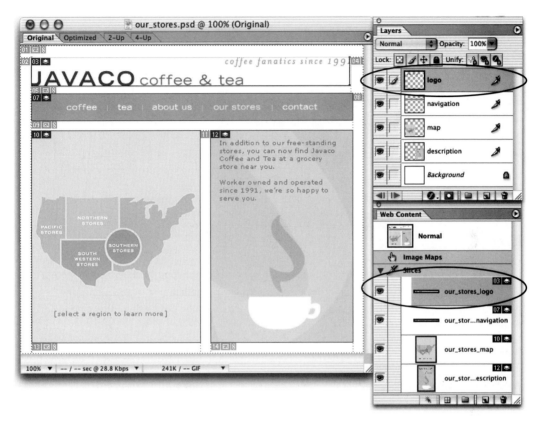

5. Click the **navigation** layer in the **Layers** palette to select it. Choose **Layer > New Layer Based Slice**. Click the **logo** layer in the **Layers** palette to select it. Choose **Layer > New Layer Based Slice**.

There are now a total of 14 slices in the image—four layer-based slices, which you created, and ten auto slices, which were automatically created to slice the rest of the image.

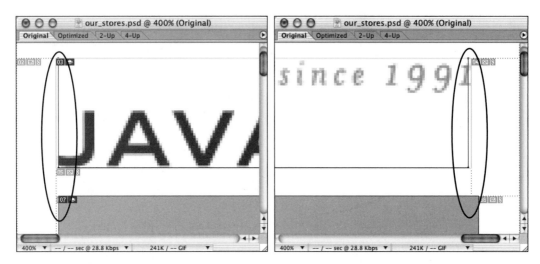

6. Select the **Zoom** tool in the **Toolbox**. Click and drag over the **Javaco** logo. Notice the **our_stores_logo** slice is not the same width as the **our_stores_navigation** slice—the left side is about one pixel too far to the left. Use the scroll bar on the document window to scroll to the right side of the image. Notice the right side is about three pixels too far to the left.

*You'll fix the slice size differences in the next steps using the **Slice Outset** fields in the **Slice** palette.*

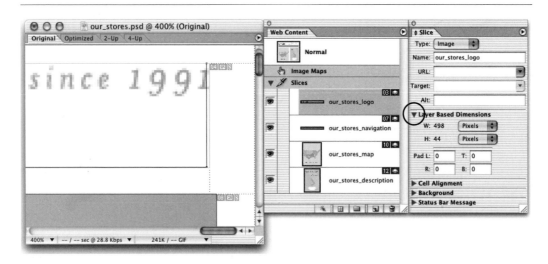

7. Choose **Window > Slice** to make the **Slice** palette visible. Expand the **Layer Based Dimensions** section of the **Slice** palette by clicking the arrow to the left of the **Layer Based Dimensions** heading. In the **Web Content** palette, click the **our_stores_logo** slice (**Slice 03**) to select it.

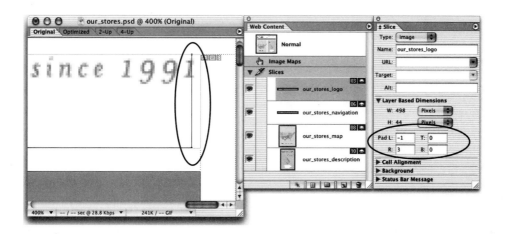

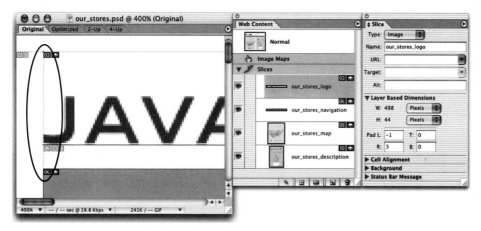

8. In the **Layer-Based Dimensions** section of the **Slice palette**, type **−1** in the **L** (left) field and type **3** in the **R** (right) field. Press **Return** (Mac) or **Enter** (Windows).

*Notice the right edge of the **our_stores_logo** slice is now the same width as the right edge of the **our_stores_navigation** slice. Using the scroll bar at the bottom of the document window, scroll to the left side of the image. Notice the left edge of the **our_stores_logo** slice is now the same width as the left edge of the **our_stores_navigation** slice.*

*Changing the **Slice Outset** does not make any changes to the image—it just increases or decreases the size of the slice based on the original dimensions of the layer. This is a great way to make sure your slice layers are perfectly aligned without changing the size of the layer. In this case, I experimented with different values until the slices aligned perfectly. When your settings offset values in your own Web graphics, be prepared to experiment with different values until the slices align perfectly.*

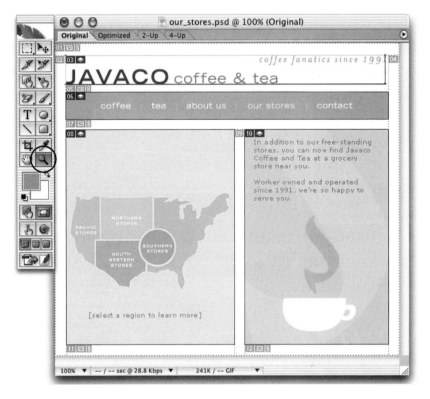

9. Double-click the **Zoom** tool in the **Toolbox** to return the image to **100%**.

Next, you'll see how layer-based slices update automatically when you move or edit layers.

10. Click the **Toggle Slices Visibility** button on the **Toolbox** to hide the slices.

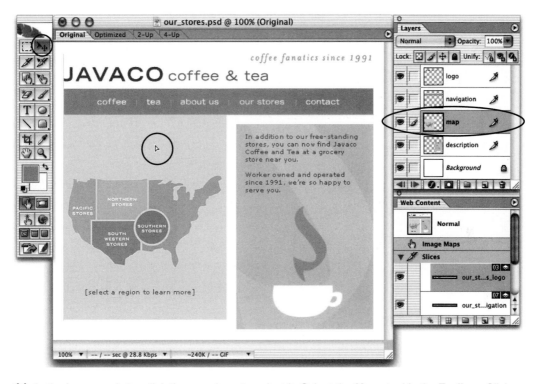

11. In the **Layers** palette, click the **map** layer to select it. Select the **Move** tool in the **Toolbox**. Click and drag the **map** layer so the top edge of the layer touches the bottom edge of the **navigation** layer, as shown here.

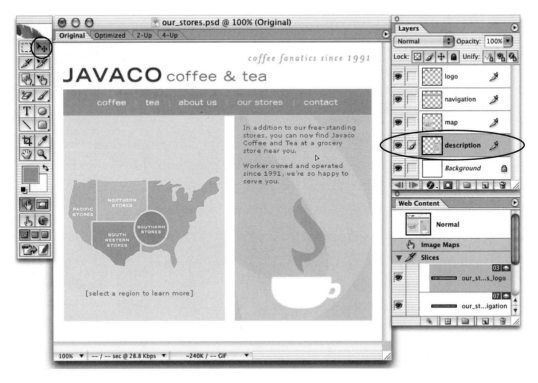

12. In the **Layers** palette, click the **description** layer to select it. With the **Move** tool selected in the **Toolbox**, click and drag the **description** layer so the top edge of the layer touches the bottom edge of the **navigation** bar, as shown here.

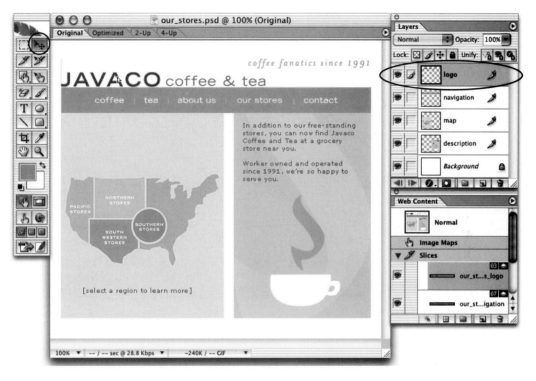

13. In the **Layers** palette, click the **logo** layer to select it. With the **Move** tool selected in the **Toolbox**, click and drag the **logo** layer so the bottom edge of the layer touches the top edge of the **navigation** layer, as shown here.

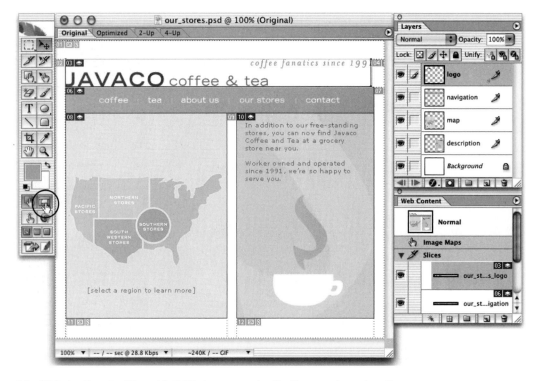

14. Click the **Toggle Slices Visibility** button on the **Toolbox** to show the slices.

Notice the slices are automatically in the same position as the layers. Layer-based slices move automatically when you move layers. This saves you a lot of time if you need to make changes to your image because you don't have to reslice it.

Next you'll see how slices resize automatically when you resize layers.

15. Click the **Toggle Slices Visibility** button on the **Toolbox** to hide the slices.

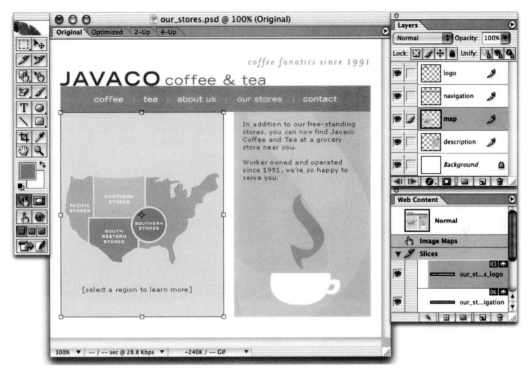

16. In the **Layers** palette, click the **map** layer to select it. Choose **Edit > Free Transform**.

*Putting the layer into **Free Transform** mode will let you resize it easily.*

17. Position your mouse over the middle node on the right side of the **map** layer until the resize cursor appears.

18. Click and drag until the right edge of the **map** layer touches the left edge of the **description** layer. Press **Return** (Mac) or **Enter** (Windows) to exit **Free Transform** mode.

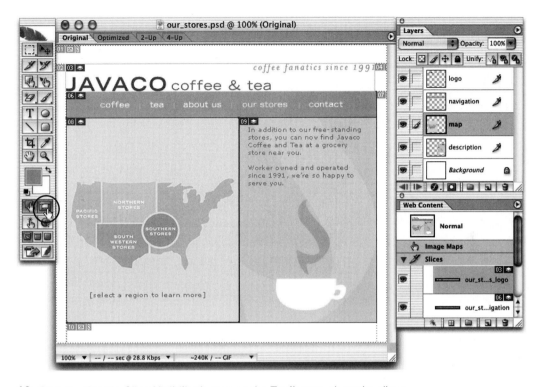

19. Click the **Toggle Slice Visibility** button on the **Toolbox** to show the slices.

Notice the slices updated automatically to reflect the new size of the map layer.

Layer-based slices offer a great deal of flexibility because they update each time you edit or move a layer. During the design process, you'll often have to make changes to your images. Using layer-based slices will save you from reslicing images each time you make changes to your layers.

20. Save and close the file.

NOTE | Promoting Layer-Based Slices to User Slices

Layer-based slices don't have the flexibility of user slices. As a result, you may want to promote layer-based slices to user slices. Here's how:

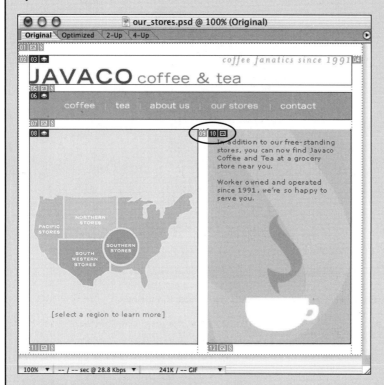

Select the layer-based slice you want to promote to a user slice with the **Slice Select** tool or by selecting it in the **Web Content** palette. Choose **Slices > Promote to User Slice**. When you promote a layer-based slice to a user slice, the slice symbol updates automatically.

3. [IR]——————Editing Slices

In the last two exercises, you learned how to create user slices, auto slices, and layer-based slices and how to promote auto slices and layer-based slices to user slices. After you've created slices, you'll often want to resize, divide, combine, or duplicate slices. Here's an exercise to show you how.

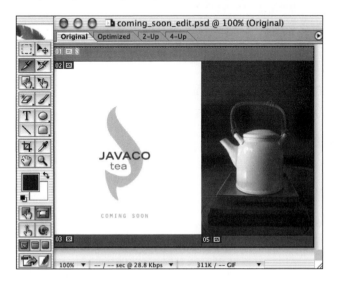

1. Open **coming_soon_edit.psd** from the **chap_10** folder you copied to your **Desktop**.

*The image contains four slices: one auto slice for the top green section of the image (**Slice 01**), one user slice for the **javaco** and **teapot** images (**Slice 02**), and two user slices for the bottom green section of the image (**Slice 03** and **Slice 04**).*

*First, you'll divide **Slice 02** into two slices.*

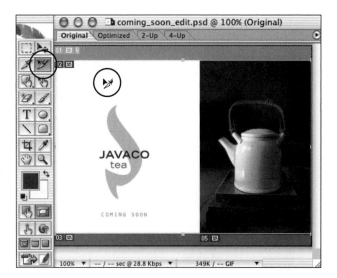

2. Select the **Slice Select** tool from the **Toolbox**. Click inside **Slice 02** to select it.

3. Choose **Slices > Divide Slice**.

*The **Divide Slice** dialog box opens automatically.*

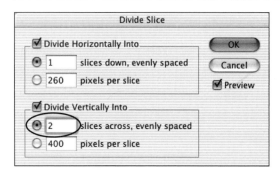

4. In the **Divide Slice** dialog box, type **2** in the **slices across, evenly spaced** field. Click **OK**.

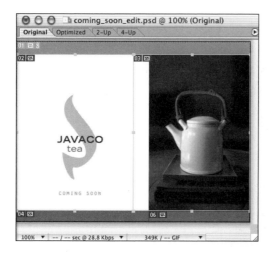 

*You should now see **Slice 02** and **Slice 03** in the javaco and teapot section of the image.*

Notice the vertical slice cuts through the javaco section of the image. Next, you'll reposition the slice line so it matches up with javaco and the teapot image.

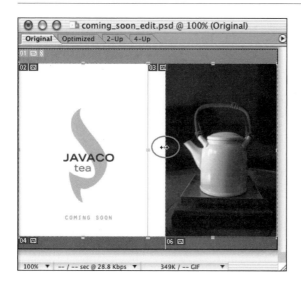

5. With the **Slice Select** tool selected in the **Toolbox**, position your mouse over the node in the middle of the vertical slice line you created in the last step. When the cursor changes to the resize cursor (the two arrows), click and drag the slice line to the right so it is positioned exactly between the **javaco** and **teapot** images.

*Next, you'll select and combine **Slice 04** and **Slice 06** into a single slice.*

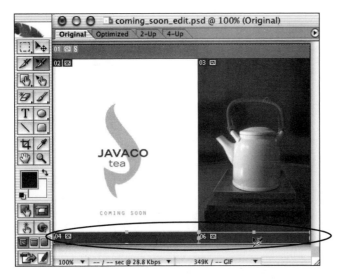

6. With the **Slice Select** tool selected in the **Toolbox**, click to select **Slice 04**. Hold down the **Shift** key and click to select **Slice 06**.

See how easy it is to select multiple slices? Next, you'll combine the slices into a single slice.

7. With **Slice 04** and **Slice 06** selected, choose **Slices > Combine Slices**.

Notice there is now a single slice at the bottom of the image—Slice 04. Next, you'll duplicate Slice 04.

8. With **Slice 04** still selected, choose **Slices > Duplicate Slice**.

*The **Duplicate Slice** dialog box opens automatically.*

9. In the **Duplicate Slice** dialog box, turn off the **Duplicate Rollover States** and **Duplicate Layers for Layer-Based Slices** options. Choose **Offset from Original** in the **Position** pop-up menu. Click **OK**.

*You should now see **Slice 06** at the bottom of the image, which is an exact copy of **Slice 04**.*

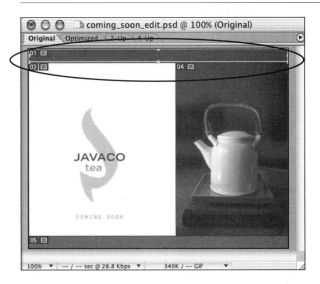

10. With the **Slice Select** tool selected in the **Toolbox**, click and drag **Slice 06** to the top of the image and position it on top of **Slice 01**.

*Notice **Slice 06** is automatically renamed to **Slice 01**. Don't worry if your slice numbers don't match up exactly as shown here.*

11. Save your changes and leave the file open for the next exercise.

4. [IR] _____**Renaming Slices**

When you're slicing images, it's important to make sure you name slices correctly; these will become the file names when you save the slices. In this exercise, you'll learn two techniques for renaming slices. Later in this chapter, you'll see how slice names are used when you save sliced images.

1. Coming_soon_edit.psd should still be open from the last exercise.

*In the **Web Content** palette, you'll notice the slices are named as follows: **coming_soon_edit_01**, **coming_soon_edit_03**, **coming_soon_edit_04**, and **coming_soon_edit_05**. Don't worry if the slice numbers don't match up exactly as shown here. Follow the exercise keeping the slice numbers you have in your image.*

*The default slice naming convention is as follows: **file name** + **underscore** + **slice number**. Sometimes, you'll want to name your slices differently from the original file name.*

Note: *This example features user slices based on a flat image. If you are working with layer-based slices from a layered image, the naming convention differs slightly: **file name** + **underscore** + **layer name**.*

*Next, you'll learn to rename slices using the **Web Content** palette.*

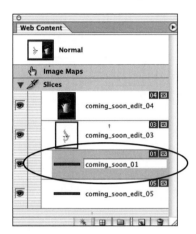

2. In the **Web Content** palette, double-click the **coming_soon_edit_01** slice. A bounding box will appear around the text, letting you rename it. Rename the slice to **coming_soon_01**. Press **Return** (Mac) or **Enter** (Windows).

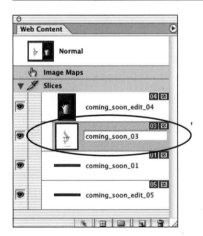

3. Repeat **Step 2** for **coming_soon_edit_03**, renaming the slice to **coming_soon_03**.

*Next, you'll rename the remaining two slices using the **Slice** palette.*

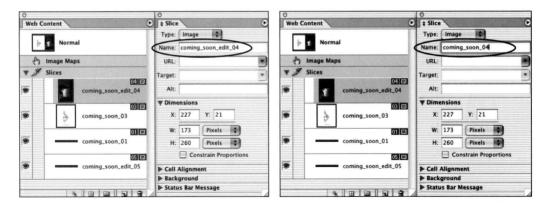

4. In the **Web Content** palette, click the **coming_soon_edit_04** slice to select it. Notice the **Slice** palette updates automatically. In the **Name** field, rename the slice to **coming_soon_04**. Press **Return** (Mac) or **Enter** (Windows).

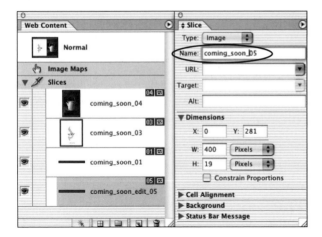

5. Select **coming_soon_edit_05** in the **Web Content** palette. Rename the slice in the **Slice** palette and press **Return** (Mac) or **Enter** (Windows).

*See how easy it is to rename slices? In this exercise, you learned to rename slices in the **Web Content** palette and in the **Slice** palette.*

6. Save and close the file.

TIP | Modifying the Default Slice-Naming Settings

The default slice naming in ImageReady CS is as follows:

User slices: file name + underscore + slice number

Layer-based slices: file name + underscore + layer name

Output Settings

Preset: Default Settings

Slices

Slice Output

● Generate Table

Empty Cells: GIF, IMG W&H

TD W&H: Auto

Spacer Cells: Auto (Bottom)

○ Generate CSS

Referenced: By ID

Default Slice Naming

doc. name + underscore + layer name or slice +

none + none + none

Example: MyFile_01

OK
Cancel
Prev
Next
Load...
Save...

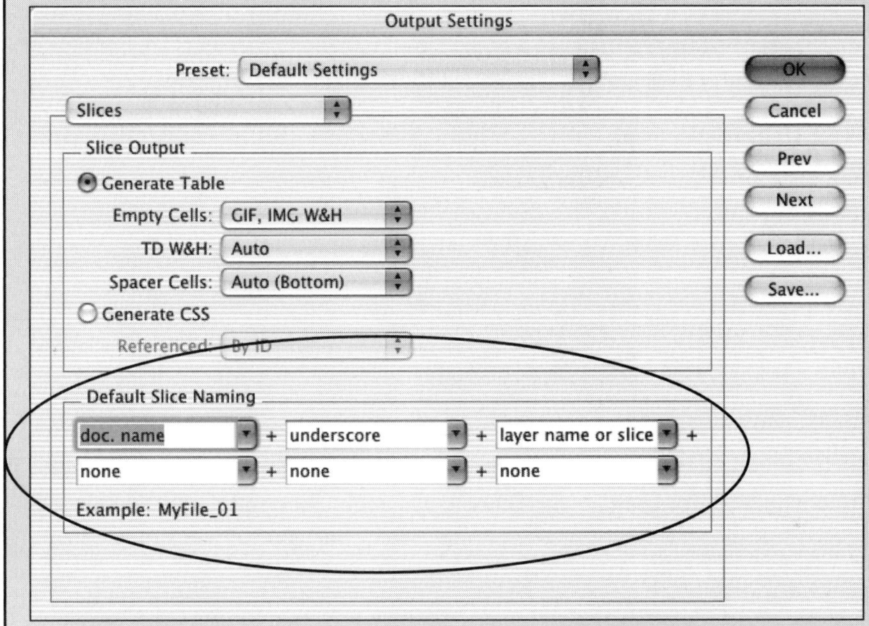

If you want to change the default slice-naming settings, choose **File > Output Settings > Slices**. In the **Output Settings** dialog box, use the **Default Slice Naming** pop-up menus to choose your own slice-naming convention.

5. [IR] _____Optimizing Slices

The benefit of slicing images is the ability to apply different optimization settings to each slice. In this exercise, you'll learn to apply different optimization settings to different slices to achieve the best overall file size and quality.

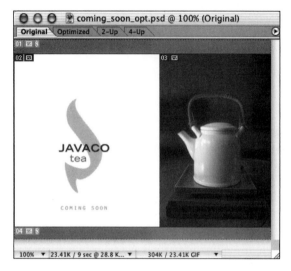

1. Open **coming_soon_opt.psd** from the **chap_10** folder you copied to your **Desktop**.

*Notice the image contains four slices: two user slices (**Slice 02** and **Slice 03**) and two auto slices (**Slice 01** and **Slice 04**).*

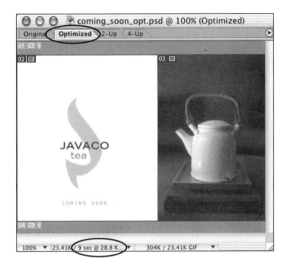

2. Click the **Optimized** tab in the document window.

Notice the current estimate to load this image is approximately nine seconds. The estimate is for the entire image, not the currently selected slice.

3. Make sure the **Optimize** palette is visible. If it's not, choose **Window > Optimize**. Click the **Slice Select** tool in the **Toolbox** and click each of the slices in the image; watch the settings in the **Optimize** palette.

*You'll notice all the slices have the same GIF settings in the **Optimize** palette. In the next few steps, you'll optimize each slice with its own optimization settings to reduce the file size while maintaining high image quality.*

4. With the **Slice Select** tool selected in the **Toolbox**, click **Slice 02** to select it.

This slice is best optimized as a GIF because it is composed of solid colors.

5. In the **Optimize** palette, choose **GIF** from the **Format** pop-up menu, **Selective** from the **Reduction** pop-up menu, **8** from the **Colors** pop-up menu, and **No Dither** from the **Method** pop-up menu.

Notice the optimization settings reduce the file size from approximately 18.44K to 1.77K.

6. With the **Slice Select** tool selected in the **Toolbox**, click **Slice 03** to select it.

Because this slice contains a photograph, it will optimize best as a JPEG, not a GIF. The great thing about slicing is you can optimize each slice differently to ensure the best quality images and the smallest file sizes.

7. In the **Optimize** palette, choose **JPEG Medium** from the **Preset** pop-up menu.

Notice the considerable file savings when you change the slice from GIF to JPEG. The download time has been reduced from nine seconds to three seconds.

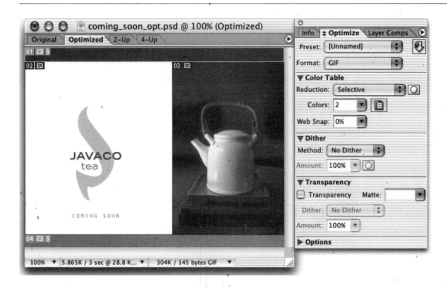

8. With the **Slice Select** tool selected in the **Toolbox**, click **Slice 01** to select it. In the **Optimize** palette choose **GIF** from the **Format** pop-up menu, **Selective** from the **Reduction** pop-up menu, **2** from the **Colors** pop-up menu, and **No Dither** from the **Method** pop-up menu.

9. With the **Slice Select** tool selected in the **Toolbox**, click **Slice 04**.

*Notice the settings you specified for **Slice 01** are automatically applied to **Slice 04**. Auto slices are linked together for optimization purposes. If you change the optimization settings for one auto slice, they will be applied to all auto slices in the image. If you don't want to use the same optimization settings for all the auto slices in an image, you must convert the auto slices to user slices by choosing Slices > Promote to User Slice.*

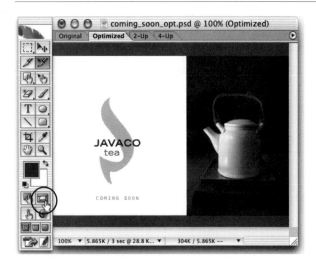

10. Click the **Toggle Slices Visibility** button on the **Toolbox** to hide the slice lines.

I like to toggle the visibility of slice lines on and off frequently so I can accurately view the optimization settings. When slice visibility is turned on, unselected slices appear slightly discolored.

11. Click the **Preview in Default Browser** button on the **Toolbox** to preview the optimized image in your default Web browser.

*Notice the image defaults against a white background? Slicing an image creates foreground images only. Next, you'll learn to set a background color that matches the green color in the auto slices (**Slice 01** and **Slice 04**).*

12. Return to ImageReady CS. Select the **Eyedropper** tool in the **Toolbox**. Click inside the **green** area to sample color.

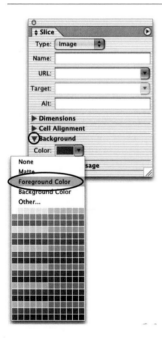

13. Make sure the **Slice** palette is visible. If it's not, choose **Window > Slice**. Expand the **Background** section of the **Slice** palette. Choose **Foreground Color** from the **Color** pop-up menu.

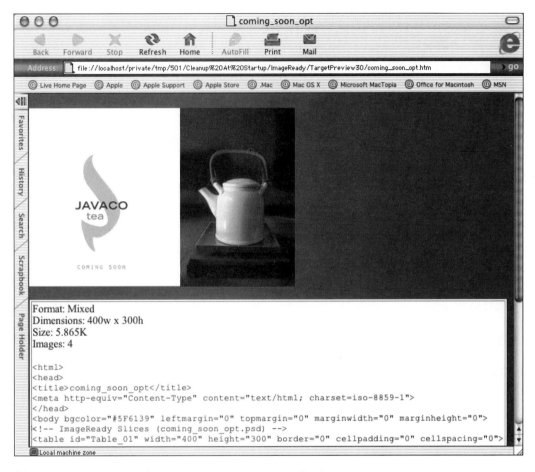

14. Click the **Preview in Default Browser** button on the **Toolbox**.

Now the sliced foreground image appears against a green background.

When you're designing Web graphics, there will be times when you want to leave the background at its default setting (white), and there will be times when you want to match it to a color in your sliced image. Now you know how to achieve both results.

---

15. Save your changes and keep the file open for the next exercise.

TIP | **Linking Slices and Copying Optimization Settings**

When you're optimizing sliced images, you'll often want to use the same optimization settings for one or more slices. There are two ways to share optimization settings: linking slices and copying optimization settings.

If you know you want to use the same optimization settings for one or more slices, you can link the slices together. Here's how:

With the **Slice Select** tool selected in the **Toolbox**, select one or more slices. Choose **Slices > Link Slices**. Notice each linked slice now has a link icon. Now when you specify settings in the **Optimize** palette, you'll be applying the settings to all the linked slices.

If you specify optimization settings in the **Optimize** palette and want to apply those settings to another slice, you can copy the optimization settings from one slice to another. Here's how:

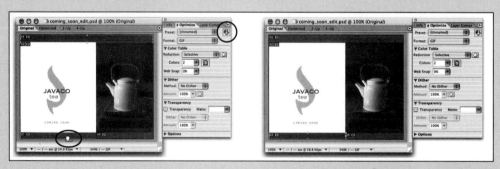

With the **Slice Select** tool selected in the **Toolbox**, select the slice with the optimization settings you want to copy. In the **Optimize** palette, drag the **Droplet** icon onto the slice you want to apply the optimization settings to.

6. [IR] _____Saving Sliced Images

Now that you've learned to optimize slices, it's time to learn how to save the slices and the required HTML table code so your sliced images display correctly in a Web browser. If it sounds complicated, don't worry; ImageReady CS makes saving the images and the HTML table code very easy!

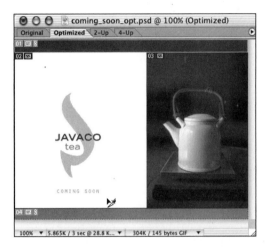

1. With **coming_soon_opt.psd** open from the last exercise, choose **File > Save Optimized As**.

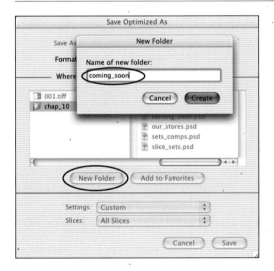

2. In the **Save Optimized As** dialog box, navigate to the **chap_10** folder you copied to your **Desktop**. Click the **New Folder** (Mac) or the **Create New Folder** (Windows) button. In the **New Folder** dialog box, name the folder **coming_soon**. Click **Create** (Mac) or **OK** (Windows).

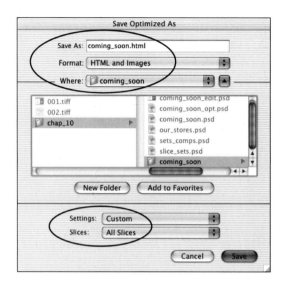

3. Choose **HTML and Images** from the **Format** pop-up menu. Name the file **coming_soon.html**. Make sure **All Slices** is selected from the **Slices** pop-up menu. Click **Save**.

*Note: You don't have to save the HTML code with the images. If you prefer, you can choose **Images** from the **Format** pop-up menu and create the HTML table code in an HTML editor, such as Adobe GoLive or Macromedia Dreamweaver. The choice is yours, but it's easiest to let ImageReady CS create the code! You'll learn how to bring the resulting HTML code into GoLive and Dreamweaver in Chapter 16, "Integration with Other Programs."*

4. Browse to the **coming_soon** folder you created in the **chap_10** folder on your **Desktop**.

*You'll see **coming_soon**.html and a folder called **images**, which contains the sliced images! Pretty cool!*

*Notice three of the images are GIFs, and one of the images is a JPEG. ImageReady CS remembered the settings you specified in the **Optimize** palette when it saved the slices.*

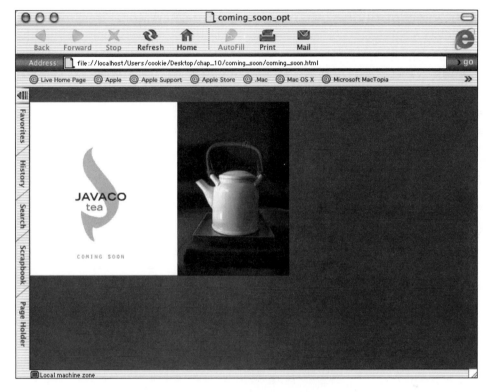

5. Double-click **coming_soon.html** to display the sliced images in your default Web browser.

The sliced images appear exactly the same as the original unsliced image.

*Notice the background image is green. ImageReady CS remembers the **Foreground Color** option you chose from the **Color** pop-up menu in the **Background** section of the **Slice** palette from the last exercise. If you want to change the background image back to its default color (white), return to ImageReady CS and choose **None** from the **Color** pop-up menu in the **Background** section of the **Slice** palette.*

6. Return to ImageReady CS. Save the file and keep it open for the next exercise.

[IR] _____**Applying Alt Text and Status Bar Messages to Slices**

To make Web pages more accessible for all viewers, you should apply alt text to critical images on your Web sites, including sliced images. Alt text lets viewers see a text description of the images on a Web page.

You can also apply status bar messages to slices. When a viewer positions his or her mouse over a slice on a Web page, the Web browser status bar changes to display the message you created. This is another helpful way to provide information about the contents of a slice.

Here's a short exercise to show you how to apply alt text and status bar messages to sliced images.

1. With **coming_soon_opt.psd** open from the last exercise, make sure the **Slice** palette is visible. If it's not, choose **Window > Slice**.

2. Select the **Slice Select** tool in the **Toolbox**. Click **Slice 02** to select it.

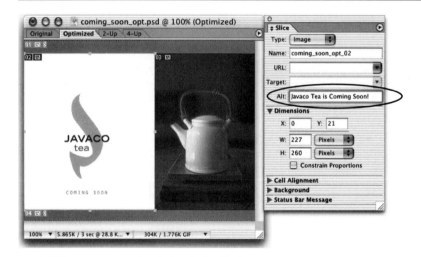

3. In the **Slice** palette, type **Javaco Tea is Coming Soon!** in the **Alt** field. Press **Return** (Mac) or **Enter** (Windows) to apply the alt text to the slice.

4. With the **Slice Select** tool selected in the **Toolbox**, click **Slice 03**.

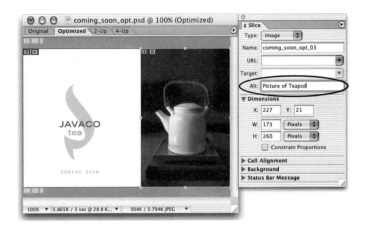

5. In the **Slice** palette, type **Picture of Teapot** in the **Alt** field. Press **Return** (Mac) or **Enter** (Windows) to apply the alt text to the slice.

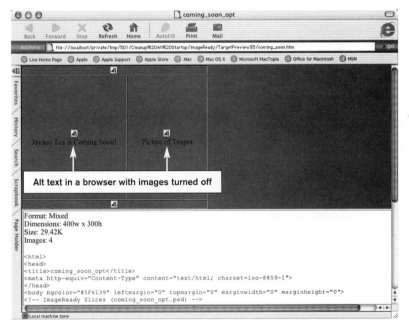

*Alt text shows in a Web browser if the user turns off images in the **Preferences** or if they are accessing Web pages with a text-only Web browser. Some viewers turn off images when they surf the Web to speed up the downloading process. Sight-impaired visitors use screen-reading software to "read" the alt text to them out loud.*

Next, you'll learn to apply status bar messages to slices.

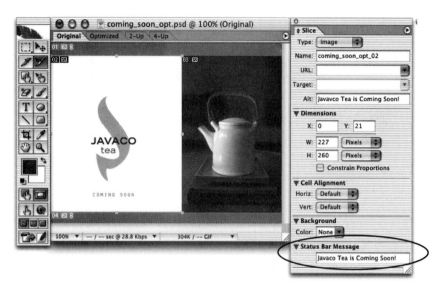

6. Select the **Slice Select** tool from the **Toolbox**. Click **Slice 02** to select it. In the **Status Bar Message** field of the **Slice** palette, type **Javaco Tea is Coming Soon!**. Press **Return** (Mac) or **Enter** (Windows).

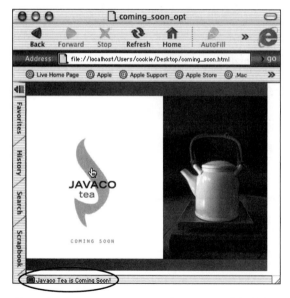

Status bar messages appear at the bottom of the Web browser window when you position your mouse over the slice. Status bar messages are a great way to provide additional information to your viewers.

7. Save your changes and keep the file open for the next exercise.

8. [IR] _____Assigning URLs to Slices

When you assign a URL to a slice, the slice automatically becomes a hot spot users can click on. When users click on a hot spot, it links them to a specific URL. ImageReady CS makes it easy to assign URLs to slices. Here's a short exercise to show you how.

1. With **coming_soon_opt.psd** open from the last exercise, make sure the **Slice** palette is visible. If it's not, choose **Window > Slice**.

2. Select the **Slice Select** tool in the **Toolbox**. Click **Slice 03** to select it.

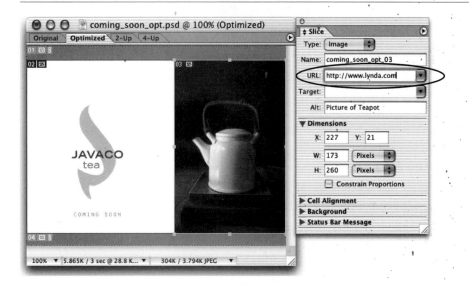

3. In the **Slice** palette, type **http://www.lynda.com** in the **URL** field. Press **Return** (Mac) or **Enter** (Windows) to assign the URL.

Notice the URL field is also a pop-up menu. The URL pop-up menu remembers the most-recently used URLs and saves them in the pop-up menu for easy access.

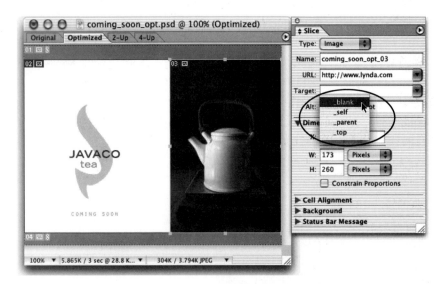

4. In the **Target** field, choose **_blank** and press **Return** (Mac) or **Enter** (Windows).

_blank indicates you want the URL to open in a new Web browser window.

5. Click the **Preview in Default Browser** button on the **Toolbox**.

6. Click the **teapot** image.

*If you have a live Web connection, a new Web browser window will open automatically to the **lynda.com** Web site. This is a quick and easy way to assign URLs to slices without using an HTML editor.*

Note: In order to test links, you must preview or open the file in a Web browser because there is no way to test a link in ImageReady CS.

*Because I linked to an external Web site, **lynda.com**, I included the **http://www** information. This type of link is called an **absolute link**. You can also link to Web pages inside the same Web site. This type of link is called a **relative link**. When you use relative links, you must know the file structure and how to link to the files. For more information about absolute and relative links, refer to the side-bar at the end of this exercise.*

7. Save and close the file.

NOTE | Understanding Relative and Absolute Links

When you design Web sites, you'll use two kinds of links: relative and absolute. Here's a brief description of each to help you understand when and why to use them.

Relative links point to a page inside your Web site. For example, if you are designing a Web site, and you want to link from the Home page to the About Us page, you don't need to include the full **http://www** information. Instead, you include information about where you want to link to in relation to where you're linking from. For example, **aboutus.html** (instead of **http://www.somedomain.com/aboutus.html**) Because relative links can become complex to program when files are nested inside and outside of folders on the Web server, you might find it easier to create and manage them in an HTML editor, such as Adobe GoLive or Macromedia Dreamweaver.

Absolute links point to external Web sites. Absolute links always link to the same, defined location. For that reason, you must include the **http://www** information when you use absolute links.

Many HTML editors, including Adobe GoLive and Macromedia Dreamweaver, have site-management features, which help you manage absolute and relative links.

About Slice Sets

Slice sets are a new feature in ImageReady CS. A **slice set** is a group of slices stored inside a folder in the Web Content palette. Slice sets keep your slices organized if you have lots of slices in an image. Specifically, slice sets are helpful if you have two different designs in a single image, and you need to create different site configurations for each design. For example, if you create two Web site mock-ups—one with vertical navigation and one with horizontal navigation—you can create a slice set for each of the the designs in the same file.

9. [IR] _____Using Slice Sets

In this exercise, you'll practice creating slice sets and adding slices to slice sets. The benefit of using slice sets is you can create different slice configurations for different designs in the same file.

1. Open **slice_sets.psd** from the **chap_11** folder you copied to your **Desktop**. Make sure the **Web Content** and **Layers** palettes are visible. If they aren't, choose **Window > Web Content** and **Window > Layers**.

2. Notice **slice_sets.psd** contains two layer sets—**Horizontal Navigation** and **Vertical Navigation**. The visibility of the **Vertical Navigation** layer set is turned on by default. Turn off the visibility of the **Vertical Navigation** layer set and turn on the visibility of the **Horizontal Navigation** layer set. Notice the file is made up of two designs for the same Web page. Next, you'll create slice sets for each design.

3. Make sure the visibility of the **Horizontal Navigation** layer set is turned on, and the visibility of the **Vertical Navigation** layer group is turned off. Click the **Slice** tool in the **Toolbox** to select it.

4. Create slices for the **STORY**, **TEA**, and **TO GO** buttons and create a slice for the **Javaco Tea** text and **teapot** image, as shown here.

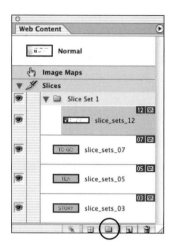

5. Click the **New slice set** button at the bottom of the **Web Content** palette to create a slice set. Notice the slice at the top of the slice stack is automatically placed inside the slice set. Next, you'll add the other slices to the slice set.

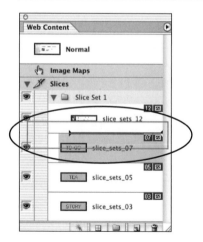

6. Click and drag **slice_sets_07** into **Slice Set 1**. Position the slice below **slice_sets_12**, as shown here.

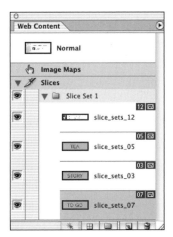

7. Repeat **Step 6** for **slice_sets_03** and **slice_sets_05**.

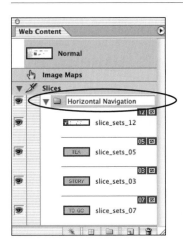

8. Double-click **Slice Set 1**. When the bounding box appears around the slice set, rename it to **Horizontal Navigation** and press **Return** (Mac) or **Enter** (Windows).

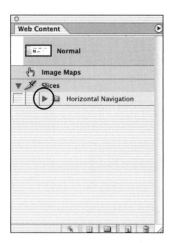

9. Collapse the **Horizontal Navigation** slice set by clicking the arrow next to it. Click **Normal** at the top of the **Web Content** palette and make sure the **Horizontal Navigation** slice set is no longer selected in the **Web Content** palette. Turn off the visibility of the **Horizontal Navigation** slice set.

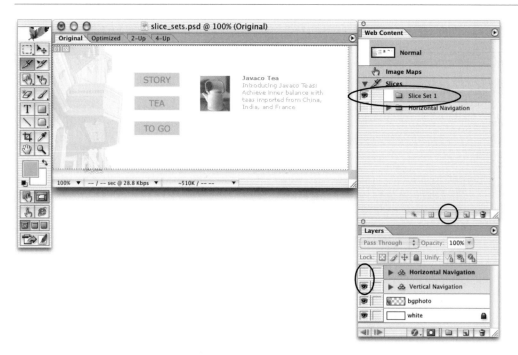

10. Click the **New slice set** button at the bottom of the **Web Content** palette to create an empty slice set. Turn off the visibility of the **Horizontal Navigation** layer set and turn on the visibility of the **Vertical Navigation** layer set in the **Layers** palette.

11. With the **Slice Tool** selected in the **Toolbox**, create slices for the **STORY**, **TEA**, and **TO GO** buttons and create a slice for the **Javaco Tea** text and **teapot** image, as shown here. Notice the slices automatically appear inside **Slice Set 1**.

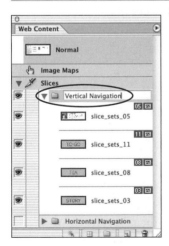

12. Double-click **Slice Set 1**. When the bounding box appears around the slice set, rename it **Vertical Navigation** and press **Return** (Mac) or **Enter** (Windows).

13. Collapse the **Vertical Navigation** slice set by clicking the arrow beside it.

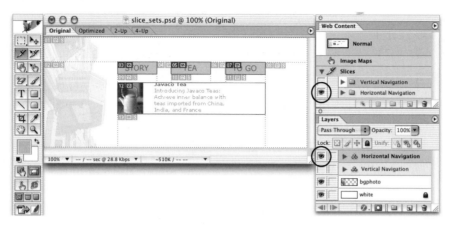

14. Turn off the visibility of the **Vertical Navigation** slice set and turn on the visibility of the **Horizontal Navigation** slice set in the **Web Content** palette. Turn off the visibility of the **Vertical Navigation** layer set in the **Layers** palette and turn on the visibility of the **Horizontal Navigation** layer set in the **Layers** palette. As you can see, ImageReady CS remembered the slices you created in the slice set.

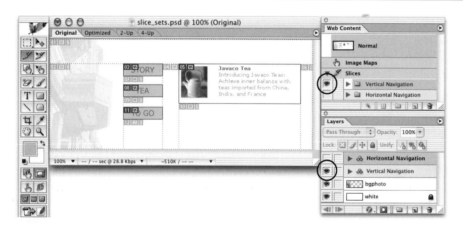

15. Turn off the visibility of the **Horizontal Navigation** slice set and turn on the visibility of the **Vertical Navigation** slice set in the **Web Content** palette. Turn off the visibility of the **Horizontal Navigation** layer set and turn on the visibility of the **Vertical Navigation** layer set in the **Layers** palette.

Using the new slice sets feature in ImageReady CS is a great way to keep your slices organized and, more importantly, is a great way to create different configurations of slices for different designs in the same file. As you can see from this exercise, slice sets are a useful new feature in ImageReady CS.

16. Save and close the file.

IO. [IR]_____Using Slices and Layer Comps

A great new feature in ImageReady CS is the **layer comps** feature. If you design a series of Web pages in the same document and save the individual pages as layer comps, you can slice one of the pages and apply the slices to all the layer comps in your document. This saves you from slicing Web pages based on the same design over and over. Sound a bit confusing? Follow this exercise and you'll understand.

Tip: For this exercise, you'll need access to the four following palettes: **Layers**, **Layer Comps**, **Optimize**, and **Web Content**. To keep your workspace tidy, I recommend docking the **Layers** and **Layer Comps** palettes together and docking the **Optimize** and **Web Content** palettes together, as shown here. For more information about how to dock palettes, refer to Chapter 2, "*Interface.*"

1. Open **sets_comps.psd** from the **chap_10** folder you copied to your **Desktop**. Click the **Layer Comps** tab.

*Notice there are six layer comps in this document: **home**, **coffee**, **tea**, **about us**, **our stores**, and **contact**. Each layer comp represents a page in the javaco Web site. You can click the **Apply Layer Comp** button beside the layer comp name if you want to preview the different layer comps. For more information about how to create layer comps, refer to Chapter 5, "Layers."*

First, you'll slice the home page.

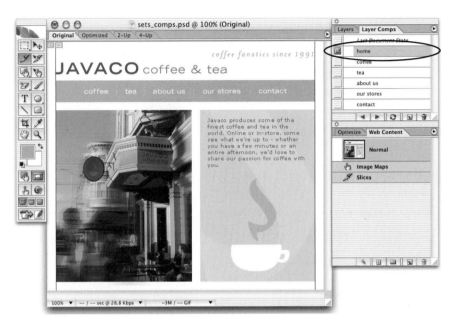

2. Select the **home** layer comp in the **Layer Comps** palette. Select the **Slice** tool from the **Toolbox**.

3. Slice each of the following elements: the **logos** at the top, the **navigation bar**, the **photograph**, and the **description box**, as shown here.

4. Click the **coffee** layer comp.

*Notice the slices you created for the **home** layer comp are automatically applied to the **coffee** layer comp. When you slice an image with layer comps, the slices you create are automatically applied to all layer comps in a document, which saves you from slicing similar images individually.*

Next, you'll set the optimization settings for the slices. Because many of the slices are the same (or very similar) in all the layer comps, you'll be able to share the optimize settings from one layer comp to another, which is another huge time saver!

5. Click the **Optimized** tab in the document window. Select the **home** layer comp in the **Layer Comps** palette. Click the **Optimize** tab to switch from the **Web Content** palette to the **Optimize** palette.

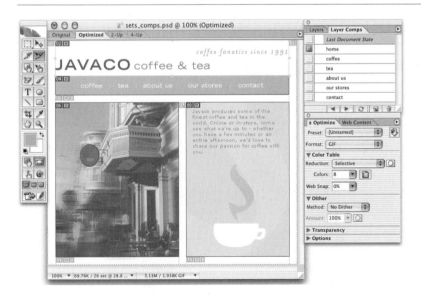

6. Select the **Slice Select** tool in the **Toolbox**. Click **Slice 02** (the **javaco** and **coffee fanatics since 1991** logos) to select it. In the **Optimize** palette, match the settings shown here.

*Tip: If you want to preview the optimized image without the slice lines, click the **Toggle Slices Visibility** button on the **Toolbox**.*

7. With the **Slice Select** tool selected in the **Toolbox**, click **Slice 04** (the **navigation bar**) to select it. In the **Optimize** palette, match the settings shown here.

8. Click to select **Slice 08** (the **description box**). In the **Optimize** palette, match the settings shown here.

9. Click **Slice 06** (the **photograph**) to select it. In the **Optimize** palette, match the settings shown here. Because this image is a photograph, it will optimize best as a JPEG, not a GIF.

Next, you'll save the HTML and images for the home page.

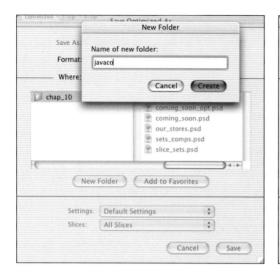
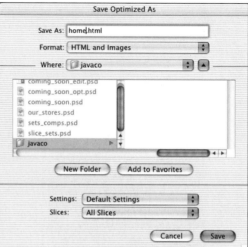

10. Choose **File > Save Optimized As**. In the **Save Optimized As** dialog box, navigate to the **chap_10** folder you copied to your **Desktop**. Click the **New Folder** (Mac) or **Create New Folder** (Windows) button. In the **New Folder** dialog box, name the folder **javaco** and click **Create** (Mac) or **OK** (Windows). Choose **HTML and Images** from the **Format** pop-up menu. Type the name **home.html** in the **Save As** field. Choose **All Slices** from the **Slices** pop-up menu. Click **Save**.

*Next, you'll optimize and save the slices in the **coffee** layer comp. Because many of the slices are the same between the **home** and the **coffee** layer comp, you won't have to adjust the settings for each slice.*

---

11. In the **Layer Comps** palette, click the **coffee** layer comp. Have a look at the slices in the image. The only slice requiring changes to the optimization settings is the **french roast** image. The other slices can keep the same optimization settings.

12. With the **Slice Select** tool selected in the **Toolbox**, click **Slice 06** (the **french roast** image) to select it. Match the optimization settings with the settings shown here.

The french roast image is tough to optimize because part of the image contains a flat graphic (which will optimize best as a GIF) and part of the image contains a photograph (which will optimize best as a JPEG). In a case like this, you'll need to experiment with different GIF and JPEG optimization settings until you find a result which gives you the best quality and the smallest file size.

---

13. Choose **File > Save Optimized As**. In the **Save Optimized As** dialog box, navigate to the **javaco** folder you created in the **chap_10** folder. Choose **HTML and Images** from the **Format** pop-up menu. Type the name **cofffee.html** in the **Save As** field. Choose **All Slices** from the **Slices** pop-up menu. Click **Save**.

Next, you'll optimize and save the slices in the tea layer comp.

---

14. In the **Layer Comps** palette, click the **tea** layer comp. Have a look at the slices in the image. The only slice requiring changes to the optimization settings is the **teapot** photograph. The other slices can keep the same optimization settings.

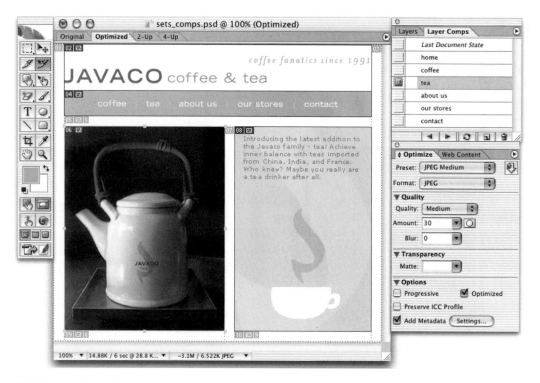

15. With the **Slice Select** tool selected in the **Toolbox**, click **Slice 06** (the **teapot** photograph) to select it. Match the optimization settings with the settings shown here.

---

16. Choose **File > Save Optimized As**. In the **Save Optimized As** dialog box, navigate to the **javaco** folder you created in the **chap_10** folder. Choose **HTML and Images** from the **Format** pop-up menu. Type the name **tea.html** in the **Save As** field. Choose **All Slices** from the **Slices** pop-up menu. Click **Save**.

*Next, you'll optimize and save the slices in the **about us** layer comp.*

---

17. In the **Layer Comps** palette, click the **about us** layer comp. Have a look at the slices in the image. In this case, you can keep the settings for all of the slices.

---

18. Choose **File** > **Save Optimized As**. In the **Save Optimized As** dialog box, navigate to the **javaco** folder you created in the **chap_10** folder. Choose **HTML and Images** from the **Format** pop-up menu. Type the name **about_us.html** in the **Save As** field. Choose **All Slices** from the **Slices** pop-up menu. Click **Save**.

*Next, you'll optimize and save the slices in the **our stores** layer comp.*

19. In the **Layer Comps** palette, click the **our stores** layer comp. Have a look at the slices in the image. The only slice requiring changes is the map image.

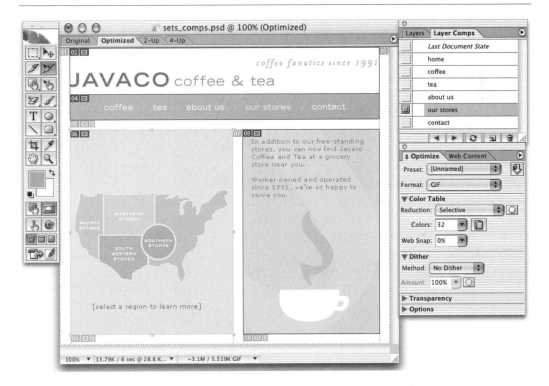

20. With the **Slice Select** tool selected in the **Toolbox**, click **Slice 06** (the **map**) to select it. Match the optimization settings with the settings shown here.

21. Choose **File > Save Optimized As**. In the **Save Optimized As** dialog box, navigate to the **javaco** folder you created in the **chap_10** folder. Choose **HTML and Images** from the **Format** pop-up menu. Type the name **our_stores.html** in the **Save As** field. Choose **All Slices** from the **Slices** pop-up menu. Click **Save**.

*Next, you'll optimize and save the slices in the **contact** layer comp.*

22. In the **Layer Comps** palette, click the **contact** layer comp. Have a look at the slices in the image. The large slices at the bottom of the page both require changes to the optimization settings.

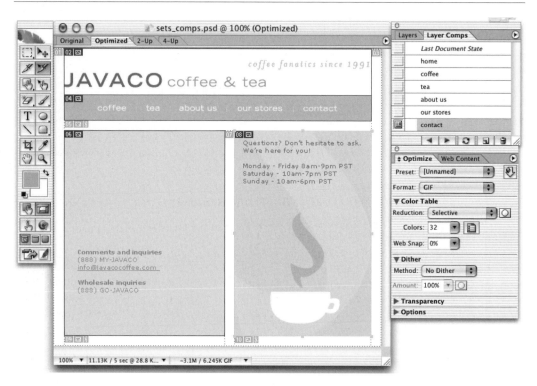

23. With the **Slice Select** tool selected in the **Toolbox**, click **Slice 06**. Match the optimization settings with the settings shown here.

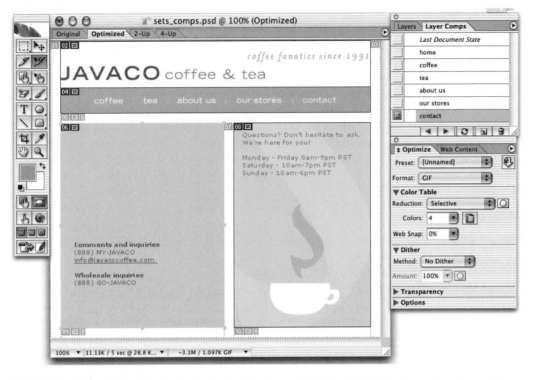

24. With the **Slice Select** tool selected in the **Toolbox**, click **Slice 08**. Match the optimization settings with the settings shown here.

25. Choose **File > Save Optimized As**. In the **Save Optimized As** dialog box, navigate to the **javaco** folder you created in the **chap_10** folder. Choose **HTML and Images** from the **Format** pop-up menu. Type the name **contact.html** in the **Save As** field. Choose **All Slices** from the **Slices** pop-up menu. Click **Save**.

You're now finished optimizing and saving the sliced layer comps, which make up the pages of the Javaco Web site. It's time to see the results of your hard work.

26. Browse to the **javaco** folder in the **chap_10** folder on your **Desktop**.

*Notice the following six html files: **about_us.html**, **coffee.html**, **contact.html**, **home.html**, **our_stores.html**, and **tea.html**.*

27. Double-click the **home.html** file to view the sliced image in your default Web browser.

Notice it looks identical to the original layer comp you started with at the beginning of the exercise. Pretty cool! If you want to view the other files, double-click the HTML files to open them in your default Web browser.

28. Open the **images** folder in the **javaco** folder.

*Notice some images are GIFs and some images are JPEGs, depending on the settings you chose in the **Optimize** palette.*

The ability to use the same slices for all layer comps in the same document saves you from slicing, saving, and optimizing images based on the same design over and over. Layer comps are an excellent new feature in ImageReady CS and will save you time when you're designing Web pages.

29. Return to ImageReady CS. Save and close the file.

MOVIE | slices_comps.mov

To learn more about working with slices and layer comps, check out **slices_comps.mov** from the **movies** folder on the **H•O•T CD-ROM**.

You've finished another complex chapter! In this chapter, you learned the basics of working with slicing in ImageReady CS. In Chapter 11, "Rollovers," you'll take slicing to the next level by using slices to create rollovers.

11.

Rollovers

| About Rollover States | About the Web Content Palette |
| Creating Rollovers with Styles | Renaming and Saving Rollovers |
| Using Rollover Styles for Multiple Buttons |
| Renaming and Saving Rollovers |
| Creating Rollovers Using Layer Visibility |
| Creating Rollovers from Layer Comps | Creating Remote Rollovers |

chap_11

Photoshop CS/ImageReady CS
H•O•T CD-ROM

A **rollover** is a type of Web graphic that changes when a user rolls his or her mouse over it or when it is clicked. Rollovers are one of the best ways to indicate a graphic is a link. To create a rollover, not only do you have to create the images for the different rollover states, you also have to create the required JavaScript and HTML code, which are necessary for making the rollover work on a Web page. The good news is when you create rollovers in ImageReady CS, it creates the required JavaScript and HTML code for you!

In this chapter, you'll learn how to create simple rollovers using rollover styles, how to create rollovers from layer-based slices, how to create rollovers manually, and how to create remote rollovers. In addition, you'll learn how to optimize and save the images and required JavaScript and HTML code to make your rollovers work on a Web page. Sounds like a lot, but you'll be amazed at how easy it easy to complete these complex tasks in ImageReady CS!

You'll learn different techniques for creating rollovers in ImageReady CS throughout this chapter. Although you can't create rollovers in Photoshop CS, you can open a rollover in Photoshop CS that was created in ImageReady CS and still retain the rollover information. The next time you open the rollover in ImageReady CS, the rollover information will remain as part of the document.

About Rollovers

A rollover is an object on a Web page that changes in appearance when a user positions his or her mouse over it or clicks it. Each rollover appearance (or state in Web design lingo) is saved as a separate image. When you create rollovers, you also need to create the required JavaScript and HTML code to make the rollover work when it is placed inside a Web page. Fortunately, ImageReady CS saves the images and required JavaScript and HTML code in a single step!

There are many different types of rollovers. In this chapter, you'll learn to create three main types of rollovers: **replacement rollovers**, which replace the original image with a new image; **addition rollovers**, which add visual elements to the existing image; and **remote rollovers**, which trigger different images in different locations on a Web page. The following illustrations show examples of each type of rollover:

Replacement rollovers: Notice the rollover replaces the image.

Addition rollovers: Notice the rollover adds color to the inside of the tiki graphic on the left side of the rollover.

Remote rollovers: Notice the rollover triggers an image beside the original image.

About Rollover States

When you create rollovers in ImageReady CS, you can specify a number of different rollover states. Here is a handy chart to help you understand the different rollover states:

Rollover States in ImageReady CS	
Rollover State	**Definition**
Normal	When a user loads a Web page, the default appearance of an image before or after a user activates a rollover state.
Over	When the user positions his or her mouse over a slice or image map region without clicking.
Down	When the user clicks over a slice or image map region. The Down state appears until the user releases the mouse.
Click	When the user clicks over a slice or image map region. The Click state appears until the user moves the mouse outside the rollover region.
Out	When the user moves the mouse outside the slice or image map region. If there is no defined Out state, the image will automatically return to the Normal state.
Up	When the user releases the mouse inside the slice or image map region. If there is no defined In state, the image will automatically return to the Over state.
Custom	When a custom-programmed event occurs. This state is available if you want to create your own JavaScript event and add it to the HTML code.
Selected	When the user clicks a slice or image map region, the Selected state appears until another rollover state is selected. Other rollover effects can occur while the Selected state is active. For example, a Selected state for one button and an Over state for another button can occur simultaneously. However, if a layer is used by both states, the layer attributes of the Selected state override those of the Over state. Use Default Selected State to activate the state initially when the document is previewed in ImageReady CS or loaded in a Web browser.
None	When you want to preserve the current state of an image for future use. Rollovers with a None state are not saved when you save rollovers.

About the Web Content Palette

When you're working with rollovers in ImageReady CS, you'll need access to the Web Content palette, which is new to ImageReady CS. In previous versions of ImageReady, you used the Rollover palette. The Web Content palette is a great addition to ImageReady CS because not only does it store information about rollovers, it also stores information about slices and image maps. As a result, you can see information about your rollovers, slices, and image maps in a single location.

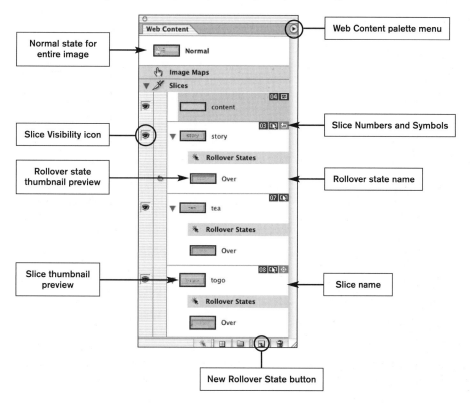

The Web Content palette lets you preview rollovers in an image. Similar to the Layers palette, the Web Content palette displays a thumbnail preview of the rollover, the rollover state, and offers the ability to turn on and off the visibility of a slice. The Web Content palette also offers a number of controls for creating and editing rollovers. It displays slice numbers and symbols, which are helpful when you're working with rollovers based on slices.

I. [IR] _____Creating Rollovers with Styles

In Chapter 7, "*Shapes and Layer Styles*," you learned how to apply layer styles to shapes using the Styles palette in Photoshop CS. What you didn't learn is the Styles palette also contains "rollover styles" that apply a layer style, create the rollover state(s), slice the image, and write the required JavaScript. As a result, you can create rollovers in no time flat. In this exercise, you'll learn how to identify rollover styles in the Styles palette, how rollover styles are constructed, and how to apply rollover styles to layers to create rollovers quickly and easily. In Exercise 2, you'll learn how to create your own rollover styles.

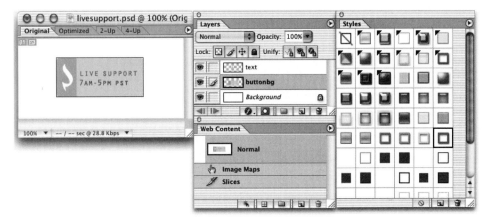

1. In ImageReady CS, open **livesupport.psd** from the **chap_11** folder you copied to your **Desktop** from the **H•O•T CD-ROM**. Make sure the **Layers**, **Web Content**, and **Styles** palettes are visible. If not, choose **Window > Layers**, **Window > Web Content**, and **Window > Styles**.

Note: Livesupport.psd was created in Photoshop CS. Although you can't create rollovers in Photoshop CS, you can create graphics in Photoshop CS and bring them into ImageReady CS when you're ready to convert them to rollovers.

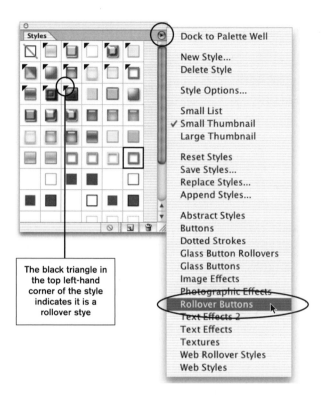

The black triangle in the top left-hand corner of the style indicates it is a rollover stye

2. Choose **Rollover Buttons** from the **Styles** palette menu. You'll be prompted with a dialog box asking if you want to replace the current styles with the styles from the **Rollover Buttons** library. Click **Replace**.

*Notice the styles in the **Styles** palette all have a small black triangle in the top-left corner. The black triangle indicates the style is a rollover style, not a layer style. For the purpose of this exercise, I want to use a rollover style from the **Rollover Buttons** library. There are rollover styles in the default styles library and many of the other style libraries; you can experiment with them when you're designing your own Web graphics.*

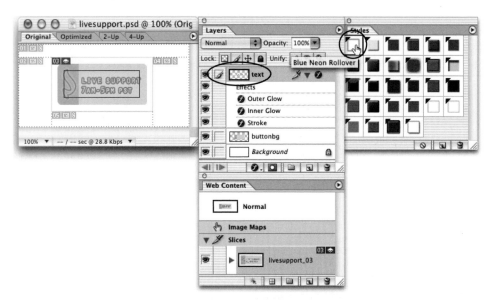

3. In the **Layers** palette, click the **text** layer to select it. In the **Styles** palette, click the **Blue Neon Rollover** style.

*Notice the changes after you apply the **Blue Neon Rollover** style. Livesupport.psd has been sliced into four auto slices and one layer-based slice, **livesupport_03**, which is displayed in the **Web Content** palette. Three layer styles (**Outer Glow**, **Inner Glow**, and **Stroke**) have been applied to the **text** layer.*

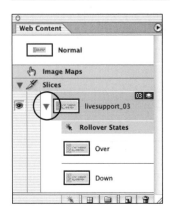

4. Click the **arrow** beside the **livesupport_03** slice in the **Slices** section of the **Web Content** palette.

*Notice an **Over** and a **Down** state automatically appear in the **Rollover States** section of the **Slices** section of the **Web Content** palette. The **Over** and **Down** rollover states are contained in the rollover style you applied in the last step.*

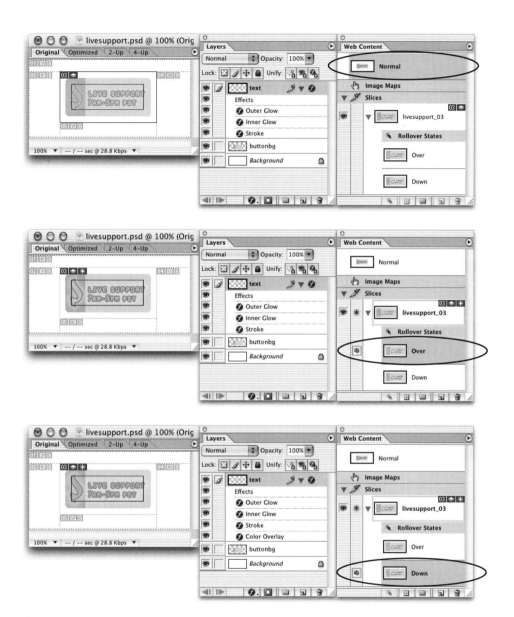

5. Click **Normal** in the **Web Content** palette. Click the **Over** rollover state. Click the **Down** rollover state. As you click through the different rollover states, you'll notice the contents of the document window change.

*Notice the layer styles on the **text** layer change when you choose the **Normal**, **Over**, or **Down** rollover states in the **Web Content** palette. These changes are all part of the rollover style you applied in **Step 3**.*

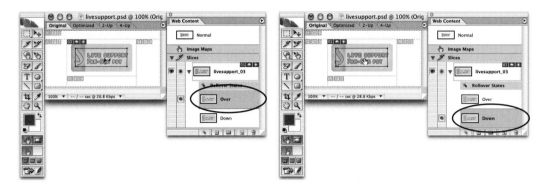

6. Click the **Preview Document** button on the **Toolbox** and take a look at the image in the document window. Position your mouse over the image and notice the image changes to the **Over** state. Next, click the image and notice it changes to the **Down** state.

*Using the **Preview Document** button is a great way to preview the rollover states.*

---

7. Click the **Preview Document** button on the **Toolbox** to deselect it.

Next, you'll optimize the images that make up the rollover.

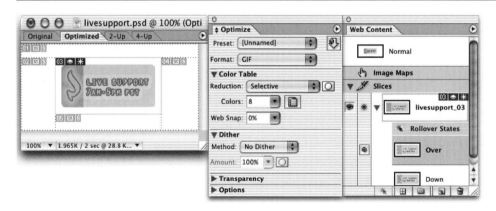

8. Click the **Optimized** tab. Make sure the **Optimize** palette is visible. If not, choose **Window > Optimize**. Experiment with different optimization settings in the **Optimize** palette until you're happy with the results. Make sure you click each of the rollover states in the **Web Content** palette; the optimization settings apply to all of the rollover states.

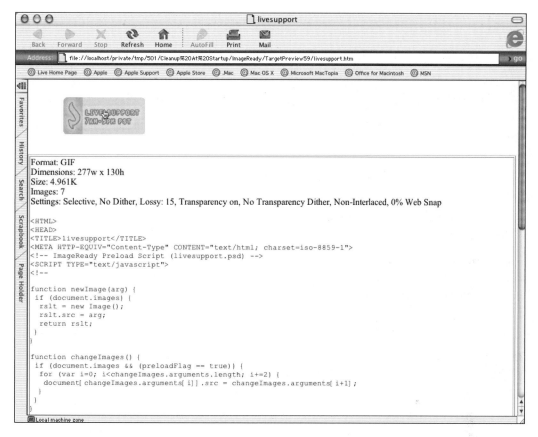

9. Click the **Preview in Default Browser** button on the **Toolbox**. When the image opens in the Web browser, position your mouse over the image and notice it changes to the **Over** state. Click the image and notice it changes to the **Down** state. Scroll down and you'll see the JavaScript ImageReady CS generated automatically.

WARNING | Microsoft Internet Explorer Problem

In some versions of Microsoft Internet Explorer, you may find rollovers have an annoying black outline after you click them. This is not through any fault of ImageReady CS. There are scripts within Adobe GoLive and Macromedia Dreamweaver that eliminate this issue. Unfortunately, there is nothing you can do with ImageReady CS to prevent the black outline.

10. Return to ImageReady CS. Choose **File > Save Optimized As**. In the **Save Optimized As** dialog box, navigate to the **chap_11** folder you copied to your **Desktop**. Click the **New Folder** (Mac) or **Create New Folder** (Windows) button. In the **New Folder** dialog box, name the folder **livesupport**. Click **Create** (Mac) or **OK** (Windows). In the **Save Optimized As** dialog box, the file name should automatically be named to **livesupport.html**. (By default, ImageReady CS uses the file name for the HTML file.) Choose **HTML and Images** from the **Format** pop-up menu. Click **Save**.

---

11. Browse to the **livesupport** folder in the **chap_11** folder on your **Desktop**.

*Notice ImageReady CS generated **livesupport.html**, which contains the JavaScript and HTML code necessary to make the rollover work, and a folder called **images**, which contains the images for the rollover states.*

---

12. Double-click **livesupport.html** to view the file in your Web browser. Position your mouse over the image to see the **Over** state. Click the image to see the **Down** state.

---

13. Return to ImageReady CS. Click **File > Save As**. In the **Save As** dialog box, name the file **livesupport_finished.psd** and click **Save**. The rollover settings will be automatically saved as part of the PSD file if you ever want to reopen it and make changes to the rollover. Close the file.

This exercise covered a lot of different concepts including rollover styles, rollover states, previewing, optimizing, and saving rollovers. In the next exercise, you'll learn how to create rollovers from layer-based slices and how to create and save custom rollover styles.

---

2. [IR] Creating Rollovers from Layer-Based Slices and Creating Custom Rollover Styles

In the last exercise, you created rollovers using rollover styles that ship with ImageReady CS. In this exercise, you'll learn to create rollovers from layer-based slices. Then you'll learn how to create and save your own custom rollover styles.

1. Open **livesupport.psd** from the **chap_11** folder you copied to your **Desktop**.

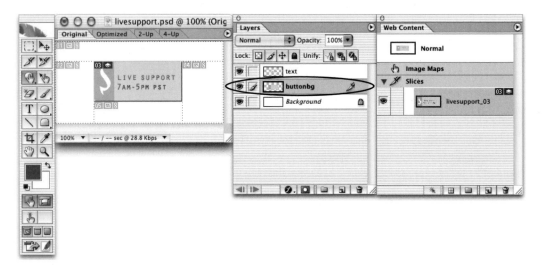

2. Select the **buttonbg** layer in the **Layers** palette. Choose **Layer > New Layer Based Slice**.

Notice the slice is the same shape and size as the contents of the layer. This is a feature of layer-based slices; they always create a slice with the exact same dimensions and shape as the layer.

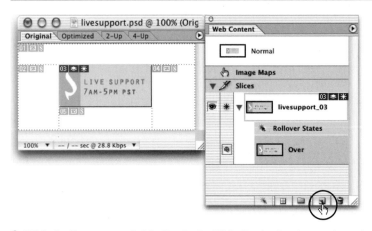

3. With the **livesuppport_03** slice in the **Web Content** palette selected, click the **Create rollover state** button at the bottom of the **Web Content** palette.

*Notice an **Over** state was created automatically and it is identical to the **livesupport_03** layer-based slice. You'll change the appearance of the **Over** state shortly.*

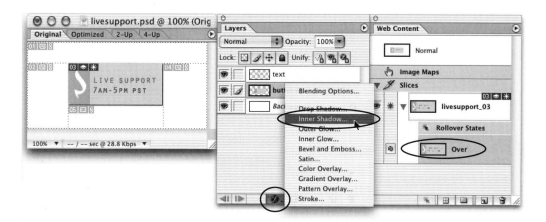

4. With the **Over** rollover state selected in the **Web Content** palette and the **buttonbg** layer selected in the **Layers** palette, choose **Inner Shadow** from the **Layer Styles** pop-up menu at the bottom of the **Layers** palette.

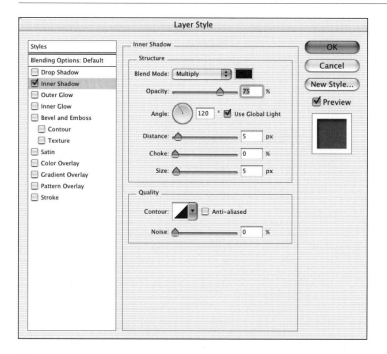

5. Leave the settings in the **Layer Style** dialog box at the default settings and click **OK**.

*Notice the **Inner Shadow** layer style has been applied to the **buttonbg** layer in the **Layers** palette.*

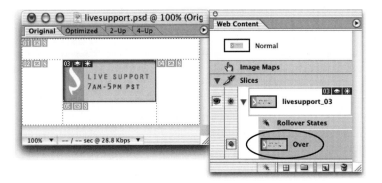

6. Click the **Normal** state in the **Web Content** palette. Click the **Over** state in the **Web Content** palette.

*Notice the **Inner Shadow** layer style was applied only to the **Over** state.*

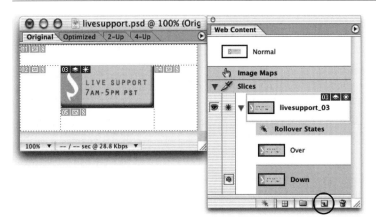

7. With the **buttonbg** layer selected in the **Layers** palette and the **Over** state selected in the **Web Content** palette, click the **Create rollover state** button at the bottom of the **Web Content** palette.

*Notice a **Down** state was created automatically. Next, you'll change the appearance of the **Down** state.*

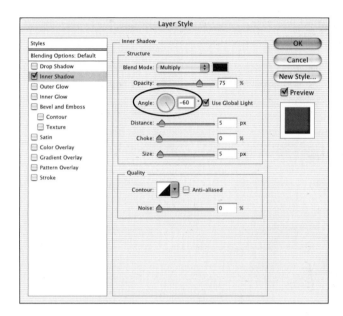

8. With the **Down** state selected in the **Web Content** palette, double-click the **Inner Shadow** layer style in the **Layers** palette. In the **Layer Styles** dialog box, change the **Angle** to **−60** degrees. Click **OK**.

*Notice the inner shadow appears in the bottom-right corner instead of the top-left corner. This change was applied to the **Down** state only. If you click the **Over** state or the **Normal** state in the **Web Content** palette, you'll notice the layer style did not affect them.*

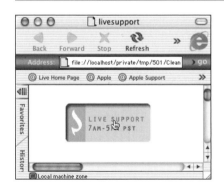
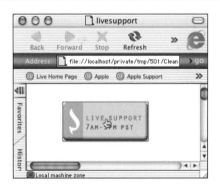

9. Click the **Preview in Default Browser** button on the **Toolbox**. Position your mouse over the graphic in the Web browser and watch it change to the **Over** state. Click the image and watch it change to the **Down** state.

*You just created a rollover from a layer-based slice with an **Over** and a **Down** state. Next, you'll save the layer styles you created for the **Over** and **Down** states as a rollover style in the **Styles** palette.*

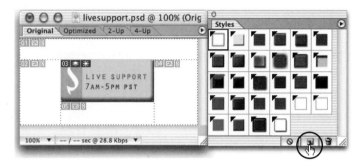

10. Return to ImageReady CS. Click the **New Style** button at the bottom of the **Styles** palette.

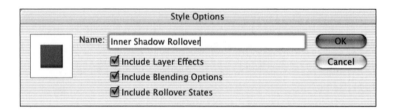

11. In the **Style Options** dialog box, type **Inner Shadow Rollover** in the **Name** field. Make sure the **Include Layer Effects**, **Include Blending Options**, and **Include Rollover States** options are turned on. Click **OK**.

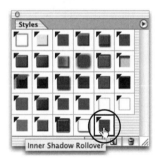

*Take a look at the **Styles** palette. Notice the **Inner Shadow Rollover** style you just created is in the **Styles** palette with a black triangle indicating it is a rollover style.*

*You'll learn how to apply the **Inner Shadow Rollover** style you just created in the next exercise.*

12. Click **File > Save As**. In the **Save As** dialog box, name the file **livesupport_style.psd**. Close the file.

3. [IR]_____**Using Rollover Styles for Multiple Buttons**

In the last exercise, you learned how to create a rollover from scratch and how to save the rollover as a rollover style in the Styles palette. In this exercise, you'll learn how to use the rollover style you made to create multiple rollover buttons. Using rollover styles is a great way to create consistent-looking buttons on a Web page.

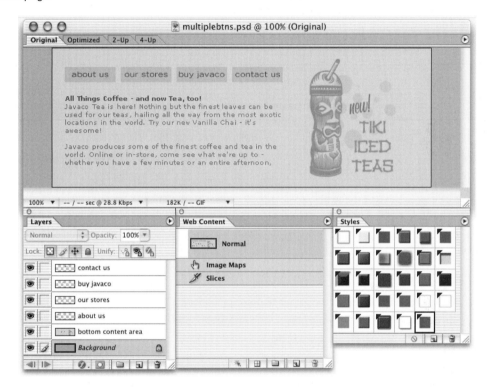

1. Open **multiplebtns.psd** from the **chap_11** folder you copied to your **Desktop**. Make sure the **Layers**, **Web Content**, and **Styles** palettes are visible. If not, choose **Window > Layers**, **Window > Web Content**, and **Window > Styles**.

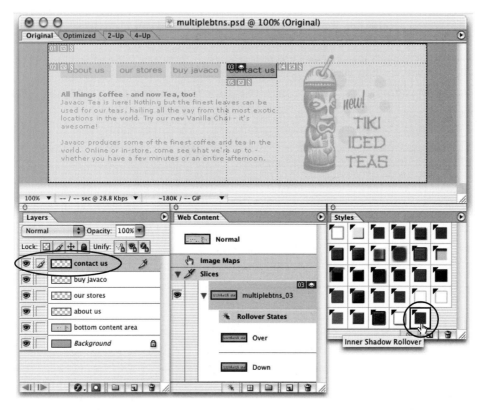

2. In the **Layers** palette, click the **contact us** layer to select it. Click the **Inner Shadow Rollover** style in the **Styles** palette. Notice a layer-based slice and **Over** and **Down** states were automatically created in the **Web Content** palette. Click the **Over** and **Down** states in the **Web Content** palette and notice they are the same as the **Over** and **Down** states you created in the last exercise.

*Next, you'll apply the **Inner Shadow Rollover** style to the other three buttons in the image.*

3. In the **Layers** palette, click the **buy javaco** layer to select it. Hold down the **Shift** key and click the **our stores** and **about us** layers.

*The **buy javaco**, **our stores**, and **about us** layers should all be selected in the **Layers** palette. The capability to select multiple layers with the **Shift** key is new to ImageReady CS.*

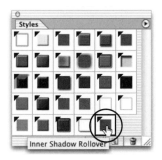

4. Click the **Inner Shadow Rollover** style in the **Styles** palette.

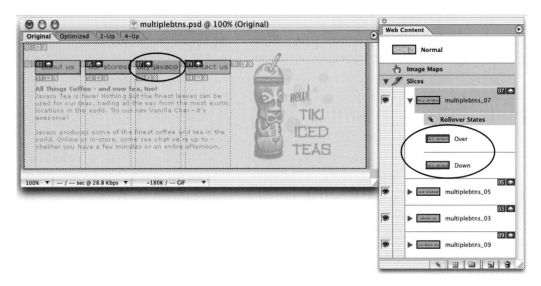

*Notice the **Inner Shadow Rollover** style was automatically applied to all three layers. In the **Web Content** palette, you'll see the new layer-based slices and the **Over** and **Down** states for each of the three layers. Selecting multiple layers in the **Layers** palette is a great way to apply rollover styles to multiple layers.*

5. Click the **Preview in Default Browser** button on the **Toolbox**. Position your mouse over each button to see the **Over** state. Click each button to see the **Down** state.

6. Return to ImageReady CS. Choose **File > Save As**. In the **Save As** dialog box, name the file **multiplebtns_final.psd**. Click **Save**. Leave the file open for the next exercise.

4. [IR] ——————**Renaming and Saving Rollovers**

In Exercise 1, you learned the basics of how to save rollovers along with the required JavaScript and HTML code. In that exercise, you used the default rollover names. In this exercise, you'll learn how to rename rollovers so they have more meaningful names. You'll also learn more advanced optimizing and saving techniques.

1. The **multiplebtns_final.psd** file should still be open from the last exercise. Make sure the **Web Content** and **Optimize** palettes are visible. If not, choose **Window > Web Content** and **Window > Optimize**.

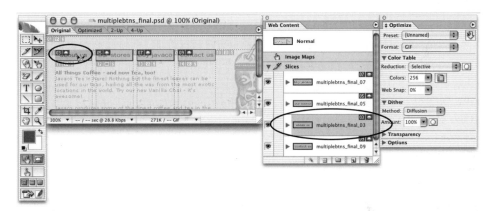

2. Select the **Slice Select** tool in the **Toolbox**. Click **Slice 03** (the **about us** slice) to select it. Notice the name of the slice in the **Web Content** palette—**multiplebtns_final_03**.

Next, you'll rename the slice so it has a more meaningful name.

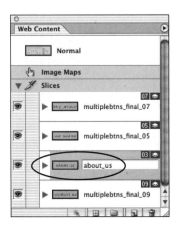

3. In the **Web Content** palette, double-click the **multiplebtns_final_03** slice. A bounding box will appear around the slice name. Rename the slice to **about_us**. Press **Return** (Mac) or **Enter** (Windows).

*When you save the file, the **about_us** slice and respective rollover states will use **about_us** in the file name, making it easier for you to identify the saved images and the references to the images in the HTML code.*

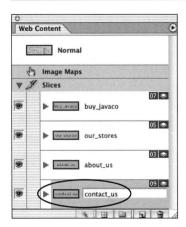

4. In the **Web Content** palette, rename the other slices as **our_stores**, **buy_javaco**, and **contact_us**.

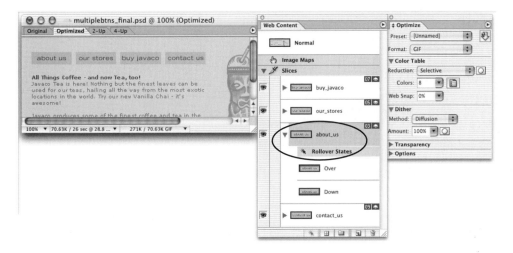

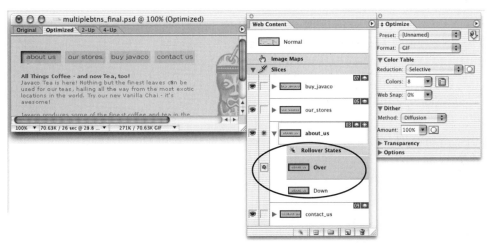

5. Click the **Optimized** tab. Select the **about_us** slice in the **Web Content** palette. Specify optimization settings of your choice in the **Optimize** palette. Be sure to preview how the settings appear in the **Normal**, **Over**, and **Down** states to make sure you're satisfied with the choices. Remember, the same optimization settings apply for the slice and the associated rollover states.

*Tip: To make it easier to preview the optimization settings, click the **Toggle Slice Visibility** button on the **Toolbox** to temporarily hide the slice lines. If you hide the slice visibility, make sure you click the **Toggle Slice Visibility** button again to show the slice visibility before you move on to the next step.*

6. With the **Slice Select** tool selected in the **Toolbox**, click the **Slice 01** auto slice to select it. Click the **Toggle Slices Visibility** button on the **Toolbox** to hide the slice lines. Specify optimization settings for the auto slices in the image in the **Optimize** palette. Remember, because auto slices are linked, the optimization settings will be applied to all the auto slices in the image.

*Tip: If you want to apply different optimization settings to part of the image, you can unlink the auto slices. To unlink slices, select the slice you want to unlink with the **Slice Select** tool. Choose **Slices > Unlink Slice**. The auto slices will automatically be converted to user slices, and you will be able to apply different optimization settings to each slice.*

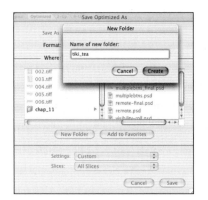
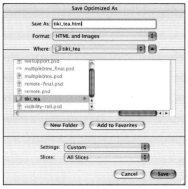

7. Choose **File > Save Optimized As**. In the **Save Optimized As** dialog box, navigate to the **chap_11** folder on your **Desktop**. Click the **New Folder** (Mac) or **Create New Folder** (Windows) button. In the **New Folder** dialog box, name the folder **tiki_tea**. Click **Create** (Mac) or **OK** (Windows). In the **Save Optimized As** dialog box, name the file **tiki_tea.html**. Choose **HTML and Images** from the **Format** pop-up menu. Click **Save**.

*Choosing **HTML and Images** in the **Format** pop-up menu tells ImageReady CS to create and save the images and the required HTML code to make the rollovers work. In Chapter 16, "Integration," you'll learn how to open the HTML files you created in ImageReady CS in an HTML editor such as Adobe GoLive or Macromedia Dreamweaver.*

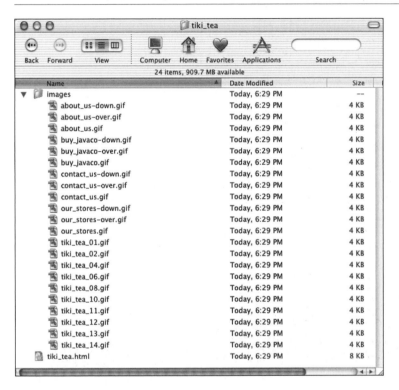

8. Browse to the **tiki_tea** folder in the **chap_11** folder on your **Desktop**. Notice ImageReady CS saved **tiki_tea.html** and a folder called **images**, which contains the images for the rollovers.

*Notice the images reflect the slice names you specified in the **Web Content** palette. The other images, which begin with "tiki_tea", were generated from the auto slices, and they reflect the file name you specified in the **Save Optimized As** dialog box.*

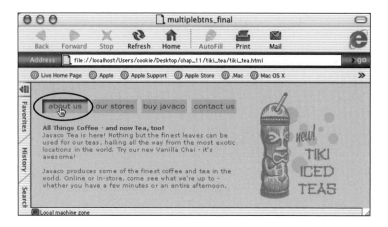

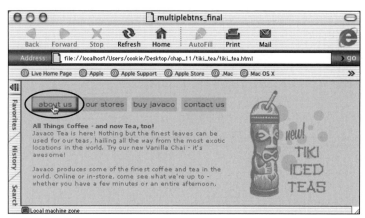

9. Double-click **tiki_tea.html** to open the file in your default Web browser. Position your cursor over the buttons to view the **Over** state. Click the buttons to view the **Down** state.

10. Return to ImageReady CS. Choose **File > Save**. It's important to save your changes to the original PSD file in case you need to go back and make changes to your image.

5. [IR] Creating Rollovers Using Layer Visibility

So far, you've learned how to create rollovers using rollover styles and layer-based slices. Depending on the kind of rollover effect you want, this isn't always the best workflow. The next exercise will show you how to build a rollover by turning layer visibility on and off as part of the rollover technique. Note that a rollover style cannot save layer visibility information.

1. Open **visibility-roll.psd** from the **chap_11** folder you copied to your **Desktop**. Make sure the **Layers** and **Web Content** palettes are visible. If not, choose **Window > Layers** and **Window > Web Content**.

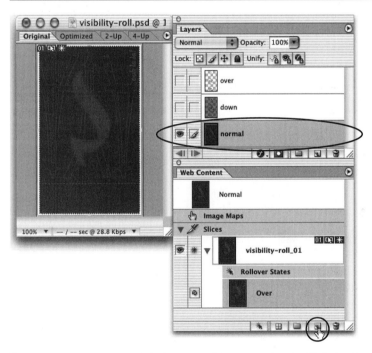

2. In the **Layers** palette, click the **normal** layer to select it. Click the **Create rollover state** button at the bottom of the **Web Content** palette.

*Notice a new slice called **visibility-roll_01** was created in the **Web Content** palette along with an **Over** state.*

3. In the **Web Content** palette, double-click the **visibility-roll_01** slice. When the bounding box appears around the slice, rename the slice as **javaco**. Press **Return** (Mac) or **Enter** (Windows).

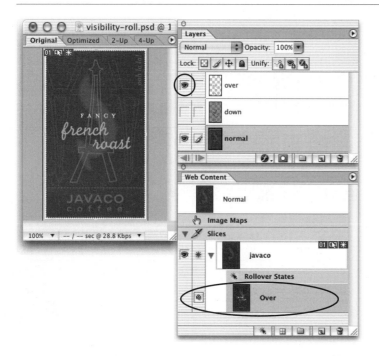

4. Click the **Over** state to select it. Turn on the visibility of the **over** layer in the **Layers** palette.

*Notice the **Over** state updated automatically to show the visibility of the **over** layer.*

5. Click the **Create rollover state** button at the bottom of the **Web Content** palette.

*Notice a **Down** state was created automatically.*

6. Click the **Down** state to select it. Turn on the visibility of the **down** layer in the **Layers** palette.

*Notice the **Down** state updated automatically to show the visibility of the **down** layer.*

7. Click the **Preview in Default Browser** button on the **Toolbox** to view the rollover in your default Web browser. Position your mouse over the image to preview the **Over** state. Click the image to preview the **Down** state.

The rollover states remembered the visibility of the layers. Pretty cool!

*Next, you'll change the size of the **Down** state so it is more targeted in the center of the image.*

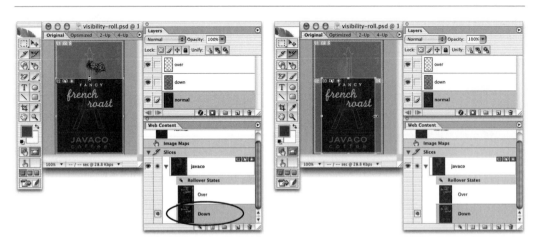

8. Return to ImageReady CS. Click the **Down** state in the **Web Content** palette to select it. Select the **Slice Select** tool in the **Toolbox**. Resize the slice as shown here. By reshaping the slice (instead of creating a new one), you keep the rollover information you specified in the first part of this exercise.

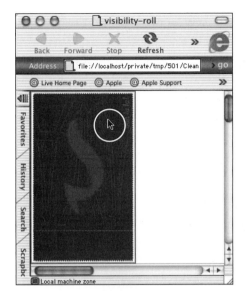 

9. Click the **Preview in Default Browser** button on the **Toolbox** to view the rollover in your default Web browser. Position your mouse over the image to preview the **Over** state. Click the image to preview the **Down** state.

*Notice the **Down** state is smaller, and it reflects the changes you made to the slice size.*

*A great way to create rollovers is from layer visibility. **Note:** You must use user slices to create rollovers that respect layer visibility changes. Layer-based slices will not work for this technique.*

10. Return to ImageReady CS. Save and close the file.

6. [IR] _____Creating Rollovers from Layer Comps

In the last exercise, you created rollovers by turning on the visibility of layers. One of the great new features in ImageReady CS is the layer comps feature. Layer comps lets you save different configurations of layer visibility, position, and appearance, which you can apply to different rollover states. Here's an exercise to show you how.

1. Open **visibility-roll-comps.psd** from the **chap_11** folder you copied to your **Desktop**. Make sure the **Layer Comps** and **Web Content** palettes are visible. If not, choose **Window > Layer Comps** and **Window > Web Content**.

2. Take a look at the **Layer Comps** palette. There are three layer comps in this file: **Normal State**, **Over State**, and **Down State**. Click each layer comp to preview what the different layer comps look like.

Note: For more information about how to create layer comps, refer to Chapter 5, "Layers."

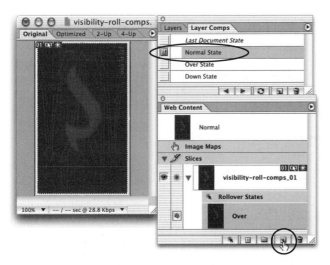

3. Click the **Normal State** layer comp to select it. Click the **Create rollover state** button at the bottom of the **Web Content** palette.

*Notice a slice called **visibility-roll-comps_01** was created in the **Web Content** palette along with an* ***Over** state.*

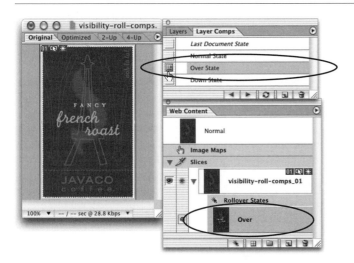

4. Click the **Over** state in the **Web Content** palette to select it. Click the **Over State** layer comp in the **Layer Comps** palette to select it.

*Notice the **Over** state in the **Web Content** palette updated automatically to look like the **Over State** layer comp.*

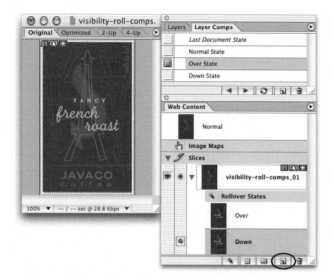

5. Click the **Create rollover state** button at the bottom of the **Web Content** palette.

*Notice a **Down** state was created automatically.*

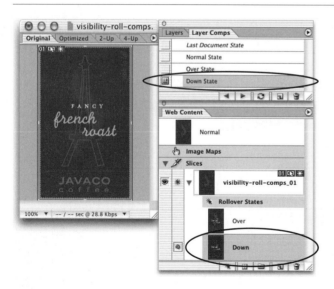

6. Click the **Down** state in the **Web Content** palette to select it. Click the **Down State** layer comp in the **Layer Comps** palette.

*Notice the **Down** state in the **Web Content** palette updated automatically to look like the **Down State** layer comp.*

7. Click the **Preview in Default Browser** button on the **Toolbox**. Position your mouse over the image to preview the **Over** state. Click the image to preview the **Down** state.

As you can see from this exercise, layer comps are a great way to apply different layer configurations to rollover states quickly and easily!

8. Return to ImageReady CS. Save and close the file.

7. [IR] Creating Remote Rollovers

The rollovers you've created so far have been replacement rollovers (which means the image representing the Normal state has been replaced with an image representing the Over state or the Down state) or addition rollovers (which means something was added to the original image in the Over or Down state). In this exercise, you'll learn how to combine replacement rollovers with remote rollovers. When you create remote rollovers, additional visual information appears elsewhere on the Web page. Sound confusing? Here's an exercise to help you understand.

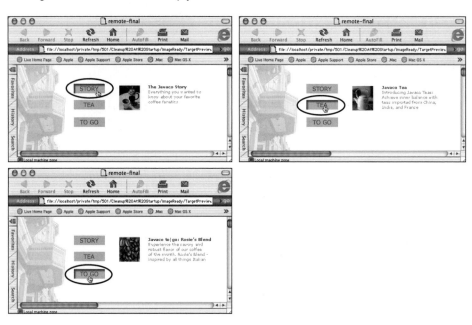

1. Before you get started, take a minute to see the final result of this exercise. It will help you understand what remote rollovers are all about. In ImageReady CS, open **remote-final.psd**. Click the **Preview in Default Browser** button on the **Toolbox**. Position your mouse over the **STORY**, **TEA**, and **TO GO** buttons.

*When you position your mouse over a button, the appearance of the button changes, and an image with text appears to the right. The change to the button is a replacement rollover (because the **Over** state replaces the **Normal** state), and the image and text to the right is a remote rollover (because the **Over** state triggers an action in another part of the Web page).*

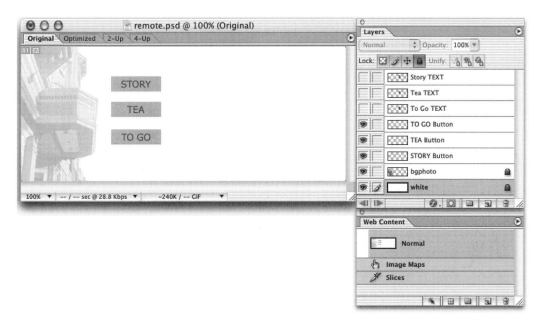

2. Open **remote.psd** from the **chap_11** folder you copied to your **Desktop**. Make sure the **Layers** and the **Web Content** palettes are visible. If not, choose **Window > Layers** and **Window > Web Content**.

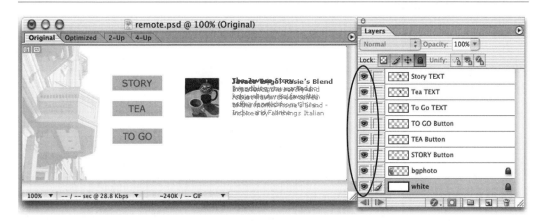

3. Turn on the visibility of all the layers in the document.

Don't worry about the appearance of the image in the document window. The purpose of turning on the visibility of all the layers is to see where to slice the image.

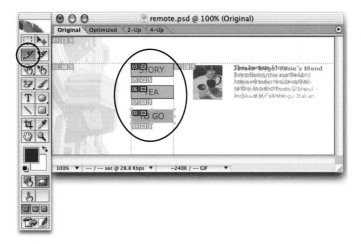

4. Click the **Slice** tool in the **Toolbox**. Click and drag to create a slice around the **STORY**, **TEA**, and **TO GO** buttons, as shown here.

5. Click and drag to create a slice around the **square photograph** and **associated text**, as shown here.

Note: When you're creating rollovers from slices, it's important to create all the slices before you create any of the rollover states.

NOTE | Slicing Layered Images

As you're slicing layered images, you may wonder which layer should be selected in the **Layers** palette. In fact, it makes no difference. Slices drill down through each visible layer in an image.

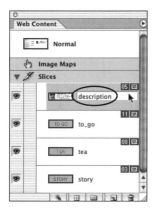

6. Rename the slices in the **Web Content** palette as **story**, **tea**, **to_go**, and **description**.

Renaming the slices to match the names on the buttons will help you keep them organized and identify them in the HTML code.

Next, you'll create the rollovers for the buttons.

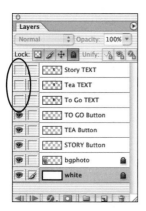

7. In the **Layers** palette, turn off the visibility of the **Story TEXT**, **Tea TEXT**, and **To Go TEXT** layers.

8. Click the **STORY Button** layer in the **Layers** palette to select it. Click the **story** slice in the **Web Content** palette to select it. Click the **Create rollover state** button at the bottom of the **Web Content** palette.

*Notice an **Over** state was created automatically for the story slice in the **Web Content** palette.*

9. Choose **Inner Shadow** from the **Layer Styles** pop-up menu on the **Layers** palette. In the **Layer Style** dialog box, click **OK**.

*Notice an **Inner Shadow** layer style has been applied to the **Over** state of the story rollover.*

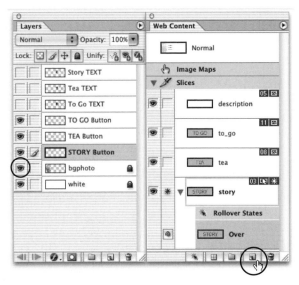

10. With the **Over** state selected in the **Web Content** palette, turn on the visibility of the **Story TEXT** layer in the **Layers** palette.

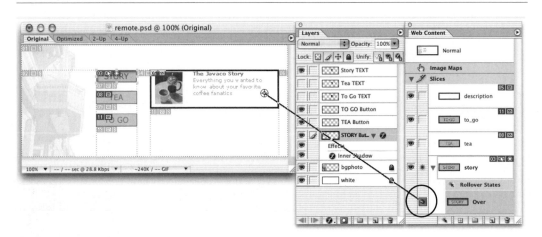

11. With the **Over** state still selected, click and drag the **Target** icon beside the **Over** state in the **Web Content** palette to the **Story TEXT** slice in the document window.

This workflow for creating remote rollovers is new in ImageReady CS.

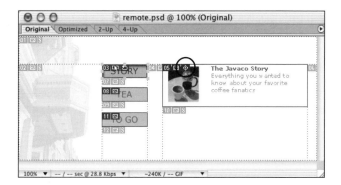

*Notice the **description** slice (**Slice 05**) now has a target icon. This icon indicates the slice is a remote rollover.*

12. Click the **tea** slice in the **Web Content** palette. Click the **Create rollover state** button at the bottom of the **Web Content** palette.

*Notice an **Over** state was created automatically for the **tea** slice.*

13. With the **Over** state selected in the **Web Content** palette and the **TEA Button** layer selected in the **Layers** palette, choose **Inner Shadow** from the **Layer Styles** pop-up menu. In the **Layer Style** dialog box, click **OK**.

*Notice an **Inner Shadow** layer style was automatically applied to the **Over** state.*

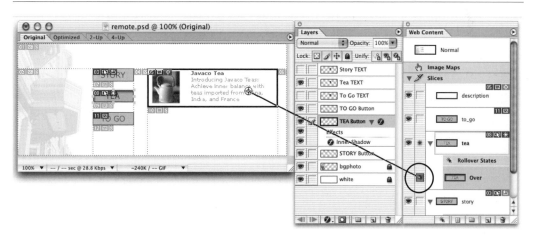

14. Turn on the visibility of the **Tea TEXT** layer in the **Layers** palette. With the **Over** state still selected, click and drag the **Target** icon beside the **Over** state in the **Web Content** palette to the **Tea TEXT** slice in the document window.

15. Click the **to_go** slice in the **Web Content** palette. Click the **Create rollover state** button at the bottom of the **Web Content** palette.

*Notice an **Over** state was created automatically for the **to_go** slice.*

16. With the **Over** state selected in the **Web Content** palette and the **TO GO Button** layer selected in the **Layers** palette, choose **Inner Shadow** from the **Layer Styles** pop-up menu. In the **Layer Styles** dialog box, click **OK**.

*Notice an **Inner Shadow** layer style was automatically applied to the **Over** state.*

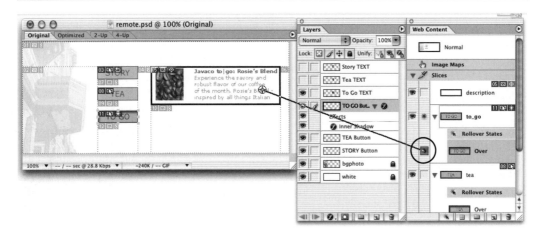

17. Turn on the visibility of the **To Go TEXT** layer in the **Layers** palette. With the **Over** state still selected, click and drag the **Target** icon beside the **Over** state in the **Web Content** palette to the **To Go TEXT** slice in the document window.

18. Click the **Preview in Default Browser** button on the **Toolbox**. Position your mouse over the button to preview the **Over** state and the remote rollover. Pretty cool!

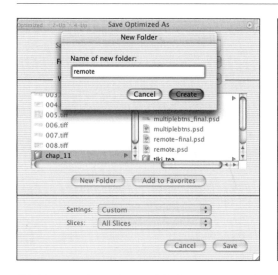 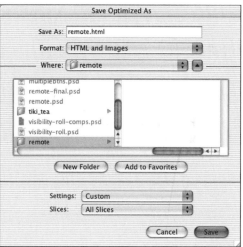

19. Return to ImageReady CS. Choose **File > Save Optimized As**. In the **Save Optimized As** dialog box, navigate to the **chap_11** folder you copied to your **Desktop**. Click the **New Folder** (Mac) or **Create New Folder** (Windows) button. In the **New Folder** dialog box, name the folder **remote**. Click **Create** (Mac) or **OK** (Windows). Keep the default file name **remote.html**. Choose **HTML and Images** from the **Format** pop-up menu. Click **OK**.

20. Browse to the **remote** folder in the **chap_11** folder on your **Desktop**.

*ImageReady CS created **remote.html** and a folder called **images** containing the images that make up the rollover states.*

---

21. Double-click the **remote.html** file to open it in your default Web browser. Position your mouse over the buttons and watch the buttons and the remote rollovers change.

---

22. Return to ImageReady CS. Save and close the file.

MOVIE | **remote_roll.mov**

To learn more about creating remote rollovers as shown in this exercise, check out **remote_roll.mov** from the **movies** folder on the **H•O•T CD-ROM**.

8. [IR]_____Creating Remote Rollovers with Selected States

In the last exercise, you learned how to create remote rollovers for Over states. In this exercise, you'll learn how to create remote rollovers for Selected states. In addition, you'll save the required HTML code and images for the pages. The capability to save multiple HTML pages for rollovers with Selected states is a great new feature in ImageReady CS.

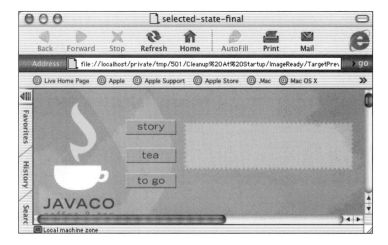

1. Before you get started, take a minute to see the final result of this exercise. Open **selected-state-final.psd** from the **chap_11** folder you copied to your **Desktop**. Click the **Preview in Default Browser** button on the **Toolbox**.

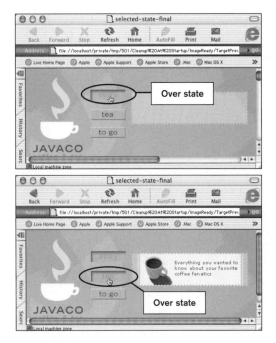

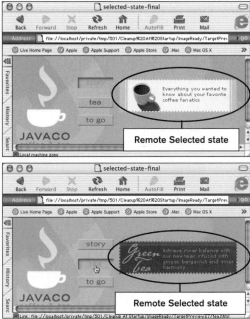

2. Position your mouse over the **Story** button to view the **Over** state. Click the **Story** button to view the **Selected** state. Position your mouse over the **Tea** button to view the **Over** state. Click the **Tea** button to view the **Selected** state. Position your mouse over the **To Go** button to view the **Over** state. Click the **To Go** button to view the **Selected** state.

*When you specify a **Selected** state, it means when the button is selected, something will change on the Web page. For example, if you click the **Tea** button, the image on the right will change to display information about tea. Likewise, if you click the **To Go** button, the image on the right will change to display information about to-go orders.*

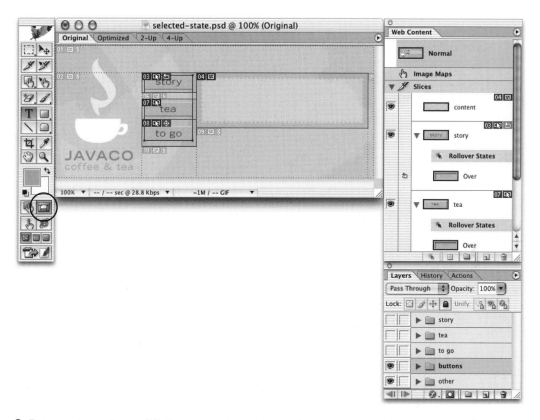

3. Return to ImageReady CS. Open **selected-state.psd** from the **chap_11** folder you copied to your Desktop. Make sure the **Layers** and **Web Content** palettes are visible. If not, choose **Window >** **Layers** and **Window > Web Content**. Turn on the slice visibility by clicking the **Toggle Slice Visibility** button on the **Toolbox**.

*Notice the image has been sliced into 10 slices, and **Over** states have been created for each of the three buttons. Click the **Over** states in the **Web Content** palettes to preview the **Over** states.*

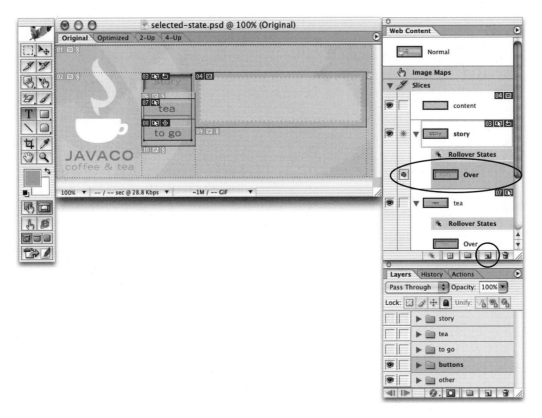

4. In the **Web Content** palette, click the **Over** state for the **story** rollover to select it. Click the **Create rollover state** button at the bottom of the **Web Content** palette.

*Notice a **Down** state was created automatically. Next, you'll change the **Down** state to a **Selected** state.*

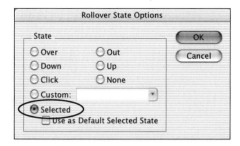

5. Double-click the **Down** state for the **story** rollover. In the **Rollover State Options** dialog box, choose **Selected**. Click **OK**.

*Notice the **Down** state changed to **Selected** state in the **Web Content** palette.*

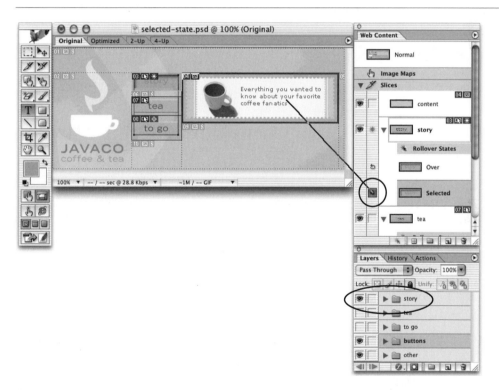

6. With the **Selected** state for the **story** rollover selected in the **Web Content** palette, turn on the visibility of the **story** layer set in the **Layers** palette. Click and drag the **target** icon beside the **Selected** state to the **story** slice, as shown here.

*Setting a remote rollover for the **Selected** state will ensure it appears in the correct position on the Web page.*

7. In the **Web Content** palette, click the **Over** state for the **tea** rollover to select it. Click the **Create rollover state** button at the bottom of the **Web Content** palette. Notice a **Down** state was created automatically. Double-click the **Down** state. In the **Rollover State Options** dialog box, choose **Selected**. Click **OK**.

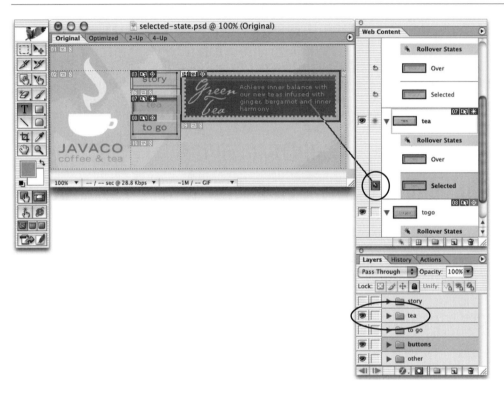

8. Turn on the visibility of the **tea** layer set in the **Layers** palette. Drag the **target** icon beside the **Selected** state to the **tea** slice, as shown here.

9. In the **Web Content** palette, click the **Over** state for the **to go** rollover to select it. Click the **Create rollover state** button at the bottom of the **Web Content** palette. Notice a **Down** state was created automatically. Double-click the **Down** state. In the **Rollover State Options** dialog box, choose **Selected**. Click **OK**.

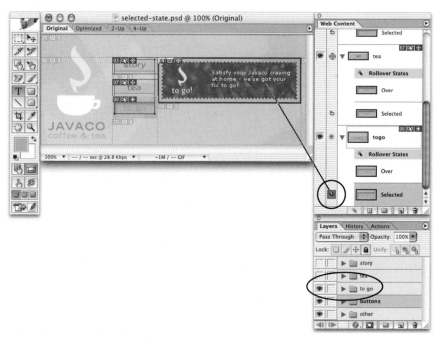

10. Turn on the visibility of the **to go** layer set in the **Layers** palette. Drag the **target** icon beside the **Selected** state to the **to go** slice, as shown here.

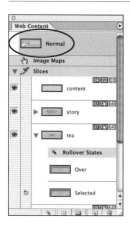

11. Click the **Normal** state at the top of the **Web Content** palette.

*Next, you'll save the required HTML and images. In this example, you need to save four pages: the **default** page and images, the **story** page and images, the **tea** page and images, and the **to go** page and images. One of the great new features in ImageReady CS is the capability to save multiple HTML pages for rollovers with selected states.*

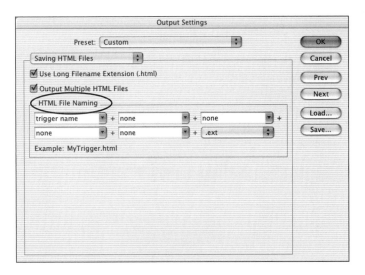

12. Choose **File > Output Settings > Saving HTML Files**. In the **Output Settings** dialog box, turn on the **Output Multiple HTML Files** option. Click **OK**.

*The **Output Multiple HTML Files** option tells ImageReady CS to save an HTML file for each rollover. This new feature in ImageReady CS saves you from saving HTML files individually for each Web page.*

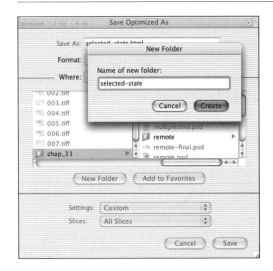

13. Choose **File > Save Optimized As**. Navigate to the **chap_11** folder on your **Desktop**. Click the **New Folder** (Mac) or **Create New Folder** (Windows) button. In the **New Folder** dialog box, name the folder **selected-state**. Click **Create** (Mac) or **OK** (Windows). Leave the default file name (**selected-state.html**) and choose **HTML and Images** from the **Format** pop-up menu. Click **Save**.

14. Browse to the **selected-state** folder in the **chap_11** folder on your **Desktop**. Notice there are four HTML files: **selected-state.html**, **story.html**, **tea.html**, and **togo.html**, along with a folder called **images** that contains the images for the rollovers. ImageReady CS automatically saved each html file and the associated images in a single step. Pretty cool, huh?

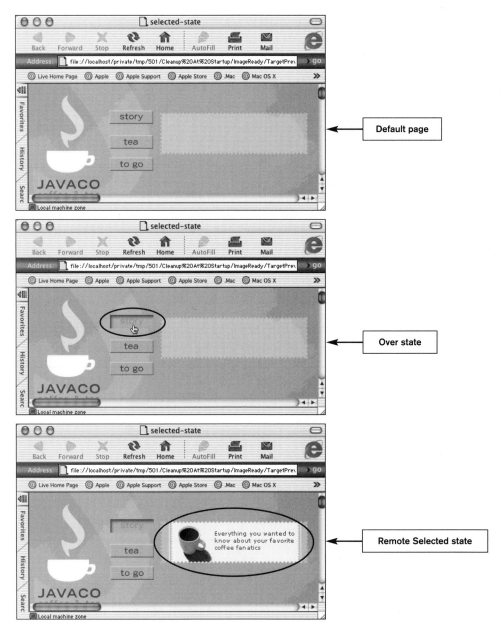

15. Double-click the **selected-state.html** file. Position your mouse over the **Story** button to view the **Over** state. Click the **Story** button to view the **Selected** state. Position your mouse over the **Tea** button to view the **Over** state. Click the **Tea** button to view the **Selected** state. Position your mouse over the **To Go** button to view the **Over** state. Click the **To Go** button to view the **Selected** state.

16. Return to ImageReady CS. Save and close the file.

 MOVIE | selected_state.mov

To learn more about creating selected states as shown in this exercise, check out
selected_state.mov from the **movies** folder on the **H•O•T CD-ROM**.

---

*You've finished another complex chapter! In this chapter, you learned how to create different kinds of
rollovers in ImageReady CS. You'll use these skills again and again when you design your own Web
graphics. In the next chapter, "Image Maps," you'll learn how to create image maps in ImageReady CS.*

I2.

Image Maps

| Creating an Image Map with the Image Map Tools |

| Creating Image Maps from Layers |

| Creating Image Maps from Type |

| Jumping to Photoshop CS with an Image Map |

| Creating Image Map–Based Rollovers |

chap_12

Photoshop CS/ImageReady CS
H•O•T CD-ROM

Most buttons and navigation bars on Web pages are composed of individual images that link to individual URLs. When you're designing Web graphics, you'll often want one image to link to multiple URLs. For example, if you have a map of the United States, you may want each state to link to a different URL. Image maps let you create multiple links from a single graphic.

In the past, you had to create image maps in HTML editors or specialized image map editing software. Fortunately, ImageReady CS makes it easy to create image maps without the need for other applications. In this chapter, you'll learn different techniques for creating image maps in ImageReady CS. Although you can't create image maps in Photoshop CS, you can open an image map created in ImageReady CS in Photoshop CS and still keep the image map information. The next time you open the image map in ImageReady CS, the image map information will remain part of the document.

Server-Side and Client-Side Image Maps

There are two types of image maps—server-side image maps and client-side image maps. In the early days of the Web, it was only possible to create server-side image maps. Today, server-side image maps are no longer used due to the difficulty involved in creating them, the extra bandwidth required to load them, and because server-side image maps do not meet current accessibility recommendations. As a result, this chapter will only focus on creating client-side image maps.

In this chapter, you'll learn different techniques for creating client-side image maps, including creating image maps with the Image Map tool, creating image maps from layers, creating image maps from type layers, and creating rollovers from image maps.

NOTE | Creating Server-Side Image Maps in ImageReady CS

This chapter focuses on creating client-side image maps in ImageReady CS. If you need to create server-side image maps in ImageReady CS, here's how:

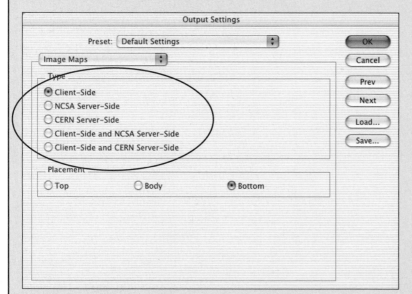

In ImageReady CS, choose **File > Output Settings > Image Maps**. The **Output Settings** dialog box opens automatically. In the **Type** section of the **Output Settings** dialog box, choose the type of server-side image map you want to create. When you build server-side image maps in ImageReady CS, the program will create an HTML file, an image file, and a separate map definition file, which you'll store on the Web server.

What Does an Image Map Look Like?

The required HTML code for client-side image maps contains **map** and **usemap** tags plus the coordinates for the image map regions. The coordinates plot the dimensions and location of the hot spots in an image map.

What's a hot spot? A **hot spot** is a clickable area on a Web page that links to another Web page. Moving your cursor over a hot spot changes the cursor to a hand, which indicates you can click on it and link to another Web page.

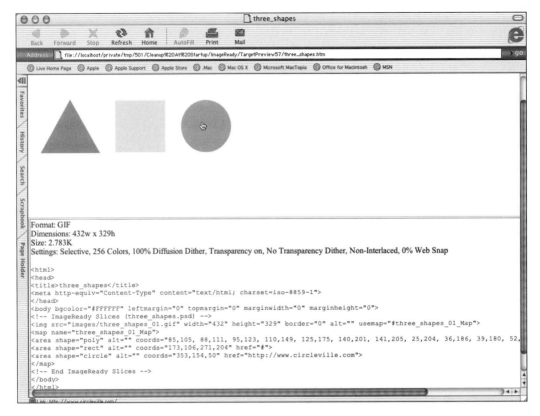

Here is an example of an image map (a single graphic containing three shapes—a triangle, a square, and a circle), including the required HTML code created in ImageReady CS.

*In the HTML code you can see the three types of **area shape** elements [**poly** (polygon), **rect** (rectangle), and **circle**), **coords** (coordinates)], and a series of comma-separated numbers. The numbers describe the coordinates of the hot spots around each shape.*

Creating Image Maps in ImageReady CS

Creating image maps in ImageReady CS is a snap! There are two ways to create image maps in ImageReady CS. You can use the image map tools, or you can create image maps from layers.

There are four image map tools in ImageReady CS. Here's a handy chart to help you understand the tools:

Image Map Tools in ImageReady CS	
Rectangle Image Map tool	Lets you create a rectangular image map
Circle Image Map tool	Lets you create a circular image map
Polygon Image Map tool	Lets you create an irregularly shaped image map
Image Map Select tool	Lets you select an image map

About the Web Content and Image Map Palettes

When you're working with image maps in ImageReady CS, you'll need to access the Web Content palette and the Image Map palette. Here is an overview of the palettes and their roles in the image map creation process.

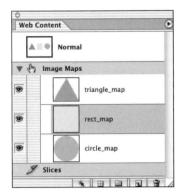

The Web Content palette lets you preview the image maps in an image. Similar to the Layers palette, the Web Content palette displays a thumbnail preview of the image map and offers the ability to turn on and off the visibility of an image map. The Web Content palette also displays information about slices and rollovers, which you learned about in Chapter 10, "*Slicing*," and Chapter 11, "*Rollovers*."

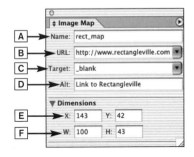
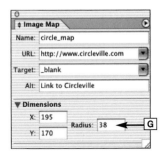
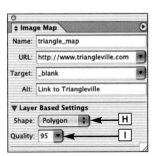

The Image Map palette lets you specify different options for image maps. It is context-sensitive and changes depending on the current image map. If you're working with a tool-based image map, the palette displays dimension information. If you're working with a layer-based image map, it displays layer-based settings. Here's a handy chart to help you understand the controls in the Image Map palette.

Image Map Palette Controls		
A	**Name field**	Specify a name for the currently selected image map.
B	**URL field pop-up menu**	Specify a URL you want the currently selected image map to link to.
C	**Target pop-up menu**	Choose one of the following target types when you specify a URL for an image map: **_blank**, **_self**, **_parent**, or **_top**.
D	**Alt field**	Specify the text you want viewers to see when images are turned off in a Web browser.
E	**X and Y Coordinates fields**	Specify the left edge (X) and top edge (Y) of an image map.
F	**Width and Height fields** (available only for image maps created with the Rectangle Image Map tool and the Polygon Image Map tool)	Specify the width and height of an image map.
G	**Radius field** (available only for image maps created with the Circle Image Map tool)	Specify the radius of an image map area.
H	**Shape pop-up menu** (available only for layer-based image maps)	Specify the shape of an image map area (rectangle, circle, or polygon).
I	**Quality pop-up menu** (available only for the polygonal layer-based image maps)	Specify the accuracy of polygon vertices.

I. [IR] _____Creating an Image Map with the Image Map Tools

Using the Image Map tools is the best way to create image maps when you're working with flattened images or images on a single layer. In this exercise, you'll learn how to create and modify an image map with the Image Map tools. You'll also learn how to optimize image maps and save the images and required HTML code.

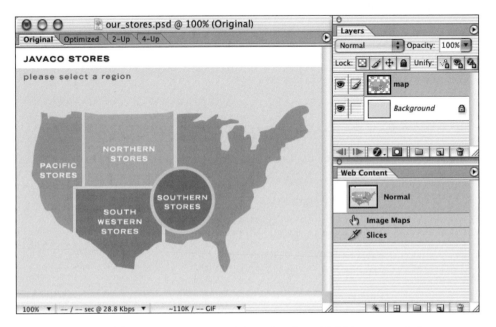

1. In **ImageReady CS**, open **our_stores.psd** from the **chap_12** folder you copied to your **Desktop** from the **H•O•T CD-ROM**.

*Because the image is on a single layer, you'll use the **Image Map** tools to create an image map and its associated hot spots. If the image was separated into individual layers, you'd have the option to create the image map from the **Image Map** tools or from the layers (which you'll learn in the next exercise).*

2. Select the **Circle Image Map** tool from the **Toolbox**.

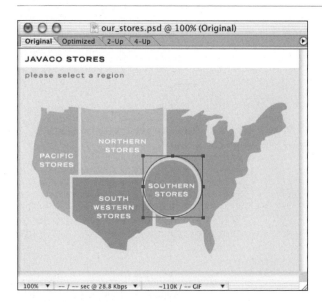

3. Click and drag over the **Southern Stores** graphic to create a circular image map.

*Tip: To draw a circular image map from the center out, hold down the **Option** (Mac) or **Alt** (Windows) key while dragging.*

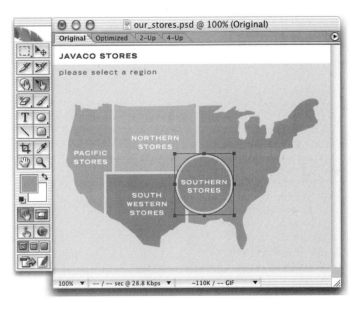

4. Select the **Image Map Select** tool in **Toolbox**. Click inside the circular image map you just drew and position it over the circle in the image using the **arrow keys** on your keyboard or by clicking and dragging.

NOTE | Resizing Image Maps

If you create an image map with one of the Image Map tools, you can resize it easily. Here's how:

With one of the Image Map tools selected in the Toolbox, position your mouse over one of the nodes on the perimeter of the image map. You'll notice the cursor change from the image map cursor to the resize cursor. When the cursor changes to the resize cursor, click and drag to resize the image map.

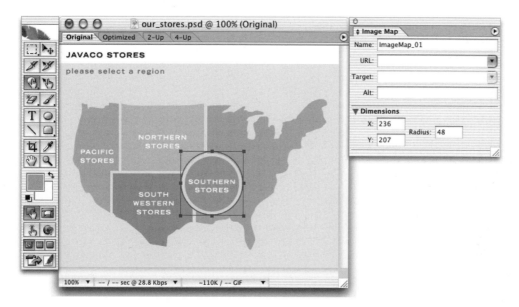

5. Make sure the **Image Map** palette is visible. If it's not, choose **Window > Image Map**.

*Tip: You can toggle the **Image Map** palette on and off using the **Image Map** palette button on the **Options** bar for the **Image Map Select** tool. (The **Image Map** palette button is only available on the **Options** bar for the **Image Map Select** tool, not the **Rectangle**, **Circle**, or **Polygon Image Map** tools.)*

6. Type **southernstores_map** in the **Name** field on the **Image Map** palette.

Tip: Avoid using spaces when you name an image map. A good substitute is an underscore or a hyphen.

Note: *It's not mandatory to type a name in the **Name** field because ImageReady CS names image maps automatically. However, you'll find giving image maps useful names makes it easier to find them in the HTML code should you need to.*

7. Type **http://www.southernstores.com** (or a URL of your choice) in the **URL** field on the **Image Map** palette. You can link to a URL on another Web site or to a URL on a page in the same Web site as your image map. **Note:** The URLs I use in this exercise are fictitious URLs, and they will not actually work. If you want to use a real URL, and you have a live Web connection, go ahead!

8. Choose **_blank** from the **Target** pop-up menu in the **Image Map** palette.

_blank *indicates you want the URL to open in a new Web browser window. You don't have to specify a target if you don't want to. If you don't choose a target, the URL will open in the same Web browser window as the page containing the image map.*

9. Type **Link to Southern Stores** in the **Alt** field of the **Image Map** palette.

Alt text shows in a Web browser if the user turns off images in the **Preferences** *or if they are access-ing Web pages with a text-only Web browser. Some viewers turn off images when they surf the Web to speed up the downloading process. Sight-impaired visitors who can't read text on a computer screen use screen readers to "read" the alt text to them because they can't see the images.*

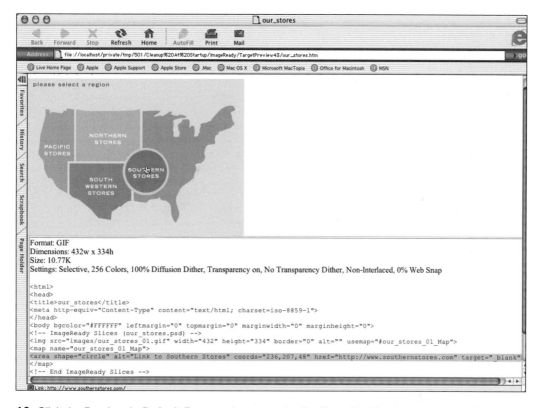

10. Click the **Preview in Default Browser** button on the **Toolbox**. Position your cursor over the **Southern Stores** graphic in the Web browser. Notice the cursor changes to a hand, indicating the image is a hot spot.

Take a look at the highlighted section of HTML code. It reads as follows: **<area shape="circle" alt="Link to Southern Stores" coords="236,207,48" href="http://www.southernstores.com" target="_blank">**. *This section of HTML code tells your Web browser the image map is a circle with coordinates of **236**, **208**, **47** and links to **http://www.southernstores.com** (or whatever URL you used) in a new Web browser window.*

11. Return to ImageReady CS.

*Next, you'll use the **Polygon Image Map** tool to create an image map for the **Northern Stores** graphic.*

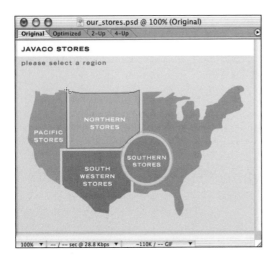
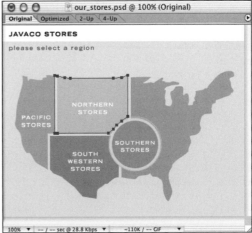

12. Select the **Polygon Image Map** tool from the **Toolbox**. Click the top-left corner of the **Northern Stores** graphic. Click and drag your cursor around the border of the graphic, clicking when you need to create a contour in the line. When you finish outlining the shape, position your cursor over the spot in the top-left corner where you began. When the cursor changes to a small circle, click to close the path.

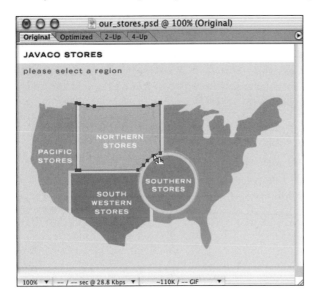

Note: To adjust the shape, position your mouse over one of the nodes on the path. When the cursor changes to the white arrow and white hand, click and drag the node into position.

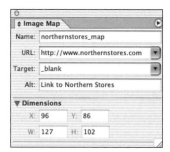

13. In the **Image Map** palette, type **northernstores_map** in the **Name** field, type **http://www.northernstores.com** in the **URL** field (or use a URL of your choice), choose **_blank** in the **Target** field, and type **Link to Northern Stores** in the **Alt** field.

14. Click the **Preview in Default Browser** button on the **Toolbox**.

*Notice there are now two hot spots in the image—**Southern Stores** and **Northern Stores**.*

---

15. Return to ImageReady CS.

*Next, you'll use the **Polygon Image Map** tool to create an image map for the **South Western Stores** graphic.*

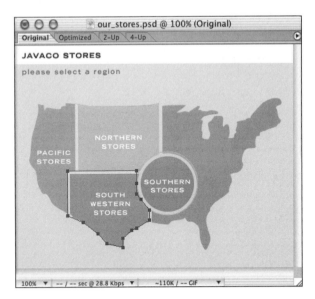

16. With the **Polygon Image Map** tool selected in the **Toolbox**, click the top-left corner of the **South Western Stores** graphic. Click and drag your cursor around the border of the graphic, clicking when you need to create a contour in the line. When you finish outlining the shape, position your cursor over the spot in the top-left corner where you began. When the cursor changes to a small circle, click to close the path.

If you need to adjust the shape, position your mouse over one of the nodes on the path. When the cursor changes to the white arrow and white hand, click and drag the node into position.

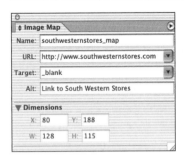

17. In the **Image Map** palette, type **southwesternstores_map** in the **Name** field, type **http://www.southwesternstores.com** (or a URL of your choice) in the **URL** field, choose **_blank** from the **Target** pop-up menu, and type **Link to South Western Stores** in the **Alt** field.

18. Click the **Preview in Default Browser** button in the **Toolbox**.

*Notice there are now three hot spots in the image—**Southern Stores**, **Northern Stores**, and **South Western Stores**.*

---

19. Return to ImageReady CS.

Next, you'll optimize and save the images and the required HTML code.

---

20. Click the **Optimized** tab. Make sure the **Optimize** palette is visible. If not, choose **Window > Optimize**.

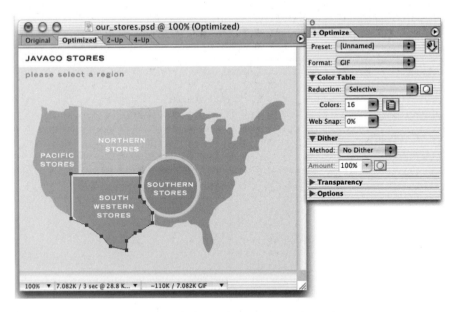

21. In the **Optimize** palette, match the settings to those shown here.

Because the image is a flat graphic, it's best to optimize it as a GIF. You can also optimize image maps as JPEGs.

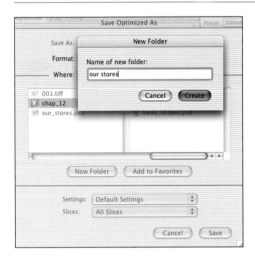

22. Choose **File > Save Optimized As**. In the **Save Optimized As** dialog box, navigate to the **chap_12** folder you copied to your **Desktop**. Click the **New Folder** (Mac) or **Create New Folder** (Windows) button. In the **New Folder** dialog box, name the folder **our stores**. Click **Create** (Mac) or **OK** (Windows).

23. Choose **HTML and Images** in the **Format** pop-up menu. Name the file **our_stores_map.html**.

*Note: You don't have to save the HTML code with the image map. If you prefer, you can choose **Images** from the **Format** pop-up menu and create the HTML code in an HTML editor such as Adobe GoLive or Macromedia Dreamweaver. The choice is yours, but it's easiest to let ImageReady CS create the code. You'll learn how to bring the resulting HTML code into Adobe GoLive and Macromedia Dreamweaver in Chapter 16, "Integration."*

24. Browse to the **our stores** folder in the **chap_12** folder on your **Desktop**.

*Notice there is a file called **our_stores_map.html** and a folder called **images**, containing **our_stores_map_01.gif**. When you create an image map, the individual sections are saved in the same file.*

25. Double-click **our_stores_map.html** to view the file in your default Web browser. You should see three hot spots in the image—**Northern Stores**, **Southern Stores**, and **South Western Stores**.

26. Save and close **our_stores.psd**. The image map information will be saved in the PSD file format.

2. [IR]_____Creating an Image Map from Layers

In the last exercise, you learned how to create image maps with the Image Map tools. In this exercise, you'll learn how to create image maps from layers.

Layer-based images are a great way to create image maps because they create hot spots the same size as the layer. Creating image maps from layers is often easier than using the Image Map tools to trace around the edges of irregularly shaped images because layer-based image maps match the exact size of the layer. Plus, if you change the contents of a layer or move a layer, the image map updates automatically. You can also move layer-based image maps without having to redraw the image maps after every move.

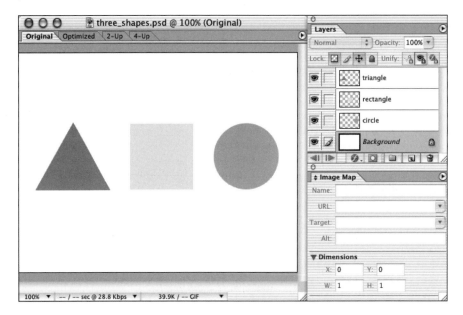

1. Open **three_shapes.psd** from the **chap_12** folder you copied to your **Desktop**.

Notice the triangle, the rectangle, and the circle are each on separate, transparent layers.
Note: *You can only create layer-based image maps from transparent layers.*

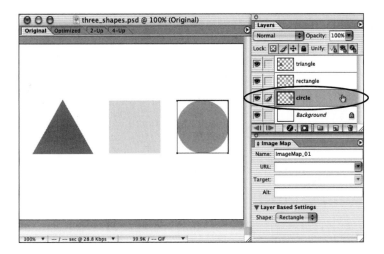

2. In the **Layers** palette, click the **circle** layer to select it. Choose **Layer > New Layer Based Image Map Area**.

*Notice the **hand** symbol to the right of the **circle** layer in the **Layers** palette. The **hand** symbol indicates the **circle** layer has an image map associated with it.*

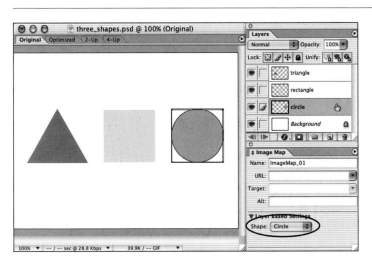

3. Choose **Circle** from the **Shape** pop-up menu in the **Layer Based Settings** section of the **Image Map** palette.

*By default, layer-based image maps are rectangular. Choosing **Circle** or **Polygon** from the **Shape** pop-up menu creates a better fit between the shape of the layer and the hot spot area of the image map. The better the fit, the easier it is to locate a hot spot in a Web browser.*

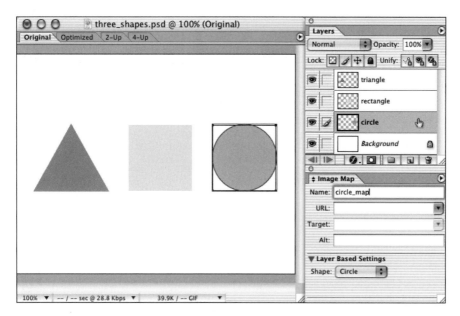

4. Type **circle_map** in the **Name** field on the **Image Map** palette.

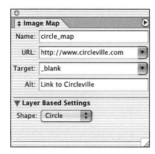

5. Type **http://www.circleville.com** (or a URL of your choice) in the **URL** field of the **Image Map** palette. Choose **_blank** from the **Target** pop-up menu. Type **Link to Circleville** in the **Alt** field.

Note: *If you are not online when you test the preview or final HTML file, the link to the URL you specified will not work.*

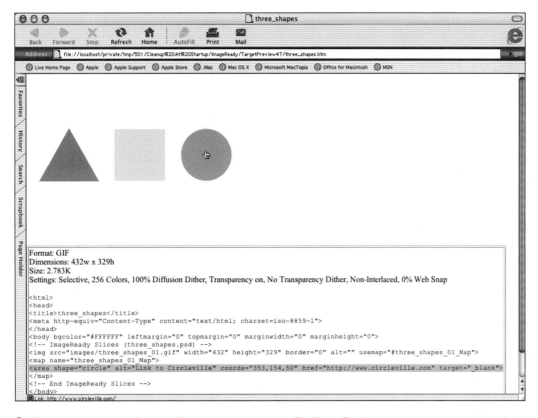

6. Click the **Preview in Default Browser** button on the **Toolbox**. Position your cursor over the circle.

*Notice the cursor changes to a hand, indicating the **circle** is a hot spot.*

---

7. Return to ImageReady CS.

*Next, you'll create layer-based image maps from the **rectangle** and **triangle** layers.*

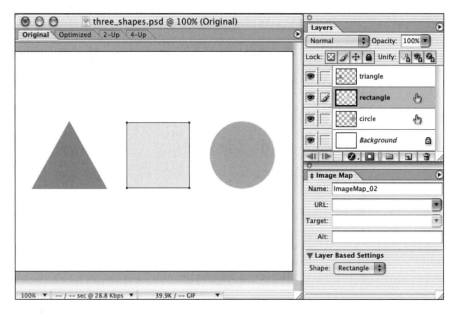

8. In the **Layers** palette, click the **rectangle** layer to select it. Choose **Layer > New Layer Based Image Map Area**.

*Notice the **Shape** pop-up menu automatically defaults to **Rectangle**, so you don't need to change it.*

9. In the **Image Map** palette, type **rectangle_map** in the **Name** field, type **http://www.rectangleville.com** in the **URL** field, choose **_blank** from the **Target** pop-up menu, and type **Link to Rectangleville** in the **Alt** field.

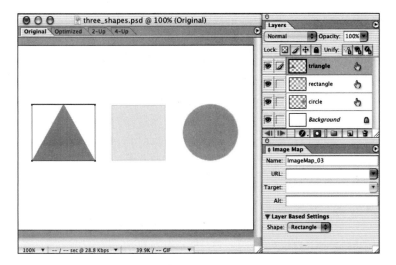

10. In the **Layers** palette, click the **triangle** layer to select it. Choose **Layer > New Layer Based Image Map Area**.

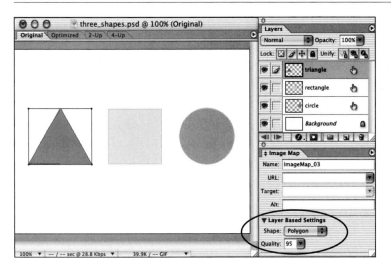

11. Choose **Polygon** from the **Shape** pop-up menu of the **Layer Based Settings** section of the **Image Map** palette. Type **95** in the **Quality** field.

*The **Quality** setting affects how tightly the polygon-shaped image map will hug the layer. The higher the tolerance, the closer the match will be between the image map and the layer.*

***Tip:** You won't always want **Quality** to be at its highest setting. In some cases, such as those involving complex shapes or text, high **Quality** settings will create hot spots too narrow for practical use.*

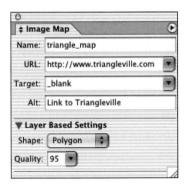

12. In the **Image Map** palette, type **triangle_map** in the **Name** field, type **http://www.triangleville.com** in the **URL** field, choose **_blank** from the **Target** pop-up menu, and type **Link to Triangleville** in the **Alt** field.

NOTE | Changing the Image Map Settings

If you need to change the settings in the **Image Map** palette, select the **Image Map Select** tool from the **Toolbox** and click inside the layer you want to change. The **Image Map** palette will change automatically to reflect the currently selected image map. If you save the file as a PSD, the image map settings will be stored with the file and can be changed easily in ImageReady CS at any time.

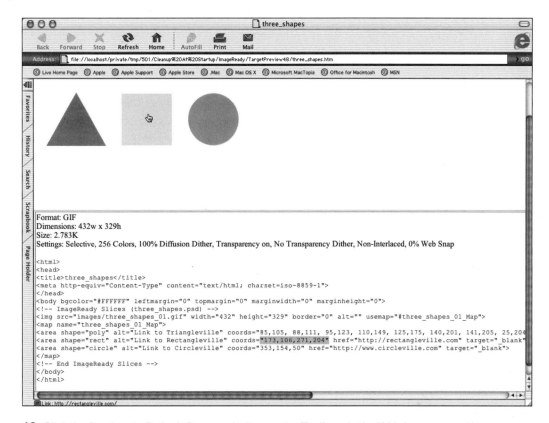

13. Click the **Preview in Default Browser** button on the **Toolbox**. In the Web browser, position your cursor over each of the three shapes. The cursor will change to a hand, indicating each shape is a hot spot.

*Notice the coordinates of the rectangle hot spot: **173**, **106**, **271**, **204**. In the next steps, you'll move the **rectangle** layer so you can see how layer-based image maps update automatically when you move a layer.*

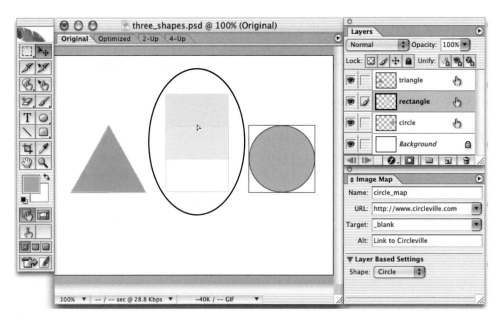

14. Return to ImageReady CS. In the **Layers** palette, click the **rectangle** layer to select it. Select the **Move** tool in the **Toolbox**. Click and drag to move the **rectangle** layer.

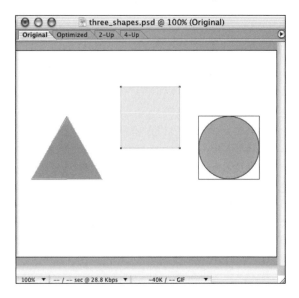

When you release the mouse, the thin blue outline of the image map moves with the layer. When you move layers, layer-based image maps update automatically.

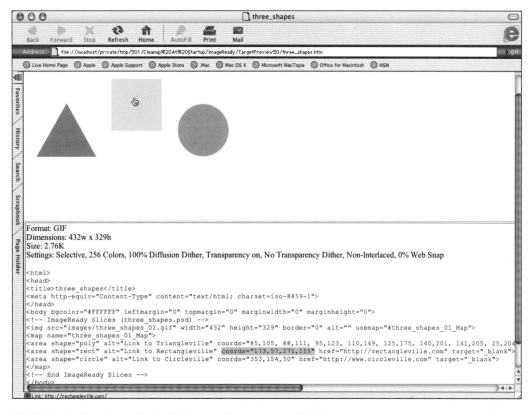

15. Click the **Preview in Default Browser** button on the **Toolbox**.

*Notice the coordinates of the rectangle image map changed to reflect the move, proving the layer-based image map moved with the layer. In my case, the new coordinates are **173**, **57**, **271**, **155**. Your coordinates may be different depending on where you moved the rectangle layer.*

---

16. Return to ImageReady CS.

Next, you'll optimize and save the image map and the required HTML code.

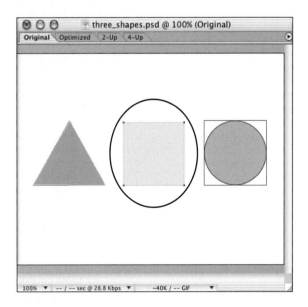

17. In the **Layers** palette, click the **rectangle** layer to select it. With the **Move** tool selected in the **Toolbox**, drag the **rectangle** layer back to its original position (in line with the **triangle** and **circle** layers).

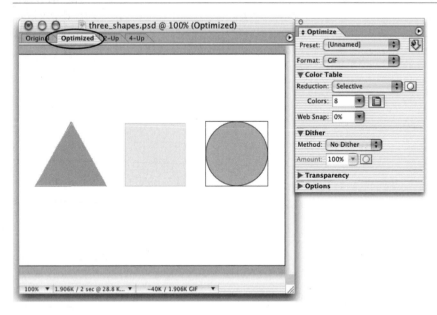

18. Click the **Optimized** tab. In the **Optimize** palette, match the optimization settings with the settings shown here.

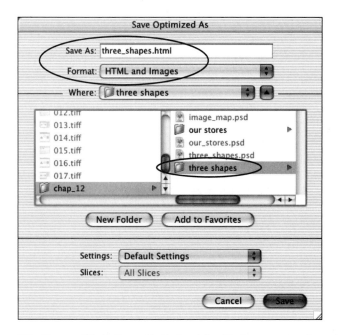

19. Choose **File > Save Optimized As**. Navigate to the **chap_12** folder you copied to your **Desktop**. Click the **New Folder** (Mac) or **Create New Folder** (Windows) button. In the **New Folder** dialog box, type **three shapes**. Click **Create** (Mac) or **OK** (Windows). Choose **HTML and Images** from the **Format** pop-up menu. Name the file **three_shapes.html**. Click **Save**.

20. Browse to the **three shapes** folder in the **chap_12** folder on your **Desktop**. Notice the **three_shapes.html** file and a folder called **images** that contains the image map file. If you want to view the file in a Web browser, double-click **three_shapes.html**.

21. Return to ImageReady CS. Leave **three_shapes.psd** open for the next exercise.

3. [IR] _____Creating Image Maps for Type

Creating an image map to fit type or other complex shapes can be tricky. In some cases, you'll need to experiment with the tool-based method you learned in Exercise 1 and the layer-based method you learned in Exercise 2 to see which technique creates the best image map. In this exercise, you'll learn to create image maps for type by experimenting with both image map creation methods.

1. Three_shapes.psd should still be open from the last exercise. Click the **Original** tab. In the **Layers** palette, click the **triangle** layer to select it.

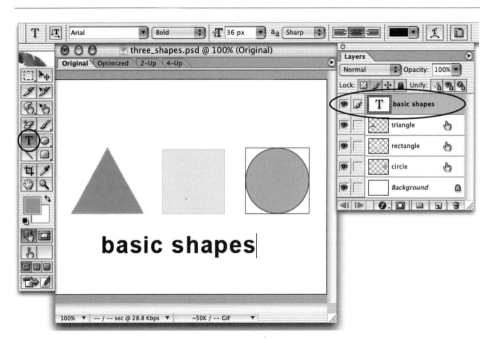

2. Select the **Type** tool from the **Toolbox**. On the **Options** bar, choose **Arial** from the **Font Family** pop-up menu, **Bold** from the **Font Style** pop-up menu, and **36 px** from the **Font Size** pop-up menu. Choose a **dark grey** or **black** from the **Font Color** picker. Click inside the document window and type **basic shapes**.

*Notice a new type layer, **basic shapes**, was created in the Layers palette automatically.*

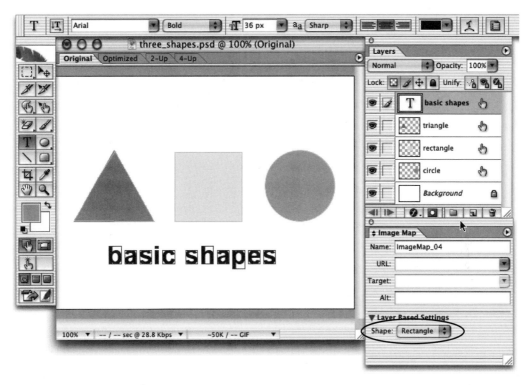

3. With the **basic shapes** type layer selected in the **Layers** palette, choose **Layer > New Layer Based Image Map Area**.

*Notice **Rectangle** is automatically selected in the **Shape** pop-up menu in the **Layer Based Settings** section of the **Image Map** palette.*

4. Click the **Preview in Default Browser** button on the **Toolbox**. In the Web browser, position your cursor over the type.

Notice when you position your mouse over some areas of type, the cursor does not change to a hand, making it difficult to discover the hot spot.

Notice several lines of code and image map coordinates were generated by the layer-based image map. Web developers usually try to avoid creating unnecessarily complex code, which is difficult to read and can increase the size of a Web page.

As you can see, creating a layer-based image map is not ideal when the underlying artwork consists of complex shapes such as type.

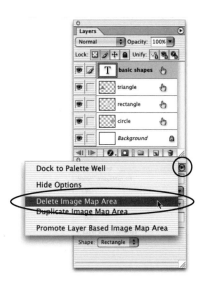

5. Return to ImageReady CS. With the **basic shapes** type layer selected in the **Layers** palette, choose **Delete Image Map Area** from the **Image Map** palette menu.

6. Select the **Rectangle Image Map** tool from the **Toolbox**.

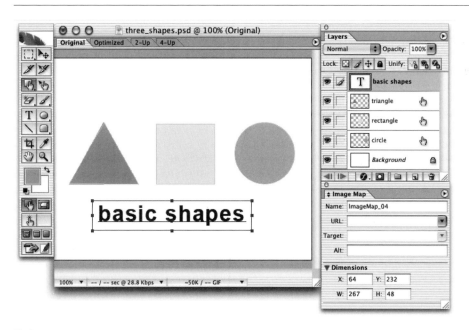

7. Click and drag to draw a rectangular image map around the type in the document window.

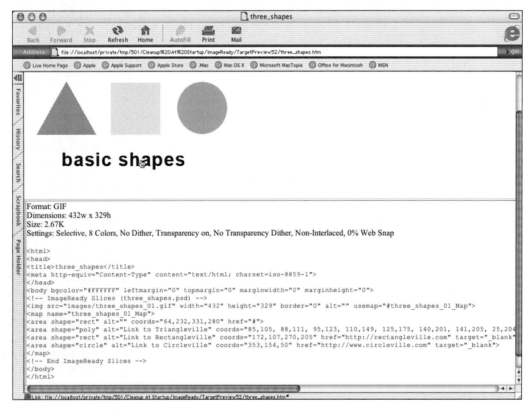

8. Click the **Preview in Default Browser** button on the **Toolbox**.

Notice when you move your cursor over the text in the Web browser window, it is easy to find the hot spot because it is a continuous area. Also notice the code is much simpler than when you created a layer-based image map.

Even though you have transparent layers in an image, creating layer-based image maps will not always give you the desired result. In some cases, it's best to create a simple rectangular image map to make it easy for your viewers to identify hot spots quickly.

9. Return to ImageReady CS. Save your changes and leave **three_shapes.psd** open for the next exercise.

[IR/PS]_____**Jumping to Photoshop CS with an Image Map**

In the introduction to this chapter, I mentioned that Photoshop CS honors image map information from ImageReady CS even though it cannot display it. Here's an exercise to show you how it works.

1. With **three_shapes.psd** open in ImageReady CS from the last exercise, click the **Jump To** button at the bottom of the **Toolbox**.

Three_shapes.psd will open automatically in Photoshop CS.

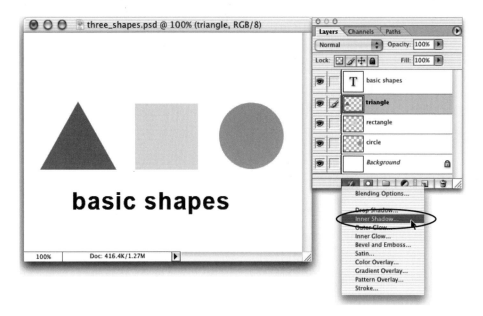

2. In Photoshop CS, click the **triangle** layer in the **Layers** palette to select it. Choose **Inner Shadow** from the **Layer Styles** pop-up menu at the bottom of the **Layers** palette. The **Layer Styles** dialog box opens automatically. Click **OK**.

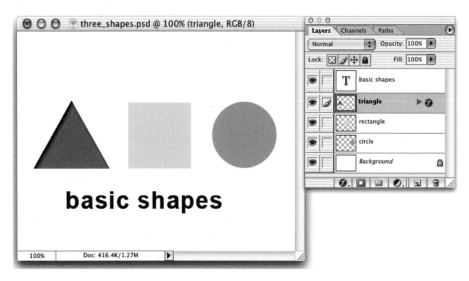

An **Inner Shadow** layer style will be applied to the **triangle** layer.

3. Click the **Jump To** button on the **Toolbox**.

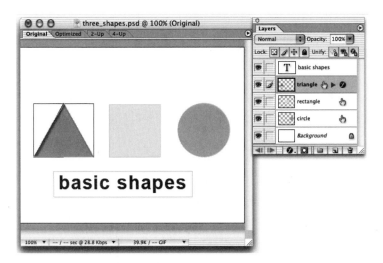

Three_shapes.psd will open automatically in ImageReady CS. Notice the changes you made with Photoshop CS appear in ImageReady CS. Notice the image map information, which was not visible in Photoshop CS, is still intact. Even though Photoshop CS does not let you create image maps, you can edit images freely between Photoshop CS and ImageReady CS without losing image map information.

If you want, you can preview, optimize, or save the image map using the techniques you learned in this chapter.

4. Save and close the file.

5. [IR] _____ Creating Image Map–Based Rollovers

In Chapter 11, "*Rollovers,*" you learned how to create rollovers from slices. You can also create rollovers from image maps. You use this technique when the shape triggering the rollover is not a rectangle or a square (slice-based rollovers can only be created from rectangles and squares). Here's an exercise to show you how.

1. Open **image_map.psd** from the **chap_12** folder you copied to your **Desktop**.

Image_map.psd is similar to a file you worked with in Chapter 11, "Rollovers."

2. Select the **Polygon Image Map** tool from the **Toolbox**.

*Note: You can use any of the **Image Map** tools to create image map-based rollovers. For this particular example, the **Polygon Image Map** tool will work best.*

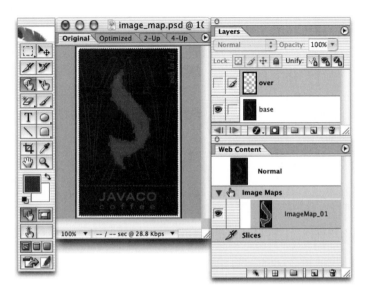

3. Click and drag around the **smoke** logo, clicking when you need to create a contour in the line. When you finish outlining the **smoke** logo, position your cursor over the spot where you began. When the cursor changes to a small circle, click to close the path.

*Notice a new image map, **ImageMap_01**, has been created in the **Web Content** palette.*

4. Double-click **ImageMap_01** in the **Web Content** palette. When the bounding box appears, rename the image map as **smoke**.

As you learned in the last chapter, the name affects how rollovers are identified in the final HTML files.

5. Select the **smoke** layer in the **Web Content** palette. Choose **New Rollover State** from the **Web Content** palette menu to create an **Over** state.

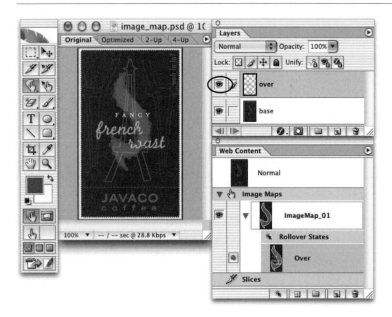

6. In the **Layers** palette, turn on the **Visibility** icon for the **over** layer.

7. Click the **Preview in Default Browser** button on the **Toolbox**.

Note: The rollover won't work until you position your mouse over the smoke logo.

This is a great technique if you want to create a rollover from an irregular shape!

---

8. Return to ImageReady CS. Save and close the file.

You've just finished another chapter! Creating image maps is fairly simple once you get the hang of it. Up next, you'll learn different animation techniques in Chapter 13, "Animated GIFs and Flash."

13.

Animated GIFs and Flash

| Creating Animations from Layer Visibility |
Setting Looping and Speed	Tweening	Saving as Animated GIFs
Creating Transparent GIF Animations	Creating Animated GIF Rollovers
Exporting Animations as SWF	Exporting Frames as Files
Designing Entire Web Interfaces

chap_13

Photoshop CS/ImageReady CS
H•O•T CD-ROM

One of the best things about designing Web graphics is the ability to create animations, which you can't do in print design. If you have a background in printing, it's possible you've never worked with animation before. No need to worry—ImageReady CS is an excellent tool to help you create animated Web graphics. If you've created animations before, you'll be surprised how easy it is to create animations in ImageReady CS.

Although animations appear to move when you view them on a computer, the movement is simulated from a series of still images. The GIF format is popular for Web animation because it can contain a series of static images and display them consecutively like a slideshow. Animated GIFs are also popular because they are backwards-compatible with older Web browsers. One of the key enhancements in ImageReady CS is the Macromedia Flash Export feature. For the first time, you can choose to save animations as animated GIFs or Macromedia Flash files.

In the first part of this chapter, you'll learn different techniques for creating animations. In the second part of this chapter, you'll learn how to how to save animations as animated GIFs, how to export animations as Macromedia Flash files, and, new to ImageReady CS, how to export individual frames as files. Photoshop CS does not support animation, so you'll use ImageReady CS for the exercises in this chapter.

The Animation Palette

When you create animations in ImageReady CS, you'll use the **Animation** palette to specify different settings. Here's an overview of the features in the Animation palette:

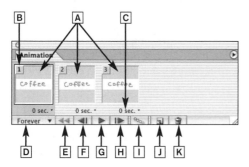

	Animation Palette Controls	
A	**Frames**	Displays a preview of the contents in a frame.
B	**Frame number**	Identifies the frame number.
C	**Frame Delay pop-up menu**	Selects the frame delay time.
D	**Looping pop-up menu**	Selects the looping option (how many times to play the animation).
E	**First Frame button**	Selects the first frame.
F	**Previous Frame button**	Selects the previous frame.
G	**Play/Stop button**	Plays or stops the animation.
H	**Next Frame button**	Selects the next frame.
I	**Tween button**	Tweens the animation. Tweening tells ImageReady CS to automatically generate frames between frames you specify.
J	**Duplicate Current Frame button**	Duplicates the current frame to make a new frame.
K	**Delete Selected Frame button**	Deletes the currently selected frame.

Controlling the Timing of Animations

Animation is a time-based medium. The timing of animations is based on how long you want the animation to play and the number of frames. Sometimes slide-show style animation is what you'll want, and other times, you'll want to make movement feel faster. The GIF and SWF format supports delays between frames and allows timing to change within a single animation file.

Video and film animation are also time-based mediums, with one key difference from animated GIFs and SWFs: video and film play back at specific frame rates (30 frames per second for video, 24 frames per second for film). Unfortunately, animated GIFs and SWFs play back at different speeds depending on the computer they're being played on. The slower the processor, the slower the animation will play. Unfortunately, there's no way to accommodate how quickly animations will play on different computers. If you can, make sure you preview your animations on a variety of different computers with different processor speeds before you create your final Web pages.

Animation Aesthetics

Animations on a Web page attract more attention than static images on a page. Make sure the subject matter you pick for animations is worthy of more attention than other images on the page. Many Web pages contain so many animations they distract viewers from the content instead of enhancing it. Good uses for animation might include ad banners, movement from certain words so they stand out, diagrams brought to life, slideshows of photographs, or cartoon characters. You'll learn how to create different kinds of animation in this chapter.

The Animated GIF Format

The GIF file format is one of the few Web file formats to support animation. A Web browser treats animated GIFs the same as static GIFs, but an animated GIF displays multiple images (called **frames** in animation terminology) in a sequence (much like a slideshow) instead of a single, static image. Different frames can have different timings, which allows you to speed up and slow down frames in an animation.

Animated GIFs do not require plug-ins to Web browsers, which means they are viewable in all Web browsers except text-only or 1.0 browsers). The HTML code required to insert animated GIFs on a Web page is no different than the code for a static GIF. You can instruct animated GIFs to repeat (called **looping** in animation lingo), to play only once, or to play a specific number of times. The looping information is stored in the animated GIF, not in the HTML code.

GIF Compression Challenges

The principles for compressing animated GIFs are similar to those for compressing static GIFs. Large areas of solid color compress better than areas with a lot of noise or detail. If you use photographic images in an animated GIF, be sure to add lossy compression. It will make a substantial difference in file savings.

Animated GIFs will always be larger than static GIFs. ImageReady CS has two animation compression features—Bounding Box and Redundant Pixel Removal, which are both enabled by default. These features ensure file size is increased only for those areas that change from one frame to the next. For example, if you have a frame with a photographic background, and the only change in the next frame is the addition of type, the photographic area will be written only once to the file, limiting the total file size. If you change every pixel of an animation, you won't be able to keep the size down using the Bounding Box and Redundant Pixel Removal features.

When you compress an animated GIF, remember the file will stream in, meaning frames will appear before the entire file has finished loading. For this reason, you should divide the file size by the number of frames to figure out the size of each frame. For example, if you have a 100K animated GIF with 10 frames, each frame is only 10K.

The Macromedia Flash File Format

One of the key enhancements in ImageReady CS is the Macromedia Flash Export feature. You can export any animation you create in ImageReady CS to the Macromedia Flash (SWF) file format. Exporting animations as SWF files is beneficial when you're working with animations containing photographs and photographic effects, as well as vector-based shapes and type.

Animated GIFs Versus Macromedia Flash

Now that you have a choice between saving animations as animated GIFs and Macromedia Flash (SWF) files, it's important to understand the issues involved with using each format. Here's a handy chart to help you understand.

Animated GIFs Versus Macromedia Flash		
Issue	Animated GIF	Macromedia Flash
Web browser plug-in requirements	The animated GIF format does not require any additional plug-ins in order to display the animation correctly in a Web browser.	The Macromedia Flash (SWF) format requires the viewer to have the Macromedia Flash Web browser plug-in installed on his or her computer in order to view the animation. Users can download the free plug-in from Macromedia's Web site at: **http://www.macromedia.com.**
HTML code requirements	The animated GIF format does not require any special HTML code to make the animation work. The HTML code required for an animated GIF is identical to the code required for a static GIF. ImageReady CS lets you save the required HTML code to make GIF files work in a Web browser.	Macromedia Flash files require an **object** and an **embed** HTML tag in order for the animation to work properly in a Web browser. It's also a good idea to write plug-in detection code (which ImageReady CS does for you if you export HTML when you export a SWF) so you can let your viewers know if they don't have the required Web browser plug-in installed in order to view the animation. ImageReady CS writes the required HTML code to make SWF files work in a Web browser.

continues on next page

Animated GIFs Versus Macromedia Flash *continued*		
Issue	Animated GIF	Macromedia Flash
Compression settings	The animated GIF format requires you to use the same compression settings for all frames in an animation, which compromises the quality of the content in each frame—especially if you use photographic content. Plus, if you include photographic content in an animated GIF file, the file size will increase significantly because GIF is not an efficient format for saving that kind of information.	The SWF format preserves vector information and keeps bitmap information separate, which means you can increase the size of animations without impacting quality. The SWF format is also ideal for creating animations with photographic content because it keeps bitmap information separate and keeps the file size small.
Font embedding		The SWF format lets you embed fonts so characters only have to download once. For example, the word "food" only requires three letters to be downloaded because the letter "o" is repeated twice.

Now that you've learned a bit about animated GIFs and Macromedia Flash, it's time to start creating animations in ImageReady CS.

I. [IR] _____**Creating Animations from Layer Visibility**

In this exercise, you'll learn how to create animations by turning on and off the visibility of layers in the Layers palette.

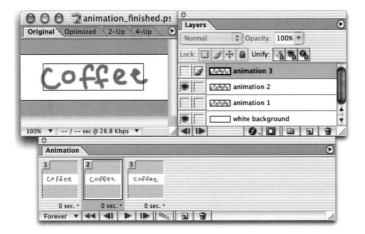

1. In ImageReady CS, open **animation_finished.psd** from the **chap_13** folder you copied to your **Desktop**. Make sure the **Animation** and **Layers** palettes are visible. If not, choose **Window > Animation** and **Window > Layers**.

2. Click **Play** at the bottom of the **Animation** palette to watch the animation play inside the document window.

Notice the letters in the word coffee move around inside the document window.

3. In **Step 2**, when you clicked the **Play** button, it immediately changed to the **Stop** button. When you're finished watching the animation, click **Stop**.

---

4. In the **Animation** palette, click **Frame 1** to select it. Notice the visibility is turned on for the **animation 1** layer in the **Layers** palette. Click **Frame 2** to select it. Notice the visibility is turned on for the **animation 2** layer in the **Layers** palette. Click **Frame 3** to select it. Notice the visibility is turned on for the **animation 3** layer in the **Layers** palette.

This animation was created by writing the word "coffee" on three separate layers. The layers were selectively turned on and off in each frame in the animation. In the next few steps, you'll learn how to create frames based on layer visibility.

---

5. Close **animation_finished.psd**. You don't need to save your changes. You'll learn to create this same file from scratch in upcoming steps.

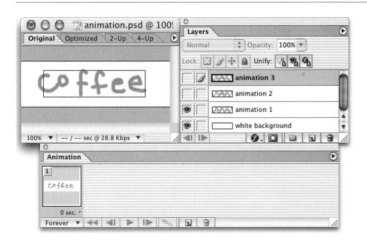

6. Open **animation.psd** from the **chap_13** folder you copied to your **Desktop**.

*Notice there is only one frame in the **Animation** palette. To make this file into an animation, there must be at least two frames with differing content. One way to create differing content in the frames is to turn on and off the visibility of different layers in the frames. The layers in this exercise have already been created for you. In the next few steps, you'll create new frames by turning on and off the visibility of layers.*

---

7. Click **Frame 1** to select it. In the **Layers** palette, make sure the visibility is turned on for the **white background** layer and the **animation 1** layer.

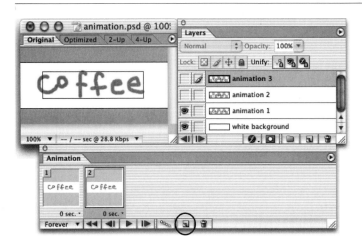

8. Click the **Duplicate current frame** button at the bottom of the **Animation** palette.

*Notice the newly created **Frame 2** is a duplicate of **Frame 1**.*

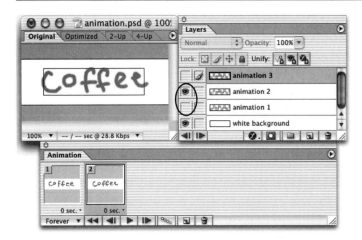

9. In the **Layers** palette, turn off the visibility of the **animation 1** layer and turn on the visibility of the **animation 2** layer.

Note: *ImageReady CS lets you turn on and off visibility of a layer without selecting the layer in the **Layers** palette.*

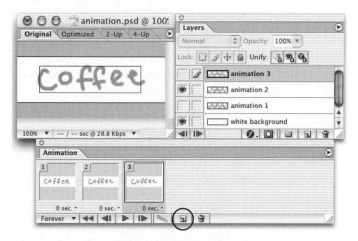

10. With **Frame 2** selected in the **Animation** palette, click the **Duplicate current frame** button.

*Notice the newly created **Frame 3** is a duplicate of **Frame 2**.*

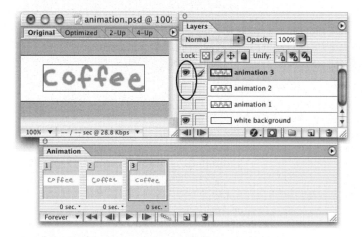

11. In the **Layers** palette, turn off the visibility of the **animation 2** layer and turn on the visibility of the **animation 3** layer.

12. Click the **Play** button on the **Animation** palette to view the animation you just created. When you're finished viewing the animation, click the **Stop** button.

13. Save the file and leave it open for the next exercise. You'll learn how save animations as animated GIFs and how to export animations as Macromedia Flash (SWF) files in later exercises.

2. [IR] _____Setting the Looping and Speed

In the last exercise, you created an animation that played at a rapid pace and repeated (or looped) until you clicked the Stop button. In this exercise, you'll learn how to decrease the speed of the animation and how to change the looping from the **Forever** setting to a specific number of repeats.

1. With **animation.psd** open from the last exercise, click the **Play** button on the **Animation** palette.

Notice the animation repeats, or loops, indefinitely.

2. Click the **Stop** button on the **Animation** palette. Choose **Once** in the **Looping** pop-up menu.

3. Click the **Play** button on the bottom of the **Animation** palette.

Notice the animation played once and stopped.

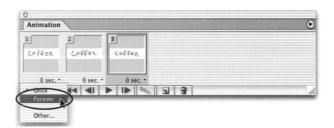

4. Choose **Forever** from the **Looping** pop-up menu to return the looping to the original setting.

TIP | Specifying the Number of Loops

If you want the animation to play more than once but not indefinitely, choose **Other** from the **Looping** pop-up menu.

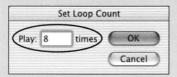

In the **Set Loop Count** dialog box, type a value in the **Play** field. Click **OK**.

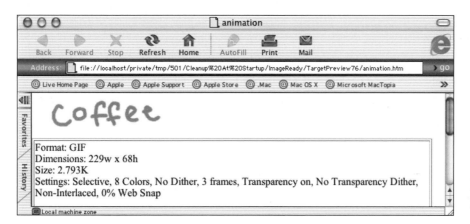

5. Make sure the **Optimize** palette is visible. If not, choose **Window > Optimize**. Choose **GIF** from the **Format** pop-up menu in the **Optimize** palette. Click the **Preview in Default Browser** button on the **Toolbox** to preview the animation in your default Web browser.

Notice the animation plays much faster in your Web browser than it did in ImageReady CS. ImageReady CS builds the animation as it plays. Web browsers play a prebuilt animated GIF, which makes it play significantly faster. If you were to upload this file to the Web, the speed might be different as well, due to bandwidth or server speed. Animation playback on the computer is an inexact science since it is dependent on so many things; processor speed: bandwidth, browsers, and operating systems!

Next, you'll learn how to reduce the speed of an animation using delay settings.

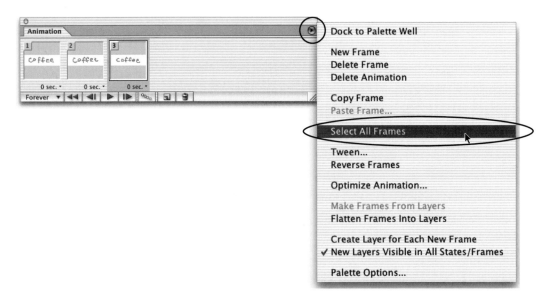

6. Return to ImageReady CS. Choose **Select All Frames** from the **Animation** palette menu.

All three frames should now be highlighted in blue, indicating they are all selected.

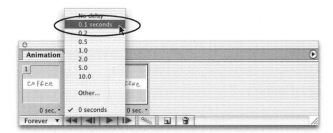

7. Choose **0.1** seconds from the **Frame Delay** pop-up menu for **Frame 2**.

*Notice the **Frame Delay** changes for all three selected frames.*

8. Click the **Preview in Default Browser** button on the **Toolbox**.

Notice the animation plays significantly slower.

*Tip: You can change the frame delay for all frames in an animation or for individual frames. To change the frame delay for individual frames, click a frame to select it and choose a frame delay time from the **Frame Delay** pop-up menu.*

9. Return to ImageReady CS. Save and close the file. You'll learn how to save animations as animated GIFs and how to export animations as Macromedia Flash (SWF) files in later exercises.

3. [IR] _____Tweening with Opacity

In the last few exercises, you created animations by turning on and off layer visibility. This technique is helpful if you have a layered file, but there will be times when you want to create animations from a flat image without having to create multiple layers for each frame. In this exercise, you'll learn how to create animations using the **Tween** feature in ImageReady CS.

1. Open **green_tea.psd** from the **chap_13** folder you copied to your **Desktop**.

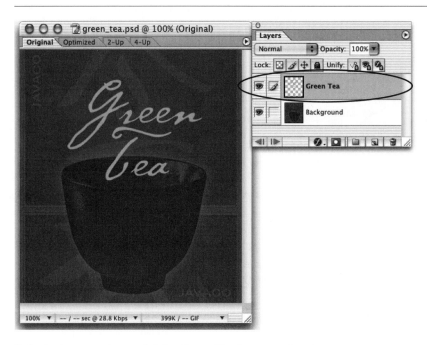

2. In the **Layers** palette, click the **Green Tea** layer to select it.

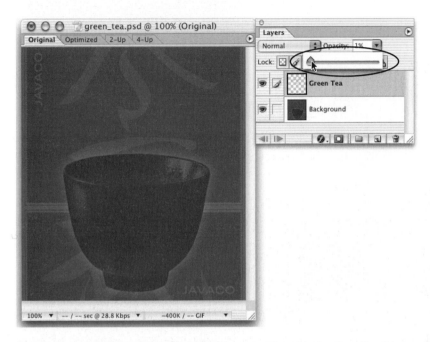

3. Reduce the **Opacity** of the **Green Tea** layer to **1%** using the **Opacity** slider on the **Layers** palette.

Notice the words "Green Tea" are no longer visible.

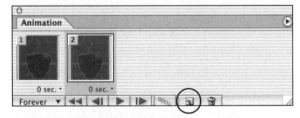

4. Click the **Duplicate current frame** button at the bottom of the **Animation** palette.

*Notice a new frame was created with the same properties as **Frame 1**. In the next step, you'll increase the opacity of **Frame 2** to **100%**.*

5. In the **Animation** palette, click **Frame 2** to select it. In the **Layers** palette, make sure the **Green Tea** layer is selected. Increase the **Opacity** to **100%** using the **Opacity** slider on the **Layers** palette.

Notice the words "Green Tea" are now visible in ***Frame 2.***

Now that you've created the two keyframes, you'll tween the animation between the two frames.

6. Click the **Tween** button on the bottom of the **Animation** palette.

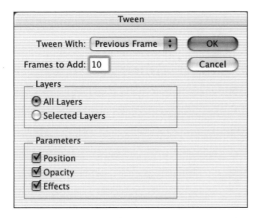

7. In the **Tween** dialog box, type **10** in the **Frames to Add** field. Make sure **Position**, **Opacity**, and **Effects** are turned on in the **Parameters** section. Click **OK**.

*You should now have 12 frames in the **Animation** palette. ImageReady CS automatically created 10 intermediary frames, which will allow the words "Green Tea" to fade in slowly. In the next step, you'll take a look at the result.*

8. Click **Play** to view the animation. You should see the words "Green Tea" fade into the image. Click **Stop** when you're finished viewing the animation.

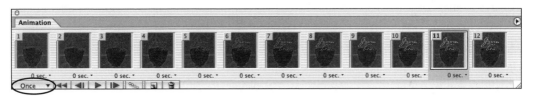

9. The **Green Tea** animation will look best in a Web browser if it plays only once. Choose **Once** from the **Looping** pop-up menu.

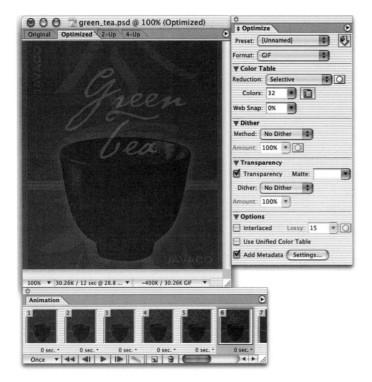

10. In the **Animation** palette, click **Frame 6** to select it. Click the **Optimized** tab. In the **Optimize** palette, match the settings to those shown in this illustration.

Note: You can choose any frame in the animation before you specify the optimization settings in the *Optimize* *palette. I chose* *Frame 6* *because it shows the text at about* *50%* *opacity, which makes it easy to choose an optimization setting that will make all the frames look good while keeping file size down.*

---

11. Click the **Preview in Default Browser** button on the **Toolbox**.

Although it's convenient to preview your animations in ImageReady CS, don't forget to test the files in a Web browser for the best indication of speed.

---

12. Return to ImageReady CS. Save the file and leave it open for the next exercise.

 MOVIE | tweening_opacity.mov

To learn more about tweening with opacity, check out **tweening_opacity.mov** from the **movies** folder on the **H•O•T CD-ROM**.

[IR] _____ **Selecting, Duplicating, and Reversing Frames**

In the last exercise, you created an animation by increasing the Opacity from 1% to 100% over the course of 12 frames. What if you want to make the words fade into 100%, hold at 100% for a few seconds, then fade out to 1%? Here's an exercise to show you how:

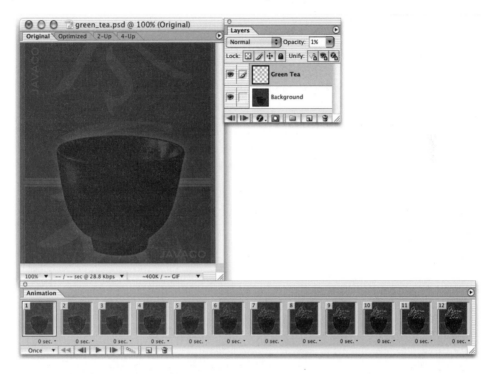

1. With **green_tea.psd** still open from the last exercise, click **Frame 1** in the **Animation** palette to select it. Hold down the **Shift** key and click **Frame 12** to multiple-select all the frames in the **Animation** palette.

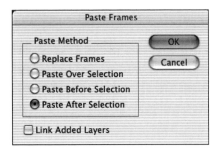

2. With all 12 frames selected, choose **Copy Frames** from the **Animation** palette menu. Click **Frame 12** to select it and choose **Paste Frames** from the **Animation** palette menu. In the **Paste Frames** dialog box, choose **Paste After Selection**. Click **OK**.

You should now have 24 frames in your animation. ImageReady CS created another full set of 12 frames from the original 12 frames in the animation and appended them to the end. As you can see, **Frames 1** *through* **12** *are the original frames.* **Frames 13** *through* **24** *are the new frames.*

Tip: Instead of copying and pasting frames, you can also use the **Duplicate current frames** *button at the bottom of the* **Animation** *palette.*

3. In the **Animation** palette, **Frame 13** through **Frame 24** (the frames you created in the last step) should already be selected. If not, click **Frame 13**, hold down the **Shift** key, and click **Frame 24** to multiple-select the frames.

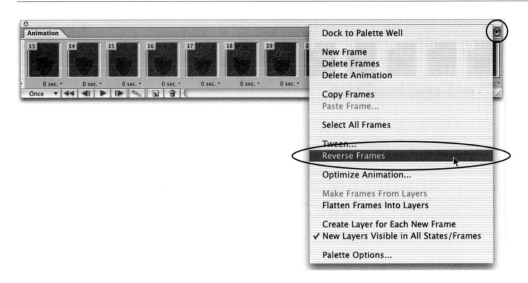

4. Choose **Reverse Frames** from the **Animation** palette menu.

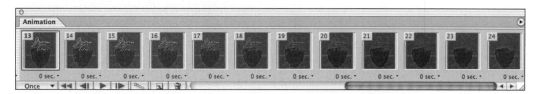

*The order of Frames 13 to 24 is reversed. The Opacity in **Frame 13** is **100%** and the opacity in **Frame 24** is **1%**.*

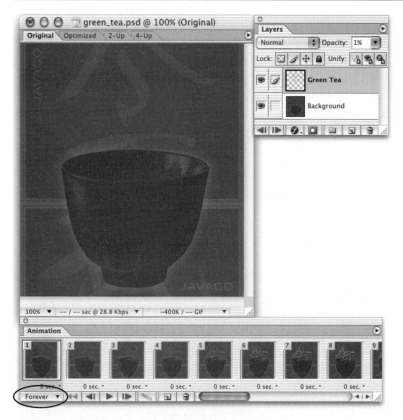

5. Choose **Forever** in the **Looping** pop-up menu. Click **Frame 1** to select it. Click **Play**. Click **Stop** when you've finished previewing the animation.

*Notice the words "Green Tea" evenly fade in and fade out. Next, you'll change the timing of **Frame 12** so the animation holds at full opacity before fading out.*

6. In the **Animation** palette, click **Frame 12** to select it. Choose **1.0** from the **Frame Delay** pop-up menu.

7. Click **Frame 1** to select it. Click **Play**. The animation should now hold at full opacity and fade out. When you're finished watching, click **Stop**.

ImageReady CS allows you to change the timing for all the frames in an animation (which you did in the last exercise) or individual frames (which you did in the last step).

8. Save the file and leave it open for the next exercise.

In this exercise, you learned how to create a loop by selecting, duplicating, and reversing frames and how to set delays for individual frames.

MOVIE | reversing.mov

To learn more about selecting, duplicating, and reversing frames, check out **reversing.mov** from the **movies** folder on the **H•O•T CD-ROM**.

The Paste Frames Dialog Box

In the last exercise, you learned how to duplicate frames using the **Copy Frames** and **Paste Frames** options from the **Animation** palette menu. The **Paste Frames** dialog box gives you a number of paste options. Here's a chart to explain them:

Paste Frames Dialog Box Options	
Replace Frames	**Replace Frames** replaces the currently selected frames with new frames. If you copy and paste frames inside the same image, ImageReady CS does not create new layers in the Layers palette; it replaces the attributes of the old frame with the attributes of the new frame. If you paste frames between two images, ImageReady CS add layers to the Layers palette. However, the layers are only visible when the pasted frame is selected in the Animation palette.
Paste Over Selection	**Paste Over Selection** adds the contents of the pasted frame to the selected frame and adds new layers to the Layers palette. The layers are only visible when the pasted frame is selected in the Layers palette.
Paste Before Selection, Paste After Selection	**Paste Before Selection** pastes the frames before the current selection. **Paste After Selection** pastes the frames after the current selection. When you paste frames from the same image, ImageReady CS does not add frames to the Layers palette. If you paste frames from a different image, ImageReady CS automatically creates new layers in the Layers palette. The layers are only visible when the pasted frame is selected in the Layers palette.
Link Added Layers	**Link Added Layers** links layers created as a result of the paste operation. For more information about the benefits of linking layers, refer to Chapter 5, "*Layers.*"

5. [IR] _____Tweening a Tweened Sequence

You can also tween an animation more than once. This is useful if you decide to change the number of frames. Here's an exercise to show you how.

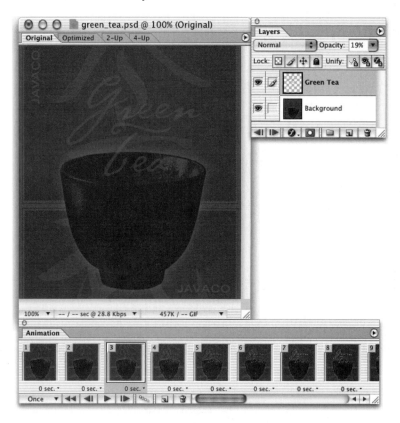

1. With **green_tea.psd** open from the last exercise, select the **Green Tea** layer in the **Layers** palette. Click **Frame 3** in the **Animation** palette to select it.

2. Increase the opacity of the **Green Tea** layer to **100%** using the **Opacity** slider on the **Layers** palette.

3. With **Frame 3** selected in the **Animation** palette, hold down the **Shift** key and click **Frame 1** to multiple-select **Frame 1** through **Frame 3**.

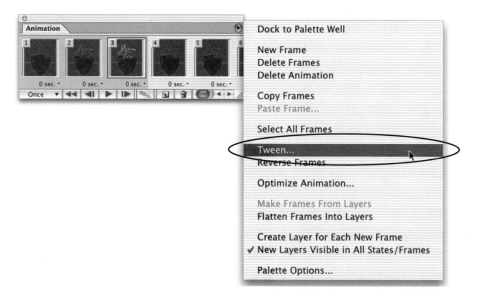

4. Choose **Tween** from the **Animation** palette menu. The **Tween** dialog box opens automatically. Notice **Selection** is selected in the **Tween With** pop-up menu and **Frames to Add** is grayed out. When you multiple-select frames, you automatically tween the frames you have selected. Click **OK**.

5. Click **Play** in the **Animation** palette menu. You'll see the words "Green Tea" fade in and out quickly at the beginning of the animation.

6. Save and close the file.

6. [IR] _____Tweening with Position

So far in this chapter, you've learned how to create animations by turning on and off layer visibility and how to create animations that fade in and out by tweening with opactiy. There are two other useful techniques when you're creating animations: tweening with position and tweening with effects. This exercise will show you how to tween with position.

1. Open **green_tea2.psd** from the **chap_13** folder you copied to your **Desktop**.

2. Click the **Green Tea** layer in the **Layers** palette to select it. Make sure the **Opacity** is set to **100%**.

3. Select the **Move** tool in the **Toolbox**. Click and drag the **Green Tea** layer to reposition it at the top of the image.

4. Click the **Duplicate current frame** button at the bottom of the **Animation** palette.

5. With the **Move** tool selected in the **Toolbox**, click and drag the **Green Tea** layer to the bottom of the image.

*Notice **Frame 2** updated automatically to reflect the move you just made.*

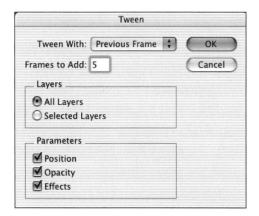

6. Click the **Tween** button at the bottom of the **Animation** palette. In the **Tween** dialog box, make sure **Previous Frame** is selected in the **Tween With** pop-up menu. Type **5** in the **Frames to Add** field. Click **OK**.

*Notice there are seven frames in the **Animation** palette.*

---

7. Click the **Play** button on the **Animation** palette to watch the animation. Click **Stop** when you've finished viewing your handiwork.

Notice the words "Green Tea" move down the page. ImageReady CS created an animation by tweening the position of the words "Green Tea."

---

8. Choose **File > Revert** to discard the changes you made in this exercise and to return the file to its original appearance.

---

7. [IR] _____Tweening with Layer Styles

You can also create animations by tweening with layer styles. Here's an exercise to show you how.

1. With **green_tea2.psd** open from the last exercise, click the **Green Tea** layer in the **Layers** palette to select it.

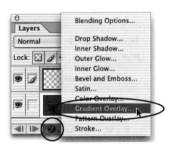

2. Choose **Gradient Overlay** from the **Add a layer style** pop-up menu at the bottom of the **Layers** palette.

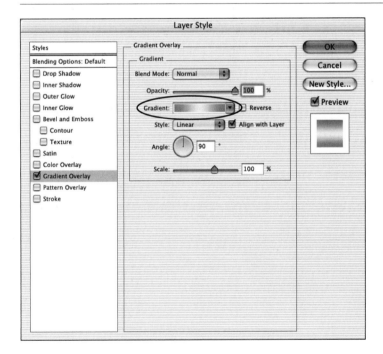

3. In the **Layer Style** dialog box, choose a gradient from the **Gradient** pop-up menu. Click **OK**.

4. In the **Animation** palette, click the **Duplicate current frame** button.

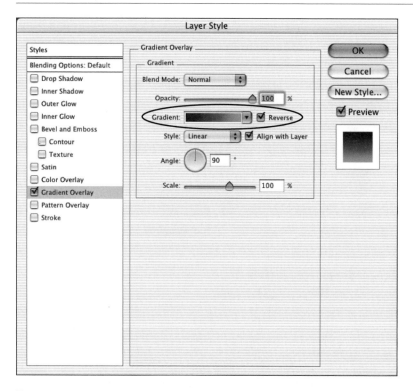

5. In the **Animation** palette, click **Frame 2** to select it. Double-click the **Gradient Overlay** layer style in the **Layers** palette. In the **Layer Style** dialog box, choose a different gradient from the **Gradient** pop-up menu. If you like, turn on the **Reverse** option. Click **OK**.

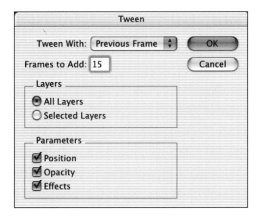

6. In the **Animation** palette, click the **Tween** button. In the **Tween** dialog box, make sure **Previous Frame** is selected in the **Tween With** pop-up menu. Type **15** in the **Frames to Add** field. Click **OK**.

You should now have a total of 17 frames in the animation.

---

7. Click the **Play** button on the **Animation** palette to preview the animation.

Notice the gradient slowly fades from the orange-yellow-orange gradient at the beginning of the animation to the purple-orange gradient at the end of the animation.

---

8. Save and close the file. You'll learn how save animations as animated GIFs and how to export animations as Macromedia Flash (SWF) files in later exercises.

NOTE | How Many Frames?

You may be wondering why you added significantly more frames to this animation than to the other animations in previous exercises. Some animations look better over a longer or shorter amount of time. The more frames you add, the smoother the animation will look. Unfortunately, the more frames you add, the larger the file size and the longer the download time. These are important considerations when you're creating animations. Deciding how many frames to include in an animation takes practice. Don't be afraid to experiment when you create animations. With ImageReady CS, you can add and subtract frames easily.

8. [IR] _____Creating an Animated Slideshow

If you have a series of photographs you want to make into a slideshow, you can do one of two things: you can put each photograph on a layer and turn the visibility of each layer on and off (similar to what you did in Exercise 1), or you can create a slideshow that fades from one image to the next (called **cross-fade** in filmmaking lingo!). ImageReady CS lets you create fading slideshows easily without setting the opacity for each frame. Here's an exercise to show you how.

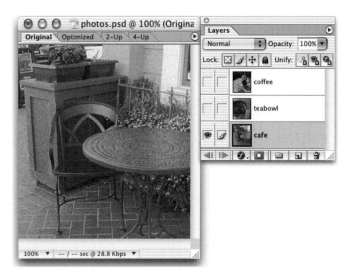

1. Open **photos.psd** from the **chap_13** folder you copied to your **Desktop**.

The file contains three layers, each with a different image. **Note:** To create an animated slideshow, you don't have to use photographic images—you can use whatever images you like!

---

2. Click the **Duplicate current frame** button in the **Animation** palette. Turn off the visibility of the **café** layer and turn on the visibility of the **teabowl** layer. Click the **Duplicate current frame** button in the **Animation** palette. Turn off the visibility of the **teabowl** layer and turn on the visibility of the **coffee** layer.

You should now have three frames in the **Animation** palette, each with different images.

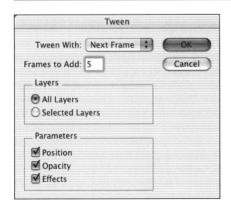

3. Click **Frame 1** to select it. Click the **Tween** button at the bottom of the **Animation** palette. In the **Tween** dialog box, make sure **Next Frame** is selected in the **Tween With** pop-up menu. Type **5** in the **Frames to Add** field. Click **OK**.

*You should now have a total of eight frames in the **Animation** palette.*

4. Click **Frame 8** to select it. Click the **Tween** button. In the **Tween** dialog box, make sure **Previous Frame** is selected in the **Tween With** pop-up menu. Type **5** in the **Frames to Add** field. Click **OK**.

5. Click the **Play** button on the **Animation** palette. Click **Stop** when you've finished viewing the animation.

*The photographs fade evenly in and out except from **Frame 13** to **Frame 1**. It would look nicer if the animation made a complete loop. You'll learn how in the next few steps.*

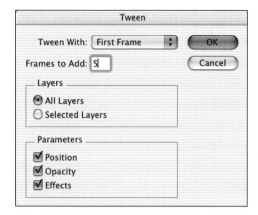

6. Click **Frame 13** (the last frame) to select it. Click the **Tween** button. In the **Tween** dialog box, choose **First Frame** from the **Tween With** pop-up menu. Type **5** in the **Frames to Add** field. Click **OK**.

There should now be a total of 18 frames in the animation.

7. Click the **Play** button on the **Animation** palette. Click **Stop** when you've finished viewing the animation.

Notice there is now a smooth fade between all the images.

The animation is complete. As you can see, it's very easy to create a cross-fading animation in ImageReady CS. Remember, when you optimize and save the animation, you must save the file as an animated GIF even though the content of the animation is photographic. Be sure to turn on lossy compression to cut down the file size if you are saving an animated GIF file.

8. Save and close the file. You'll learn how save animations as animated GIFs and how to export animations as Macromedia Flash (SWF) files in later exercises.

MOVIE | slideshow.mov

To learn more about creating animated slideshows, check out **slideshow.mov** in the **movies** folder on the **H•O•T CD-ROM**.

[IR] _____**Optimizing and Saving Animated GIFs**

In the last two exercises, you learned how to create animations, set the looping, and change the speed. In this exercise, you'll learn how to optimize and save animations as animated GIFs.

1. Open **animation_gif_final.psd** from the **chap_13** folder you copied to your **Desktop**. Click the **Optimized** tab. Make sure the **Animation** and **Optimize** palettes are visible. If not, choose **Window > Animation** and **Window > Optimize**.

> ### NOTE | The JPEG and PNG Formats Do Not Support Animation!
>
> When you create animations in ImageReady CS, you must optimize and save them as GIFs or export them as Macromedia Flash SWFs. JPEG and PNG do not support animations. If you save an animation as a JPEG or PNG, you'll see only the first frame of the animation in the Web browser, and the animation will not play.

2. In the **Optimize** palette, adjust the settings to match those shown here. You don't need to specify optimization settings for each frame.

The optimization settings you specify for an individual frame will be automatically applied to the other frames in the animation. If you use graphics in your animations that look very different from each other, make sure you view each frame to ensure the optimization settings look good on all frames. This isn't an issue with the animation in this exercise because the graphics in the individual frames are very similar to each other.

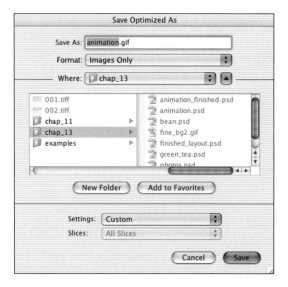

3. Choose **File > Save Optimized As**. Navigate to the **chap_13** folder you copied to your **Desktop**. Name the file **animation.gif**. Choose **Images Only** from the **Format** pop-up menu. Click **Save**.

You may wonder why you chose Images Only in the Format pop-up menu and not HTML and Images, which you've done in the last several chapters. Animated GIFs do not require additional HTML code to make them work in a Web browser. You can insert an animated GIF into an HTML editor just like any other GIF. You can even load an animated GIF into a Web browser without creating any HTML code.

4. Open a Web browser (any one will do!). Choose **File > Open**. Navigate to the **chap_13** folder on your **Desktop** and choose **animation.gif**. Click **Open**.

As you can see, the animated GIF plays in a Web browser without any need for additional HTML code.

5. Return to ImageReady CS. Save the file and leave it open for the next exercise.

IO. 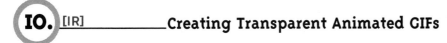[IR]_____Creating Transparent Animated GIFs

In the last few exercises, you've created animated GIFs with solid backgrounds. In this exercise, you'll learn how to create animated GIFs with transparent backgrounds.

1. With **animation_gif_final.psd** open from the last exercise, click the **Original** tab.

2. In the **Animation** palette, click **Frame 1**, **Frame 2**, and **Frame 3** to select them. Turn off the visibility of the **white background** layer in the **Layers** palette.

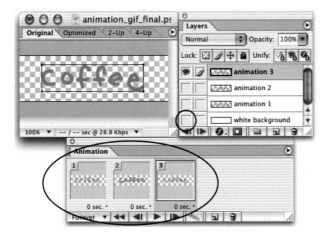

Notice the backgrounds of all three frames are now transparent.

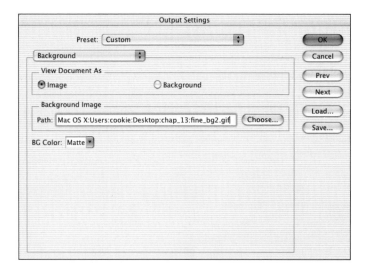

3. Choose **File > Output Settings > Background**. In the **Output Settings** dialog box, click the **Choose** button. Browse to the **chap_13** folder on your **Desktop** and choose **fine_bg2.gif**. Click **Open**. In the **Output Settings** dialog box, choose **Matte** from the **BG Color** pop-up menu. Click **OK**.

4. Click the **Optimized** tab. In the **Optimize** palette, match the settings to those shown here. Make sure the **Transparency** option is turned on.

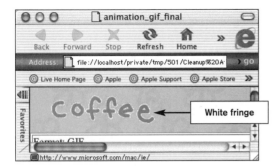

White fringe

5. Click the **Preview in Default Browser** button on the **Toolbox**.

Notice the transparent animation appears over the background image you specified in the Output Settings dialog box. Notice also the ugly white fringe around the edges of the frames. You'll learn how to eliminate the white fringe in the next step.

6. Return to ImageReady CS. Choose **File > Open** and browse to the **chap_13** folder on your Desktop. Choose **fine_bg2.gif** and click **Open**. Select the **Eyedropper** tool from the **Toolbox**. Sample the light **green** from the **fine_bg2.gif** image.

7. Return to **animation.psd** by choosing **Window > Documents > animation.psd**.

8. In the **Optimize** palette, choose **Foreground Color** from the **Matte** pop-up menu.

9. Click the **Preview in Default Browser** button on the **Toolbox**.

Notice the white fringe is gone!

For more information about creating transparent GIFs, refer to Chapter 9, "Transparent GIFs." The techniques you learned in Chapter 9 also apply to transparent, animated GIFs.

10. Return to ImageReady CS. Save and close **animation_gif_final.psd**. Close **fine_bg2.gif**.

[IR] _____Creating Animated GIF Rollovers

ImageReady CS lets you create animated rollovers. If you've never created animated rollovers in ImageReady CS before, you may find the process a bit strange. Not to worry, the steps will make more sense once you've finished the entire exercise.

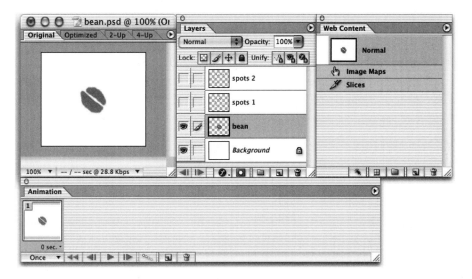

1. Open **bean.psd** from the **chap_13** folder you copied to your **Desktop**. Make sure the **Web Content**, **Layers**, and **Animation** palettes are visible. If not, choose **Window > Web Content**, **Window > Layers**, and **Window > Animation**.

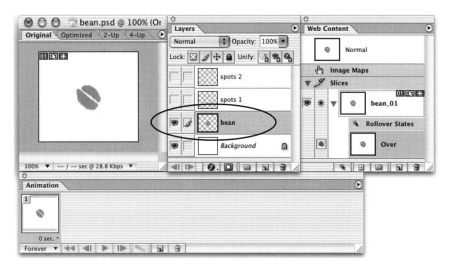

2. Make sure the **bean** layer is selected in the **Layers** palette. Click the **Create rollover state** button at the bottom of the **Web Content** palette.

*Notice a slice called **bean_01** and an **Over** state were automatically created in the **Web Content** palette. Also notice **Frame 1** in the **Animation** palette and the **Normal** state in the **Web Content** palette look the same, indicating there will be no animation in the **Normal** state. Next, you'll create the animation that will appear when a user positions his or her mouse over the image.*

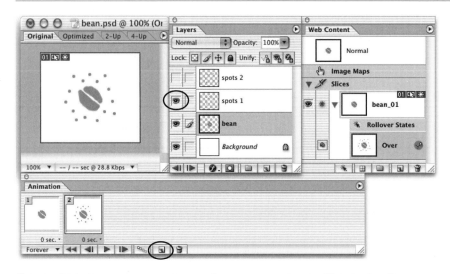

3. In the **Web Content** palette, click the **Over** state to select it. Click the **Duplicate current frame** button on the bottom of the **Animation** palette. In the **Layers** palette, turn on the visibility for the **spots 1** layer.

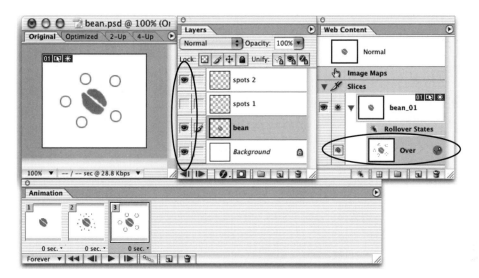

4. With the **Over** state still selected in the **Web Content** palette, click the **Duplicate current frame** button at the bottom of the **Animation** palette. Turn off the visibility of the **spots 1** layer and turn on the visibility of the **spots 2** layer.

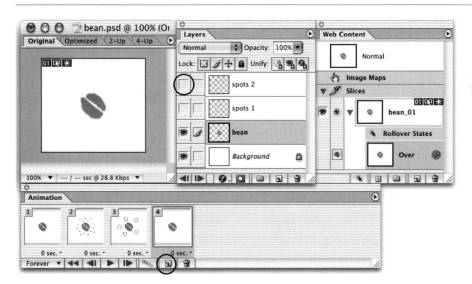

5. In the **Animation** palette, make sure **Frame 3** is selected. Click the **Duplicate current frame** button at the bottom of the **Animation** palette. Turn off the visibility for the **spot 2** layer in the **Layers** palette.

NOTE | Preload Issues

When you design animated rollovers, you need to set **Looping** to a minimum of **2**. ImageReady CS automatically writes a script that "preloads" the animation frames. If the animation is set to play one time only, it will play during the preloading process and will not play when you see the image in the Web browser.

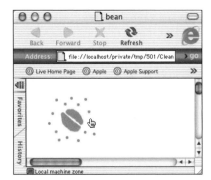

6. Click the **Preview in Default Browser** button on the **Toolbox**. Position your mouse over the image to play the animation.

You've just learned how to create an animated rollover in ImageReady CS! One of the benefits of working with ImageReady CS is the capability to transform any static rollover to an animated rollover.

WARNING | Netscape Animation Bug

If you click an animated rollover in Netscape, the animation will not resume the next time you position your mouse over the image. The problem is not with the file ImageReady CS generates; the problem is the way Netscape renders animated GIF files. Unfortunately, there is nothing you can do to work around this issue.

---

7. Return to ImageReady CS. Save and close the file.

MOVIE | animated_roll.mov

To learn more about creating animated rollovers, check out **animated_roll.mov** in the **movies** folder on the **H•O•T CD-ROM**.

---

12. [IR] _____Exporting Animations as Macromedia Flash Files

In the last few exercises, you learned how to save animations as animated GIFs. In this exercise, you'll learn how to export animations as Macromedia Flash (SWF) animations. Exporting animations as Macromedia Flash files is ideal if you have animations containing vector information or photographic content. The SWF format will create smaller, better-quality animations and will preserve vector information.

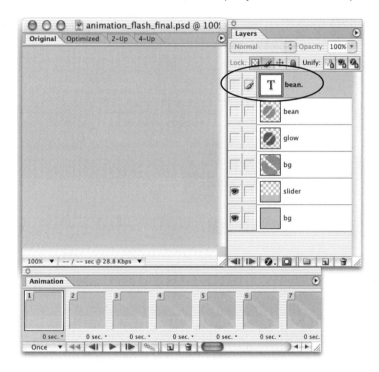

1. Open **animation_flash_final.psd** from the **chap_13** folder you copied to your **Desktop**. Make sure the **Animation** and **Layers** palettes are visible. If not, choose **Window > Animation** and **Window > Layers**.

Notice the type in the animation has been created from a vector-based type layer. When you export animations as Macromedia Flash files, you preserve all vector-based information, including vector-based type.

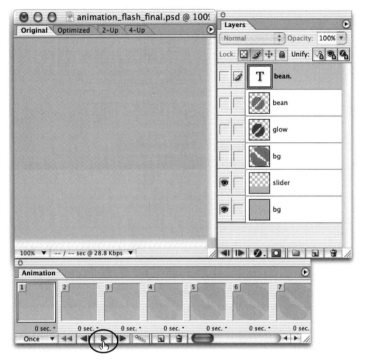

2. Click the **Play** button in the **Animation** palette to watch the animation. The looping is set to **Once** so it will stop automatically when it finishes playing.

Although most of this animation is made up flat graphics, there are drop shadows and glows in some areas. As a result, you'll get a better quality animation if you export it as a Macromedia Flash animation. In addition, the type will remain vector-based if you export the file as a Macromedia Flash animation.

3. Choose **File > Export > Macromedia Flash (SWF)**. The **Macromedia Flash Export** dialog box opens automatically.

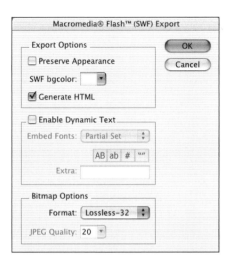

4. In the **Macromedia Flash Export** dialog box, turn on the **Generate HTML** option. Choose **Lossless-32** from the **Format** pop-up menu. Make sure the **Preserve Appearance** and the **Enable Dynamic Text** options are turned off.

*If you turn on the **Preserve Appearance** option, you'll risk rasterizing the type layer. Because the image contains five individual characters, embedding fonts using the **Enable Dynamic Text** option won't save any download time.*

5. In the **Export as Macromedia SWF** dialog box, navigate to the **chap_13** folder you copied to your **Desktop**. Leave the file name as the default (**animation_flash_final.swf**). Click **Save**.

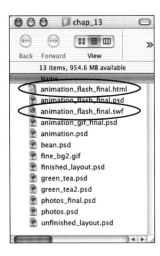

6. Browse to the **chap_13** folder on your **Desktop**. Notice ImageReady CS automatically saved two files: **animation_flash_final.html** and **animation_flash_final.swf**.

7. Double-click the **animated_flash_final.html** file to view the file in your default Web browser.

It's that easy to export an animation as a Macromedia Flash (SWF) file. This is a great new feature in ImageReady CS!

Note: *For more information about exporting SWF files from ImageReady CS, including how to edit vector-based type created in ImageReady CS in Macromedia Flash, refer to Chapter 16, "Integration with Other Programs."*

8. Return to ImageReady CS. Save and close the file.

I3. [IR] Exporting Frames as Files

One of the useful new features in ImageReady CS is the **Export Frames As Files** feature. You'll find this feature really helpful if you want to take the frames you created in ImageReady CS into another application such as Macromedia Flash or 3D Studio Max. In this exercise, you'll export frames as Macromedia Flash files; however, you can also export frames as GIFs, JPEGs, PNGs, WBMPs, and PSDs.

1. Open **photos_final.psd** from the **chap_13** folder you copied to your **Desktop**.

Notice the animation has 18 frames. In the next few steps, you'll save the frames as individual files.

2. Choose **Export > Animation Frames as Files**.

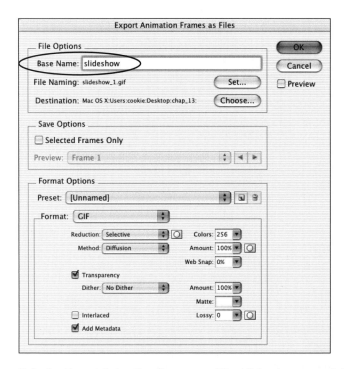

3. In the **Export Animation Frames as Files** dialog box, type **slideshow** in the **Base Name** field.

4. Click the **Choose** button. In the **Select an Export Destination Folder** dialog box, navigate to the **chap_13** folder on your **Desktop**. Click the **New Folder** (Mac) or **Create New Folder** (Windows) button. In the **New Folder** dialog box, type **slideshow_files**. Click **Create** (Mac) or **OK** (Windows). Select the **slideshow_files** folder in the **Select an Export Destination Folder** dialog box and click **Choose**.

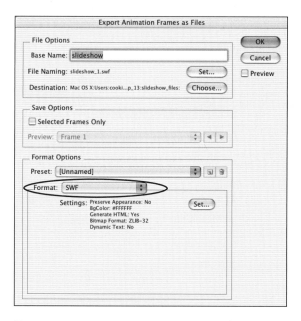

5. Choose **SWF** from the **Format** pop-up menu. The options in the **Format Options** section of the **Export Animation Frames as Files** dialog box update automatically to display the current settings for the **SWF** format. Click the **Set** button to open the **Macromedia Flash Export** dialog box.

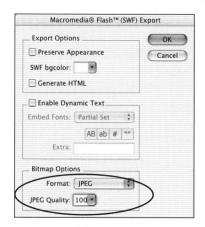

6. Leave all the options turned off and choose **JPEG** from the **Format** pop-up menu. Set the **JPEG Quality** to **100**. Click **OK**.

*Note: If you plan to open and edit the file in another application, make sure you set the **JPEG Quality** to **100** so you keep the files at their highest quality when you export them. If you're planning to use the images directly on the Web, set the **JPEG Quality** lower so the file size is kept as small as possible.*

7. In the **Export Animation Frames as Files** dialog box, click **OK**.

8. Browse to the **slideshow_files** folder in the **chap_13** folder on your **Desktop**.

*Notice the **slideshow_files** folder contains 18 SWFs—one for each of the frames in the animation. Pretty easy, huh? As you can see, being able to export frames as individual files is a helpful new feature in ImageReady CS! Remember, in addition to being able to export frames as individual SWF files, you can also export individual frames as GIFs, JPEGs, PNGs, WBMPs, and PSD files.*

9. Return to ImageReady CS. Save and close the file.

TIP | Exporting Selected Frames as Files

In the last exercise, you learned how to save animation frames as files. In that example, you saved all the frames in the file as individual files. ImageReady CS also lets you save selected frames. Here's how:

In the **Animation** palette, multiple-select the frames you want to save as individual files by holding down the **Cmd** (Mac) or **Ctrl** (Windows) key and clicking each frame.

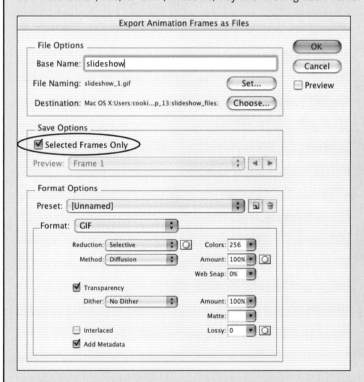

Choose **File > Export > Animation Frames as Files**. In the **Export Animation Frames as Files** dialog box, turn on the **Selected Frames Only** option. When you click **OK**, only the selected frames will save as individual files.

[IR] _____Designing Entire Web Interfaces

In the last three chapters, you learned about slicing, rollovers, and animations. You can use all of these techniques to design an entire Web interface. This next exercise will bring into practice a lot of the skills you learned and open your eyes to further possibilities. This is a complex exercise. Don't be surprised if you have to try it more than once or watch the movie over and over. ImageReady CS is a powerful yet complex program, and this exercise shows off its strengths and challenges.

1. Open **finished_layout.psd** from the **chap_13** folder you copied to your **Desktop**. Before you start creating the Web interface, take a few minutes to look at how the interface was constructed. It will help you understand what the final results will look like.

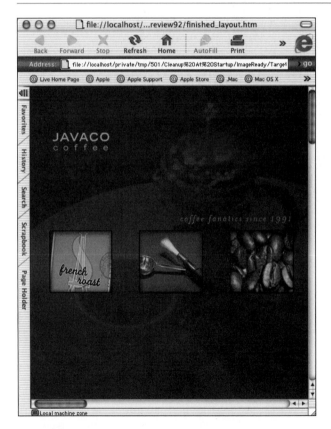

2. Click the **Preview in Default Browser** button on the **Toolbox**. Notice the **coffee cup** at the bottom of the page is an animation with the looping set to **Forever**. Notice the three photographs in the image have **Over** states and are also remote rollovers.

3. Return to ImageReady CS. Make sure the slices are visible. If not, click the **Toggle Slice Visibility** button on the **Toolbox**. Select the **Slice Select** tool in the **Toolbox**. Click to select the slices in the Web interface. Make note of the different rollover states in the **Web Content** palette.

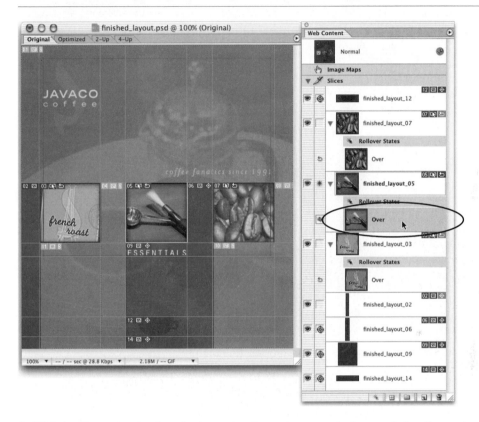

4. Click the **Over** state for the rollovers and notice text appears in the area below the center photograph, showing the **Over** state is also a remote rollover.

Deconstructing the finished Web interface will help you over the next few steps as you slice and create rollovers and animations to build the final Web interface yourself.

5. Close **finished_layout.psd**. You don't need to save your changes.

6. Open **unfinished_layout.psd** from the **chap_13** folder on your **Desktop**. Make sure the slice lines are visible. If not, click the **Toggle Slice Visibility** button on the **Toolbox**.

*First, you'll set up the **coffee cup** animation. Why? Because you want the animation to appear as the **Normal** state of every slice on the Web page. Whenever you want an animation to play when the page first loads, you must set it up in the **Normal** state.*

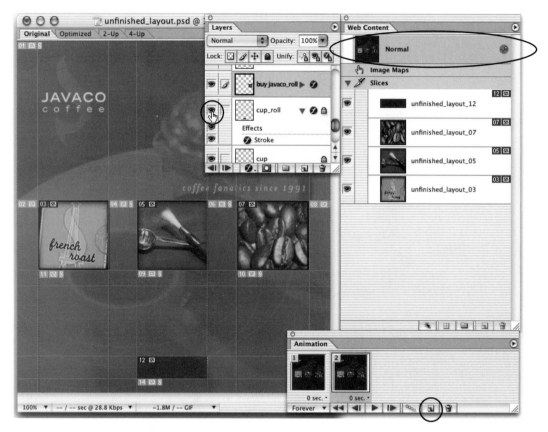

7. Click the **Normal** state in the **Web Content** palette. Click the **Duplicate current frames** button at the bottom of the **Animation** palette. With **Frame 2** selected in the **Animation** palette, turn on the visibility of the **cup_roll** layer in the **Layers** palette.

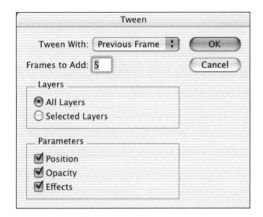

8. With **Frame 2** selected in the **Animation** palette, click the **Tween** button. In the **Tween** dialog box, make sure **Previous Frame** is selected in the **Tween With** pop-up menu. Type **5** in the **Frames to Add** field. Click **OK**.

There should now be seven frames in the animation.

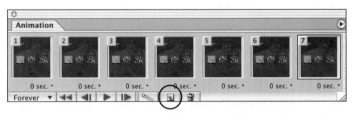

9. In the **Animation** palette, click **Frame 7**. Hold down the **Shift** key and click **Frame 1** to multiple-select all the frames. Click the **Duplicate current frames** button.

*There should now be 14 frames in the animation with **Frames 8** through **14** selected in the*
***Animation** palette.*

10. Choose **Reverse Frames** from the **Animation** palette menu.

*You now have a smooth, tweened animation of the **coffee cup** fading in and out. If you want to preview the animation, click the **Preview in Default Browser** button on the **Toolbox**. The **coffee cup** will be animated, but the rollovers will not work because you haven't set them up yet. When you build entire Web interfaces, it's a good idea to preview often and after you create each element.*

Next, you'll create the rollovers for the three photographs in the image.

11. Click the **Slice Select** tool in the **Toolbox**. Click **Slice 03** to select it. Click the **Create rollover state** button at the bottom of the **Web Content** palette.

*Notice an **Over** state was created automatically.*

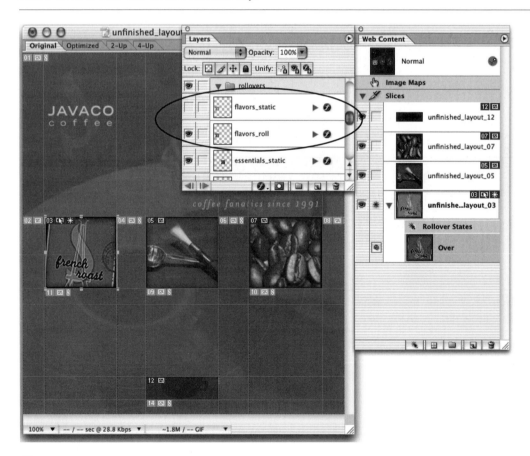

12. In the **Layers** palette, turn off the visibility of the **flavors_static** layer and turn on the visibility of the **flavors_roll** layer.

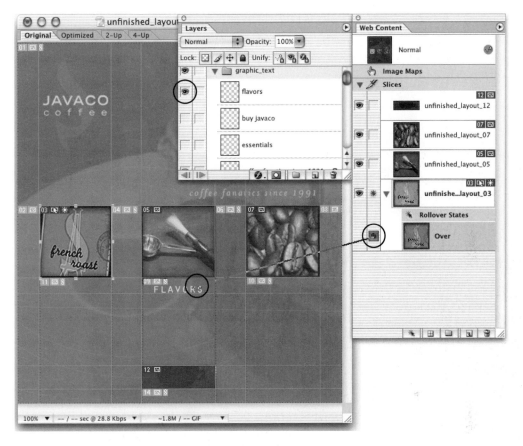

13. Turn on the visibility of the **flavors** layer in the **Layers** palette. Drag the **target** icon from the **Over** state to the **flavors** slice, as shown here.

14. Click the **Preview in Default Browser** button on the **Toolbox**. Position your mouse over the **flavors** image. The image changes to the **Over** state, and the word "Flavor" appears below the center image.

15. Return to ImageReady CS. With the **Slice Select** tool selected in the **Toolbox**, click **Slice 05** to select it. Click the **Create rollover state** button at the bottom of the **Web Content** palette.

*Notice an **Over** state was created automatically.*

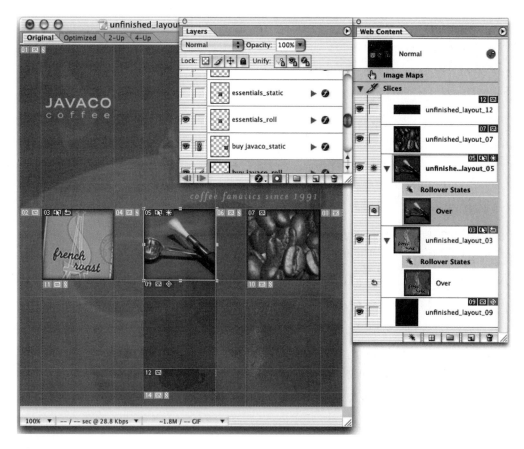

16. In the **Layers** palette, turn off the visibility of the **essentials_static** layer and turn on the visibility of the **essentials_roll** layer.

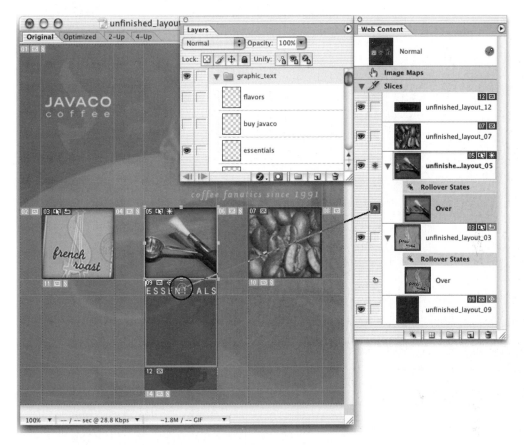

17. Turn on the visibility of the **essentials** layer. Click and drag the **target** icon from the **Over** state to the **essentials** slice, as shown here. Click the **Preview in Default Browser** button on the **Toolbox**. Position your mouse over the **essentials** image. The image changes to the **Over** state and the word "Essentials" appears below the center image.

18. With the **Slice Select** tool selected in the **Toolbox**, click **Slice 07** to select it. Click the **Create rollover state** button at the bottom of the **Web Content** palette.

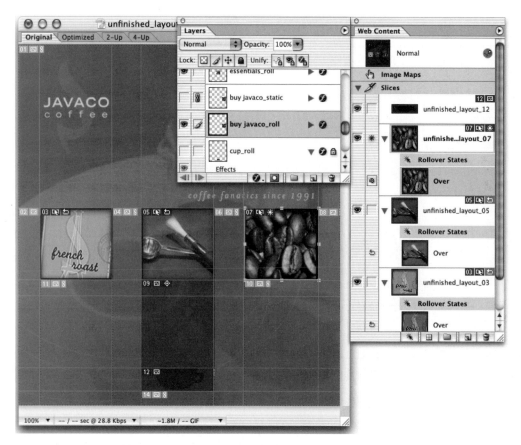

19. In the **Layers** palette, turn off the visibility of the **buy javaco_static** layer and turn on the visibility of the **buy javaco_roll** layer.

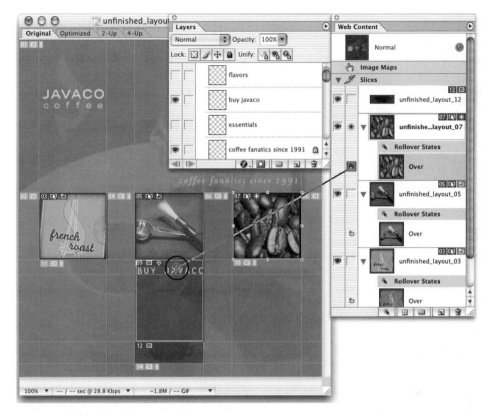

20. Turn on the visibility of the **buy javaco** layer. Click and drag the **target** icon from the **Over** state to the **buy javaco** layer, as shown here. Click the **Preview in Default Browser** button on the **Toolbox**. Position your mouse over the **flavors** image. The image changes to the **Over** state and the words "BUY JAVACO" appear below the center image.

21. You're done! Save and close the file. Remember, **Save Optimized As** will not only save the images but the required HTML and JavaScript code to make the slices and rollovers work.

 MOVIE | web_interface.mov

To learn more about how to create the Web interface in this exercise, check out **web_interface.mov** from the **movies** folder on the **H•O•T CD-ROM**.

You've finished another challenging chapter! In Chapter 14, "Automation," you'll learn how to automate common tasks.

I4.
Automation

| Creating a Web Photo Gallery |
| Customizing a Web Photo Gallery |
| Collaborating with a Web Photo Gallery |
| Creating a PDF Presentation | Creating Actions |
| Creating Droplets | Creating Conditional Actions |

chap_14

Photoshop CS/ImageReady CS
H•O•T CD-ROM

Photoshop CS and ImageReady CS offer many practical and creative tools to help you design Web graphics. This chapter shows you how to automate tasks. Automating tasks is a huge timesaver—who wants to repeat the same operations over and over when Photoshop CS or ImageReady CS can do the work for you?

Photoshop CS offers a number of new and enhanced automation features to help you convert a single image or a folder of images into a variety of useful formats, including a **Web Photo Gallery**, a **PDF slideshow**, or a **PDF presentation**, without the need for HTML or PDF authoring programs.

Photoshop CS and ImageReady CS both offer **actions**, which allow you to store a series of operations as a recording and play the recording back over a single image or multiple images in the same folder. New to ImageReady CS, you can apply conditional logic to actions. ImageReady CS will look for image characteristics you specify (file name, dimensions, and so on) and perform an automated action only if the image meets the specified criteria.

ImageReady CS has another automation feature called **droplets**, which store optimization settings. You can drag and drop the droplets to a single image or to a folder of images and instantly apply optimization settings without having to adjust settings for each image in the Optimize palette.

In this chapter, you'll learn how to create and customize a Web Photo Gallery, a PDF slideshow, and a PDF presentation in Photoshop CS; how to use actions and conditional actions in ImageReady CS; and how to use the droplet feature to optimize a folder of images quickly. This is the stuff computers were made for. Enjoy!

What Is the Web Photo Gallery?

The Web Photo Gallery lets you take a folder of images and instantly convert it into a Web page. The Web Photo Gallery feature automatically optimizes the images and writes HTML code to produce a Web site suitable for publishing online. The Web Photo Gallery feature is a quick and easy way for anyone to display their work: for architects to show renderings to clients, for photographers to display proofs, or for families to share personal photos on the Web. Plus, new to Photoshop CS, you can use one of the feedback templates, which provides an interface for clients and contacts to approve and comment on images in a Web Photo Gallery, without having to do any complicated programming!

New to Photoshop CS, you can now create a Web Photo Gallery directly from the File Browser. The File Browser is an excellent interface for creating a Web Photo Gallery because it lets you preview and organize images before you create the Gallery. This will save you time spent opening and editing images.

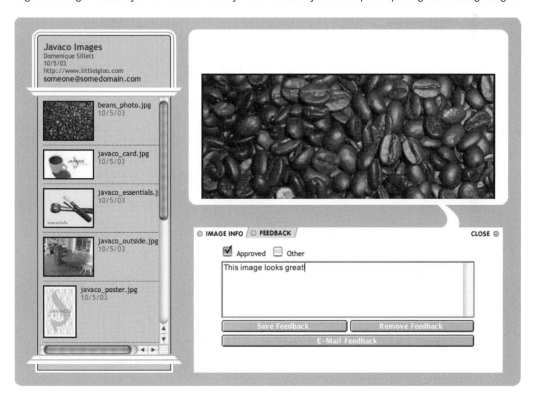

You can customize the Web Photo Gallery with many different appearances. In this example, I created a Web Photo Gallery using the **Centered Frame 2 – Feedback** template. The feedback templates are new in Photoshop CS and allow others to approve and comment about images in a Web Photo Gallery without any extra programming required! In the next few exercises, you'll learn how easy it is to create, customize, and use the feedback templates with the Web Photo Gallery feature in Photoshop CS.

When you create a Web Photo Gallery, Photoshop CS performs the following tasks automatically:

• Copies, resizes, and optimizes the images

• Creates thumbnails of the images

• Writes the required HTML code for the Web site

• Includes file information you specify such as the file name, who created the image, a description of the file, and copyright information

• Generates Next, Previous, and Home buttons to help you navigate around the Web page

Photoshop CS provides numerous options for customizing your Web Photo Gallery. You'll learn about these options in the next two exercises. If you want to make further modifications to your Web Photo Gallery, you can edit the files in an HTML editor such as Adobe GoLive or Macromedia Dreamweaver.

I. [PS] _____ Creating a Web Photo Gallery

In this exercise, you'll learn how to create a Web Photo Gallery in Photoshop CS using images provided on the **H•O•T CD-ROM**. When you're finished the exercise, try it on a folder of your own images; you'll be amazed at how easy it is to create an entire Web site without having to write HTML code!

1. In Photoshop CS, click the **Toggle File Browser** button on the **Options** bar.

2. Navigate to the **create web gallery** folder in the **chap_14** folder you copied to your **Desktop**. Hold down the **Shift** key and multiple-select the images in the **create web gallery** folder.

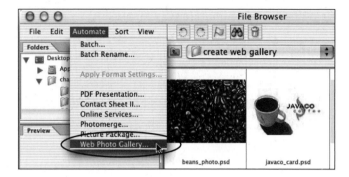

3. In the **File Browser**, choose **Automate > Web Photo Gallery**.

*The **Web Photo Gallery** dialog box launches automatically.*

*Tip: You can also open the **Web Photo Gallery** dialog box by choosing **File > Automate > Web Photo Gallery** from Photoshop CS. I prefer to use the **File Browser** to create a Web Photo Gallery because it's a more visual interface and lets me preview and organize my images before creating the Gallery. Creating a Web Photo Gallery from the **File Browser** is a new feature in Photoshop CS.*

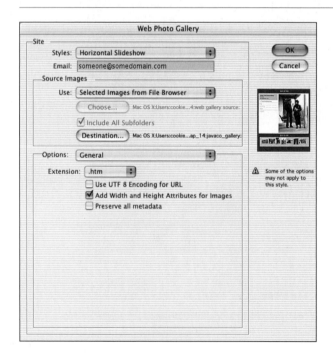

4. Choose **Horizontal Slideshow** from the **Styles** pop-up menu. Type your email address in the **Email** field. Choose **Selected Images from File Browser** in the **Use** pop-up menu.

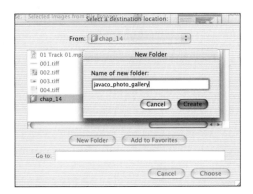

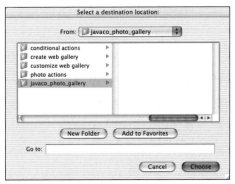

5. Click the **Destination** button. Navigate to the **chap_14** folder you copied to your **Desktop**. Click the **New Folder** (Mac) or the **Create New Folder** (Windows) button. In the **New Folder** dialog box, type **javaco_photo_gallery** in the **Name** field. Click **Create** (Mac) or **OK** (Windows). In the **Select a destination location** dialog box, select the **javaco_photo_gallery** folder you just created. Click **Choose**.

6. Click **OK** in the **Web Photo Gallery** dialog box.

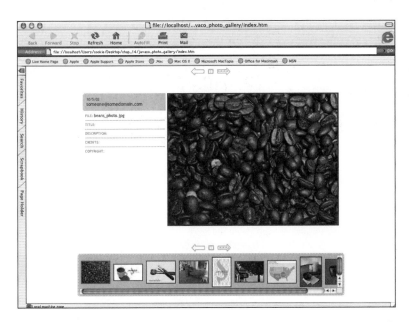

Now you can sit back and watch Photoshop CS do all the work for you! Photoshop CS will resize and optimize the images, create the HTML for the Web site, and display the Web Photo Gallery in your default Web browser!

Note: *This process can take seconds or minutes depending on the speed of your computer and the number of images in the source folder.*

7. Take a look at the Web Photo Gallery you just created in your default Web browser. Click the thumbnails to see larger versions of the images. Click the **Previous** and **Next** buttons to navigate through the images in the Web Photo Gallery.

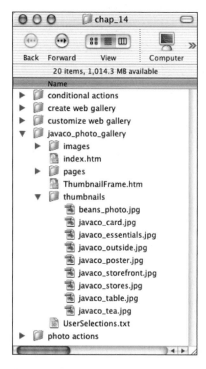

8. Browse to the **javaco_gallery** folder in the **chap_14** folder you copied to your **Desktop**. As you can see, Photoshop CS created a series of HTML pages, images, and thumbnails, which are the components of the Web Photo Gallery site.

Note: In the next exercise, you'll learn how to change the appearance of the Web Photo Gallery.

9. Return to the **File Browser** in Photoshop CS for the next exercise.

[PS] _____**Customizing a Web Photo Gallery**

If you want to change the content or appearance of a Web Photo Gallery, you can use the customization features in the Web Photo Gallery dialog box. Here's an exercise to show you how.

1. In Photoshop CS, the **File Browser** should still be open with the images in the **create web gallery** folder selected. Choose **Automate > Web Photo Gallery** from the **File Browser** menu.

Notice the **Web Photo Gallery** dialog box has the same settings from the last exercise. The settings in the **Web Photo Gallery** dialog box are sticky: Photoshop CS remembers the settings you last specified.

Notice the warning on the right-hand side of the **Web Photo Gallery** dialog box. The warning indicates this style cannot be fully customized. You'll change the style to one you can customize in the next step.

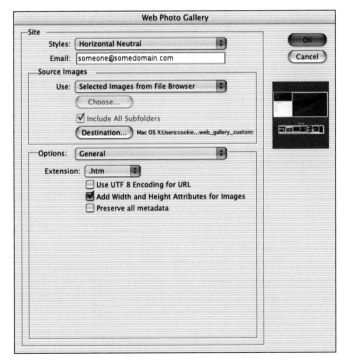

2. Choose **Horizontal Neutral** from the **Styles** pop-up menu.

Notice the warning on the right-hand side of the **Web Photo Gallery** dialog box disappears, and the thumbnail preview changes. You've chosen a style that can be customized. You'll learn how in the next steps.

3. Click the **Destination** button. Navigate to the **chap_14** folder you copied to your **Desktop**. Click the **New Folder** (Mac) or **Create New Folder** (Windows) button. In the **New Folder** dialog box, name the folder **javaco_web_gallery_custom**. Click **Create** (Mac) or **OK** (Windows). Click **Choose**.

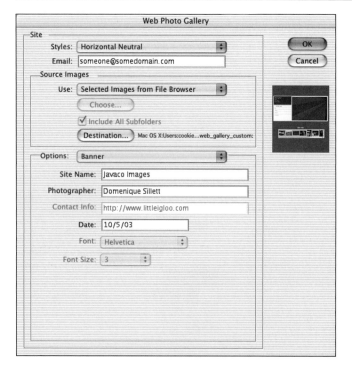

4. Choose **Banner** from the **Options** pop-up menu. Notice the settings in the **Options** section of the **Web Photo Gallery** dialog box have changed. Type info for the **Site Name**, **Photographer**, **Contact Info**, and **Date** fields. You don't have to use the info shown here—you can type anything you want.

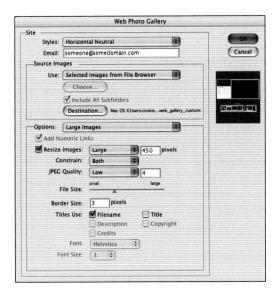

5. Choose **Large Images** from the **Options** pop-up menu. Notice the settings in the **Options** section of the **Web Photo Gallery** dialog box have changed. In this section, you can change the appearance of the large images. Choose **Large** from the **Resize Images** pop-up menu. Type **3** in the **Border Size** field.

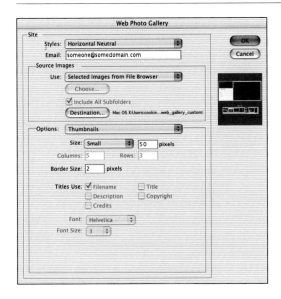

6. Choose **Thumbnails** from the **Options** pop-up menu. Notice the settings in the **Options** section of the **Web Photo Gallery** dialog box have changed. In this section, you can change the appearance of the thumbnail images. Choose **Small** from the **Size** pop-up menu. Type **2** in the **Border Size** field.

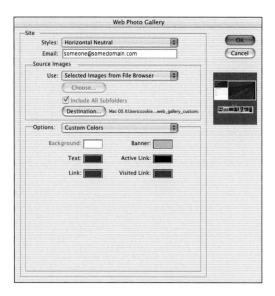

7. Choose **Custom Colors** from the **Options** pop-up menu. Click the color swatches and choose a color in the **Color Picker** dialog box for any or all of the items in the **Options** section of the **Web Photo Gallery** dialog box.

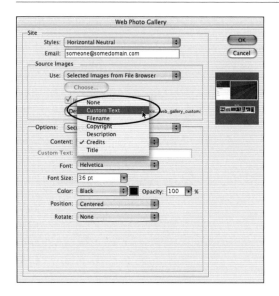

8. Choose **Security** from the **Options** pop-up menu. Take a look at the options in the **Content** pop-up menu. These settings relate to **metadata**. Wondering what metadata is? Have a look at the note following this step for more information. You don't need to change any settings in this step.

NOTE | Metadata and Security Settings

Photoshop CS can store special information called metadata that is invisible to the user. Metadata can include the file name, copyright information, a caption describing the image, creator credits, and the image title.

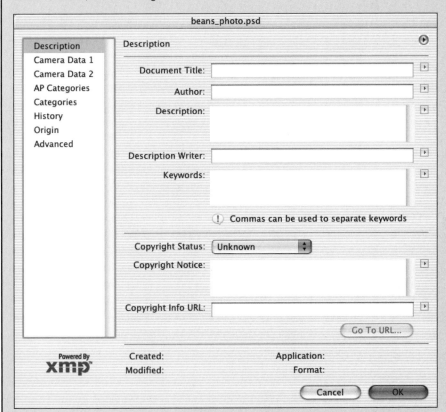

You can specify metadata for any file by choosing **File > File Info** from the **File Browser** or by opening the image in Photoshop CS and choosing **File > File Info**. When you specify information in the **File Info** dialog box, you can format the images to include some of the metadata in the **Security** settings section of the **Web Photo Gallery** dialog box.

9. Click **OK** in the **Web Photo Gallery** dialog box. Photoshop CS will automatically generate the **Web Photo Gallery** using the settings you just specified in the **Web Photo Gallery** dialog box and display the final result in your default Web browser.

10. Return to the **File Browser** in Photoshop CS for the next exercise.

NOTE | Tokens

Adobe created its own programming language called **Tokens**, which allows you to customize the HTML for a Web Photo Gallery. Tokens are an advanced feature designed to help programmers edit the HTML code. For more information about Tokens, refer to the **Using Tokens** section of the Photoshop CS online Help. To access the online Help, choose **Help > Help Topics**.

What Do All the Web Photo Gallery Settings Do?

The Photoshop CS Web Photo Gallery dialog box contains many settings. Here is an overview:

Web Photo Gallery Settings	
Setting	**Description**
SITE SETTINGS	
Styles pop-up menu	Choose a preset Web Photo Gallery site layout.
Email field	Specify an email address.
SOURCE IMAGES SETTINGS	
Use pop-up menu	Specify the images you want to use in the Web Photo Gallery. You can choose a folder of images or selected images in the File Browser.
Choose button	Choose the folder of images to use for the Web Photo Gallery.
Include All Subfolders check box	Specify if you want to include the subfolders in the Web Photo Gallery.
Destination button	Choose the location where you want to save the Web Photo Gallery.
GENERAL OPTIONS	
Extension pop-up menu	Specify if you want to save the HTML file as an .htm or a .html file.
BANNER OPTIONS	
Site Name field	Specify the name of the Web Photo Gallery.
Photographer field	Specify the name of the individual(s) who created the images.
Contact Info field	Specify contact info, such as a Web site address.
Date field	Specify the date the images were photographed or posted to the Web.
Font pop-up menu	Choose the font you want to use in the banner in the Web Photo Gallery.
Font Size pop-up menu	Choose the font size you want to use in the banner in the Web Photo Gallery.

continues on next page

Web Photo Gallery Settings *continued*	
Setting	**Description**
LARGE IMAGES OPTIONS	
Resize Images pop-up menu	Choose the size of the large images (**Small**, **Medium**, **Large**, or **Custom**).
Constrain pop-up menu	Choose if you want to constrain the width and/or height of the images when they are resized.
JPEG Quality pop-up menu	Choose the quality of JPEG optimization (**Low**, **Medium**, **High**, or **Maximum**).
File Size slider	Specify file size (large or small).
Border Size field	Specify a border size for the large images.
Titles Use check boxes	Specify if you want the file name, title, description, copyright, or credits information to appear beside the large images in the Web Photo Gallery.
Font pop-up menu	Choose the font for the text that appears beside the large images.
Font Size pop-up menu	Choose the font size for the text that appears beside the large images.

continues on next page

Web Photo Gallery Settings *continued*	
Setting	**Description**
Thumbnails Options	
Size pop-up menu	Choose the size of the thumbnail images (**Small**, **Medium**, **Large**, or **Custom**).
Columns and Rows fields	Specify how many columns and rows of thumbnail images to include in the Web Photo Gallery.
Border Size field	Specify a border size for the thumbnail images.
Titles Use check boxes	Specify if you want the file name, title, description, copyright, or credits information to appear beside the thumbnail images in the Web Photo Gallery.
Font pop-up menu	Choose the font for the text that appears beside the thumbnail images.
Font Size pop-up menu	Choose the font size for the text that appears beside the thumbnail images.
Custom Colors Options	
Background	Specify a color for the background in Web Photo Gallery.
Banner	Specify a color for the banner in the Web Photo Gallery.
Text	Specify a color for the text in the Web Photo Gallery.
Active Link	Specify a color for active links in the Web Photo Gallery.
Link	Specify a color for links in the Web Photo Gallery.
Visited Link	Specify a color for visited links in the Web Photo Gallery.

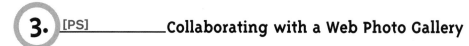

3. [PS] _____Collaborating with a Web Photo Gallery

One of the new features in Photoshop CS is the capability to collaborate with a Web Photo Gallery. Photoshop CS includes Web Photo Gallery templates that let clients approve or provide feedback about images in a Web Photo Gallery. Collaborating through the Web Photo Gallery interface is easy because it doesn't require any extra programming. Here's an exercise to show you how.

1. In Photoshop CS, you should have the **File Browser** open with the images in the **create web gallery** folder selected. Choose **Automate > Web Photo Gallery** from the **File Browser** menu.

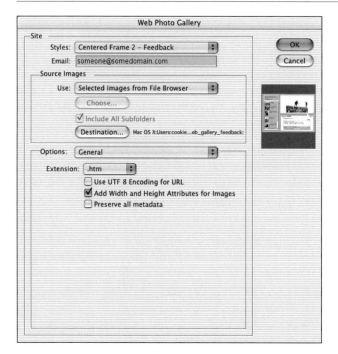

2. Choose **Centered Frame 2 – Feedback** from the **Styles** pop-up menu.

3. Click the **Destination** button. Navigate to the **chap_14** folder you copied to your **Desktop**. Click the **New Folder** (Mac) or **Create New Folder** (Windows) button. In the **New Folder** dialog box, name the folder **javaco_web_gallery_feedback**. Click **Create** (Mac) or **OK** (Windows). Click **Choose**.

4. Customize the **Web Photo Gallery** dialog box using the skills you learned in the last exercise. When you're finished, click **OK**.

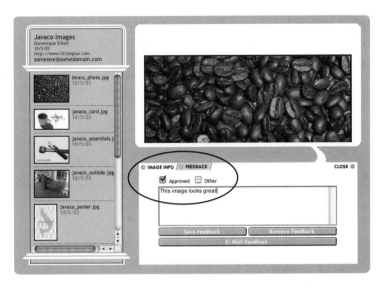

5. Take a look at the Web Photo Gallery Photoshop CS created. Click the **Feedback** button. Turn on the **Approved** option and type a message in the **Feedback** field.

6. Click the **Save Feedback** button and notice the word "Saved" appears above the top-right corner of the text field.

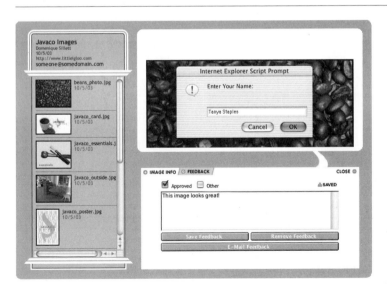

7. Click the **E-Mail Feedback** button. Type your name in the **Enter Your Name** field of the dialog box and click **OK**. An email will be automatically created in your default email application.

Notice the email address you specified in the **Web Photo Gallery** *dialog box automatically populates the* **To** *field, "Feedback from Tanya Staples" (or whatever name you specified in* **Step 7**) *automatically populates the* **Subject** *field, and the name of the image, approval status, and the comments you typed in the text field automatically populate the body of the email. Very cool!*

Tip: *If you want to change any of the information in the email, you can! Just delete and retype the information you want to change.*

8. When you're finished, return to the **File Browser** in Photoshop CS for the next exercise.

4. [PS] Creating a PDF Presentation

One of the new automation features in Photoshop CS is the capability to create a PDF presentation from a series of images in the File Browser. Photoshop CS automatically creates a slideshow presentation in PDF format. This is a fast and easy way to create a slideshow presentation without having to use presentation applications. Here's an exercise to show you how.

Note: For this exercise, you must have Adobe Reader installed on your computer. If you don't, you can download and install it from **www.adobe.com**, Adobe's Web site.

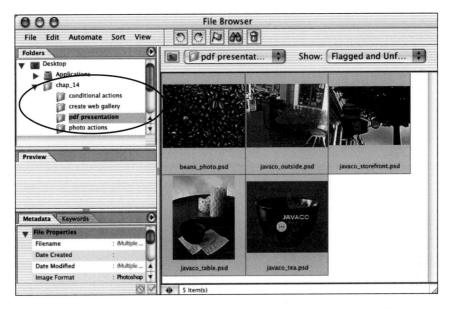

1. In Photoshop CS, you should have the **File Browser** open. Click the **pdf presentation** folder. Hold down the **Shift** key and multiple-select the images in the **pdf presentation** folder. Choose **Automate > PDF Presentation** from the **File Browser** menu.

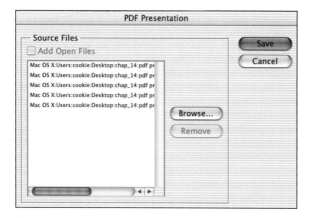

2. In the **PDF Presentation** dialog box, notice the images you selected in the **File Browser** are automatically listed in the **Source Files** box.

*Tip: If you want to add additional images, you can do so by clicking the **Browse** button to browse to the location where the images are stored on your computer. If you want to remove images, click to select the images you want to remove. Notice the **Remove** button becomes enabled. Click **Remove.***

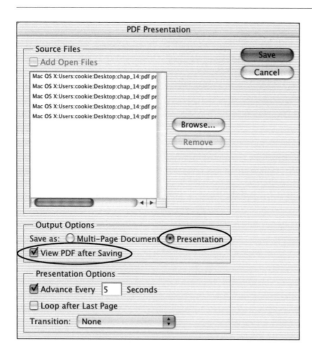

3. Choose **Presentation** from the **Output Options** section of the **PDF Presentation** dialog box. Turn on the **View PDF after Saving** option.

4. Adjust the settings in the **Presentation Options** section of the dialog box. The **Advance Every** option specifies the amount of time each slide is displayed onscreen. The **Loop After Last Page** option plays the presentation continually (until you press the **Esc** key to exit). The **Transition** pop-up menu lets you choose different options for how the slideshow will transition between images. When you're satisfied with your choices, click **Save**.

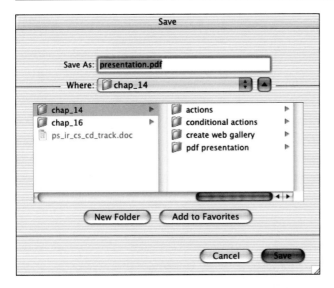

5. In the **Save** dialog box, navigate to the **chap_14** folder on your **Desktop**. Type **presentation.pdf** in the **Save As** field. Click **Save**.

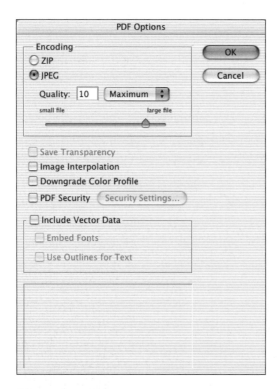

6. In the **PDF Options** dialog box, leave the options as the defaults and click **OK**.

Photoshop CS will now convert the images you selected into a PDF presentation and open it in Adobe Reader. The presentation will automatically appear in full-screen mode, as shown here.

7. When you've finished viewing the results, press **Esc**. You'll return to Adobe Reader. Quit Adobe Reader and return to Photoshop CS. Close the **File Browser** and quit Photoshop CS. You'll use ImageReady CS for the next exercises.

TIP | Creating a Multi-Page PDF

In the last exercise, you created a PDF presentation. Photoshop CS also lets you create a multi-page PDF document from selected files in the **File Browser**. Here's how:

In the **Output Options** section of the **PDF Presentation** dialog box, select **Multi-Page Document**. Save the file. Instead of creating a PDF presentation, Photoshop CS created a multi-page PDF. The PDF presentation features in the **Automate** menu help you quickly create PDFs you can share on the Web without having to use other programs.

What Are Actions?

An **action** is a series of commands you can play back on a single image or on a folder of images. For example, you can create an action that opens, crops, optimizes, and saves images.

Most of the commands and tool operations in Photoshop CS and ImageReady CS can be recorded as actions. Photoshop CS and ImageReady CS both allow stops, which let actions stop so you can perform tasks that can't be recorded, and modal controls, which let you enter values in a dialog box while playing an action. New to ImageReady CS, you can insert a conditional step, which scans for specific image characteristics such as size or file name and performs a step only if the characteristics match.

If you want to apply an action to a single image, click the Play button at the bottom of the Actions palette. If you want to apply the action to a series of images, you can use the Batch command in Photoshop CS or the droplet feature in ImageReady CS. You'll learn how in the next few exercises.

Using Predefined Actions

Photoshop CS and ImageReady CS include predefined actions, which you can access in the Actions palette. Some of the actions have words in parentheses, such as **Vignette (selection)**, **Cast Shadow (type)**, and **Sepia Toning (layer)**. These words indicate the action will only work under certain conditions, such as when the image contains an active selection, editable or rendered type, or a layer.

It's easy to use the predefined actions in Photoshop CS or ImageReady CS. Simply open an image, click to select the action you want to play in the Actions palette, and click the Play button at the bottom of the Actions palette.

5. [IR] _____ Creating Actions in ImageReady CS

Actions are a great way to automate repetitive tasks such as creating thumbnails for a Web page, which you'll learn to do in this exercise. You'll create an action that resizes a copy of an image to thumbnail size and saves it as an optimized JPEG. For this exercise, you'll use ImageReady CS, but it works the same way in Photoshop CS. In Exercise 6, you'll apply the action to a whole folder of images using the droplet feature in ImageReady CS.

1. In ImageReady CS, open **beans_photo.psd** from the **actions** folder in the **chap_14** folder you copied to your **Desktop**. Make sure the **Actions** palette is visible. If it's not, choose **Window > Actions**.

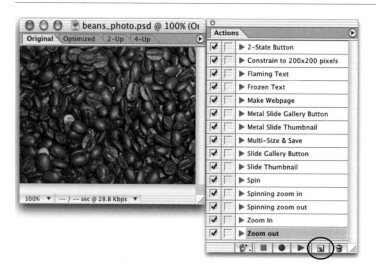

2. Click the **Create new action** button at the bottom of the **Actions** palette.

3. In the **New Action** dialog box, type **Thumbnail** in the **Name** field. Click **Record**.

*Notice an entry named **Thumbnail** now appears in the **Actions** palette. Clicking **Record** begins the recording process. All operations you perform in ImageReady CS will be recorded in the **Thumbnail** action.*

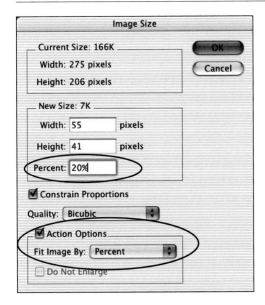

4. Choose **Image > Image Size**. In the **Image Size** dialog box, type **20%** in the **Percent** field. Make sure **Constrain Proportions** is turned on. Turn on **Action Options** and choose **Percent** from the **Fit Image By** pop-up menu. Click **OK**.

5. Make sure the **Optimize** palette is visible. If it's not, choose **Window > Optimize**.

6. Click the **Optimized** tab in the document window. Choose **JPEG Medium** from the **Preset** pop-up menu.

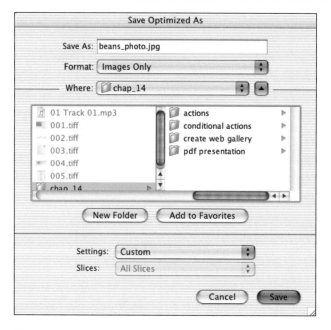

7. Choose **File > Save Optimized As**. In the **Save As** dialog box, browse to the **actions** folder in the **chap_14** folder you copied to your **Desktop**. Click **Save** to save **beans_photo.jpg** in the **actions** folder.

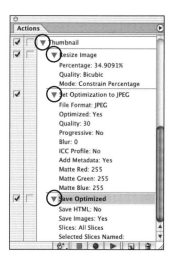

8. Click the **Stop** button at the bottom of the **Actions** palette. Click the arrows beside the **Resize Image**, **Set Optimization as JPEG**, and **Save Optimized** steps in the **Actions** palette. Take a look at the information that was recorded.

You successfully recorded an action! ImageReady CS recorded everything you did in the last few steps. Next, you'll play back the recording over an image to test the results.

9. Open **café_photo.psd** from the **actions** folder in the **chap_14** folder you copied to your **Desktop**. Click the **Play** button at the bottom of the **Actions** palette. The **Thumbnail** action will resize, optimize, and save the file.

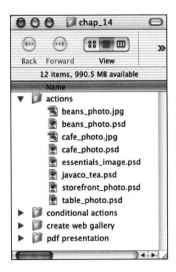

10. Browse to the **actions** folder in the **chap_14** folder on your **Desktop**. Notice **beans_photo.jpg** and **cafe_photo.jpg** were saved in the **actions** folder. If you like, you can open the files to see how they look.

It's that easy to create and save actions in ImageReady CS. In the next exercise, you'll learn how to apply the action to an entire folder of images using droplets.

11. With the **actions** folder still open, delete the **beans_photo.jpg** and **cafe_photo.jpg** files.

12. Return to ImageReady CS. Close **cafe-photo.psd** and **beans_photo.psd**. Do not save the changes.

NOTE | Recording Actions in Photoshop CS

Now that you've learned how to create an action in ImageReady CS, you might wonder if you can do the same thing in Photoshop CS. You can indeed! Photoshop CS also includes an Actions palette, and the process for recording actions is the same as that in ImageReady CS.

Editing Actions

Once you've created an action in Photoshop CS or ImageReady CS, you can always make changes to it later. Here's a handy chart that outlines how to add, delete, or move steps in an action.

Editing Actions	
Operation	**Method**
Add	To add a step to an action, choose **Start Recording** from the **Actions** palette menu. Perform the operations you want to add. Click the **Stop** button at the bottom of the **Actions** palette. The steps you recorded will be automatically added to the end of the action. If you want to add steps to the middle of an action, click the action you want to come after the insertion and begin the recording process.
Delete	To delete a step from an action, click the step to select it in the **Actions** palette. Drag the step to the **Trash** icon at the bottom of the **Actions** palette or choose **Delete** from the **Actions** palette menu.
Move	 To move a step inside an action, click the step to select it, then drag and drop the step until a black line appears where you want the step moved.
Turn On/ Off Step	 To turn on or off a step, click the **Toggle item on/off** check box in the **Actions** palette. When you play an action with a step turned off, it will skip over that step.
Turn On/Off Dialog Box	 To turn on or off a dialog box so you can specify individual settings for the step, click the **Toggle dialog on/off** button in the **Actions** palette. When you play the action, the appropriate dialog box will open and prompt you to specify settings before completing the rest of the steps in the action.

About Droplets

A droplet is a small application created by Photoshop CS or ImageReady CS that applies an action to a folder of images or to a series of selected images.

When you create a droplet, Photoshop CS and ImageReady CS create a droplet icon. To apply the droplet, drag and drop a folder or a series of selected images onto the droplet icon.

The process for creating droplets in Photoshop CS and ImageReady CS is identical. However, if you want to optimize images using a droplet, you must use ImageReady CS. If you want to optimize a series of images in Photoshop CS, you must use the Batch command. For more information about the Batch command in Photoshop CS, refer to the note at the end of Exercise 6.

Here are a few other fun facts about droplets to keep in mind as you learn to use them:

- You can create droplets from actions in the Actions palette in Photoshop CS or ImageReady CS.

- You can save droplets to your Desktop or any location on your computer.

- You can use a droplet without first opening Photoshop CS or ImageReady CS. The application will launch automatically when you drag a folder or series of files onto the droplet.

- You can share droplets between Mac and Windows computers because they are cross-platform. **Note:** If you create a droplet on a Mac, make sure you add the .exe file extension so Windows computers will recognize it.

6. [IR] Creating Droplets in ImageReady CS

In the last exercise, you learned how to create an action and apply it to a single image. In this exercise, you'll learn how to create a droplet, which lets you apply an action to a folder or series of images. For this exercise, you'll use ImageReady CS. You can create droplets in Photoshop CS, but you cannot use the droplet feature to optimize images. If you want to optimize a folder or series of images in Photoshop CS, you need to use the Batch command, which is described in the note at the end of this exercise.

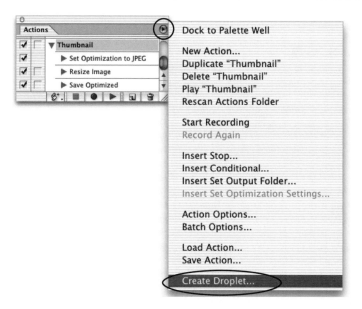

1. Click the **Thumbnail** action in the **Actions** palette to select it. Choose **Create Droplet** from the **Actions** palette menu.

2. In the **Save this action as a droplet** dialog box, navigate to your **Desktop**. Type **Thumnbail.exe** in the **Save As** field. Click **Save**.

*Note: On Windows, the .exe extension will automatically be applied to the file name in the **Save this action as a droplet** dialog box.*

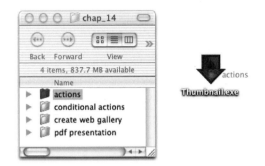

3. Browse to your **Desktop** and open the **chap_14** folder. Drag the **actions** folder onto the **Thumbnail.exe** droplet.

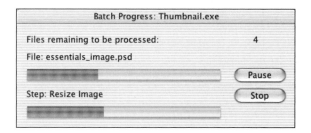

*You can watch the progress of the action in the **Batch Progress** dialog box. If you need to pause or stop the action, you can click the **Pause** or **Stop** buttons.*

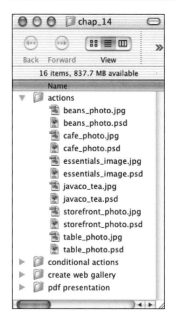

4. Open the **actions** folder in the **chap_14** folder on your **Desktop**. The droplet worked! Notice each PSD file now has an associated JPG file. If you want to view the results, open the JPG files in ImageReady CS.

TIP | Changing the Save Location for Droplets

By default, droplets save optimized images in the same folder as the original images. If you want to save the optimized images in a different folder, you can specify a location in the Batch Options dialog box. Here's how:

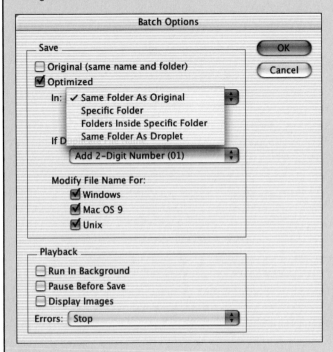

In the **Actions** palette, choose **Batch Options** from the **Actions** palette menu. Choose one of the following options: **Same Folder As Original** (which is the default setting), **Specific Folder**, **Folders Inside Specific Folder**, or **Same Folder as Droplet**.

---

5. Return to ImageReady CS for the next exercise.

 MOVIE | droplets.mov

To learn more about creating droplets in ImageReady CS, check out **droplets.mov** in the **movies** folder on the **H•O•T CD-ROM**.

NOTE | Batch Processing Actions in Photoshop CS

In addition to droplets, Photoshop CS also includes a Batch feature, which lets you apply actions to a folder of images or a series of selected images. Because the droplets feature in Photoshop CS does not allow you to apply optimization settings to images, you'll need to use the Batch feature. Here's how it works:

In Photoshop CS, choose **File > Automate > Batch**.

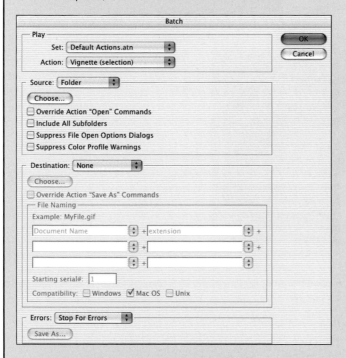

In the **Batch** dialog box, choose a set and an action from the **Set** and **Action** pop-up menus. Choose the source images in the **Source** section. Choose the destination in the **Destination** section. Specify the file naming convention you want to use. When you're happy with the settings in the **Batch** dialog box, click **OK**.

Browse to the location where you saved the destination images. The images you batch-processed should be present in the destination folder.

7. [IR] _____ Creating Conditional Actions in ImageReady CS

One of the new features in ImageReady CS is the conditional actions feature. With conditional actions, you can scan images for specific image characteristics, such as dimensions or file name, and perform a step if the characteristics match the setting. For example, if you have a series of images you want to optimize and save but some images are larger than others, you can add a conditional step to resize any images larger than a specific height. Here's an example to show you how. **Note:** Conditional actions are only available in ImageReady CS.

1. Open the images in the **conditional actions** folder in the **chap_14** folder you copied to your **Desktop**. There should be a total of eight images.

Notice some of the images are 200 pixels tall, and other images are significantly taller. In this exercise, you'll set a conditional action to resize images taller than 200 pixels, then optimize and save all the images as GIFs.

2. Close all the images except **blue_poster.psd**. Make sure the **Actions** palette is visible. If it's not, choose **Window > Actions**.

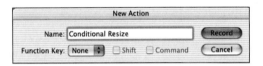

3. Click the **Create new action** button at the bottom of the **Actions** palette. In the **New Action** dialog box, type **Conditional Resize** for the **Name** and click **Record**.

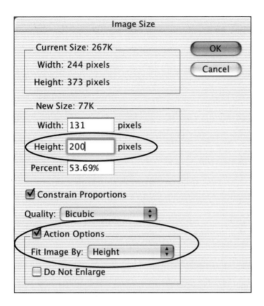

4. Choose **Image > Image Size**. In the **Image Size** dialog box, type **200** in the **Height** field. Make sure the **Constrain Proportions** option is turned on. Turn on **Action Options** and choose **Height** from the **Fit Image By** pop-up menu. Click **OK**.

5. Make sure the **Optimize** palette is visible. If it's not, choose **Window > Optimize**.

6. Click the **Optimized** tab in the document window. Choose **GIF 64 No Dither** from the **Preset** pop-up menu in the **Optimize** palette.

7. Click the **Stop** button at the bottom of the **Actions** palette.

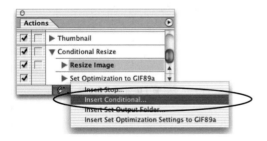

8. Click the **Resize Image** step in the **Actions** palette to select it. Choose **Insert Conditional** from the **Insert a step** pop-up menu at the bottom of the **Actions** palette.

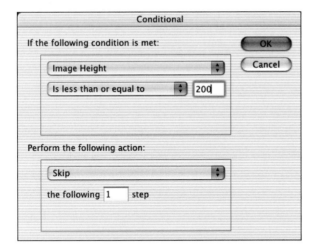

9. In the **Conditional** dialog box, match the settings to the illustration shown here. Click **OK**.

These settings will tell ImageReady CS to skip one step in the action if the image is less than or equal to 200 pixels tall. This will resize the images taller than 200 pixels to be 200 pixels tall and will leave the images that are already 200 pixels tall the same size.

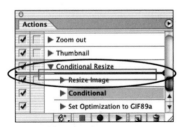

10. Notice the **Conditional** step appears between the **Resize Image** and the **Set Optimization to GIF** steps. Click and drag the **Conditional** step above the **Resize Image** step. This will ensure ImageReady CS skips the **Resize Image** step if the image is less than or equal to 200 pixels tall.

11. Click the **Conditional Resize** action in the **Actions** palette to select it. Choose **Create Droplet** from the **Actions** palette menu.

12. Name the droplet **Conditional_Resize.exe** and save it to your **Desktop**.

13. Close **blue_poster.psd**. Do not save your changes.

14. Browse to the **conditional actions** folder in the **chap_14** folder you copied to your **Desktop**.

15. Drag and drop the **conditional actions** folder onto the **Conditional_Resize.exe** droplet.

16. Browse to the **conditional actions** folder. Notice a GIF file was created for each of the original PSD images.

17. Return to ImageReady CS and open the GIF files you created in the **conditional actions** folder.

Notice the images are all 200 pixels tall. ImageReady CS recognized that some of the images in the conditional actions folder were already 200 pixels tall and did not resize them based on the information you provided in the Conditional step. The other images, which were more than 200 pixels tall, were resized to 200 pixels tall to match the height of the other images. Very cool!

18. Close any open images in ImageReady CS. You don't need to save your changes.

 MOVIE | conditional.mov

To learn more about creating conditional actions in ImageReady CS, check out **conditional.mov** in the **movies** folder on the **H•O•T CD-ROM**.

You've finished another chapter! As you can see, the automation features in Photoshop CS and ImageReady CS can save you time and prevent error. In the next chapter, "Data Sets," you'll learn how to create data-driven graphics by using the data sets feature in ImageReady CS.

15.
Data Sets

| Buzzwords and Definitions |
| Understanding Data Sets and Variables |
| Creating Data Sets and Variables |
| Creating Pixel Replacement Variables |
| Importing Data Sets from Text Files |

chap_15

Photoshop CS/ImageReady CS
H•O•T CD-ROM

In the early days of Web design, designers and developers built Web sites page-by-page and graphic-by-graphic. Today, they can reap the benefits of using data-driven templates and dynamic content. For example, if you need to create 25 Web banners that are the same size, use the same font, and have a same-sized image in the same position, you can build a data set with different variables to generate the Web banners for you. All you have to do is assemble the template and specify the data!

Confused by the buzzwords and how they relate to Photoshop CS and ImageReady CS? Not to worry, you'll learn about these terms early in this chapter. You'll also learn how to specify variables and create data sets in ImageReady CS. Plus, you'll learn some of the new features in ImageReady CS, such as how to populate data sets from text files. In Chapter 16, "*Integration with Other Programs*," you'll learn how to manipulate data sets in Adobe GoLive.

Buzzwords and Definitions

Before you begin working with data sets, you'll need to familiarize yourself with industry lingo. Here is an overview of common terms you'll need to understand:

Data-driven: Data-driven refers to the process of feeding content to a template so data changes from page to page without having to create each page individually. When you work with data-driven templates, you design an overall page layout that accepts data and formats it according to the template. Usually, templates and data are text-based; however, you can create templates that are image-based. In this chapter, you'll learn how to create image-based data-driven templates using ImageReady CS.

Dynamic content: Dynamic content refers to data or text content that changes from page to page. Dynamic content is generated on the fly and populates data-driven templates.

Dynamic graphics: Dynamic graphics refers to graphics or images that change from page to page. Dynamic graphics are generated on the fly and populate data-driven templates. In this chapter, you'll learn how to create data sets that let you create Web pages with dynamic graphics.

Variables: Variables determine which images in a template are dynamic. There are three types of variables in ImageReady CS: **Text Replacement** variables, which replace vector-based type; **Visibility** variables, which replace images using layer visibility; and **Pixel Replacement** variables, which replace pixels in a layer with pixels from a different file. You'll learn how to create all three types of variables in this chapter.

Data sets: Data sets store all the variables for a template. Once you define data sets, you can output images as PSD files, optimized images (JPEGs or GIFs), or Macromedia Flash (SWF) files.

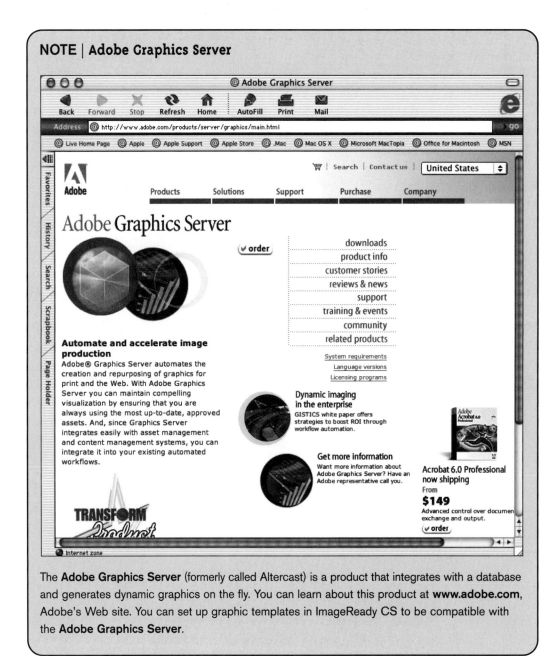

The **Adobe Graphics Server** (formerly called Altercast) is a product that integrates with a database and generates dynamic graphics on the fly. You can learn about this product at **www.adobe.com**, Adobe's Web site. You can set up graphic templates in ImageReady CS to be compatible with the **Adobe Graphics Server**.

I. [IR]_____Understanding Data Sets and Variables

The best way to understand data sets and variables is to look at a file that contains them. For the exercises in this chapter, you'll use ImageReady CS. You cannot create data sets and variables in Photoshop CS.

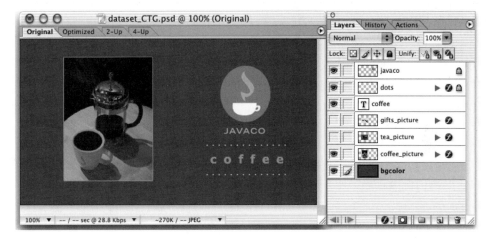

1. In ImageReady CS, open **dataset_CTG.psd** from the **chap_15** folder you copied to your **Desktop**.

Notice the image contains one text layer and five layers with graphics. Some of the layers contain layer styles.

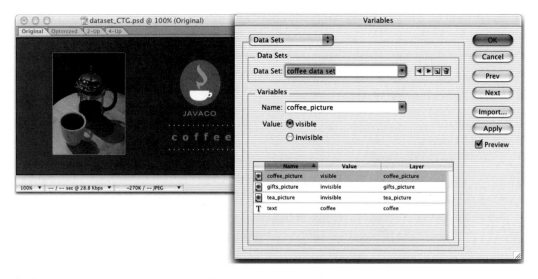

2. Choose **Image > Variables > Data Sets**.

*In the **Variables** dialog box, notice **coffee data set** is selected in the **Data Set** pop-up menu. Take a look at the contents of the **Variables** chart. Notice the **coffee_picture** variable is **visible**, the gifts_picture variable is **invisible**, and the **tea_picture** variable is **invisible**. These are examples of visibility variables because they are based on the visibility of the respective layers in the **Layers** palette.*

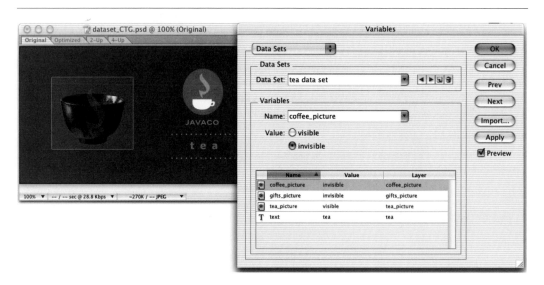

3. Choose **tea data set** from the **Data Set** pop-up menu.

Notice the coffee_picture layer is invisible, the gifts_picture is invisible, and the tea_picture layer is visible. Notice coffee_picture is selected in the Name pop-up menu. This indicates the coffee_picture layer variable is dynamic and will change based on the currently selected data set. In this example, the visibility of the coffee_picture layer has been turned off, and the visibility of the tea_picture layer has been turned on. Also notice the value of the text layer has been changed to "tea," and the word coffee has been replaced with the word "tea." The text is an example of a Text Replacement variable because the text has been replaced using the value specified in the variable.

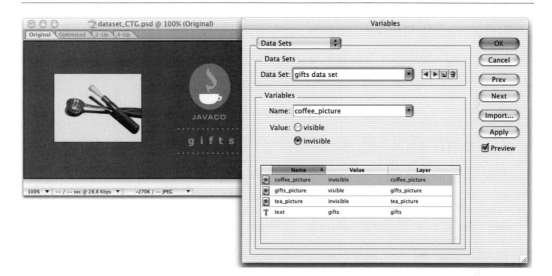

4. Choose **gifts data set** from the **Data Set** pop-up menu.

Notice the coffee_picture layer is invisible, the gifts_picture layer is visible, and the tea_picture layer is invisible. Notice coffee_picture is still selected in the Name pop-up menu. Similar to the last step, the gifts_picture layer is now visible in the image, and the text has been replaced with the word "gifts."

5. Close **dataset_CTG.psd**. You don't need to save your changes.

Now that you've had a chance to look at an image with variables and data sets, it's time to re-create this example to learn how to create variables and data sets.

Creating Data Sets and Variables

In the last exercise, you saw an example of how to use Visibility variables and Text Replacement variables to create data sets. In this exercise, you'll re-create that example from scratch so you can understand how to create data sets and variables.

1. In ImageReady, open **coffee-tea-gifts.psd** from the **chap_15** folder you copied to your **Desktop**.

2. Choose **Image > Variables > Define**. The **Variables** dialog box opens automatically.

*First, you'll define **Text Replacement** variables, which will allow you to change the text on the page without creating new text layers.*

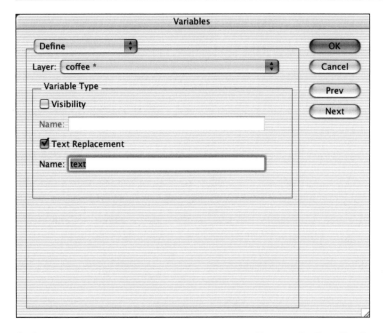

3. Choose **coffee** from the **Layer** pop-up menu. Turn on the **Text Replacement** option and type **text** in the **Name** field.

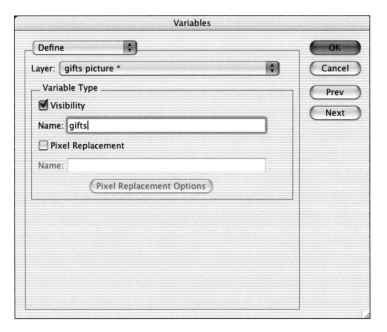

4. Choose **gifts picture** from the **Layer** pop-up menu. Turn on the **Visibility** option and type **gifts** in the **Name** field.

*Notice an **asterisk** appears beside the gifts picture in the **Layer** pop-up menu? The **asterisk** indicates you've set a variable for that layer.*

5. Choose **coffee picture** from the **Layer** pop-up menu. Turn on the **Visibility** option. Type **coffee** in the **Name** field. Choose **tea picture** from the **Layer** pop-up menu. Turn on the **Visibility** option and type **tea** in the **Name** field.

6. Choose **Data Sets** from the pop-up menu at the top of the **Variables** dialog box.

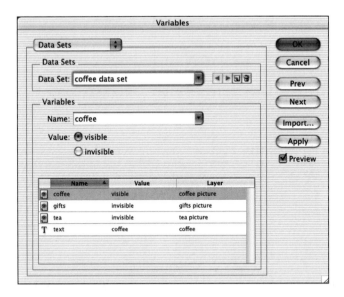

7. Type **coffee data set** in the **Data Set** field. You cannot create a data set until you define variables, which is why you created variables in the last steps. For this particular data set, you can leave the settings as they are with the **coffee picture** layer visible, the **tea picture** and **gifts picture** layers invisible, and **coffee** as the value for the **text** variable.

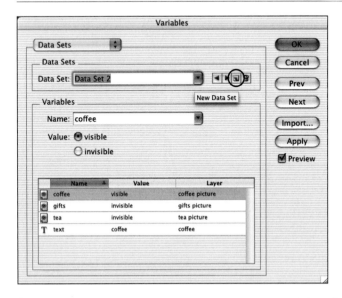

8. Click the **New Data Set** button. A new data set called **Data Set 2** will be automatically created with the same properties as the data set you just created in **Step 7**.

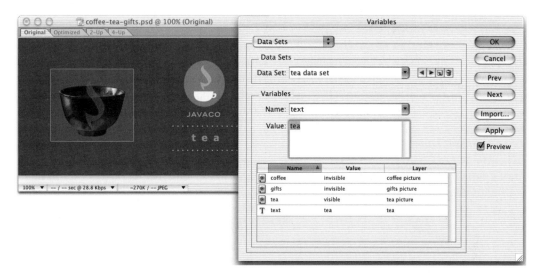

9. Type **tea data set** in the **Data Set** field. Click the **coffee picture** layer and set the **Value** to **invisible**. Click the **tea picture** layer and set the value to **visible**. Click the **coffee** layer (the text variable) and type **tea** in the **Value** field. Notice the image and the text updated automatically in the document window!

10. Click the **New Data Set** button. Type **gifts data set** in the **Data Set** field. Click the **tea picture** layer and set the **Value** to invisible. Click the **gifts picture** layer and set the value to **visible**. Click the **tea** layer (the text variable) and type **gifts** in the **Value** field. Notice the image and the text update automatically in the document window.

11. Click the **Previous** and **Next** buttons beside the **Data Set** pop-up menu to cycle through the data sets you just created. Notice the image in the document window updates each time you choose a different data set. Click **OK** and leave the file open for the next exercise.

MOVIE | datasets.mov

To learn more about creating data sets in ImageReady CS, check out **datasets.mov** from the **movies** folder on the **H•O•T CD-ROM**.

3. [IR] _____Creating Pixel Replacement Variables

In the last exercise, you learned how to create Text Replacement and Visibility Replacement variables. In this exercise, you'll learn how to create Pixel Replacement variables. Pixel Replacement variables allow you to locate and load external images into an ImageReady CS document. Using Pixel Replacement variables is the easiest way to set up a template with dynamic graphics.

1. With **coffee-tea-gifts.psd** open from the last exercise, choose **Images > Variables > Define**.

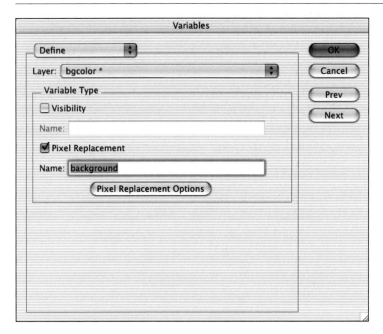

2. In the **Variables** dialog box, choose **bgcolor** from the **Layer** pop-up menu. Turn on the **Pixel Replacement** option. Type **background** in the **Name** field. Click the **Pixel Replacement Options** button.

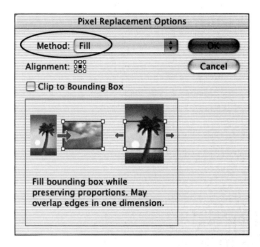

3. In the **Pixel Replacement Options** dialog box, choose **Fill** from the **Method** pop-up menu. Click **OK**.

*For more information about the choices in the **Pixel Replacement Options** dialog box, refer to the table at the end of this exercise.*

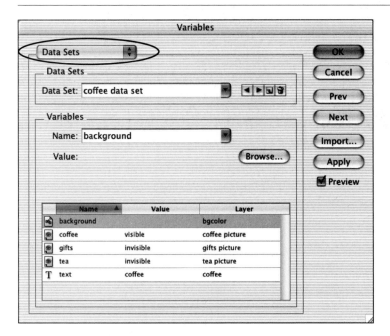

4. Choose **Data Sets** from the pop-up menu at the top of the **Variables** dialog box. The **coffee data set** will automatically appear with **background** selected in the **Name** pop-up menu, which indicates the **coffee data set** contains a variable called **background**. Click the **Browse** button.

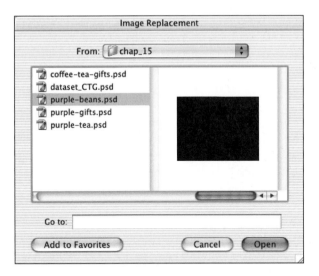

5. In the **Image Replacement** dialog box, browse to the **chap_15** folder you copied to your **Desktop** and select **purple-beans.psd**. Click **Open**.

*The **purple-beans.psd** file will now replace the background in the image.*

6. Choose **tea data set** from the **Data Set** pop-up menu. Click the **Browse** button. Browse to the **chap_15** folder you copied to your **Desktop**. Choose **purple-tea.psd** and click **Open**.

*The **purple-tea.psd** file will now replace the background in the image.*

7. Choose **gifts data set** from the **Data Set** pop-up menu. Click the **Browse** button. Browse to the **chap_15** folder you copied to your **Desktop**. Choose **purple-gifts.psd** and click **Open**.

*The **purple-gifts.psd** file will now replace the background in the image.*

8. Click **OK** to close the **Variables** dialog box. Save and close the file.

The benefit of using data sets and variables is best realized in an HTML editor such as Adobe GoLive or a dynamic graphics environment such as the Adobe Graphics Server. You'll learn how to use data sets in Adobe GoLive in Chapter 16, "Integration with Other Programs."

	Pixel Replacement Options
Fit	
	Scales the image to fit the height. (**Note:** This may leave undesirable gaps on the sides of the image when you put the image into a Web page.)
Fill	
	Fills the entire layer with the image while constraining the proportions. (**Note:** This may cause part of the image to be cut off when you put the image into a Web page.)
As Is	
	Makes no modifications to the image.
Conform	
	Scales the image without keeping the original proportions of the image.
Alignment	
	Aligns the image on a Web page based on which square you click in the **Alignment** icon in the **Pixel Replacement Options** dialog box.
Clip to Bounding Box	Clips areas of the image that do not fit. (**Note:** This option is available when the **Fill** or **As Is** options are selected in the **Method** pop-up menu.)

NOTE | Setting Up PSD Files

Here are a few helpful tips for creating PSD files with data sets and variables:

- Center or left-align your text (depending on the layout) to make sure the text looks consistent in all data sets.

- Test the length of your text to ensure it fits in the space.

- Use layer styles liberally to format your layers. Layer styles work on text and pixel-based layers.

[IR]_____**Importing Data Sets from Text Files**

In the last two exercises, you created data sets manually using the Variables dialog box in ImageReady CS. This process works well if you only have to create a few data sets. If you need to create a large number of data sets, that process would be very time-consuming. Fortunately, ImageReady CS lets you import data sets from a tab-delimited or comma-delimited text file. Here's an exercise to show you how this new feature works.

1. Before you get started, take a look at the **import-file.txt** file in the **chap_15** folder you copied to your **Desktop**. When you double-click the file, it should automatically open in **TextEdit** (Mac) or **Notepad** (Windows).

The first line in the text file indicates the variable names. The remaining lines, which are defined inside quotations, represent the words that will appear in the text and details variables for the data sets in the image. For this example, I created a simple text file in TextEdit. If you have a lot of data, you may want to export a tab-delimited or comma-delimited text file from a spreadsheet or database application.

_____

2. Return to ImageReady CS. Open **coffee-tea-gifts-import.psd** from the **chap_15 folder** you copied to your **Desktop**.

_____

3. Choose **Image > Variables > Data Sets**.

*Notice there are two **Text Replacement** variables: **details** and **text**.*

_____

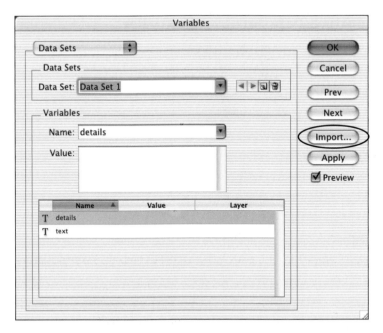

4. Click the **Import** button in the **Variables** dialog box. Browse to the **chap_15** folder you copied to your **Desktop**. Select **import-file.txt** and click **Open**. This imports the text file, which will result in new data sets and **Text Replacement** variables once you change a few settings.

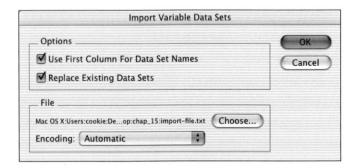

5. In the **Import Variable Data Sets** dialog box, turn on the **Use First Column For Data Set Names** option and turn on the **Replace Existing Data Sets** option. Click **OK**.

*The **User First Column For Data Set Names** option uses the first entry in the text file for the name of the data sets. In this case, it will use **coffee, tea,** and **gifts**. If you do not turn this option on, ImageReady CS will create data set names for you. The **Replace Existing Data Sets** option replaces any existing data set that matches a data set specified in the text file. If you do not turn this option on, it will create a new data set for each entry in the text file.*

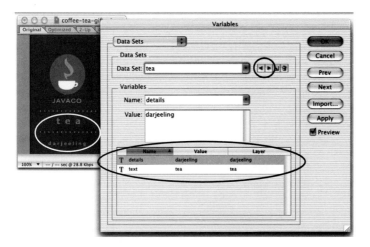

6. Browse through the data sets using the **Previous** and **Next** buttons beside the **Data Set** pop-up menu.

*As you can see, ImageReady CS created three data sets: **coffee**, **tea**, and **gifts**. Each data set has two **Text Replacement** variables. In this illustration, the **tea** data set is selected, and you can see the value of the **text** variable is "tea," and the value of the **details** variable is "darjeeling."*

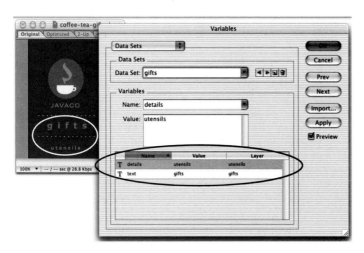

*In this illustration, the **gifts** data set is selected, and you can see the value of the **text** variable is "gifts," and the value of the **details** variable is "utensils." As you can see, if you have a large number of **Text Replacement** variables, the ability to import data sets from text files can save a lot of time!*

7. Close the file. You don't need to save your changes.

That's a wrap! You may not put these skills to work right away, but they are the workflow of the future. Next up: learning to integrate Photoshop CS and ImageReady CS files with other programs.

16.

Integration with Other Programs

| Updating HTML | Integrating with GoLive CS |
| Integrating with Dreamweaver MX 2004 |
| Integrating with Flash MX 2004 | Integrating with Illustrator CS |
| Integrating with QuickTime | Converting PSDs to PDF |

chap_16

Photoshop CS/ImageReady CS
H•O•T CD-ROM

When you're designing Web graphics and entire Web sites, you'll often need to use other programs. The exercises in this chapter provide information about how to integrate the Web graphics you created in Photoshop CS or ImageReady CS with other applications, such as Adobe GoLive, Macromedia Dreamweaver, Macromedia Flash, Adobe Illustrator, QuickTime, and Adobe Acrobat. In this chapter, you'll learn how to import and export files (other than PSD, GIF, and JPG) to and from Photoshop CS and ImageReady CS and to and from other applications. You may or may not have the programs described in this chapter and you may or may not know how to use them. Some sections in this chapter are intended for advanced users who know how to perform tasks in other applications without much coaching. Most books cover only a single program; however, since Web development almost always involves more than one program, I had an idea this chapter might be useful to many readers. ;-)

I. [IR]_____Updating HTML in ImageReady CS

When you save graphics in ImageReady CS with HTML, you'll often want to make changes after the fact. For example, if you create a remote rollover in ImageReady CS, save the HTML and images, and a client looks at your files and notices a spelling error, it would be easy to correct the spelling mistake in ImageReady CS, but then you would have to re-export all the optimized images and HTML. Or would you? The Update HTML command lets you make changes to a file and helps you update and manage the HTML files and the required images. It saves you managing multiple versions of a document because it updates the HTML and images to reflect any changes you make to the PSD file. Here's an exercise to show you how:

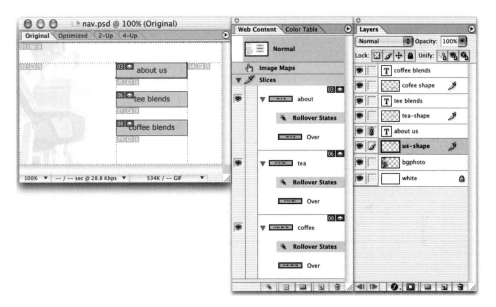

1. In ImageReady CS, open **nav.psd** from the **chap_16** folder you copied to your **Desktop**.

The file you opened is a sliced image with rollovers. The optimization settings have already been set in ImageReady CS and have been saved with the image. Any time you specify optimization settings and save the file in the PSD format, the optimization settings are automatically saved with the file.

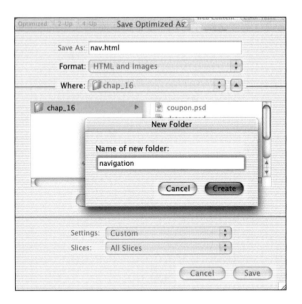

2. Choose **File > Save Optimized As**. Navigate to the **chap_16** folder you copied to your **Desktop**. Click the **New Folder** button. In the **New Folder** dialog box, name the folder **navigation**. Click **Create** (Mac) or **OK** (Windows). Leave the default file name (**nav.html**) and choose **HTML and Images** from the **Format** pop-up menu. Click **Save**.

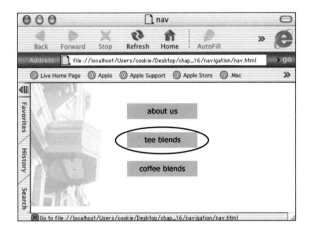

3. Browse to the **navigation** folder in the **chap_16** folder on your **Desktop**. Double-click **nav.html** to open the file in your default Web browser. Notice the spelling mistake—the word "tea" is spelled "tee."

Next, you'll return to ImageReady CS, fix the problem, and update the required files.

4. Return to ImageReady CS.

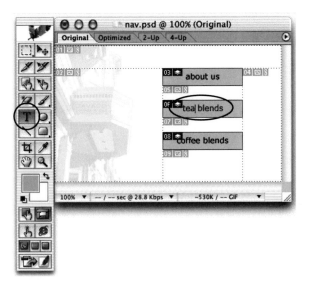

5. Select the **Type** tool from the **Toolbox**. Position your mouse and click beside the second letter "e" in the word "tee." Press **Delete** (Mac) or **Backspace** (Windows) to delete the letter "e." Type the letter "a."

Next, you'll update the HTML and images with the change you just made.

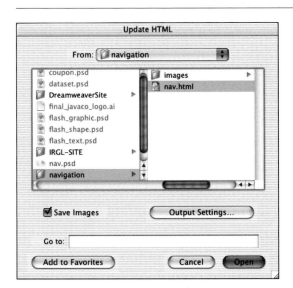

6. Choose **File > Update HTML**. In the **Update HTML** dialog box, browse to the **navigation** folder in the **chap_16** folder on your **Desktop**. Choose **nav.html** and click **Open**.

7. In the **Replace Files** dialog box, click **Replace** to replace the images inside the **navigation** folder and the **nav.html** file.

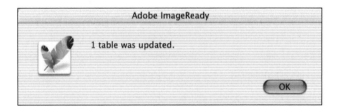

8. A dialog box will pop-up indicating one table was updated. Click **OK**.

*ImageReady CS just rewrote all the files you created in **Step 2**, and you avoided having to resave or create a duplicate set of files just to make this one change. Whenever you make changes to an ImageReady CS–generated HTML file or images, use the **Update HTML** command so you don't end up with multiple folders with multiple versions of images and HTML files.*

*The **Update HTML** command is useful for more than just fixing spelling errors. You could change anything about the document—its styles, the type, its position, slice names, layers visibility, and so on.*

Next, you'll view the changes you made in a Web browser.

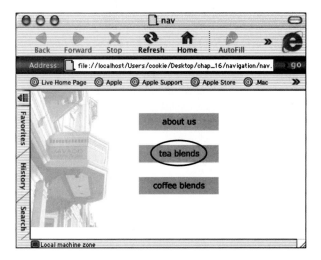

9. Browse to the **navigation** folder in the **chap_16** folder on your **Desktop**. Double-click **nav.html** to open the file in your default Web browser.

Notice the spelling mistake has been fixed, which means the files were updated properly.

Note: *If you do not see the changes you made when you open the file, click the* **Refresh** *button to reload the page and to clear the Web browser cache.*

---

10. Return to ImageReady CS. Leave **nav.psd** open for the next exercise.

2. [IR] _____ Importing ImageReady CS Rollovers into GoLive CS

In Chapter 11, you learned how to create rollovers in ImageReady CS. As you followed the exercises in the chapter, you may have been wondering, "How do I get this into an HTML editor?" You can open an HTML file that was created in ImageReady CS in any HTML editor, and the rollovers will work beautifully. The biggest challenge is integrating rollovers you created in ImageReady CS into another Web site you created in an HTML editor. For example, you may design the rollovers in ImageReady CS and then use the rollovers on an existing HTML page you created. In this exercise, you'll learn how to import rollovers created in ImageReady CS into an existing HTML page that was created in GoLive CS.

1. If you followed the last exercise, you should still have **nav.psd** open in ImageReady CS.

2. Choose **File > Save Optimized As**. Navigate to the **chap_16** folder on your **Desktop**. Click the **New Folder** button. In the **New Folder** dialog box, type **navigationGL**. Click **Create** (Mac) or **OK** (Windows). Keep the default filename (**nav.html**) and make sure **HTML and Images** is selected from the **Format** pop-up menu. Click **Save**.

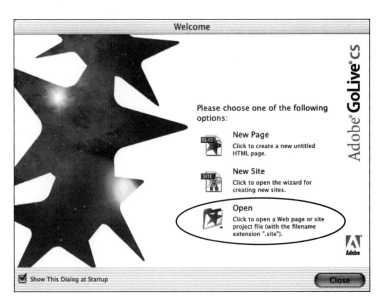

3. Open GoLive CS. When you first open GoLive CS, you'll be prompted with the **Welcome Screen**. Click **Open**.

Note: If the ***Welcome Screen*** *does not appear when you open GoLive CS, choose* ***File > Open.***

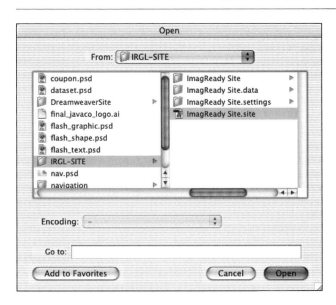

4. Navigate to the **IRGL-SITE** folder in the **chap_16** folder on your **Desktop**. Click the **ImagReady Site.site** file and click **Open**.

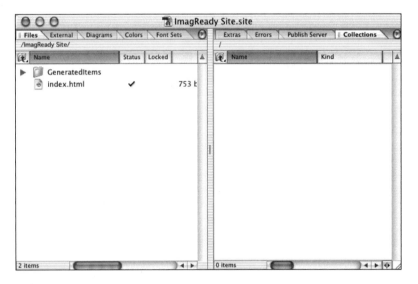

ImagReady Site.site will automatically open in GoLive CS. Notice there are two items in the Site window: *index.html* and a **GeneratedItems** folder. Next, you will learn how to import the ImageReady CS HTML file and images into this GoLive CS site.

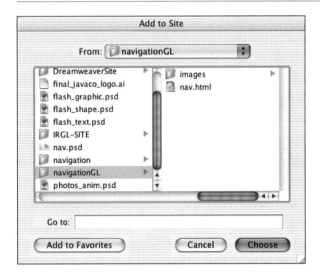

5. Click **index.html** to select it. Choose **File > Import > File to Site**. Navigate to the **navigationGL** folder in the **chap_16** folder on your **Desktop**. Click **Choose**. The **Copy Files** dialog box will open automatically.

6. In the **Copy Files** dialog box, click **OK**.

This is how GoLive CS updates the ImageReady CS HTML so it works with the GoLive CS site. One of the benefits of using GoLive is the site management tools. They ensure all links generated in ImageReady CS translate to GoLive CS properly.

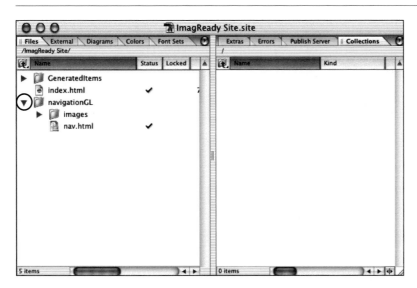

7. You should now see the **navigationGL** folder in the **Site** window. This is the folder you created in Step 2. Click the arrow beside **navigationGL** to expand the folder so you can see the contents. Double-click **nav.html** to open it.

8. With **nav.html** open, choose **Edit > Select All**. Then, choose **Edit > Copy**.

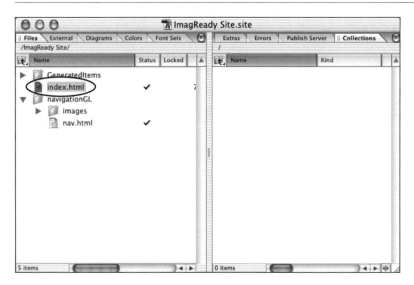

9. Choose **Window > ImagReady Site.site** to return to the **Site** window. Double-click **index.html** to open it.

Index.html will open in its own window.

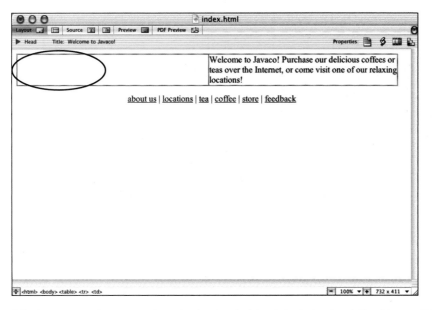

10. Click inside the table cell on the left-hand side of the **index.html** file. Choose **Edit > Paste**.

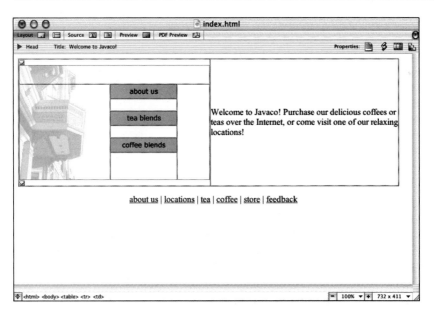

*The contents of **nav.html** you selected and copied should now be pasted inside the table cell in **index.html**.*

Next, you'll preview the site in a Web browser to make sure the rollovers still work.

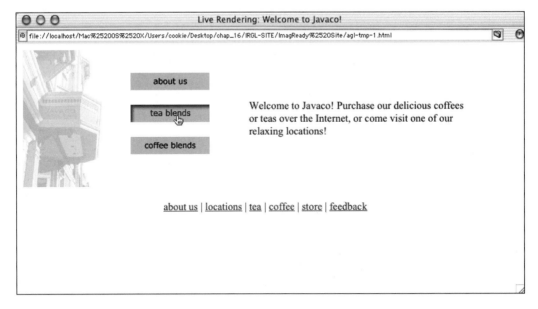

11. Press **Cmd+T** (Mac) or **Ctrl+T** (Windows) to preview **index.html** in your default Web browser. Position your mouse over the buttons.

Notice the rollovers work exactly as they did in ImageReady CS!

12. Return to GoLive CS and leave the file open for the next exercise.

MOVIE | golive_rollovers.mov

To learn more about importing rollovers created in ImageReady CS into GoLive CS, check out **golive_rollovers.mov** in the **movies** folder on the **H•O•T CD-ROM**.

3. [PS/IR] Using Smart Objects in GoLive CS

One of the useful features in GoLive CS is **Smart Objects**. Smart Objects let you open a PSD file directly into GoLive CS, which eliminates the need to save HTML code and optimized images from ImageReady CS. This is a GoLive CS exercise, not a Photoshop CS or ImageReady CS exercise; however, it's a helpful workflow when you need to go between the two applications, which is why I've included it in this chapter.

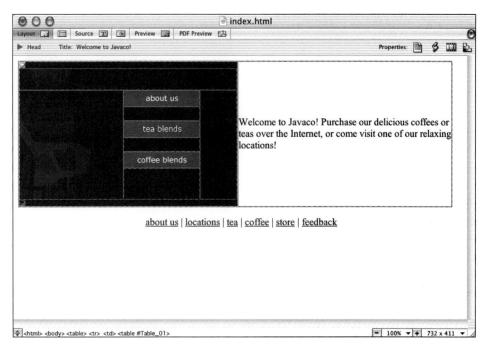

1. In GoLive CS, choose **Window > index.html**. Click and drag to select the content you pasted into **index.html** from the last exercise, including all the comments, and press **Delete** to remove them.

The table will be left with an empty cell on the left-hand side.

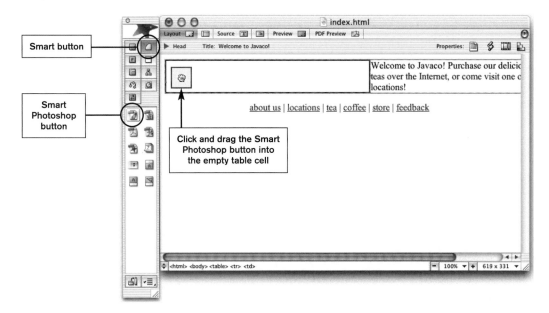

2. Make sure the **Objects** palette is visible. If it's not, choose **Window > Objects**. In the **Objects** palette, click the **Smart** button. The contents of the **Objects** palette will change to show the **Smart Objects** options. Click and drag the **Smart Photoshop** button into the empty table cell.

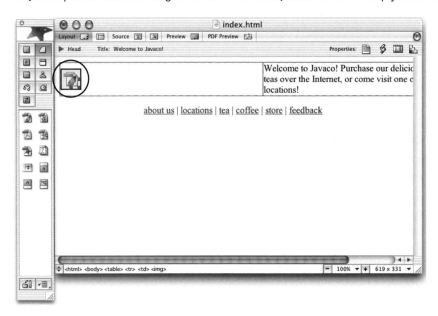

You'll see a Photoshop CS icon inside the table cell, which is the Smart Photoshop object.

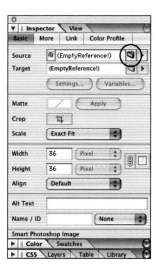

3. Click the **Photoshop Smart Object** to select it. Make sure the **Inspector** palette is visible. If it's not, choose **Window > Inspector**. Click the **Source Folder** icon. The **Open** dialog box opens automatically.

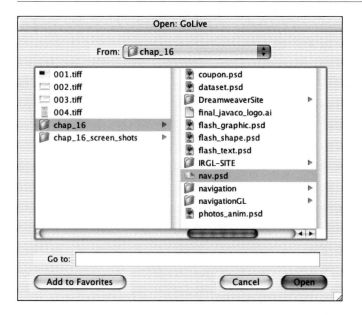

4. In the **Open** dialog box, browse to the **chap_16** folder on your **Desktop**. Choose **nav.psd** and click **Open**. The **Variable Settings** dialog box opens automatically.

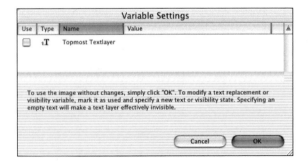

5. In the **Variable Settings** dialog box, click **OK**. The **Save for Web** dialog box opens automatically.

*Note: Because there aren't any variables set up in **nav.psd**, you don't need to worry about making any changes in the **Variable Settings** dialog box. You learned about variables in Chapter 15, "Data Sets." In an upcoming exercise, you'll have a chance to import variables from ImageReady CS into GoLive CS.*

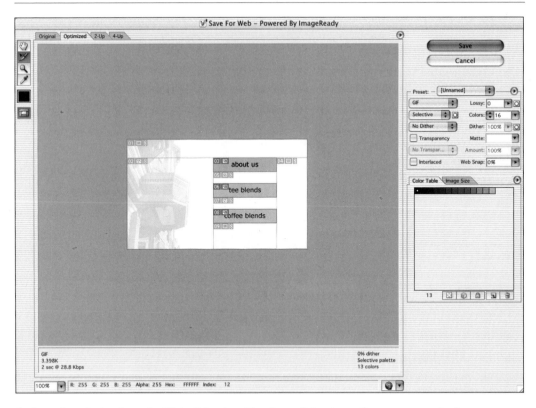

6. Click **Save** in the **Save for Web** dialog box. The **Save** dialog box will open automatically.

*Did you notice the **Save for Web** dialog box looks familiar? It's identical to the **Save for Web** dialog box in Photoshop CS. Notice the slices you saw when **nav.psd** was open in ImageReady CS are visible in the **Save for Web** dialog box. The optimization settings have also been kept. When you use the Smart Objects feature in GoLive CS, it automatically keeps the slices and optimization settings you saved in the PSD file. Pretty cool, huh?*

*You may notice the spelling error "tee" is still present in this document. When you fixed this problem earlier, you fixed it in the HTML and images, but not in the master PSD file. You'll get a chance to fix it in the next exercise when you learn how to use the **Edit Original** feature in GoLive CS.*

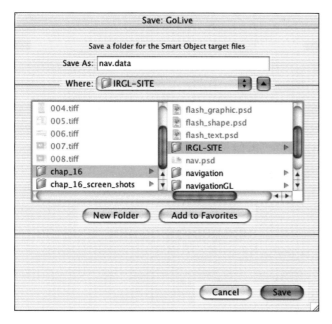

7. In the **Save** dialog box, browse to the **IRGL-SITE** folder in the **chap_16** folder on your **Desktop**. Click **Save**.

*In **Exercise 2**, you imported the ImageReady CS content into the GoLive CS site. This step achieves the same result but in a different way. The HTML and images will now be stored inside the GoLive CS site.*

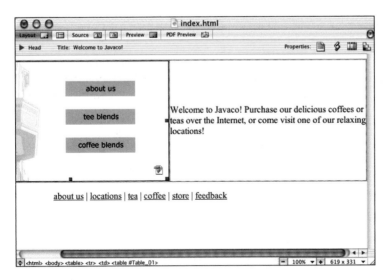

8. The contents of **nav.psd** should now appear inside the cell on the left-hand side of the table. Press **Cmd+T** (Mac) or **Ctrl+T** (Windows) to preview the results in your default Web browser.

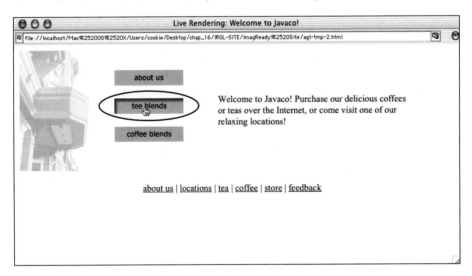

*The rollovers work, and the end result is identical to **Exercise 2**. Why would you use this technique over the one you learned in **Exercise 2**? It's just a matter of convenience—why go through saving the HTML and images in ImageReady CS when you can do the same thing in GoLive CS? Most people who use the two programs together prefer to use the method you learned in this exercise.*

9. Return to GoLive CS and leave **index.html** open for the next exercise.

4. [PS/IR] _____**Using the Edit Original Feature in GoLive CS**

The Edit Original feature in GoLive CS lets you edit the PSD files you use with Smart Objects. When you use the Edit Original feature, you can make a change to the PSD file, and the changes will be updated in GoLive CS as well as in the slices and optimized images. In this exercise, you'll change the color of the background image to see how this works.

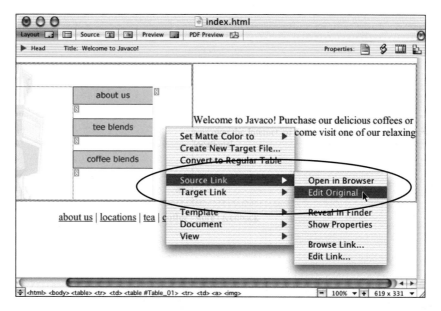

1. In GoLive CS, **Ctrl+click** (Mac) or **right-click** (Windows) anywhere on the **Smart Object** you created in the last exercise. Choose **Source Link > Edit Original** from the contextual menu.

You'll return to ImageReady CS to the **nav.psd** file you were working with in Exercises 1 and 2. Notice the word "tea" is spelled correctly.

---

2. Make sure the **Layers** palette is visible. If it's not, choose **Window > Layers**. In the **Layers** palette, click the **bgphoto** layer to select it.

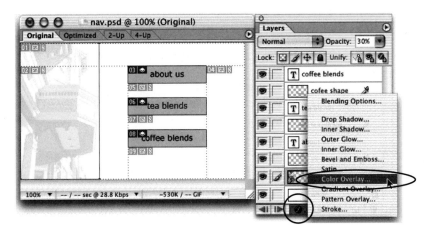

3. Choose **Color Overlay** from the **Layer Styles** pop-up menu. The **Layer Style** dialog box will open automatically.

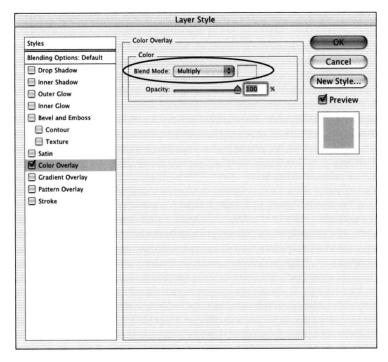

4. In the **Layer Style** dialog box, choose **Multiply** from the **Blend Mode** pop-up menu. Click the color swatch to open the **Color Picker** dialog box. Choose a bright **yellow**. Click **OK**. In the **Layer Style** dialog box, click **OK**.

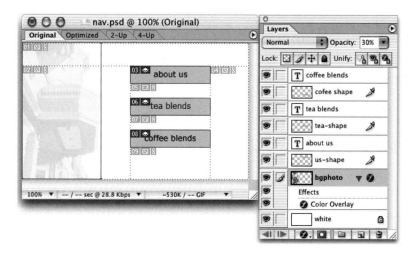

*The **Color Overlay** layer style will automatically be applied to the **bgphoto** layer.*

---

5. Choose **File > Save** to save your changes.

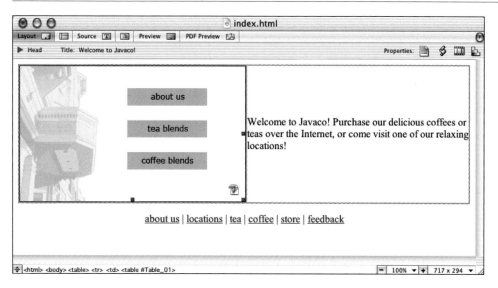

6. Return to GoLive CS. It may take a few minutes, but eventually the changes will appear!

What was taking so long? GoLive CS was generating the images, updating the HTML, and changing the preview on the screen. Not bad for a few minutes work, huh?

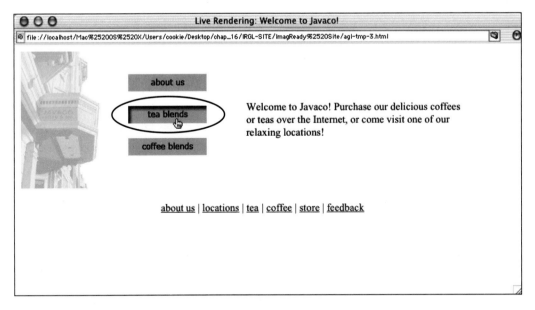

7. Press **Cmd+T** (Mac) or **Ctrl+T** (Windows) to preview the results in your default Web browser. If you don't see the changes right away, click the **Refresh** button in your Web browser.

Notice all the changes you made in ImageReady CS appear in the Web browser.

8. Return to GoLive CS and leave the file open for the next exercise.

5. [IR] _____ Working with ImageReady CS Data Sets in GoLive CS

In Chapter 15, "*Data Sets*," you learned how to create data sets in ImageReady CS. Data sets become much more powerful when you work with them in GoLive CS. This exercise shows you how you can use a data set you created in ImageReady CS in GoLive CS. In this example, the variables have been defined for text layers in a rollover. In GoLive CS, you'll learn how to change the button names and how to generate rollovers with new text labels without using ImageReady CS. Hold on to your hats—this is an amazing feature!

Before starting this exercise, you might wonder how the file was prepared first in ImageReady CS. We made three text layers and defined them as variables—button_one, button_two, and button_three. The text layers are set up for text replacement variables—you learned about these in Chapter 15, "*Data Sets*."

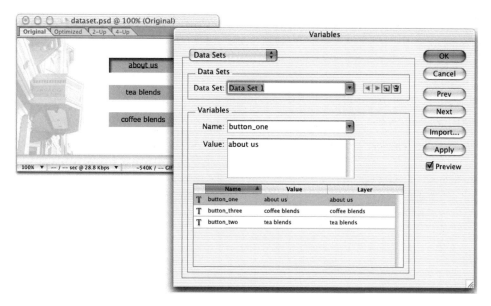

1. Before you get started in GoLive CS, take a look at how the data sets were defined in ImageReady CS. In ImageReady CS, open **dataset.psd** from the **chap_16** folder you copied to your **Desktop**. Choose **Image > Variables > Data Sets**. In the **Variables** dialog box, notice there is one data set in this document (**Data Set 1**) with three Text Replacement variables (**button_one**, **button_three**, and **button_two**). The Text Replacement variables were created using the same method you learned in Chapter 15, "*Data Sets*." Click **Cancel** in the **Variables** dialog box. Close the file and return to GoLive CS.

2. Click and drag to select the content you pasted into **index.html** from the last exercise, including all the comments, and press **Delete** to remove them.

The table will be left with an empty cell on the left-hand side.

3. Make sure the **Objects** palette is visible. If it's not, choose **Window > Objects**. In the **Objects** palette, click the **Smart** button. The contents of the **Objects** palette will change to show the **Smart Objects** options. Click and drag the **Smart Photoshop** button into the empty table cell.

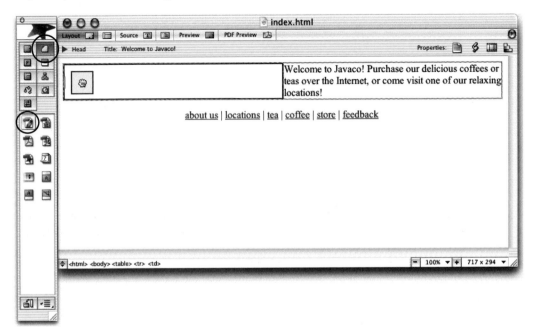

You'll see a Photoshop CS icon inside the table cell, which is the Smart Photoshop object.

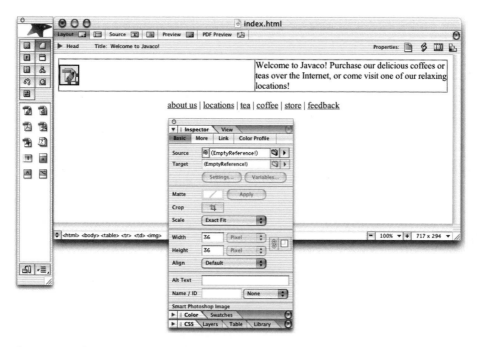

4. Click the **Smart Photoshop Object** to select it. Make sure the **Inspector** palette is visible. If it's not, choose **Window > Inspector**. Click the **Source Folder** icon. The **Open** dialog box opens automatically.

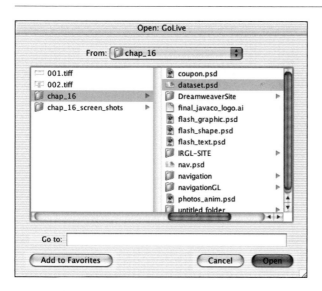

5. In the **Open** dialog box, browse to the **chap_16** folder on your **Desktop**. Choose **dataset.psd** and click **Open**. The **Variable Settings** dialog box opens automatically.

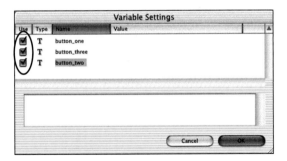

6. In the **Variable Settings** dialog box, check **button_one**, **button_three**, and **button_two**. Click **OK**. The **Save for Web** dialog box opens automatically.

*In **Exercise 3**, there wasn't anything in the **Variable Settings** dialog box because the file did not have any data sets or variables saved with it.*

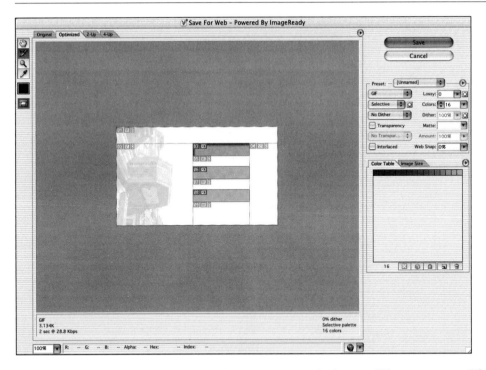

7. In the **Save for Web** dialog box, notice there is no text on the buttons. When you open a PSD file with Text Replacement variables, you can create new text labels for the buttons in GoLive CS. This is very powerful because you can apply different text labels to buttons to create different pages of your site while still using the slices you created in ImageReady CS for each. Click **Save**. The **Save** dialog box opens automatically.

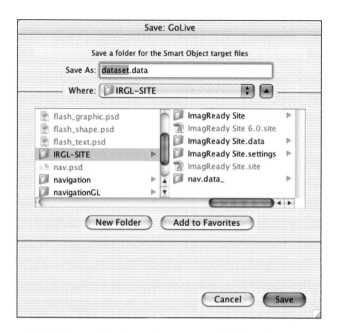

8. In the **Save** dialog box, choose the **IRGL-SITE** folder in the **chap_16** folder on your **Desktop**. Click **Save**.

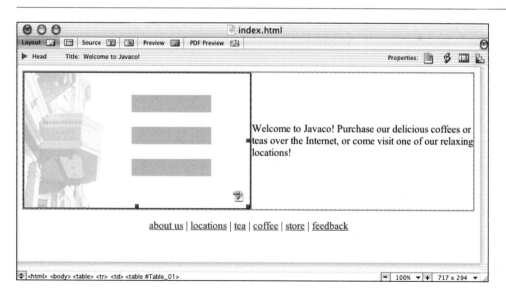

9. The contents of **dataset.psd** automatically appear inside the table cell.

Notice there are no text labels on the buttons. Not to worry—you'll remedy that in the next few steps!

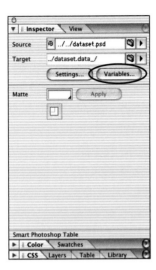

10. Make sure the **Inspector** palette is visible. If it's not, choose **Window > Inspector**. Click the **Variables** button on the **Inspector** palette. The **Variable Settings** dialog box opens automatically.

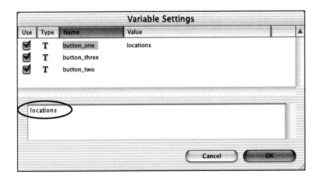

11. In the **Variable Settings** dialog box, click **button_one** to select it and type **locations** in the text field. Click **OK**.

Notice the word "locations" now appears on button 1 using the same formatting (font, size, style, and color) as the text labels that were originally created in ImageReady CS.

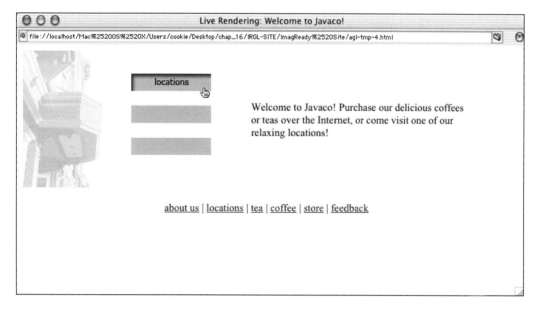

12. Press **Cmd+T** (Mac) or **Ctrl+T** (Windows) to preview the results in your default Web browser. If you don't see the changes right away, click the **Refresh** button in your Web browser.

Notice the rollovers work, and the text is bitmap text, not HTML! GoLive CS used the formatting information from ImageReady CS to create the text label.

The power of this workflow is truly amazing. You could take the same PSD file and use it as a Smart Object on multiple pages, changing the navigation buttons on every page. You could make a header graphic and change its name on every page. You could also make animated GIF files that change! The possibilities are endless. Cool, huh?

13. Return to GoLive CS. Save your changes and quit GoLive CS.

Next, you'll move on to Macromedia Dreamweaver MX 2004!

6. [IR] Importing ImageReady CS Rollovers into Dreamweaver MX 2004

In Exercise 2, you learned how to import rollovers that were generated by ImageReady CS into GoLive CS. In this exercise, you'll learn how to do the same thing using Dreamweaver MX 2004. Like GoLive CS, Dreamweaver MX 2004 is an HTML editor. Just like with GoLive CS, if all you only want to do is use the HTML and images from ImageReady CS in their original form, you can simply open the HTML file in Dreamweaver MX 2004. However, if you want to import rollovers created in ImageReady CS into an existing file, it's a bit trickier. Here's an exercise to show you how.

1. Before you get started, you need to install an extension called **ImageReadyHTML.mxp** from the **software** folder on the **H•O•T CD-ROM**. **ImageReadyHTML.mxp** is a Macromedia Extension Manager file written by Massimo Foti for Lynda.com. This extension converts code from ImageReady CS to native Dreamweaver MX 2004 code. Before you install the extension, you must have the Macromedia Extension Manager installed onto your computer. The Macromedia Extension Manager can be installed from the Dreamweaver MX 2004 CD-ROM. To install the extension, copy the **ImageReadyHTML.mxp** file from the **software** folder on the **H•O•T CD-ROM** to your **Desktop**. Double-click the file and follow the instructions onscreen. If you want to be sure it's installed correctly, open Dreamweaver MX 2004 and take a look at the **Insert** bar. Make sure **Common** is selected from the pop-up menu. If the **ImageReadyHTML.mxp** file is installed correctly, you'll see an **ImageReady HTML** icon on the **Insert** bar.

NOTE | What Is the ImageReady HTML.mxp File?

Lynda.com commissioned well-known Dreamweaver Extension developer, Massimo Foti, to create an extension for Dreamweaver that converts ImageReady rollover code into a native Dreamweaver behavior. Since Adobe isn't likely to create a product for Dreamweaver users, and Macromedia isn't likely to create a product for Photoshop users, the folks at Lynda.com saw this as an opportunity to support customers who might be using these two products together. Lynda.com offers the ImageReady HTML extension for free from the Lynda.com Web site. You can find it (and other helpful files) at: http://www.lynda.com/files/.

2. Once the extension is successfully installed, open Dreamweaver MX 2004. Choose **Site > Manage Sites**. In the **Manage Sites** dialog box, click the **New** button and choose **Site** from the **New** pop-up menu.

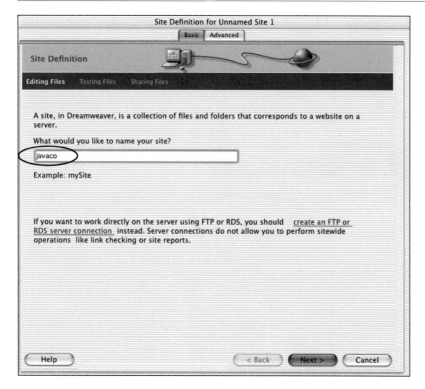

3. In the **Site Definition** dialog box, type **javaco** in the **What would you like to name your site?** field. Click **Next**.

4. Choose the **No, I do not want to user a server technology** option. Click **Next**.

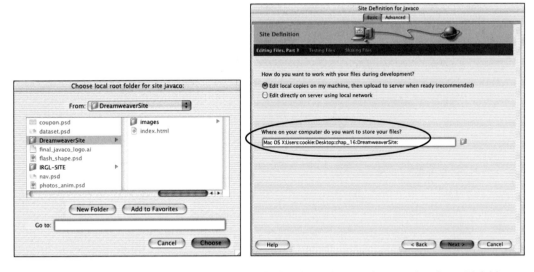

5. Click the **folder** icon. In the **Choose local root folder** dialog box, navigate to the **chap_16** folder on your **Desktop**. Click the **DreamweaverSite** folder to select it and click **Choose**. In the **Site Definition** dialog box, click **Next**.

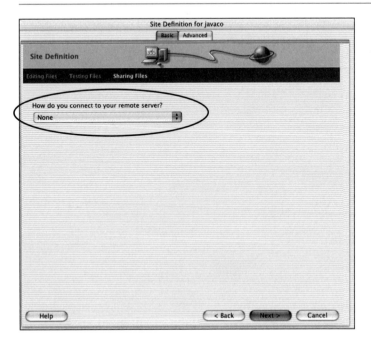

6. Choose **None** from the **How do you connect to your remote server?** pop-up menu. Click **Next**.

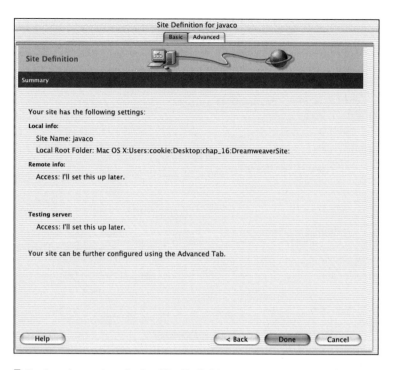

7. Review the settings in the **Site Definition** summary and click **Done**.

8. In the **Manage Sites** dialog box, notice there is now an entry called **javaco**. Click **Done**.

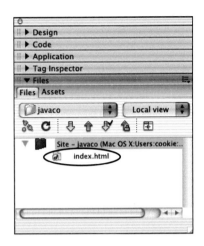

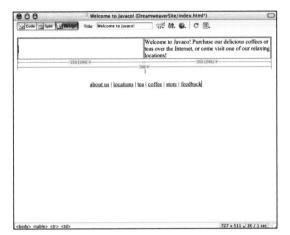

9. Make sure the **Files** palette is visible. If it's not, choose **Window > Files**. Notice the **Files** palette now contains an entry for the **javaco** Web site you created in the last few steps. Double-click the **index.html** file to open it.

Index.html was made ahead of time so you can simulate the workflow of importing rollovers created in ImageReady CS into Dreamweaver MX 2004. If you followed Exercise 2, you'll notice this file looks very similar to the file you opened in GoLive CS.

Next, you'll create an empty file so you can import the rollovers from ImageReady CS.

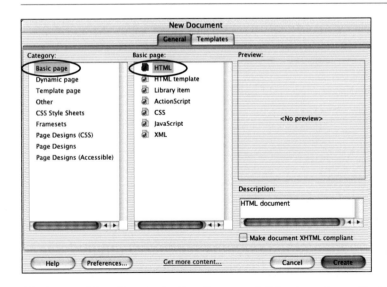

10. Choose **File > New**. In the **New Document** dialog box, choose **Basic page** from the **Category** options and choose **HTML** from the **Basic page** options. Click **Create**.

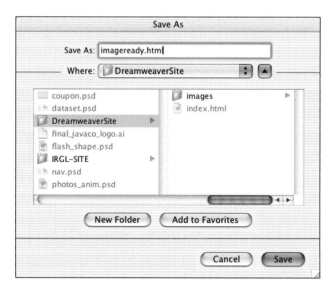

11. Choose **File > Save As**. Navigate to the **DreamweaverSite** folder in the **chap_16** folder on your **Desktop**. Name the file **imageready.html**. Click **Save**.

12. Make sure **Common** is selected in the **Insert** bar pop-up menu. Click the **ImageReady HTML** button. The **ImageReady HTML** dialog box opens automatically.

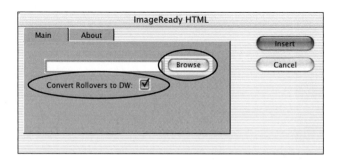

13. In the **ImageReady HTML** dialog box, make sure the **Convert Rollovers to DW** option is turned on. Click the **Browse** button. The **Select ImageReady 2 File** dialog box opens automatically.

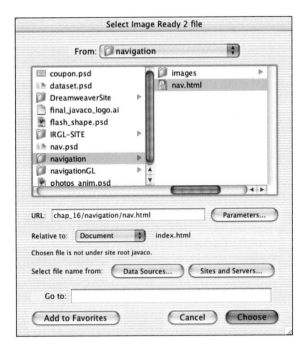

14. Browse to the **navigation** folder in the **chap_16** folder you copied to your **Desktop**. Choose **nav.html** and click **Choose**. In the **ImageReady HTML** dialog box, click **Insert**. You will be warned that this process may take a few minutes. Click **OK** to proceed.

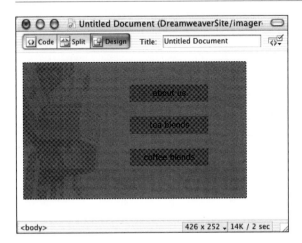

15. The contents of the **nav.html** file should now be visible inside the document window. Choose **Edit > Select All** to select the contents of the file. Choose **Edit > Copy** to copy the contents of the file to the clipboard.

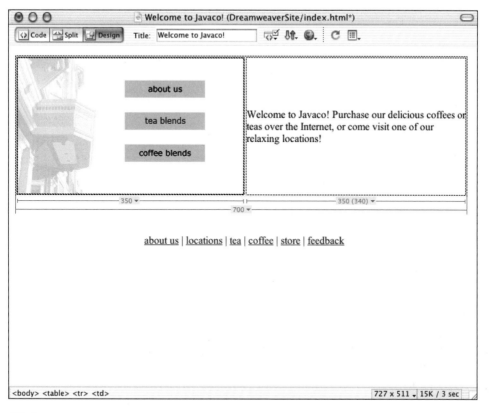

16. Choose **Window > index.html**. Click inside the empty table cell on the left-hand side of the document window and choose **Edit > Paste HTML**.

*Voila! The contents of the **nav.html** file now appear inside the table!*

---

17. Press **F12** to preview the file in your default Web browser. You'll be prompted to save your changes. Click **Save**. If you do not save your changes, you will not see any of the changes you made in this exercise.

18. Position your mouse over the buttons. The rollovers work the same way they did in the ImageReady CS file!

*The **ImageReady HTML** command not only allowed you to browse to find the HTML file, but it also copied and moved the HTML code and the required images in the **DreamweaverSite** directory. That's why it's important that you define the **Site** settings before you begin this type of operation.*

19. Return to Dreamweaver MX 2004. Save the file and exit the application.

Next, you'll learn how to work with Macromedia Flash MX 2004 files!

MOVIE | dreamweaver_rollovers.mov

To learn more about importing rollovers created in ImageReady CS into Dreamweaver MX 2004, check out **dreamweaver_rollovers.mov** in the **movies** folder on the **H•O•T CD-ROM**.

NOTE | Learning Dreamweaver MX 2004 Resources

If you're interested in learning more about Dreamweaver MX 2004, check out the following resources available from lynda.com:

Macromedia Dreamweaver MX 2004 Hands-On Training (H•O•T)
By Garo Green, developed with Lynda Weinman
lynda.com/books and Peachpit Press
ISBN: 032120297X
$44.99

Learning Dreamweaver MX 2004 Movie Training
By Garo Green
http://www.lynda.com

7. [IR] _____Exporting Vector Images as Macromedia Flash Files

In Chapter 4, "*Optimization*," you learned how to export images to the Macromedia Flash (SWF) format. In this exercise, you'll learn how to export an image with a vector object and how to open the exported SWF file in Macromedia Flash MX 2004. The benefit of exporting files to Macromedia Flash is that the SWF format maintains the vector objects and does not rasterize them, which means you can open the SWF file in Macromedia Flash MX 2004 and edit the vector objects. Here's an exercise to show you how.

1. In ImageReady CS, open **flash_shape.psd** from the **chap_16** folder you copied to your **Desktop**. Make sure the **Layers** palette is visible. If it's not, choose **Window > Layers**.

Notice the image is made up of two layers: a shape layer and a background layer. In this exercise, you'll learn how to export the image as a SWF file while keeping the shape layer as a vector-based object.

2. Choose **File > Export > Macromedia Flash SWF**. The **Macromedia Flash Export** dialog box opens automatically.

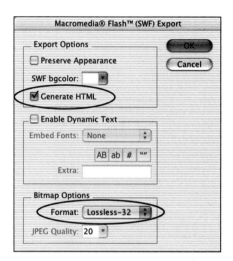

3. In the **Macromedia Flash Export** dialog box, turn on the **Generate HTML** option and choose **Lossless-32** from the **Format** pop-up menu. **Lossless-32** is the best format to use when you export flat graphic content. Make sure the **Preserve Appearance** option is turned off to ensure the shape layer remains as vector-based information. Click **OK**.

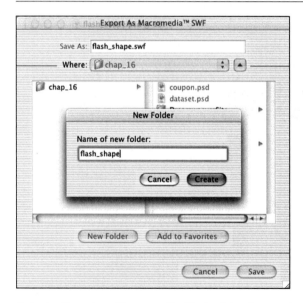

4. In the **Export as Macromedia Flash** dialog box, navigate to the **chap_16** folder you copied to your **Desktop**. Click the **New Folder** button. In the **New Folder** dialog box, type **flash_shape** and click **Create** (Mac) or **OK** (Windows). Leave the file name as the default—**flash_shape.swf**. Click **Save**.

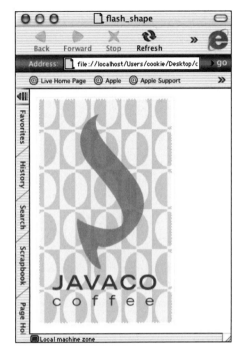

5. Browse to the **flash_shape** folder in the **chap_16** folder you copied to your **Desktop**. Double-click the **flash_shape.html** file to preview how the file looks in a Web browser.

Note: The shape layer in this file was maintained as vector information. Next, you'll open the SWF file in Macromedia Flash MX 2004 to see how the vector information has been kept and how you can edit it easily.

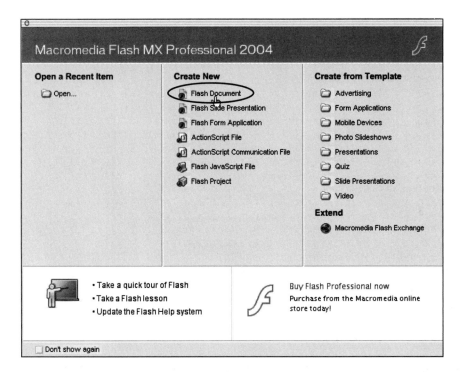

6. Open Macromedia Flash MX 2004. When you first open Macromedia Flash MX 2004, you'll see a **Welcome Screen**. Click the **Create New Flash Document** option. A new untitled file will be created automatically.

*Note: If the **Welcome Screen** does not appear when you open Macromedia Flash MX 2004, choose File > New.*

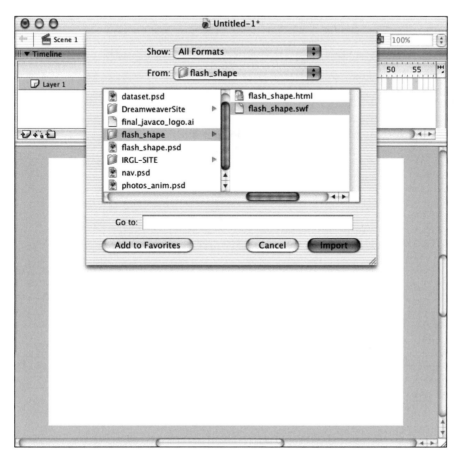

7. Choose **File > Import > Import to Stage**. Navigate to the **flash_shape** folder in the **chap_16** folder on your **Desktop**. Choose **flash_shape.swf** and click **Import**.

*The file you just saved in ImageReady CS should now be open in the **Stage** area.*

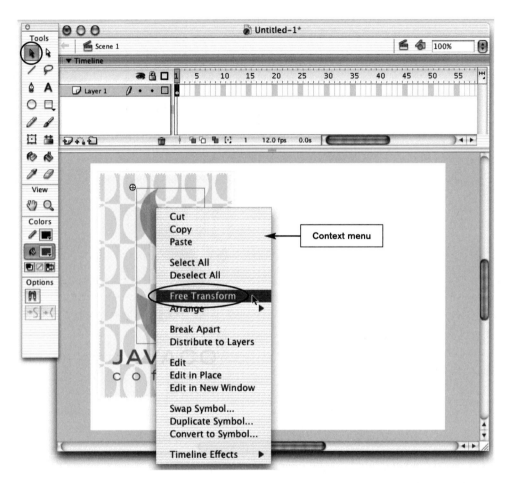

8. With the **Select** tool selected in the **Toolbox**, **Ctrl+click** (Mac) or **right-click** (Windows) the **javaco smoke**. Choose **Free Transform** from the contextual menu.

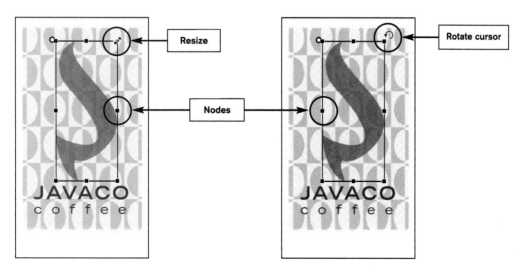

9. You should now see nodes around the perimeter of the javaco smoke shape. You can resize, rotate, and change the shape the same way you can in Photoshop CS. As you can see, the vector-based properties have been kept, which means you can increase size without losing any image quality.

Next, you'll learn how to optimize the image for the Web.

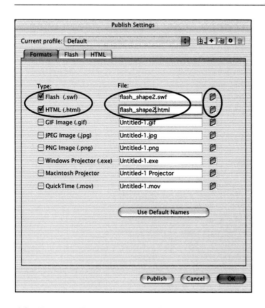

10. Choose **File > Publish Settings**. In the **Publish Settings** dialog box, make sure the **Flash** and **HTML** options are selected. Name the files **flash_shape2.swf** and **flash_shape2.html**. Click the **Select Publish Destination** button beside each file.

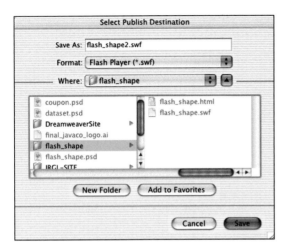

11. In the **Select Publish Destination** dialog box, navigate to the **flash_shape** folder in the **chap_16** folder you copied to your **Desktop** and click **Save**.

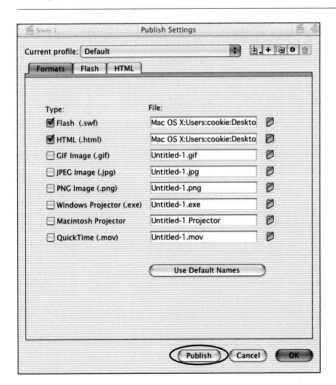

12. With the formats, file names, and destinations set in the **Publish Settings** dialog box, click **Publish**. When the files are finished publishing, click **OK**.

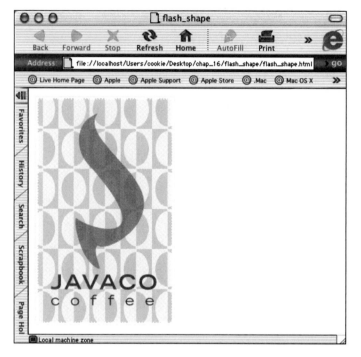

13. Browse to the **flash_shape** folder in the **chap_16** folder on your **Desktop**. Double-click **flash_shape2.html** to preview the file in your default Web browser.

*As you can see, the **Macromedia Flash Export** feature in ImageReady CS makes it easy to export files and open them in Macromedia Flash MX 2004. The added bonus is that vector information for type layers and shape layers are kept, which means you can still edit the shapes and type while keeping crisp edges.*

14. Return to Macromedia Flash MX 2004. Save and close the file.

15. Return to ImageReady CS. Save **flash_shape.psd** and leave it open for the next exercise.

Preserving the Appearance of ImageReady CS Files with SWF Export

1. With **flash_shape** open from the last exercise, make sure the **Layers** palette is visible. If it's not, choose **Window > Layers**. In the **Layers** palette, click the **Shape 1** layer to select it. Choose **Drop Shadow** from the **Layer Styles** pop-up menu at the bottom of the **Layers** palette. The **Layer Styles** dialog box opens automatically.

2. Leave the default settings in the **Layer Styles** dialog box and click **OK**.

Drop shadow

Now that you've applied a drop shadow to the shape layer, you'll export the file.

3. Choose **File > Export > Macromedia Flash SWF**. The **Macromedia Flash Export** dialog box opens automatically.

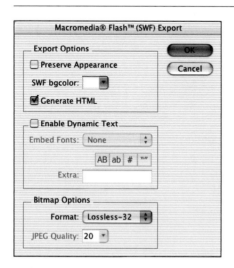

4. In the **Macromedia Flash Export** dialog box, use the same settings you used in the last exercise, as shown here. Click **OK**.

5. In the **Export as Macromedia Flash** dialog box, navigate to the **flash_shape** folder in the **chap_16** folder on your **Desktop**. Name the file **flash_shape_shadow.swf**. Click **Save**.

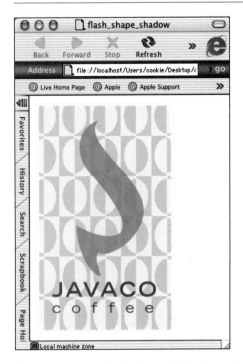

6. Browse to the **flash_shape** folder in the **chap_16** folder on your **Desktop**. Double-click the **flash_shape_shadow.swf** file to open it in your default Web browser.

Notice the drop shadow disappeared? In order to keep the shape as a vector-based object, the drop shadow had to be removed during the export process. The only way to keep the drop shadow is to rasterize the shape layer during the export process. You'll learn how in the next few steps.

7. Return to ImageReady CS. Choose **File > Export > Macromedia Flash SWF**. The **Macromedia Flash Export** dialog box opens automatically.

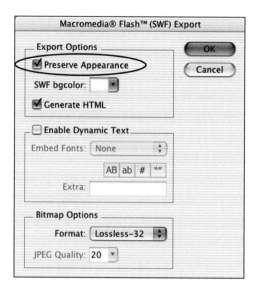

8. In the **Macromedia Flash Export** dialog box, turn on the **Preserve Appearance** option. Click **OK**.

9. In the **Export as Macromedia Flash** dialog box, navigate to the **flash_shape** folder in the **chap_16** folder on your **Desktop**. Name the file **flash_shape_shadow.2swf**. Click **Save**.

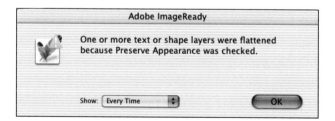

10. After you click **Save**, a message will appear on your screen indicating one or more text or shape layers were flattened because the **Preserve Appearance** option was turned on. Click **OK**.

In order to keep the appearance of the shape with the drop shadow, ImageReady CS must flatten and rasterize the shape layer and the layer style. As a result, the shape layer will no longer be vector-based.

11. Browse to the **flash_shape** folder in the **chap_16** folder on your **Desktop**. Double-click the **flash_shape_shadow2.swf** file to open it in your default Web browser.

*Notice the shape now has its shadow. When you apply layer styles to vector-based shape or type layers, you have to rasterize the layers when you export files to the SWF format. If you open the SWF file in Macromedia Flash MX 2004, you won't be able to edit the shapes the same way you did in the **Exercise 7**.*

12. Return to ImageReady CS. Save and close the file.

NOTE | Learning Macromedia Flash MX 2004 Resources

If you're interested in learning more about Macromedia Flash MX 2004, check out the following resources available from lynda.com:

Macromedia Flash MX 2004 Hands-On Training (H•O•T)
By Rosanna Yeung, developed with Lynda Weinman
lynda.com/books and Peachpit Press
ISBN: 0321202988
$44.99

Learning Macromedia Flash MX 2004 Movie Training
By Shane Rebenschied
http://www.lynda.com

9. [PS/IR] _____Exporting Illustrator CS Files

If you create images in Illustrator CS and you want to import them into Photoshop CS or ImageReady CS, it's best to create layered files and then export the file to the PSD format. Here's an exercise to show you how.

1. In Illustrator CS, open **final_javaco_logo.ai** from the **chap_16** folder on your **Desktop**. Make sure the **Layers** palette is visible. If it's not, choose **Window > Layers**.

Notice the file contains four layers. In this exercise, you'll export the file to the PSD format, keeping the layers intact so you can edit them in Photoshop CS.

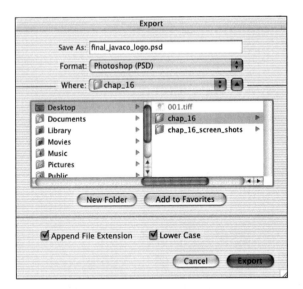

2. Choose **File > Export**. In the **Export** dialog box, navigate to the **chap_16** folder on your **Desktop** and choose **Photoshop (PSD)** from the **Format** pop-up menu. Click **Export**.

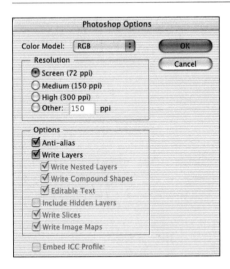

3. In the **Photoshop Options** dialog box, choose **RGB** from the **Color Model** pop-up menu, choose **Screen (72 ppi)** from the **Resolution** section, and turn on **Anti-alias** and **Write Layers** from the **Options** section. Click **OK**.

It's very important to choose RGB and Screen (72 ppi) because it's the only color mode and resolution that works in Web browsers.

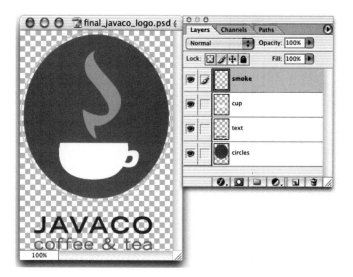

4. Open Photoshop CS or ImageReady CS. Open **final_javaco_logo.psd** from the **chap_16** folder on your **Desktop**.

Notice the layers are the same in Photoshop CS as they were in Illustrator CS!

Exporting PSD files from Illustrator CS and keeping the layers intact makes it easy for you to create Web graphics that rely heavily on layers, such as rollovers, animated GIFs, and so on.

5. Close the file. You don't need to save the changes.

NOTE | Save For Web in Illustrator CS

The Save for Web window in Illustrator CS is identical to the Save for Web window in Photoshop CS and GoLive CS. As a result, you can save GIF, JPEG, PNG, and even Macromedia Flash files directly from Illustrator CS. Because you already know how to use the Save For Web window in Photoshop CS, you'll be able to apply those skills to Illustrator CS.

IO. [IR] _____Exporting ImageReady CS Files to QuickTime

In addition to creating animated GIFs and Macromedia Flash animations, ImageReady CS also lets you export animations as QuickTime files. You may find this useful if you're working on a multimedia project instead of an HTML project.

1. In ImageReady CS, open **photos_anim.psd** from the **chap_16** folder you copied to your **Desktop**.

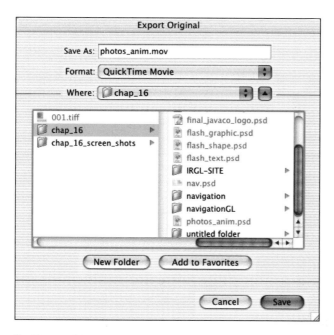

2. Choose **File > Export > Original Document**. In the **Export Original** dialog box, navigate to the **chap_16** folder on your **Desktop**. Choose **QuickTime Movie** from the **Format** pop-up menu and click **Save**.

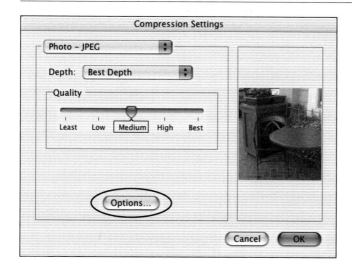

3. In the **Compression Settings** dialog box, make sure **Photo – JPEG** is selected form the pop-up menu. This is a good format if your animation includes photographs. Click the **Options** button.

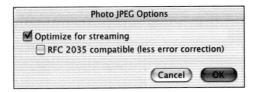

4. In the **Photo JPEG Options** dialog box, turn on the **Optimize for streaming** option if you plan to use the QuickTime movie on the Web. Click **OK**. Click **OK** in the **Compression Settings** dialog box.

5. Browse to the **chap_16** folder on your **Desktop**. Double-click **photos_anim.mov** to view the file in QuickTime Player.

6. Return to ImageReady CS. Save and close the file.

II. [IR]————————Opening QuickTime Movies in ImageReady CS

In addition to exporting QuickTime movies from ImageReady CS, you can also open QuickTime movies into ImageReady CS. Once you've opened the file, you can then save it as an animated GIF or export it as a Macromedia Flash animation.

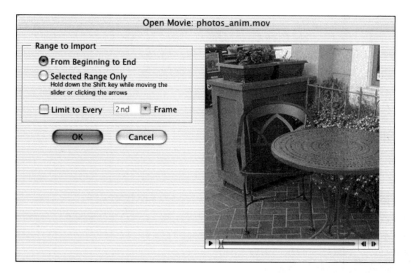

1. In ImageReady CS, open the **photos_anim.mov** file you created in the last exercise. The **Open Movie** dialog box opens automatically. In the **Open Movie** dialog box, you have a number of options. You can choose to import the entire movie, select a range of frames, or you can skip frames to specified increments such as every five frames. Click **OK** and leave the settings as the defaults for this example.

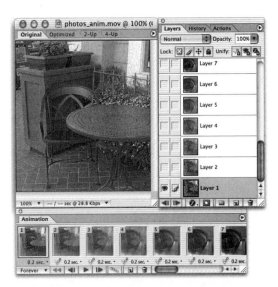

When you open the file, each frame will automatically be converted to a layer. You can see the individual frames in the **Animation** and **Layers** palettes. The timing of the animation will be based on the time of the original MOV file. If the **Animation** and **Layers** palettes are not visible, choose **Window >** **Animation** and **Window > Layers**. Next, you'll save the file as an animated GIF.

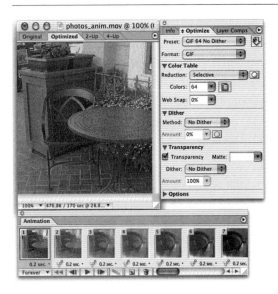

2. Click the **Optimized** tab. Make sure the **Optimize** palette is visible. If it's not, choose **Window >** **Optimize**. Choose **GIF** from the **Format** pop-up menu in the **Optimize** palette. Adjust the settings in the **Optimize** palette until you're happy with the result.

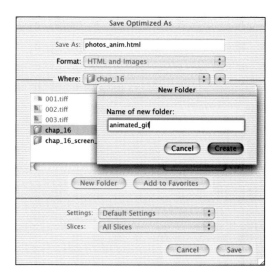

3. Choose **File > Save Optimized As**. Navigate to the **chap_16** folder on your **Desktop**. Click the **New Folder** button. In the **New Folder** dialog box, name the folder **animated_gif** and click **Create** (Mac) or **OK** (Windows). Choose **HTML and Images** from the **Format** pop-up window. Click **Save**.

4. Browse to the **animated_gif** folder in the **chap_16** folder on your **Desktop**. Double-click **photos_anim.html** to preview the file in your default Web browser.

5. Return to ImageReady CS. Close and save the file.

12. [PS]_____Converting PSD files to PDF

One of the coolest new features in Photoshop 7 is the capability to easily save a PDF from a Photoshop document. PDF (**P**ortable **D**ocument **F**ormat) is used to exchange documents when the formatting of the document is critical, but the end party might not have the application the document was created with (in this case, Photoshop or ImageReady). Sure, you could send a GIF or a JPEG and they wouldn't need Photoshop either, but PDF has a few other neat features, like the capability to set password protection, and leave all the text accessible to someone who has visual impairments! We're excited about this new feature for these reasons, and it's great to end the book and this chapter on this wonderful new feature.

1. In Photoshop CS, open **coupon.psd** from the **chap_16** folder you copied to your **Desktop**.

Notice the image contains a vector-based type layer and a Background layer.

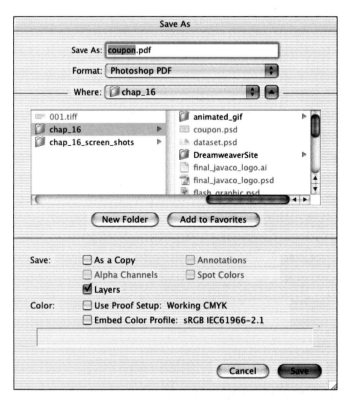

2. Choose **File > Save As**. In the **Save As** dialog box, navigate to the **chap_16** folder you copied to your **Desktop**. Choose **Photoshop PDF** from the **Format** pop-up menu. Turn on the **Layers** option at the bottom of the **Save As** dialog box. Click **Save**.

Note: For more information about the PDF options in the **Save As** *dialog box, refer to the chart at the end of this exercise.*

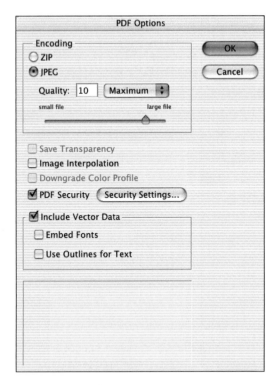

3. In the **PDF Options** dialog box, select **JPEG** from the **Encoding** section, turn on the **PDF Security** option, and turn on the **Include Vector Data** option. Click the **Security Settings** button.

*Note: For more information about the options in the **PDF Options** dialog box, refer to the chart at the end of this exercise.*

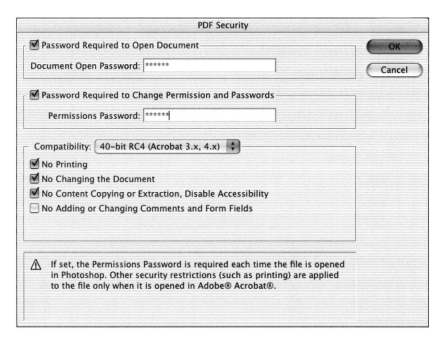

4. In the **PDF Security** dialog box, turn on the **Password Required to Open Document** option and type **javaco** in the **Document Open Password** field. Turn on the **Password Required to Change Permission and Passwords** option and type **coffee** in the **Permissions Password** field. Turn on the **No Printing**, **No Changing the Document**, and **No Content Copying or Extraction, Disable Accessibility** options. Click **OK**.

*The **Document Open Password** is what a viewer will type in order to view this document in Adobe Reader. The **Permissions Password** is so you can change the security options in the file if you need to. I picked the passwords **javaco** and **coffee** as simple examples. You might want to create more original passwords when you work with this feature in the future!*

Note: *For more information about the options in the **PDF Security** dialog box, refer to the chart at the end of this exercise.*

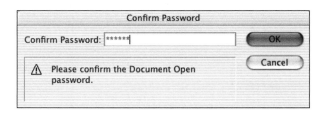

5. In the **Confirm Password** (Document Open Password) dialog box, type **javaco**. Click **OK**.

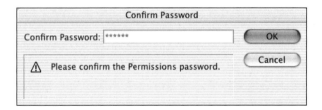

6. In the **Confirm Password** (Permissions Password) dialog box, type **coffee**. Click **OK**.

7. Browse to the **chap_16** folder on your **Desktop**. Double-click **coupon.pdf**. Notice the file opened in Photoshop CS and it maintained the vector-based type layer.

Wondering why the file didn't open in Adobe Reader? When you open a PDF created in Photoshop CS, it will automatically open in Photoshop CS if you have it installed on your computer. If you don't have it installed on your computer, the file will open in Adobe Reader. Next, you'll learn how to open the file in Adobe Reader.

8. Open Adobe Reader. Open **coupon.pdf** from the **chap_16** folder on your **Desktop**. In the **Password** dialog box, type **javaco** (the **Document Open Password**). Click **OK**.

The file opens! You won't be able to print the file because you disabled printing in the **Security Settings** *dialog box.*

That's all there is to saving a PDF from Photoshop CS! It's an easy way to communicate information to clients, copy editors, team members, and so on.

9. Close **coupon.pdf**. Return to Photoshop CS. Save and close the files you have open.

PDF Save Settings	
Category	**Description**
SAVE	
As a Copy	Saves a flattened copy of the PSD document
Alpha Channels	Includes alpha channels in the PDF document
Annotations	Includes annotations in the PDF document
Spot Colors	Includes spot colors in the PDF document
Layers	Includes Photoshop layers in the PDF document
COLOR	
Use Proof Setup: Working CMYK	Retains CMYK settings
Embed Color Profile	Embeds a color profile in the PDF document

PDF Options	
Category	**Description**
ZIP	Encodes the file as a ZIP, which is best for images with large areas of solid color.
JPEG	Encodes the file as a JPEG, which is best for photographic or continuous tone images.
Quality	Lets you specify the JPEG quality.
Save Transparency	Includes transparent layer information.
Image Interpolation	Anti-aliases the printed appearance of a low-resolution image.
Downgrade Color Profile	Allows programs that don't support color profiles to view the image.
PDF Security	Turns on the PDF security settings using settings in the Security Settings dialog box. For more information, refer to the "PDF Security" chart that follows.
Include Vector Data	Preserves vector graphics as resolution-independent objects.
Embed Fonts	Ensures all fonts in the file will display and print properly. **Note:** This option will increase the file size of the PDF.
Use Outlines for Text	Saves text as paths. Use this option when embedded fonts don't display properly.

PDF Security	
Category	**Description**
Password Required to Open Document	Requires anyone who is opening the file to type in a password you specify.
Password Required to Change Permissions and Passwords	Requires anyone who tries to change the security settings to provide a password. Using this option allows you to ensure no one can print, copy, or change the file.
Compatibility	Lets you choose the level of encryption (40-bit or 128-bit).
No Printing	Disables the Print command, which prevents users from printing the PDF. The PDF can only be viewed onscreen.
No Changing the Document	Disables the Editing tools, which prevents users from adding form fields, link, bookmarks, articles, and movies. It also prevents users from changing or moving text with the Touch Up Text tool. Users can still add comments to the PDF.
No Content Copying or Extraction, Disable Accessibility	Disables **Edit > Copy**, which prevents users from copying text or images from the document. Disables **File > Export > Extract Images As**, which prevents users from extracting images from the PDF. This option also disables the Accessibility interface.
No Adding or Changing Comments and Form Fields	Disables the Comment tools and the Form tools, which prevents users from filling in form fields.

> ## NOTE | Learning Adobe Acrobat 6
>
> If you're interested in working with advanced PDF features, you may want to try Adobe Acrobat 6. If you're interested in learning about Adobe Acrobat 6, check out the following resources from lynda.com:
>
> **Adobe Acrobat 6 Hands-On Training (H·O·T)**
> By Garrick Chow, developed with Lynda Weinman
> lynda.com/books and Peachpit Press
> ISBN: 0321202996
> $44.99
>
> **Learning Adobe Acrobat 6 Movie Training**
> By Garrick Chow
> **http://www.lynda.com**

Congratulations! You just finished the last chapter! Now it's time to start designing your own Web graphics. Enjoy! ;-)

A.

Troubleshooting FAQ and Technical Support

| Appendix A |

H·O·T

Photoshop CS/ImageReady CS for the Web

If you've run into any problems following the exercises in this book, this Troubleshooting FAQ (Frequently Asked Questions) should help. This document will be maintained and expanded upon at this book's companion Web site: **http://www.lynda.com/ books/pscshot**.

If you don't find what you're looking for here or in the companion Web site, please send an email to **pscshot@lynda.com**.

If you have a question related to Photoshop CS or ImageReady CS that is not related to a specific exercise in this book, visit Adobe's Web site (**http://www.adobe.com**) or call their tech support hotline at: (206) 675-6203 (Mac) or (206) 675-6303 (Windows).

Q: I'm using a Windows computer, and all the files on the **H•O•T CD-ROM** are locked even though I transferred them to my hard drive. What should I do?

A: Unfortunately, some versions of the Windows operating system treat files copied from a CD-ROM as read-only files, which means you can't make changes to any of the files until you remove the read-only property. For specific instructions about how to do this, take a look at the Introduction.

Q: What if I use color profiles for my print work? It's kind of disconcerting to turn them off, as you suggested in Chapter 3, "*Color*."

A: You can always create an **action** that will turn them off or back on. You learned how to make actions in Chapter 14, "*Automation*." Start recording an action before you turn profiles on or off, and the action will remember your steps. Once you've finished recording, click the **Stop** button. Bingo, you have an action for that turns your color profiles on or off!

Q: If I create a CMYK image for print, can I use it on the Web?

A: You can't use CMYK images for the Web. You'll have to convert CMYK images to RGB first. To convert CMYK images to RBG in Photoshop CS, choose **Image > Mode > RGB Color**. You may see some color shifting during this process because CMYK and RGB are different color spaces, and you cannot achieve an exact color translation when you convert the files.

Q: In Chapter 4, "*Optimization*," you suggest I leave the **Save For Web** dialog box open for many exercises in a row. What happens if I have to quit and come back to the exercise another time?

A: You're in luck! The **Save For Web** dialog box remembers the last settings you used, even if you quit Photoshop CS. You can quit the application without having to redo the exercises again from scratch.

Q: Sometimes when I'm in the **Save For Web** dialog box, I see an orange warning triangle. What should I do?

A: Choose **Repopulate Views** from the **Save For Web** menu to refresh all views. The warning icon will disappear.

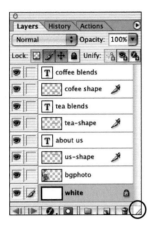

Q: My **Layers** palette doesn't look like yours! What's up with that?

A: To access any palette in its entirety, not just the **Layers** palette, just drag its bottom-right corner to increase or decrease its size.

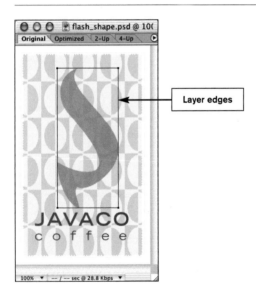

Layer edges

Q: When I work with layered images in ImageReady CS, I often see an outline around the edges of the selected layers. Sometimes it's helpful, but sometimes it's distracting. What are these lines, and how can I turn them off?

A: ImageReady CS has a feature called layer edges, which let you see where the edges in a layer begin and end. Layer edges can be helpful when you need to visualize the size of a layer. To turn the layer edges off, choose **View > Show > Layer Edges**.

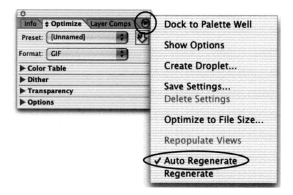

Q: When I click the **Optimized** tab in the ImageReady CS document window, I see a checkerboard pattern instead of the background of the image.

A: If you're having trouble seeing an image when you click the **Optimized** tab, make sure **Auto Regenerate** is turned on in the **Optimize** palette menu. Remember, the checkerboard pattern indicates a file is a transparent GIF.

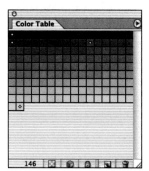

Q: When I'm optimizing a GIF in ImageReady CS, sometimes I don't see any color swatches in the **Color Table** palette. Why not?

A: Click the yellow triangle at the lower left of the **Color Table** palette to regenerate the color table.

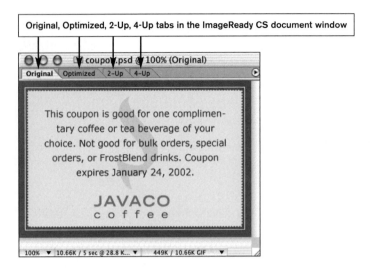

Q: What are each of the tabs in the ImageReady CS document window?

A: The ImageReady CS document window has four tabs: **Original**, **Optimized**, **2-Up**, and **4-Up**. The **Original** tab shows the original, non-optimized image. The **Optimized** tab shows the optimized image using the settings you specify in the **Optimize** palette. I prefer to do all my image creation and image-editing with the **Original** tab selected. The **Optimized** tab can really slow things down because the image constantly updates each time you make a change. The **2-Up** and **4-Up** tabs let you view two and four versions of the image, respectively. They're useful for comparing the image with different optimization settings.

Q: Every time I save a file, I get this annoying box asking me where I want to update it.

A: You're in luck! There is a simple way to fix this in both programs. Choose **Photoshop > Preferences > General** (Mac) or **Edit > Preferences > General** (Windows). Turn on the **Auto-Update Open Documents** option. Click **OK** and you'll never have to see that pesky box again! These steps work for both Photoshop CS and ImageReady CS.

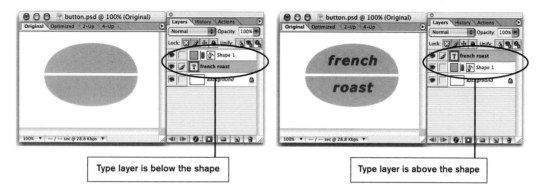

Type layer is below the shape

Type layer is above the shape

Q: When I create a Web button, the type shows behind the button, not over it. Why does this happen and how can I fix it?

A: The stacking order of layers in the **Layers** palette is from bottom to top. If your type layer is the shape layer (or whatever layer makes up the button), it may be hidden. Drag the type layer above the button layer and you'll see it. Also, make sure you're not typing with the same color as the button. Hey, it happens even to the pros!

Q: Not to complain, but I get sick of zooming in and out. Is there a quick way to get a large view of an image or to return to 100%?

A: If you double-click the **Hand** tool in the **Toolbox**, the image will expand to fill your screen. If you double-click the **Zoom** tool in the **Toolbox**, it will change to **100%**. The trick is to double-click the tool, not inside your image.

Q: When I'm working in ImageReady CS, it's taking forever for the program to accept my edits, and it's driving me crazy.

A: It sounds like you're working in the **Optimized** tab, which tells ImageReady CS to constantly optimize your graphic while you're editing it. Switch over to the **Original** tab. It will go faster—I promise.

Q: Is there a quick, one-step way to hide all the palettes? Sometimes I find it overwhelming to have them all visible onscreen.

A: Photoshop CS and ImageReady CS have a handy keyboard shortcut to toggle the visibility of the palettes on and off. Just press the **Tab** key! It's a beautiful thing!

Q: I keep trying to select a slice, but for some reason, I can't. Help!

A: Are you using the **Slice Select** tool? Use the **Slice** tool to divide an image into slices and then use the **Slice Select** tool to adjust those slices. The **Slice Select** tool lets you drag, reposition, delete, and select one or more slices. To select multiple slices, hold down the **Shift** key.

B.

Online Resources

| Appendix B |

H·O·T

Photoshop CS/ImageReady CS for the Web

The Web is full of great resources for Photoshop CS and ImageReady CS users. There are a variety of newsgroups and third-party Web sites that can help you get the most out of the new skills you've developed by following the exercises in this book. This appendix lists some of the best resources for learning and extending Photoshop CS and ImageReady CS.

Adobe User-to-User Forums

Adobe has set up several discussion boards (newsgroups) for Photoshop CS and ImageReady CS. This is a great place to ask questions and get help from thousands of Photoshop CS and ImageReady CS users. The newsgroup is composed of beginning to advanced users, so you should have no problem finding the type of help you need. You can access all of the Adobe User Forums at the following location: **http://www.adobe.com/support/forums/main.html**. You will need to register to log in, read, and post messages. Here are some of the forums that might interest you:

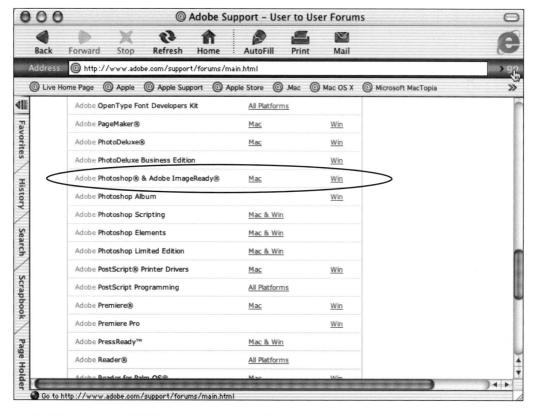

Adobe Photoshop and Adobe Image Ready for Mac
Adobe Photoshop and Adobe ImageReady for Windows

Adobe Design Forums

Adobe also offers a number of design forums to help you find information about design.

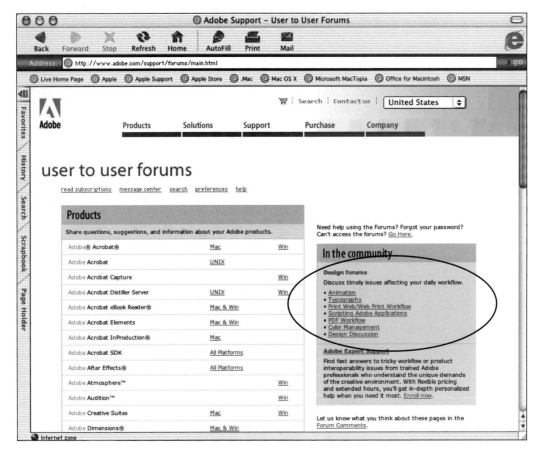

You can access the design forums from the following location: **http://www.adobe.com/support/forums/main.html**. Here are a few design forums that might interest you:

Animation
Typography
Print Web/Web Print Workflow
Design Discussion

Adobe Studio

Adobe also offers a design resource Web site, which provides resources for graphics professionals.

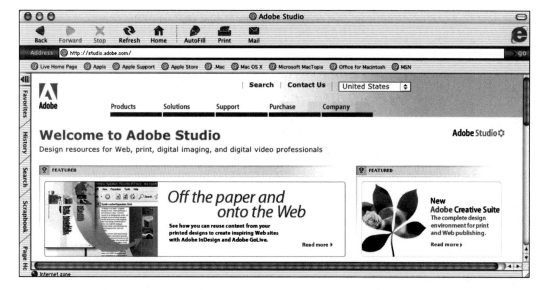

You can check out the **Adobe Studio** Web site at the following location: **http://studio.adobe.com**.

National Association of Photoshop Professionals (NAPP)

The **National Association of Photoshop Professionals** (NAPP) is an organization dedicated to providing Photoshop CS and ImageReady CS users with the latest education, training, and news. Membership with NAPP provides you with access to the **Resource Center**, which provides useful tutorials, tips, and news about Photoshop CS and ImageReady CS. Members also receive a subscription to *Photoshop User* magazine, help with technical questions, and special offers on training, videos, and seminars. NAPP also holds a useful conference twice a year called **Photoshop World**.

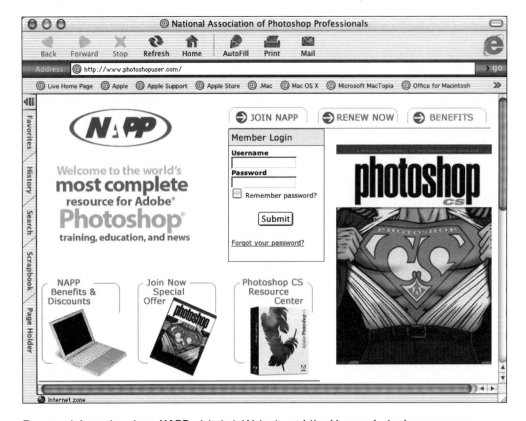

For more information about **NAPP**, visit their Web site at **http://www.photoshopuser.com**.

Planet Photoshop

Planet Photoshop also offers tutorials, user forums, education materials, books, seminars, and more to help you learn Photoshop CS and ImageReady CS.

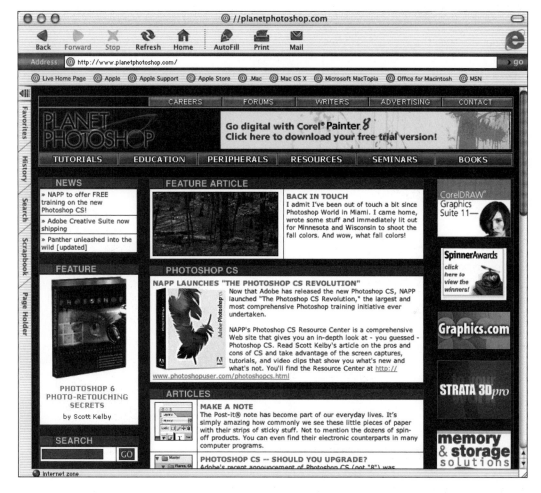

For more information about **Planet Photoshop**, visit their Web site at **http://www.planetphotoshop.com.**

Index

H•O•T

Photoshop CS/ImageReady CS for the Web

Symbols

* (asterisk) character, 699
8-bit transparency, 367
256-level transparency, 367

A

absolute links, 463
Accessing Offset Filter (ImageReady CS), 345
actions, 675
    creating, 676-680
    droplets, 682
        changing save locations, 686
        creating, 683-685
    editing, 681
    predefined, 675
Actions palette, 675
adding
    images to PDF presentations, 670
    slices to slice sets, 466-469
addition rollovers, 487
Adjustment, Hue/Saturation command
        (ImageReady CS Image menu), 351
adjustment layers, 230-232
    creating, 234
    Hue/Saturation dialog box, 233
Adobe Acrobat 6, 783
Adobe Graphics Server, 694
Adobe Tokens, 662
Adobe Web site, 669
aliased images, 249
aligning linked layers, 176-179
Alignment option (Pixel Replacement
        variable), 706
alpha channels, 124-126, 142-144
alt text, applying to slices, 458-459
Altercast, 694
Angle option (Layer Styles dialog box), 303
Animation palette, 585
animations, 7, 107, 584
    aesthetic benefits, 586
    compression, 587
    creating
        from layer visibility, 590-593
        optimization, 602
        tweening with opacity, 598-601
    delaying frames, 606
    designing Web interfaces, 641-642
    duplicating frames, 604
    exporting as SWF files, 631-634
    frames, exporting as files, 635-639
        GIFs, 107, 586
            rollovers, 627-630
            vs. Macromedia Flash, 588-589
        JPEG and PNG formats, 621
        looping, 605
        lossy compression, 620
        reversing frames, 605
        selecting frames, 603
        slideshows, 618-620
        speed, 594-597
        SWF, 107
        timing, 586
        tweening
            with layer styles, 615-617
            with position, 611-614
            a tweened sequence, 608-610
Anti-Alias option (Layer Styles dialog box), 303
anti-aliasing (graphics), 249, 369
Anti-Aliasing Method pop-up menu, 248
applying
    alt text and status bar messages to slices,
        458-460
    custom layer styles, 308-311
As Is option (Pixel Replacement variable) 706
Assigning keywords (File Browser), 57-60
asterisk (*) character, 699
Auto Select Layer option, 173
auto slices, 411
    converting to user slices, 418
    creating, 416
    optimizing, 450
    resizing, 417
automation (PDF presentations), 669, 672
    adding images, 670
    multi-page PDF documents, 674
    presentation options, 671

B

background images, 5, 315
    BODY tag, 315
    colors, 316, 324
    creating, 316
    defining, 327
    directional tiles, 363-365
    fast-loading, 353
    full-screen, 353-356
    full-screen photographic, 357-362
    layers, 315
    non-symmetrical, 338-345
    previewing, 320, 350
    saving, 326-331

seamless, from photographs, 346-352
size, 317-318, 322-323
specifying, 319-325
symmetrical, 332-337
tiles, 315
Background layers, 164, 184
background tiles. *See* background images
backgrounds
broad backgrounds (GIFs), 385-388
filling with color (layered images), 90
slices, 452
Batch Progress dialog box, 685
Bevel and Emboss layer style, 300, 304
beveled edge effect, 296
bit depth (GIFs), 111
bitmaps vs. vector graphics, 283
Blend Mode option (Layer Styles
dialog box), 303
Blending graphics, 369
blurring graphics, 122
BODY tag (HTML), 315
bold text, 254
bounding boxes, 259
brightness, 74
broad backgrounds, 385-388
Browse for Folder dialog box, 212
browsers
offset in, 372
previewing graphics, 146
Brush tool, 169
buttons
linked, 178
rollovers, 6, 503-505
buzzwords, 693

C

Canvas Size command (ImageReady CS Image
menu), 322
changing
Image Map palette settings, 566
ImageReady CS-generated HTML files, 714
Slice Outset, 427
type color, 248
Channels palette, 124-126
Character palette, 250
All Caps button, 255
editing type, 252
Kerning pop-up menu, 253
Leading pop-up menu, 254
Tracking pop-up menu, 253
type settings, 256

Check Spelling dialog box, 263
checkerboard pattern (graphics), 370
Circle Image Map tool, 545
client-side image maps, 543
Clip to Bounding Box option (Pixel Replacement
variable), 706
clipping groups, 236-239
Cmd+H command (Mac), 248
Cmd+Z shortcut key, 91
code (HTML), 394
collaborating with Web Photo Galleries,
666-667
color
background images, 316, 324
changing settings, 67-68
custom swatches, 81-88
dithering, 71, 137
fonts, 246
gamma, 65
HTML, 101-102
ICC profiles, 65
locking colors in a GIF, 138
Macintosh settings, 65
management help, 69
matte, 152-153, 381
recoloring layered images, 89, 94
background color, 90
Color Replacement tool, 95-98
higher layers, 90
Lock Transparent Pixels feature, 92
text, 92
sRGB, 65
unpredictable shifts online, 70
Wacom tablet, 100
the Web, 65
Web-safe, 69-70
choosing from Color palette, 76
choosing from Color Picker, 72-74
choosing from Swatches palette, 77-79
writing as HTML in ImageReady CS, 154
Color Balance dialog box, 235
Color option (Layer Styles dialog box), 303
Color palette, choosing Web-safe colors, 76
Color Picker
choosing Web-safe colors, 72-73
differences between Photoshop CS and
ImageReady CS, 75
viewing by brightness, 74
viewing by hue, 75
viewing by saturation, 73
Color Picker dialog box, 220, 290
Font Color box, 247

Color Reduction Palette settings
    changing colors to Web-safe colors, 134
    GIFs, 132, 135-140
    Web-safe colors, 135
    when to use, 134
Color Replacement tool
    recoloring images, 95-98
    Wacom tablet, 100
Color Stops (gradient bar), 226
Combining slices, 440-441
commands
    File menu
        Other, Offset (ImageReady CS), 334
        Other, Offset (Photoshop), 337
        Output Settings, Background
            (ImageReady CS), 335,
            343-347, 375
        Output Settings (ImageReady
            CS), 319
        Save For Web (Photoshop CS), 396
        Save Optimized (ImageReady CS),
            327, 350
        Save Optimized As (ImageReady
            CS), 394
    HTML command, 711
    Image menu (ImageReady CS)
        Adjustment, Hue/Saturation, 351
        Canvas Size, 322
        Rotate Canvas, 90°CW, 364
    Optimize menu, 400
    Transform, 279-281
    View menu, 330
Commit Current Edits button (Type Options bar),
    248, 254
Commit Transform button (Options bar), 280
Compressing animated GIFs, 587
conditional actions, 688-691
Conform option (Pixel Replacement
    variable), 706
context-sensitive properties (GIFs), 116
Contour option (Layer Styles dialog box), 303
Convert Rollovers to DW option (ImageReady
    HTML dialog box), 745
Converting PSD files to PDF, 774-779
Copy Color as HTML feature, 101-102
Copying layers, 197
cover overlay effect, 296
creating
    actions, 676-680, 688-691
    animated GIFs
        rollovers, 627-630
        transparent, 623-625
    animations
        delaying frames, 606

        duplicating frames, 604
        from layer visibility, 590-593
        looping, 605
        optimization, 602
        reversing frames, 605
        selecting frames, 603
        slideshows, 618-620
        tweening with layer styles, 615-617
        tweening with opacity, 598-601
        tweening with position, 611-614
        tweening a tweened sequence,
            608-610
auto slices, 416
background images, 316
bitmaps, 283
custom swatches, 81-85
    adding colors, 86-88
data sets, 698-701
droplets, 682-685
image maps
    changing Image Map palette
        settings, 566
    for types, 572-575
    from layers, 560-570
    HTML code, 559
    Image Map tools, 548-549
    naming, 551
    optimization, 557
    previewing, 555
    quality settings, 565
    resizing, 550-551
    rollovers, 580-583
    shaping, 556
layer-based slices, 422-432
layer comps, 472
layer sets, 182
layer styles, 297-298
    Bevel and Emboss layer style, 300
    Outer Glow layer style, 301
paragraph type, 258
PSD files with data sets and variables, 706
remote rollovers, 522-529
remote rollovers with selected states,
    531-540
rollovers, 490-493
    from layer-based slices, 498-501
    layer comps, 518-520
    layer visibility, 513-516
    multiple buttons from a saved style,
        503-505
server-side images, 543-544
shapes, 288
slices, 442

tool presets, 34-35
type on a path, 268-273
user slices, 415-420
variables, 698
    * (asterisk) character, 699
    Pixel Replacement variables, 702-703
vector graphics, 283
warped type, 266, 274
Web graphics, 3
Web Photo Galleries, 651-655
cross-fades, 618
Ctrl+H command (Windows), 248
Ctrl+Z shortcut key, 91
Custom Colors options (Web Photo Gallery
    dialog box), 665
custom layer styles
    applying, 308-311
    saving, 304-307
Custom Shapes Picker, 295
Custom Shapes tool, 285, 295
custom swatches, 81-88
custom workspaces, saving, 38-39
customizing Web Photo Galleries, 651, 657,
    660-662
    photo info, 658
    sizing options, 659

D

data-driven, 693
data sets, 693-696
    creating, 698-701, 706
    HTML editors, 705
    importing from text files, 707-709
    working with in GoLive CS, 733-738
defining
    background images, 327
    Text Replacement variables, 698
delaying frames, 606
deleting
    layer styles from Styles palette, 313
    slices, 419
Depth option (Layer Styles dialog box), 303
designing
    Web graphics
        setting preferences for the Web, 63
        Web-safe color, 69
    Web interfaces, 640-649
dialog boxes
    Batch Progress dialog box, 685
    Browse for Folder, 212
    Check Spelling dialog box, 263

Color Balance dialog box, 235
Color Picker dialog box, 72, 220, 290
Divide Slice dialog box, 438
Duplicate Slice dialog box, 441
Export Animation Frames as Files dialog
    box, 636
Export Layers as Files dialog box, 210
Find and Replace Text dialog box, 265
Gaussian Blur dialog box, 278
Gradient Fill dialog box, 223, 226
Hue/Saturation dialog box, 232, 351
Image Replacement dialog box, 704
Image Size dialog box, 677
Import Variable Data Sets dialog box, 708
Keyboard Shortcuts dialog box, 41
Layer Set Properties dialog box, 186
Layer Styles dialog box, 297, 303, 382, 615
Macromedia Flash Export dialog box,
    632, 751
Modify Dither Setting dialog box, 145
Modify Lossiness Setting dialog box, 144
Modify Quality Setting dialog box, 126
New Layer Comp dialog box, 204
New Layer dialog box, 164
New Style dialog box, 305
New Tool Preset dialog box, 36
Offset dialog box, 334
Output Setting dialog box, 319, 343, 375
Paste Frames dialog box, 607
Pattern Fill dialog box, 228
PDF Options dialog box, 776
Pixel Replacement Options dialog box, 703
Replace Files dialog box, 714
Rollover State Options dialog box, 536
Save Optimized As dialog box, 147, 394, 496
Save Optimized dialog box, 327
Save this action as a droplet dialog box, 684
Search dialog box, 61
Select an Export Destination Folder dialog
    box, 636
Set an Export Destination Folder dialog
    box, 212
Set Loop Count dialog box, 595
Shape Name dialog box, 293
Tile Maker dialog box, 349
Variables dialog box, 696
Warp Text dialog box, 266
Diffusion Transparency Dither, 389-391
Direct Selection tool, 292
directional tiles, 363-365
dithering, 71, 137, 392
Divide Slice dialog box, 438
Dividing slices, 438-439
docking palettes, 26-33

downloading
Adobe Reader, 669
fonts, 244
dragging layers, 356
Dreamweaver MX 2004
importing ImageReady CS rollovers, 740-744
creating a new folder, 744
previewing files in Web browser, 747
saving files to new folder, 745
selecting file contents, 746
Site Definition summary settings, 743
Manage Sites dialog box, 741
drop-down panels (palettes), 25
Drop Shadow option (Layer Styles
dialog box), 303
drop shadows (GIFs), 382-384
droplets, 682
changing save locations, 686
creating, 683-685
Duplicate Layer command, 198
Duplicate Slice dialog box, 441
duplicating
frames, 593, 604, 629
layers, 197
dynamic content, 693
dynamic graphics, 693

E

edges of transparent GIFs, 377-381
Edit Original feature (GoLive CS), 729
Edit Output Settings (Photoshop CS Optimize
menu), 400
editing
actions, 681
ImageReady CS-generated HTML files, 714
layer-based slices, 428
PSD files in GoLive CS, 729-731
shapes, 288
text
find and replace feature, 265
spell checking, 263-264
warped, 267
type, 252
after a clipping group has been
applied, 239
faux bold/italic, 254
leading, 254
tracking, 253
uppercasing, 255
Ellipse Options box, 289
Ellipse tool, 268

embossed edge effect, 296
Eraser tool, keyboard shortcut, 40
.exe extension, 684
expanding layer sets, 187
Export Animation Frames as Files dialog box,
635-639
Export Layers as Files dialog box, 210, 214
Export Layers dialog box, 218
Export Original option (ImageReady CS), 331
exporting
animations as SWF files, 631-634
as SWF, 106, 117-118, 157-159
frames as files, 635-636
quality settings, 637
selected frames, 639
selecting destination folder, 636
Illustrator CS, 765-766
ImageReady CS files to QuickTime, 768-769
layers as files, 210-212
Export Layers dialog box options, 218
optimization, 214-216
selected layers, 219
to Macromedia Flash, 12
vector images as SWF files, 750-758
Free Transform option, 756
manipulating the graphic, 757
Eyedropper tool, 40, 87

F

faux bold, 254
faux italic, 254
fast-loading background images, 353
File Browser
adding folders, 54
assigning keywords, 57-60
closing, 56
flagging images, 52
hiding images, 51-53
overview, 46
searching, 57-62
viewing and organizing images, 47-51, 55
Web Photo Galleries, 654
file compression, 108
GIFs, 110
optimization, 129
reducing colors, 136-140
JPEGs, 108
File menu commands
Output settings (ImageReady CS), 319
Output Settings, Background (ImageReady
CS), 335, 343, 347, 375

Save For Web (Photoshop CS), 396
Save Optimized (ImageReady CS), 327, 350
Save Optimized As (ImageReady CS), 394
files
data sets, 695
exporting frames as, 635-636
quality settings, 637
selected frames, 639
selecting destination folder, 636
exporting from Illustrator CS, 765-766
exporting from ImageReady CS to QuickTime,
768-769
exporting layers as, 210-212
Export Layers dialog box options, 218
optimization, 214-216
selected layers, 219
flattening, 170
ImageReady CS, preserving appearance with
SWF Export, 760-764
PDF, converting from PSD, 774-779
fill layers, 220, 287
Gradient layers, 223-226
Pattern layers, 228-230
solid colors, 220-221
Fill option (Pixel Replacement variable), 706
Fill slider, 168
Filter menu commands
Output Settings, Background (ImageReady
CS), 335
Other, Offset (ImageReady CS), 334
Other, Offset (Photoshop), 337
Find and Replace Text dialog box, 265
Fit option (Pixel Replacement variable), 706
flagging images, 51-52
Flash (Macromedia), 4
animation, 107
exporting to, 12
exporting files as, 117-118, 157-159
SWF, 105
transparencies, 107
flattening files, 170
fly-out menus, 23
folders, adding in File Browser, 54
fonts
attributes, 250
Character palette controls, 250
color, 246
downloading, 244
selecting, 245
sizing, 248-249

formatting
text, 257
alignment, 260
paragraph type, 258-260
type, 243, 257
alignment, 260
creating paragraph type, 258-260
rasterizing, 275-277
Transform commands, 279-281
Foti, Massimo, 740
frames
animations, 586, 591
GIF rollovers, 628
layer visibility, 590
delaying, 606
exporting as files, 635
duplicating, 593
frame delay settings, 597
optimization settings, 621
Paste Frames dialog box, 607
Free Transform mode, 279, 433
Freeform Pen tool, 271, 289
From Center option, 289
full-screen background images, 353-356
full-screen photographic background images,
357-362

G

galleries (photo), 7
gamma, 65, 68
Gaussian Blur dialog box, 278
Geometry Options box, 289
GIFs (Graphic Interchange Format), 105, 371
animations, 107, 586
Netscape animation bug, 630
optimizing, 621-622
rollovers, 627-630
transparent, 623-625
vs. SWF files, 588-589
anti-aliasing, 369
background images, 315
BODY tag, 315
colors, 316, 324
creating, 316
defining, 327
directional tiles, 363-365
fast-loading, 353
full-screen, 353-356
full-screen photographic, 357-362
layers, 315
non-symmetrical, 338-345

previewing, 320, 350
saving, 326-331
seamless from photographs, 346-352
size, 317-323
specifying, 319-325
symmetrical, 332-337
tiles, 315
bit depth, 111
Color Reduction Palette settings, 132-135
context-sensitive properties, 116
file compression, 110, 136-140
halos, 377
limitations, 391
locking colors, 138
lossy, 108
optimizing
with alpha channels, 142-144
ImageReady CS, 147-148
slices as, 448
options, 114-115
previewing in Web browsers, 146
saving for the Web, 129-131
sizing, 141
slice, 409
transparent, 107, 367, 371
1-bit masking, 368
broad backgrounds, 385-388
creating, 373-376
creating in Photoshop CS, 396-402
Diffusion Transparency Dither, 389-391
drop shadows, 382-384
fixing edges, 377-381
from non-transparent, 403-407
saving, 393-395
saving in Photoshop CS, 396-402
viewing in browser, 373-376
Gloss Contour option (Layer Styles dialog
box), 303
GoLive CS
editing PSD files, 729-731
ImageReady CS data sets, 733-738
importing ImageReady CS rollovers, 716-717
copying files, 718-721
previewing sites, 722
Save for Web dialog box, 726
Site window, 718
Smart Objects, 723
options, 724
Photoshop Smart Objects, 725
saving for the Web, 726-727
Gradient Editor dialog box, 226
Gradient Fill dialog box, 223

Gradient layers, 223-224
Color Stops, 226
Gradient Editor dialog box, 226
Gradient Presets, 225
Gradient option (Layer Styles dialog box), 303
gradient overlay effect, 296
gradients (animations), 615
Graphic Interchange Format. *See* GIFs
graphics. *See also* images
8-bit transparency, 367
aliased, 249
animation
SWF files, 588-589
animations, 7, 107, 584
aesthetic benefits, 586
compression, 587
creating from layer visibility,
590-593
delaying frames, 606
duplicating frames, 604
exporting as SWF files, 631-634
exporting frames as files, 635-639
GIFs, 586
looping, 605
optimization, 602
reversing frames, 605
selecting frames, 603
speed, 594-597
timing, 586
tweening a tweened sequence,
608-610
tweening with layer styles, 615-617
tweening with opacity, 598-601
tweening with position, 611-614
anti-aliased, 249
anti-aliasing, 369
background images, 5
blending, 369
checkerboard pattern, 370
clipping groups, 236-239
designing Web graphics
setting preferences for the Web, 63
dynamic, 693
editing HTML, 712
exporting as SWF, 157-159
GIFs, 105
1-bit masking, 368
animation, 107
bit depth, 111
Color Reduction Palette settings,
132-135
context-sensitive properties, 116
file compression, 110

GIF options, 114-115
locking colors, 138
lossy, 108
optimizing with alpha channels,
        142-144
reducing colors, 136-140
saving for the Web, 129-131
transparencies, 107
transparency, 367
halos, 377
image maps, 543
        appearance, 544
        changing Image Map palette
                settings, 566
        creating, 549
        creating for type, 572-575
        creating with layers, 560-570
        HTML code, 559
        moving to Photoshop CS, 577-579
        naming, 551
        optimizing, 557, 571
        previewing, 555
        quality settings, 565
        resizing, 550-551
        rollovers, 580-583
        server-side, 543
        shaping, 556
        text-only browsers, 552
JPEGs, 105
        file compression, 108
        JPEG options, 112
        optimizing with alpha channels,
                124-127
        saving for the Web, 119-122
layers, 160, 162
        adjustment layers, 230-234
        aligning linked layers, 176-179
        Background layers, 184
        duplicating, 197
        exporting as files, 210-219
        fill, 220-221
        flattening, 170
        Free Transform mode, 433
        Gradient layers, 223-226
        ImageReady CS, 193-196
        Layer Comps feature, 202-208
        linked layers, 200-201
        merging, 198
        moving, 171-175
        Pattern layers, 228-230
        saving as different formats, 213
        selecting, 197

selecting multiple layers, 194, 200-201
        sets, 180, 182-192, 200-201
        transparent, 370
masks, 371
measuring, 63
optimization in ImageReady CS, 147-148
        JPEGs, 149-151
        matte colors, 152-153
previewing in Web browsers, 146
rollovers, 486
        addition rollovers, 487
        creating, 492-493
        creating from layer comps, 518-520
        creating from layer-based slices,
                498-501
        creating multiple buttons from saved
                styles, 503-505
        creating with layer visibility, 513-516
        naming, 507-508, 511
        optimizing, 494
        previewing, 494
        problems with Internet Explorer, 495
        remote rollovers, 487
        remote, creating, 522-529
        remote, creating with selected states,
                531-540
        replacement rollovers, 487
        saving settings, 496
        states, 488
shapes, 286
sizing, 141
slices
        naming conventions, 442
SWF, 105
        animation, 107
transparent, 106, 371
transparent GIFs
        broad backgrounds, 385-388
        creating, 373-376
        creating in Photoshop CS, 396-402
        Diffusion Transparency Dither, 389-391
        drop shadows, 382-384
        fixing edges, 377-381
        from non-transparent, 403-407
        saving, 393-395
        saving in Photoshop CS, 396-402
        viewing in browser, 373-376
type, 240
vector vs. bitmap images, 283
Web, creating, 3

H

halos (GIFs), 377
Hand tool, 40
Healing Brush tool, 97
Hide/Show Slices tool, 40
hiding
    HTML text box, 376
    images in File Browser, 51, 53
highlighting type, 248
Horizontal Type tool, 245
hot spots, 544
HTML
    BODY tag, 315
    color, 101-102
    editors
        animated GIFs, 622
        data sets and variables, 705
    previewing, 154-156
    rollover graphics, 511
    saving, 328, 394
    simulating HTML type with system
        layout, 256
    type, 240
    updating in ImageReady CS, 711-715
    uploading to ImageReady CS, 156
HTML text box, hiding, 376
HTML.mxp files, 740
Hue/Saturation dialog box, 232, 351

I

ICC (International Color Consortium) profiles, 65
Illustrator CS, exporting files, 765-766
Image Map palette
    changing setting, 566
    Layer Based Settings section, 561, 573
image map-based rollovers, 580-583
Image Map tools
    naming image maps, 551
    optimizing image maps, 557
    previewing image maps, 555
    resizing image maps, 550-551
    shaping image maps, 556
image maps, 6, 543-544
    changing Image Map palette settings, 566
    creating
        Image Map tools, 548-549
        ImageReady CS tools, 545
        from layers, 560-570

    quality settings, 565
        for type, 572-575
hot spots, 544
HTML code, 559
layer-based drawbacks, 576
moving to Photoshop CS, 577-579
naming, 551
optimizing, 557, 571
Polygon Image Map tool, 554
previewing, 555
resizing, 550-551
server-side, 543
shaping, 556
targets, 552
text-only browsers, 552
Web Content palette, 546
Image menu commands (ImageReady CS)
    Adjustment, Hue/Saturation, 351
    Canvas Size, 322
    Rotate Canvas, 90°CW, 364
Image Replacement dialog box, 704
Image Size dialog box, 677
ImageReady CS
    actions. *See* actions
    Color Picker, 75
    creating
        image maps, 545
        server-side image maps, 543
    data sets, working with in GoLive CS,
        733-738
    editing text, 262
    Export Frames As Files feature, 635
    exporting files
        to QuickTime, 768-769
        as SWF, 117
        copying files, 718-721
        previewing sites, 722
    graphic optimization, 147-148
        JPEGs, 149-151
        matte colors, 152-153
    HTML
        previewing, 154-156
        uploading, 156
    HTML.mxp files, 740
    importing rollovers into Dreamweaver MX
        2004, 740-744
        creating a new folder, 744
        previewing files in Web browser, 747
        saving files to new folder, 745
        selecting file contents, 746
        Site Definition summary settings, 743
    importing rollovers into GoLive CS, 716-717
    keyboard shortcuts, 40

Layer Comps feature, 202-208, 471-484
    basic element visibility, 205
    New Layer Comp dialog box, 204
layers
    exporting as files, 211
    multiple layers, 193-196
    visibility, 592
new features, 10-16
Offset Filter, accessing, 345
opening QuickTime movies, 771
    previewing the file, 773
    saving the file as a GIF, 772
optimizing JPEGs, 124
Options bar, 30
Output Multiple HTML Files option (File menu), 538
palettes, 25
    default settings, 29
    docking, 26-33
preserving file appearance with SWF Export, 760-764
resetting tool options, 37
rollover states, 488
Save options, 331
slices, 421
slideshows, 618
Swatches palette, 77
Toolbox, 22
Tween feature, 598-601
type, 241-243
updating HTML, 711-715
variables, 693
vs. Photoshop CS (when to use), 7-8
ImageReady HTML command, 748
ImageReady HTML dialog box, 745
images. *See also* graphics
    actions, 675
        conditional, 688-691
        creating, 676-680
        droplets, 682-685
        editing, 681
        predefined, 675
    background, 315
        BODY tag, 315
        colors, 316, 324
        creating, 316
        defining, 327
        directional tiles, 363-365
        fast-loading, 353
        full-screen, 353-356
        full-screen photographic, 357-362
        layers, 315
        non-symmetrical, 338-345

        previewing, 320, 350
        saving, 326-331
        seamless, from photographs, 346-352
        size, 317-318, 322-323
        specifying, 319-325
        symmetrical, 332-337
        tiles, 315
    blurry, 93
    editing HTML, 712
    exporting as SWF, 157-159
    layered, recoloring, 89-94
    organizing in File Browser, 48
    PDF presentations, 669, 672
        adding images, 670
        multi-page PDF documents, 674
        presentation options, 671
    recoloring, 95-98
    rotating, 50
    shapes, 286
    slices, 409
        applying alt text and status bar messages to slices, 458-460
        assigning URLs, 461-462
        auto, 416
        backgrounds, 452
        combining, 440-441
        copying optimization settings, 454
        deleting, 419
        dividing, 438-439
        layer comps, 471-484
        layer-based, 422-432
        linking, 454
        modifying default slice naming settings, 445
        optimizing, 446-450
        previewing, 451
        promoting layer-based slices to user slices, 436
        renaming, 442-444
        saving, 455-457
        Slice palette, 413
        slice sets, 464-470
        types, 411
        user, 415-418, 420
        visibility, 450
        Web Content palette, 413
    slideshows, 618-620
Import Variable Data Sets dialog box, 708
importing
    data sets from text files, 707-709
    ImageReady CS rollovers into Dreamweaver MX 2004, 740-744
        creating a new folder, 744

previewing files in Web browser, 747
 saving files to new folder, 745
 selecting file contents, 746
 Site Definition summary settings, 743
ImageReady CS rollovers into GoLive CS,
 716-717
 copying files, 718-721
 previewing sites, 722
inner shadow effect, 296
Inner Shadow layer style (rollover graphics), 500
insertion cursor, 252
Inspector palette, 735
Internet, speed, 105
Internet Explorer
 rollover problems, 495
 View menu commands, 330
italic text, 254

J

Jitter option (Layer Styles dialog box), 303
JPEGs (Joint Photographic Experts Group), 105
 animation limitation, 621
 blurring, 122
 file compression, 108
 optimizing
  ImageReady CS, 147-151
  matte colors, 152-153
  slices as, 449
 optimizing with alpha channels, 124-127
 options, 112
 previewing in Web browsers, 146
 saving for the Web, 119-122

K

kerning, 253
key palettes, 21
keyboard shortcuts
 Cmd+G (Mac), 195
 Ctrl+G (Windows), 195
 customizing, 41, 43
 list of, 40
 saving and printing sets, 45
Keyboard Shortcuts dialog box, 41
keywords, assigning (File Browser), 57-60
Keywords palette (File Browser), 58

L

Large Images options (Web Photo Gallery dialog
 box), 664
layer-based slices, 411
 creating, 422-432
 deleting, 419
 editing, 428
layer comps, 518-520
 slices, 471-484
Layer Comps feature, 202-208
 basic element visibility, 205
 New Layer Comp dialog box, 204
Layer Comps palette, 518
Layer Knocks Out option (Layer Styles dialog
 box), 303
Layer Set Properties dialog box, 186
Layer Style dialog box, 297
 editing PSD files in GoLive CS, 730
 Gradient option, 615
layer styles, 296
 accessing from Layers palette, 307
 applying custom, 308-311
 Bevel and Emboss layer style, 300, 304
 creating, 297-298
 deleting from Styles palette, 313
 Outer Glow layer style, 301
 saving custom, 304-307
 terminology, 303
 turning off visibility, 302
Layer Styles dialog box, 303, 382
layered images
 recoloring, 89, 94
  background color, 90
  higher layers, 90
  Lock Transparent Pixels feature, 92
  text, 92
 slicing, 524
layers, 160-162
 adjustment, 230-232
  creating, 234
  Hue/Saturation dialog box, 233
 aligning linked layers, 176-179
 background images, 315
 Background layers, 164, 184
 creating image maps, 560-570
 dragging between documents, 356
 duplicating, 197
 exporting as files, 210-212
  Export Layers dialog box layers, 218
  optimization, 214-216
  selected layers, 219

fill, 220
    Gradient layers, 223-226
    Pattern layers, 228-230
    solid colors, 220-221
flattening, 170
Free Transform mode, 433
ImageReady CS, 193-196
Layer Comps feature, 202-208
    basic element visibility, 205
    New Layer Comp dialog box, 204
merging, 198
moving, 171
    layer selection, 172
    linked layers, 174-175
saving as different formats, 213
screen resolutions, 355
selecting
    multiple layers, 194, 505
    shortcut keys, 197
sets, 180-182, 200-201
    creating, 182-183
    expanding, 187
    functionality, 180
    linking, 188
    luminosity, 191
    nesting, 192
    opacity, 190
    organizing, 186
    saving as individual files, 212
    visibility, 190
shapes, 286
transparent, 224, 370
tweening with layer styles, 615
type, 242
variables, 699
Layers palette, 89
    accessing layer styles, 307
    Bevel and Emboss layer style, 300
    Color Replacement tool, 95-100
    creating animations, 590-593
    Hue/Saturation options, 233
    layer sets, 180-182
        creating, 182-183
        expanding, 187
        functionality, 180
        linking, 188
        luminosity, 191
        nesting, 192
        opacity, 190
        visibility, 190
    Lock All button, 245

Lock Transparent Pixels button, 91
Merge Layers option, 198
New Layer icon, 168
Opacity slider, 599
Outer Glow layer style, 301
shortening, 185
Visibility icon, 163
leading, 254
Line tool, 285
linked buttons, moving, 178
linked layers, 200-201
    aligning, 176-179
    moving, 174-175
linking layer sets, 188
links, 287
    absolute links, 463
    relative links, 463
    rollovers, 486
        addition rollovers, 487
        creating, 492-493
        creating from layer comps, 518-520
        creating from layer-based slices,
            498-501
        creating multiple buttons from saved
            styles, 503-505
        creating with layer visibility, 513-516
        naming, 507-508, 511
        optimizing, 494
        previewing, 494
        problems with Internet Explorer, 495
        remote rollovers, 487
        remote, creating, 522-529
        remote, creating with selected states,
            531-540
        replacement rollovers, 487
        saving settings, 496
        states, 488
Lock All button (Layers palette), 245
Lock Transparent Pixels feature, 89-93
locking colors in a GIF, 138
logos, 3
looping, 586
    forever setting, 605
    minimum settings, 630
lossiness, 144
lossless file compression, 108
lossy compression (animations), 620
lossy file compression, 108
luminosity (layer sets), 191

M

Macintosh
  assigning URLs to slices, 462
  color settings, 65
    changing, 67
    setting gamma, 68
Macromedia Flash, 4
  animation, 107
  exporting files as, 117-118, 157-159
  exporting to, 12
  SWF, 105
  transparencies, 107
  vs. animated GIFs, 588-589
Macromedia Flash Export dialog box, 632, 751
  Generate HTML option, 633
  Preserve Appearance option, 763
Macromedia Flash MX 2004
  Create New Flash Document option, 753
  Publish Settings dialog box, 757
Magic Wand tool, 30
Manage Sites dialog box (Dreamweaver
    MX 2004), 741
masks (graphics), 371
matte color, 152-153, 381
measuring graphics, 63
menus, 23
Merge functions (Layers palette), 170
Merge Layers option (Layers palette), 198
metadata, 660
Modify Color Reduction dialog box, 143
Modify Dither Setting dialog box, 145
Modify Lossiness Setting dialog box, 144
Modify Quality Setting dialog box, 126
Move tool, 171
  keyboard shortcut, 40
  Options bar
    Align horizontal centers button, 179
    Align top edges button, 177
    Align vertical centers, 195
    Distribute horizontal centers
      button, 178
moving
  layers, 171
    layer selection, 172
  linked layers, 174-175
  shapes on a shape layer, 291
  slices, 429
multi-page PDF documents, 674
multiple layers, 200-201

N

naming
  image maps, 551
  layers, 211
  rollovers, 507-511
  slices, 442
  Web sites, 741
nesting
  layer sets, 192
  palettes, 27
Netscape Navigator
  animation bug, 630
  View menu commands, 330
New Layer Comp dialog box, 204
New Layer dialog box, 164
New Layer icon, 168
New Style dialog box, 305
New Tool Preset dialog box, 36
Noise option (Layer Styles dialog box), 303
non-symmetrical background images, 338-345
non-transparent GIFs, 403-407

O

Offset dialog box, 334
offset filter, 230, 345
offset in browsers, 372
opacity, 180, 190
Opacity option (Layer Styles dialog box), 303
Opacity slider (Layers palette), 599
opening
  File Browser, 47
  palette drop-down panels, 25
  QuickTime movies in ImageReady CS, 771
    previewing the file, 773
    saving file as a GIF, 772
  Swatches palette, 77
  Welcome screen, 19
Optimize menu commands, 400
Optimize palette, 326, 570
  optimizing rollover graphics, 494
  optimizing slices, 447
optimizing
  animations, 602
  exporting layers as files, 214
  GIFs, 129
    animated GIFs, 621-622

Color Reduction Palette settings, 132-135
locking colors, 138
reducing colors, 136-140
selective optimization with alpha channels, 142-144
sizing, 141
image maps, 557, 571
ImageReady CS options, 147-148
JPEGs, 149-151
matte colors, 152-153
images using droplets, 682
JPEGs, 124-127
rollover graphics, 494
slices, 446-447, 454
as GIFs, 448
as JPEGs, 449
auto slices, 450
copying optimization settings, 454
in layer comps, 474-484
Options bar, 21, 30
Commit Current Edits button, 254
Commit Transform button, 280
Custom Shapes Picker, 295
Ellipse Options box, 289
Geometry Options box, 289
Palette button, 31
Rectangle Shape tool, 291
Shape Layers button, 290
shape tools, 289
Toggle File Browser button, 47
Tool Presets button, 35
Tools options, 37
Warp Text button, 266
organizing layer sets, 186
Outer Glow layer style, 301
Output Settings command, 343
Output Settings dialog box, 319, 375
Over and Down rollover states, 492

P

Page Source command (Netscape Navigator View menu), 330
Palette button (Options bar), 31
Palette Wall, 32-33
palettes
Actions palette, 675
Animation palette, 585
Character palette, 250
Color palette, choosing Web-safe colors, 76

Color Reduction palette, 132
default settings, 29
docking, 26-33
drop-down panels, 25
Inspector palette, 735
Keywords palette (File Browser), 58
Layer Comps palette, 204, 518
Layers palette, 89, 95-98, 100, 162
nesting, 27
Optimize palette, 570
overview, 25
Paragraph palette, 257
Slice palette, 413
Swatches palette
choosing Web-safe colors, 77-79
coloring layered images, 89-94
creating custom swatches, 81-88
toggling on/off, 21
Tool Presets palette, 36
Web Content palette, 15, 489, 546
Paragraph palette, 257
aligning type, 260
controls (list of), 257
creating paragraph type, 258-260
Paste Frames dialog box, 607
Path Selection tool, 273
Path Type cursor, 270
paths
shapes, 293
warped type, 274
Pattern Fill dialog box, 228
Pattern layers, 228-230
Pattern Maker, 230
patterns (graphics), 370
PDF (Portable Document Format), 774-779
PDF Options dialog box, 776, 781
PDF presentations, 669, 672
adding images, 670
multi-page PDF documents, 674
presentation options, 671
PDF Save Settings dialog box, 780
PDF Security dialog box, 782
Pen tool, 289
photo galleries. See Web Photo Galleries
Photo JPEG Options dialog box, 770
photographic images
clipping groups, 236-239
recoloring, 95-98
slideshows, 618-620
Photoshop CS
actions. See actions
Color Picker, 72, 75

Color Picker dialog box, 247
color settings, 65. *See also* color
    changing, 67
    gamma, 65
    setting gamma on a Mac, 68
Copy Color as HTML feature, 101
custom workspaces, saving, 38-39
File Browser
    adding folders, 54
    assigning keywords, 57-60
    overview, 46
    viewing and organizing images,
        47-51, 55
flattening files, 170
image maps, 577-579
interface overview, 20
keyboard shortcuts
    customizing, 41-43
    list of, 40
    saving and printing sets, 45
Layer blending modes, 166
Layer Comps feature, 202-208
    basic element visibility, 205
    New Layer Comp dialog box, 204
metadata, 661
new features, 10-16
optimizing JPEGs, 124
Options bar, 30
palettes, 25
    default settings, 29
    docking, 26-33
PDF presentations, 669-672
    adding images, 670
    multi-page PDF documents, 674
    presentation options, 671
Preset Manager, 81
resetting tool options, 37
rollovers, 490
Save For Web option, 111
setting preferences for the Web, 63
Swatches palette, 77
Toolbox, 22, 34-35
type, 241-242
    creating on a path, 268
    Type Options bar, 243-244
vs. ImageReady CS (when to use), 7-8
Web Photo Gallery
    collaborating with, 666-667
    creating, 651-655
    customizing, 651, 657, 660-662
    Horizontal Slideshow option, 654
    photo info, 658
    sizing options, 659

Photoshop Smart Objects, 725
Pill Rectangle tool, 285
Pixel Replacement Options dialog box, 703
Pixel Replacement variables, 693
    creating, 702-703
    options, 706
pixels, 63
playing animations, 591
PNG format, animation limitation, 621
Polygon Image Map tool, 545, 553
Polygon tool, 285
Portable Document Format. *See* PDF
    presentations
position, tweening (animation), 611
predefined actions, 675
preferences, setting for the Web, 63
preloading animated GIF rollovers, 630
Preserve Appearance option (Macromedia Flash
    Export dialog box), 633
Preset Manager, creating custom swatches, 81
Preset Type pop-up menu, 81
preview pane (File Browser), 48
previewing
    background images, 320
    changes made to HTML files, 715
    graphics in Web browsers, 146
    HTML in ImageReady CS, 154-156
    image maps, 555
    optimized slices, 451
    rollover graphics, 494-496
    transparent animated GIFs, 625
printing keyboard shortcut sets, 45
promoting auto slices to user slices, 419
PSD files
    converting to PDF, 774-779
    creating with data sets and variables, 706
    editing in GoLive CS, 729-731
    opening in GoLive CS, 723
    opening with Text Replacement variables, 736
Publish Settings dialog box (Macromedia Flash
    MX 2004), 757

Q

Quality slider, file compression, 126
QuickTime
    importing files from ImageReady CS,
        768-769
    opening movies in ImageReady CS, 771
        previewing the file, 773
        saving the file as a GIF, 772

R

rasterizing type, 275-277
recording. *See* creating
Rectangle Image Map tool, 545
Rectangle Shape tool, 291
Rectangle tool, 285
relative links, 463
remote rollovers, 487
    creating, 522-529
    creating with selected states, 531-540
renaming slices, 442-445, 525
Replace Files dialog box, 714
replacement rollovers, 487
resizing
    image maps, 550-551
    user slices, 417
Resolution field, 288
reversing frames, 605
Rollover Buttons library, 491
Rollover State Options dialog box, 536
rollovers, 6, 486
    addition rollovers, 487
    animated GIFs
        creating, 627-629
        preloading, 630
    creating, 492-493
        from layer-based slices, 497-501
        layer comps, 518-520
        layer visibility, 513-516
        multiple buttons from saved styles,
            503-505
    GoLive CS Smart Objects, 728
    image map-based, 580-583
    importing from ImageReady CS into
            Dreamweaver MX 2004, 740-744
        creating a new folder, 744
        previewing files in Web browser, 747
        saving files to new folder, 745
        selecting file contents, 746
        Site Definition summary settings, 743
    importing ImageReady CS rollovers into
            GoLive CS, 716-717
        copying files, 718-721
        previewing sites, 722
    naming, 507-508, 511
    optimizing, 494
    previewing, 494
    problems with Internet Explorer, 495
    remote rollovers, 487
        creating, 522-529
        creating with selected states, 531-540
    replacement rollovers, 487
    saving settings, 496
    states, 488, 492
    styles, 490, 502
    unlinking slices, 510
    Web Content palette, 489
    working with ImageReady CS data sets in
            GoLive CS, 739
Rotate Canvas, 90°CW (ImageReady CS), 364
rotating images, 50
Rounded Rectangle tool, 285

S

satin effect, 296
saturation, 73
Save As option (ImageReady CS), 331
Save For Web command (Photoshop CS File
        menu), 396
Save for Web dialog box (GoLive CS), 726
Save For Web option, 111
    GIFs, 129-131
    JPEGs, 119-122
Save Optimized As command (Image Ready CS
        File menu), 394
Save Optimized As dialog box, 147, 394,
        455, 496
Save options (ImageReady CS), 331
Save this action as a droplet dialog box, 684
saving
    actions, 680
    background images, 326-331
    custom layer styles, 304-307
    custom workspaces, 38-39
    flattened files, 170
    GIFs for the Web, 129-131
    HTML code, 328, 394
    JPEGs for the Web, 119-122
    keyboard shortcut sets, 45
    layers as different formats, 213
    rollover settings, 496
    sliced images, 455-457
    transparent GIFs, 393-402
screen resolutions layer, 355
seamless background images from photographs,
        346-352
Search dialog box (File Browser), 61
searching (File Browser), 57-62

security
    metadata, 661
    Web Photo Galleries, 660
Select an Export Destination Folder dialog
      box, 636
Select Browser pop-up menu, 146
Select Slice tool, 40
selected states, creating remote rollovers, 532
selecting
    fonts, 245
    layers
        exporting layers as files, 219
        for movement, 172
        multiple layers, 194, 505
        shortcut keys, 197
selective optimization
    GIFs, 142-144
    JPEGs, 124
server-side image maps, 543
    appearance, 544
    creating, 543
Set an Export Destination Folder dialog box, 212
Set Loop Count dialog box, 595
setting
    matte color, 381
    preferences for the Web, 63
Shadow Mode pop-up menu, 299
shadows, 382-384
Shape Layers button, 290
Shape Name dialog box, 293
shape tools, 282-285, 294
    Custom Shapes tool, 295
    Ellipse tool, 289
    Rectangle Shape tool, 291
    shape layers, 286
    shape overview, 286
shapes
    changing paths, 293
    creating, 288
    custom, 295
    drawing from scratch, 289
    layer styles, 287, 291, 296-301
shaping image maps, 556
shortcut keys
    filling layered images with color, 90
    highlighting text, 248
    menus, 23
    Move tool, 171
    palette drop-down panels, 25
    undo, 91

simulating HTML type with system layout, 256
Site settings (Web Photo Gallery
      dialog box), 663
sizing
    background images, 317-323
    bounding boxes, 259
    fonts, 248
    graphics, 141
    type, 249
slice numbers, 412
Slice palette, 413
    controls, 414
    Layer Based Dimensions section, 427
    renaming slices, 444
    Slice Outset fields, 426
Slice Select tool, 510
slice symbols, 412
Slice tool
    keyboard shortcut, 40
slices, 409
    applying alt text and status bar messages to,
      458-460
    assigning URLs, 461-462
    backgrounds, 452
    colors, 412
    combining, 440-441
    copying optimization settings, 454
    creating
        auto slices, 416
        layer-based slices, 422-432
        user slices, 415-420
    deleting, 419
    dividing, 438-439
    layer comps, 471-484
    lines, 412
    linking, 454
    modifying default slice naming settings, 445
    moving, 429
    naming conventions, 442
    optimizing, 446-447
        auto slices, 450
        as GIFs, 448
        as JPEGs, 449
    previewing, 451
    promoting layer-based slices to user
      slices, 436
    renaming, 442-444, 525
    saving sliced images, 455-457

Slice palette, 413
slice sets, 464-465
    adding slices, 466-469
    benefits of, 470
    types, 411
    visibility, 450
    Web Content palette, 413
slideshows, 618-620, 669. *See also* PDF
    presentations
Smart Objects
    GoLive CS, 723
    options, 724
    Photoshop Smart Objects, 725
    saving for the Web, 726-727
Smart Photoshop button (Objects palette), 724
Soften option (Layer Styles dialog box), 303
solid color layers, 221
Source command (Internet Explorer View
    menu), 330
Source Images settings (Web Photo Gallery
    dialog box), 663
specifying background images, 319-325
speed
    animations, 594-597
    Web, 105
spell checking, 263-264
Spread/Choke option (Layer Styles
    dialog box), 303
sRGB, 65
status bar messages, applying to slices,
    458, 460
stickiness, 37
stroke effect, 296
styles
    rollover styles, 490
    rollovers, 493
Styles palette
    applying custom layer styles, 308-311
    deleting styles, 313
    rollover styles, 490
sub slices, 411
Swatches palette, 26
    choosing Web-safe colors, 77-79
    coloring layered images, 89-94
    creating custom swatches, 81-88
    opening, 77
SWF, 105
    animations, 107
    exporting, 106, 117-118, 157-159
        animations as, 631-634
        vector images as, 750-751, 754, 758

    Free Transform option, 756
    lossy/lossless, 108
    manipulating the graphic, 757
    transparencies, 107
    vs. animated GIFs, 588-589
SWF Export, preserving ImageReady CS file
    appearance, 760-764
Switch Background/Foreground Colors tool, 40
symmetrical background images, 332-337

T

Tab Rectangle tool, 285
targets (image maps), 552
text
    alt text, 459
    animations, 603
    attributes, 250
    bounding boxes, 259
    creating on a path, 268-273
    editing, 252
        faux bold/italic, 254
        leading, 254
        tracking, 253
        uppercasing, 255
    find and replace feature, 265
    formatting, 257
        alignment, 260
        paragraph type, 258-260
    insertion cursor, 252
    kerning, 253
    sizing, 249
    spell checking, 263-264
    warped type, 266, 274
text boxes, 376
text files, importing data sets from, 707-709
Text Replacement variables, 693, 697-698, 736
text-only browsers, image maps, 552
textured images, coloring, 95, 97-98
thumbnails, 48
    actions, 677
    Web Photo Gallery options, 659
Thumbnails options (Web Photo Gallery dialog
    box), 665
Tile Maker dialog box, 349
Tile Maker filter (ImageReady CS), 346
tiles
    background images, 315
    background tiles. *See* background images

defined, 315
directional tiles, 363-365
time-based mediums, 586
timing (animations), 586
Toggle File Browser button (Options bar), 47
Toggle Slice Visibility button, 432, 509
Tokens, 662
Tool Presets button (Options bar), 35
Toolboxes, 21
    Brush tool, 169
    creating tool presets, 34-35
    Direct Selection tool, 292
    Ellipse tool, 268
    Eyedropper tool, 86
    fly-out menus, 23
    Freeform Pen tool, 271
    Horizontal Type tool, 245
    ImageReady CS/Photoshop CS
        comparison, 22
    locating, 22
    Move tool, 171
    Options bar, 30
    Path Selection tool, 273
    Photoshop version differences, 22
    Slice Select tool, 510
    Toggle Slices Visibility button, 432
tracking text, 253
Transform commands, 279-281
transforming type, 279-281
transparencies, 371
    1-bit masking, 368
    8-bit, 367
    animated GIFs, 623-625
    Macromedia Flash, 107
transparent GIFs, 106-107, 371
    broad backgrounds, 385-388
    creating, 373-376, 396-402
    Diffusion Transparency Dither, 389-391
    drop shadows, 382-384
    fixing edges, 377-381
    from non-transparent, 403-407
    saving, 393-402
    viewing in browser, 373-376
transparent layers, 224, 370
turning off layer style visibility, 302
Tween button (Animation palette), 585
Tween feature, 598-601
tweening
    with layer styles, 615-617
    with opacity, 599
    with position, 611-614
    a tweened sequence, 608-610

type
    anti-aliased, 249
    attributes, 250
    bounding boxes, 259
    Character palette controls, 250
    clipping groups, 236-239
    color, changing, 248
    creating on a path, 268-273
    editing, 252
        faux bold/italic, 254
        leading, 254
        tracking, 253
        uppercasing, 255
    fonts, 244
        color, 246
        selecting, 245
        sizing, 248
    formatting, 243, 257
        alignment, 260
        paragraph type, 258-260
        Transform commands, 279-281
        warped type, 266, 274
    highlighting, 248
    image maps, 572-575
    insertion cursor, 252
    jagged-edged, 248
    kerning, 253
    Photoshop CS/ImageReady CS comparison,
        241-242
    rasterizing, 275, 277
    simulating HTML type with system
        layout, 256
    sizing, 249
    Type Options bar, 244
    Web pages, 240
Type Options bar, 242-244
    Commit Current Edits button, 248
    features, 243
    formatting control, 243
Type tool, 40

U

unflagging images, 51, 53
Update HTML command, 711
Update HTML option (ImageReady CS), 331
updating HTML, 711-715
uploading HTML from ImageReady CS, 156
uppercasing text, 255
URLs, assigning to slices, 461-462

user slices, 411
    creating, 415-420
    deleting, 419
    promoting auto slices to, 419
    resizing, 417

V

variables, 693-696
    creating, 698
        * (asterisk) character, 699
        PSD files, 706
        GoLive CS Smart Objects, 726
        HTML editors, 705
        Pixel Replacement variables
            creating, 702-703
            options, 706
        Text Replacement variable, 697
Variables dialog box, 696, 702
vector graphics
    exporting as SWF files, 750-751, 754, 758
        Free Transform option, 756
        manipulating the graphic, 757
    vs. bitmap images, 283
vector masks, 287
View menu commands, 330
viewing transparent GIFs in browser, 373-376
visibility
    animation, 590
    layer sets, 190
    layer styles, turning off, 302
    layers, 180
Visibility icon, 163
Visibility variable, 693

W-Z

Wacom tablet, 100
Warp Text dialog box, 266
warped type, 266, 274
Web (the), 65
    browsers
        alt text, 459
        animations, 595
        Netscape, 630
    color, 65
        Copy Color as HTML feature, 101-102
        dithering, 71
        shifting, 70
        Web-safe, 69-70

GIFs
    Color Reduction Palette settings,
        132-135
    locking colors, 138
    reducing colors, 136-140
    saving for Web, 129-131
    selective optimization with alpha
        channels, 142-144
    sizing, 141
graphics. *See* Web graphics
JPEGs, saving for Web, 119-122
previewing graphics in browsers, 146
speed, 105
Web Content palette, 15, 489, 546
    Create rollover state button, 500, 628
    creating user slices, 415
    New Rollover State option, 582
    renaming slices, 443
    slices, 413
Web graphics
    creating, 3
    rollovers, 486
        addition rollovers, 487
        creating, 492-493
        creating from layer comps, 518-520
        creating from layer-based slices,
            498-501
        creating multiple buttons from a saved
            style, 503-505
        creating with layer visibility, 513-516
        naming, 507-508, 511
        optimizing, 494
        previewing, 494
        problems with Internet Explorer, 495
        remote, creating, 522-529
        remote, creating with selected states,
            531-540
        replacement rollovers, 487
        saving settings, 496
        states, 488
Web interfaces, designing, 640-649
Web pages
    animations. *See* animations
    image maps
        hot spots, 544
        targets, 552
    slicing, 472
    type, 240

Web Photo Galleries, 651
    collaborating with, 666-667
    creating, 651-655
    customizing, 651, 657-662
    Horizontal Slideshow option, 654
    sizing options, 659
Web Photo Gallery dialog box, 657
    Email Feedback option, 668
    security settings, 661
    settings, 663
Web-safe color, 69-70
    choosing from Color palette, 76
    choosing from Color Picker, 72-74
    choosing from Swatches palette, 77-79
    Color Reduction Palette, 134-135
    dithering, 71
Web sites
    Adobe, 669
    alt text, 459
    buttons, rollovers, 6
    graphics, transparencies, 106
    naming, 741
    photo galleries, 7, 653
    Wacom, 100
    Web interfaces. *See* Web interfaces
Welcome screen
    color management help, 69
    opening, 19
Windows
    assigning URLs to slices, 462
    .exe extension, 684
    sRGB, 65
workspaces, custom, 38-39
WWW. *See* Web (the)

Zoom tool, 40

www.informit.com

YOUR GUIDE TO IT REFERENCE

New Riders has partnered with **InformIT.com** to bring technical information to your desktop. Drawing from New Riders authors and reviewers to provide additional information on topics of interest to you, **InformIT.com** provides free, in-depth information you won't find anywhere else.

Articles

Keep your edge with thousands of free articles, in-depth features, interviews, and IT reference recommendations—all written by experts you know and trust.

Online Books

Answers in an instant from **InformIT Online Books'** 600+ fully searchable online books.

POWERED BY

Safari

Catalog

Review online sample chapters, author biographies, and customer rankings and choose exactly the right book from a selection of more than 5,000 titles.

New Riders

www.newriders.com

Go Beyond the Book

with lynda.com Training CD-ROMs:

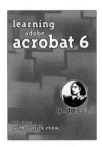

**Learning Adobe
Acrobat 6**

**Learning Macromedia
Flash MX 2004**

**Learning Macromedia
Dreamweaver MX 2004**

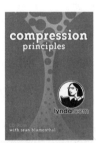

**QuickTime Compression
Principles**

- Watch industry experts lead you step-by-step.
- Learn by viewing, and then by doing.
- Maximize your learning with high-quality tutorial source files.
- Over 33 active titles in our collection.

Visit http://www.lynda.com/videos/

lynda.com

Hands-on Training Books, CDs, & Online Movie Library.

Keep Learning

with More Hands-On Training Books:

Flash MX 2004
Hands-On Training

Dreamweaver MX 2004
Hands-On Training

Adobe Acrobat 6
Hands-On Training

Adobe After Effects 6
Hands-On Training

- Learn by doing.
- Follow real-world examples.
- Benefit from exercise files and QuickTime movies included on CD-ROM.
- Many other titles to choose from.

Visit http://www.lynda.com/books/

lynda.com™

Hands-on Training Books, CDs, & Online Movie Library.

CD-ROM LICENSE AGREEMENT

THIS SOFTWARE LICENSE AGREEMENT CONSTITUTES AN AGREEMENT BETWEEN YOU AND, LYNDA.COM, LLC. . YOU SHOULD CAREFULLY READ THE FOLLOWING TERMS AND CONDITIONS BEFORE OPENING THIS ENVELOPE. COPYING THIS SOFTWARE TO YOUR MACHINE, BREAKING THE SEAL, OR OTHERWISE REMOVING OR USING THE SOFTWARE INDICATES YOUR ACCEPTANCE OF THESE TERMS AND CONDITIONS. IF YOU DO NOT AGREE TO BE BOUND BY THE PROVISIONS OF THIS LICENSE AGREEMENT, YOU SHOULD PROMPTLY DELETE THE SOFTWARE FROM YOUR MACHINE.

TERMS AND CONDITIONS:

1. GRANT OF LICENSE. In consideration of payment of the License Fee, which was a part of the price you paid for this product, LICENSOR grants to you (the "Licensee") a nonexclusive right to use and display this copy of a Software program, along with any updates or upgrade releases of the Software for which you have paid (all parts and elements of the Software as well as the Software as a whole are hereinafter referred to as the "Software") on a single computer only (i.e., with a single CPU) at a single location, all as more particularly set forth and limited below. LICENSOR reserves all rights not expressly granted to you as Licensee in this License Agreement.

2. OWNERSHIP OF SOFTWARE. The license granted herein is not a sale of the original Software or of any copy of the Software. As Licensee, you own only the rights to use the Software as described herein and the magnetic or other physical media on which the Software is originally or subsequently recorded or fixed. LICENSOR retains title and ownership of the Software recorded on the original disk(s), as well as title and ownership of any subsequent copies of the Software irrespective of the form of media on or in which the Software is recorded or fixed. This license does not grant you any intellectual or other proprietary or other rights of any nature whatsoever in the Software.

3. USE RESTRICTIONS. As Licensee, you may use the Software only as expressly authorized in this License Agreement under the terms of paragraph 4. You may physically transfer the Software from one computer to another provided that the Software is used on only a single computer at any one time. You may not: (i) electronically transfer the Software from one computer to another over a network; (ii) make the Software available through a time-sharing service, network of computers, or other multiple user arrangement; (iii) distribute copies of the Software or related written materials to any third party, whether for sale or otherwise; (iv) modify, adapt, translate, reverse engineer, decompile, disassemble, or prepare any derivative work based on the Software or any element thereof; (v) make or distribute, whether for sale or otherwise, any hard copy or printed version of any of the Software nor any portion thereof nor any work of yours containing the Software or any component thereof; (vi) use any of the Software nor any of its components in any other work.

8. THIS IS WHAT YOU CAN AND CANNOT DO WITH THE SOFTWARE. Even though in the preceding paragraph and elsewhere LICENSOR has restricted your use of the Software, the following is the only thing you can do with the Software and the various elements of the Software:DUCKS IN A ROW ARTWORK: THE ARTWORK CONTAINED ON THIS CD-ROM MAY NOT BE USED IN ANY MANNER WHATSOEVER OTHER THAN TO VIEW THE SAME ON YOUR COMPUTER, OR POST TO YOUR PERSONAL, NON-COMMERCIAL WEB SITE FOR EDUCATIONAL PURPOSES ONLY. THIS MATERIAL IS SUBJECT TO ALL OF THE RESTRICTION PROVISIONS OF THIS SOFTWARE LICENSE. SPECIFICALLY BUT NOT IN LIMITATION OF THESE RESTRICTIONS, YOU MAY NOT DISTRIBUTE, RESELL OR TRANSFER THIS PART OF THE SOFTWARE DESIGNATED AS "CLUTS" NOR ANY OF YOUR DESIGN OR OTHER WORK CONTAINING ANY OF THE SOFTWARE DESIGNATED AS "DUCKS IN A ROW ARTWORK" NOR ANY OF YOUR DESIGN OR OTHER WORK CONTAINING ANY SUCH "DUCKS IN A ROW ARTWORK," ALL AS MORE PARTICULARLY RESTRICTED IN THE WITHIN SOFTWARE LICENSE.

5. COPY RESTRICTIONS. The Software and accompanying written materials are protected under United States copyright laws. Unauthorized copying and/or distribution of the Software and/or the related written materials is expressly forbidden. You may be held legally responsible for any copyright infringement that is caused, directly or indirectly, by your failure to abide by the terms of this License Agreement. Subject to the terms of this License Agreement and if the software is not otherwise copy protected, you may make one copy of the Software for backup purposes only. The copyright notice and any other proprietary notices which were included in the original Software must be reproduced and included on any such backup copy.

6. TRANSFER RESTRICTIONS. The license herein granted is personal to you, the Licensee. You may not transfer the Software nor any of its components or elements to anyone else, nor may you sell, lease, loan, sublicense, assign, or otherwise dispose of the Software nor any of its components or elements without the express written consent of LICENSOR, which consent may be granted or withheld at LICENSOR's sole discretion.

7. TERMINATION. The license herein granted hereby will remain in effect until terminated. This license will terminate automatically without further notice from LICENSOR in the event of the violation of any of the provisions hereof. As Licensee, you agree that upon such termination you will promptly destroy any and all copies of the Software which remain in your possession and, upon request, will certify to such destruction in writing to LICENSOR.

8. LIMITATION AND DISCLAIMER OF WARRANTIES. a) THE SOFTWARE AND RELATED WRITTEN MATERIALS, INCLUDING ANY INSTRUCTIONS FOR USE, ARE PROVIDED ON AN "AS IS" BASIS, WITHOUT WARRANTY OF ANY KIND, EXPRESS OR IMPLIED. THIS DISCLAIMER OF WARRANTY EXPRESSLY INCLUDES, BUT IS NOT LIMITED TO, ANY IMPLIED WARRANTIES OF MERCHANTABILITY AND/OR OF FITNESS FOR A PARTICULAR PURPOSE. NO WARRANTY OF ANY KIND IS MADE AS TO WHETHER OR NOT THIS SOFTWARE INFRINGES UPON ANY RIGHTS OF ANY OTHER THIRD PARTIES. NO ORAL OR WRITTEN INFORMATION GIVEN BY LICENSOR, ITS SUPPLIERS, DISTRIBUTORS, DEALERS, EMPLOYEES, OR AGENTS, SHALL CREATE OR OTHERWISE ENLARGE THE SCOPE OF ANY WARRANTY HEREUNDER. LICENSEE ASSUMES THE ENTIRE RISK AS TO THE QUALITY AND THE PERFOR-

MANCE OF SUCH SOFTWARE. SHOULD THE SOFTWARE PROVE DEFECTIVE, YOU, AS LICENSEE (AND NOT LICENSOR, ITS SUPPLIERS, DISTRIBUTORS, DEALERS OR AGENTS), ASSUME THE ENTIRE COST OF ALL NECESSARY CORRECTION, SERVICING, OR REPAIR. b) LICENSOR warrants the disk(s) on which this copy of the Software is recorded or fixed to be free from defects in materials and workmanship, under normal use and service, for a period of ninety (90) days from the date of delivery as evidenced by a copy of the applicable receipt. LICENSOR hereby limits the duration of any implied warranties with respect to the disk(s) to the duration of the express warranty. This limited warranty shall not apply if the disk(s) have been damaged by unreasonable use, accident, negligence, or by any other causes unrelated to defective materials or workmanship. c) LICENSOR does not warrant that the functions contained in the Software will be uninterrupted or error free and Licensee is encouraged to test the Software for Licensee's intended use prior to placing any reliance thereon. All risk of the use of the Software will be on you, as Licensee. d) THE LIMITED WARRANTY SET FORTH ABOVE GIVES YOU SPECIFIC LEGAL RIGHTS AND YOU MAY ALSO HAVE OTHER RIGHTS WHICH VARY FROM STATE TO STATE. SOME STATES DO NOT ALLOW THE LIMITATION OR EXCLUSION OF IMPLIED WARRANTIES OR OF INCIDENTAL OR CONSEQUENTIAL DAMAGES, SO THE LIMITATIONS AND EXCLUSIONS CONCERNING THE SOFTWARE AND RELATED WRITTEN MATERIALS SET FORTH ABOVE MAY NOT APPLY TO YOU.

9. LIMITATION OF REMEDIES. LICENSOR's entire liability and Licensee's exclusive remedy shall be the replacement of any disk(s) not meeting the limited warranty set forth in Section 8 above which is returned to LICENSOR with a copy of the applicable receipt within the warranty period. Any replacement disk(s)will be warranted for the remainder of the original warranty period or thirty (30) days, whichever is longer.

10. LIMITATION OF LIABILITY. IN NO EVENT WILL LICENSOR, OR ANYONE ELSE INVOLVED IN THE CREATION, PRODUCTION, AND/OR DELIVERY OF THIS SOFTWARE PRODUCT BE LIABLE TO LICENSEE OR ANY OTHER PERSON OR ENTITY FOR ANY DIRECT, INDIRECT, OR OTHER DAMAGES, INCLUDING, WITHOUT LIMITATION, ANY INTERRUPTION OF SERVICES, LOST PROFITS, LOST SAVINGS, LOSS OF DATA, OR ANY OTHER CONSEQUENTIAL, INCIDENTAL, SPECIAL, OR PUNITIVE DAMAGES, ARISING OUT OF THE PURCHASE, USE, INABILITY TO USE, OR OPERATION OF THE SOFTWARE, EVEN IF LICENSOR OR ANY AUTHORIZED LICENSOR DEALER HAS BEEN ADVISED OF THE POSSIBILITY OF SUCH DAMAGES. BY YOUR USE OF THE SOFTWARE, YOU ACKNOWLEDGE THAT THE LIMITATION OF LIABILITY SET FORTH IN THIS LICENSE WAS THE BASIS UPON WHICH THE SOFTWARE WAS OFFERED BY LICENSOR AND YOU ACKNOWLEDGE THAT THE PRICE OF THE SOFTWARE LICENSE WOULD BE HIGHER IN THE ABSENCE OF SUCH LIMITATION. SOME STATES DO NOT ALLOW THE LIMITATION OR EXCLUSION OF LIABILITY FOR INCIDENTAL OR CONSEQUENTIAL DAMAGES SO THE ABOVE LIMITATIONS AND EXCLUSIONS MAY NOT APPLY TO YOU.

11. UPDATES. LICENSOR, at its sole discretion, may periodically issue updates of the Software which you may receive upon request and payment of the applicable update fee in effect from time to time and in such event, all of the provisions of the within License Agreement shall apply to such updates.

12. EXPORT RESTRICTIONS. Licensee agrees not to export or re-export the Software and accompanying documentation (or any copies thereof) in violation of any applicable U.S. laws or regulations.

13. ENTIRE AGREEMENT. YOU, AS LICENSEE, ACKNOWLEDGE THAT: (i) YOU HAVE READ THIS ENTIRE AGREEMENT AND AGREE TO BE BOUND BY ITS TERMS AND CONDITIONS; (ii) THIS AGREEMENT IS THE COMPLETE AND EXCLUSIVE STATEMENT OF THE UNDERSTANDING BETWEEN THE PARTIES AND SUPERSEDES ANY AND ALL PRIOR ORAL OR WRITTEN COMMUNICATIONS RELATING TO THE SUBJECT MATTER HEREOF; AND (iii) THIS AGREEMENT MAY NOT BE MODIFIED, AMENDED, OR IN ANY WAY ALTERED EXCEPT BY A WRITING SIGNED BY BOTH YOURSELF AND AN OFFICER OR AUTHORIZED REPRESENTATIVE OF LICENSOR.

14. SEVERABILITY. In the event that any provision of this License Agreement is held to be illegal or otherwise unenforceable, such provision shall be deemed to have been deleted from this License Agreement while the remaining provisions of this License Agreement shall be unaffected and shall continue in full force and effect.

15. GOVERNING LAW. This License Agreement shall be governed by the laws of the State of California applicable to agreements wholly to be performed therein and of the United States of America, excluding that body of the law related to conflicts of law. This License Agreement shall not be governed by the United Nations Convention on Contracts for the International Sale of Goods, the application of which is expressly excluded. No waiver of any breach of the provisions of this License Agreement shall be deemed a waiver of any other breach of this License Agreement.

16. RESTRICTED RIGHTS LEGEND. Use, duplication, or disclosure by the Government is subject to restrictions as set forth in subparagraph (c)(1)(ii) of the Rights in Technical Data and Computer Software clause at 48 CFR § 252.227-7013 and DFARS § 252.227-7013 or subparagraphs (c) (1) and (c)(2) of the Commercial Computer Software-Restricted Rights at 48 CFR § 52.227.19, as applicable. Contractor/manufacturer: LICENSOR: LYNDA.COM, LLC, c/o PEACHPIT PRESS, 1249 Eighth Street, Berkeley, CA 94710.